Instructor's Manual with Test Bank

for Miller's

Environmental Science
Working With The Earth

~~Seventh~~ Edition
Tenth

Irene Kokkala
North Georgia College & State University

THOMSON

BROOKS/COLE

Australia • Canada • Mexico • Singapore • Spain • United Kingdom • United States

Printed in the United States of America
1 2 3 4 5 6 7   07 06 05 04 03

Printer: Victor Graphics, Inc.

ISBN 0-534-42414-7

For more information about our products, contact us at:
Thomson Learning Academic Resource Center
1-800-423-0563

For permission to use material from this text, contact us by:
Phone: 1-800-730-2214
Fax: 1-800-730-2215
Web: http://www.thomsonrights.com

Brooks/Cole—Thomson Learning
10 Davis Drive
Belmont, CA 94002-3098
USA

Asia
Thomson Learning
5 Shenton Way #01-01
UIC Building
Singapore 068808

Australia/New Zealand
Thomson Learning
102 Dodds Street
Southbank, Victoria 3006
Australia

Canada
Nelson
1120 Birchmount Road
Toronto, Ontario M1K 5G4
Canada

Europe/Middle East/South Africa
Thomson Learning
High Holborn House
50/51 Bedford Row
London WC1R 4LR
United Kingdom

Latin America
Thomson Learning
Seneca, 53
Colonia Polanco
11560 Mexico D.F.
Mexico

Spain/Portugal
Paraninfo
Calle/Magallanes, 25
28015 Madrid, Spain

CONTENTS

PREFACE

What's new in this edition? Outlines and summaries of the chapters have been added. The test bank has been revised: Additions and deletions reflect the new material in the textbook. In addition, all questions have the same number of answer choices (5). The choice "all of the above" has been replaced with "all of these answers" so that answer choices may be scrambled more easily; also, the number of these questions has been reduced. Answers to the review and critical thinking questions at the end of the chapters have been added in Appendix E. Suggested topics or questions integrating the Interactive Concepts in Environmental Science CD-ROM are included in Appendix F. We have continued to increase possibilities for integration of other ancillary publications into an overall educational plan.

The manual continues to focus on the major goal of environmental education by emphasizing integration of concepts, values, participation, and skills needed by environmentally literate citizens.

ORGANIZATION

This manual is divided into two sections. Section I contains the following subsections for each chapter:

<u>Thinking</u>

- *Concept Maps.* Overview concept maps are provided for each chapter in Appendix A. They are one way to show connections among concepts within the chapter. They can be used as introductory material when beginning a chapter and/or summarizing material when ending a chapter. However, students learn most when they make the maps themselves.

- *Objectives.* These objectives will help students identify and master the most important content of the chapter. We have included objectives that require basic intellectual skills (define, describe, compare) and objectives that require more advanced intellectual skills (analyze, evaluate, predict).

- *Key Terms.* These terms are shown in **boldface** or *italics* in the text. The list of terms also includes the text page on which it is found. It might be worthwhile to photocopy both the Objectives and Key Terms sections and assign them to your students.

- *Outlines.* These chapter outlines provide a detailed overview of the chapter content, organized in sections. After reading these outlines the students should be able to understand the main points of the chapters.

- *Summaries.* These chapter summaries are numbered lists of main points of the chapters. In general these summaries provide key information to answer the goals of each chapter.

- *Multiple-Choice Questions.* This section refers to the page numbers of Section II where multiple-choice questions for the chapter will be found.

- *More Depth: Conceptual Term Paper Topics.* This section provides topics to deepen students' understanding of the concepts introduced in the chapter.

- *More Breadth: Interdisciplinary Activities and Projects.* This section provides ideas to broaden students' interdisciplinary understanding of environmental studies.

- *Multisensory Learning: Audiovisuals.* This section provides title, synopsis, source abbreviation, and other statistics for potentially useful films and videos. Information to obtain each source is in Appendix B.

Attitudes/Values

- *Assessment.* Assessment offers some questions to evaluate students' awareness, attitudes, and values pertinent to the content of the chapter.

- *More Depth: Discussion and Term Paper Topics.* These topics raise questions that deepen students' understanding of how different worldviews, values, and attitudes interact with environmental issues. Students are directed to critical thinking questions at the end of each chapter of the text. For further work in this area, students may refer to *Critical Thinking and the Environment* by Jane Heinze-Fry and G. Tyler Miller, Jr.

Participation

- *Lifestyle and Campus Community.* This section refers to appropriate chapters of the book *Green Lives/Green Campuses,* which is designed to help students explore how their lifestyles and campuses interact with the environment.

- *More Depth: Action-Oriented Term Paper Topics.* These topics explore in more depth actions that can be taken from individual to global levels with respect to the chapter's environmental issues.

Skills

- *Environmental Problem-Solving Skills: Projects.* These projects offer students opportunities to develop research, problem-solving, and interpersonal skills needed to address environmental problems.

- *Laboratory Skills.* This section refers to appropriate chapters of the Laboratory Manual designed to go with the textbook.

- *Computer Skills.* This section refers to a variety of computer programs that enable students to explore interactions of many environmental variables appropriate for particular chapters. For more in depth work, students may use *Introduction to the Internet for Miller's Environmental Science Texts* by Daniel J. Kurland and Jane Heinze-Fry.

Section II consists of multiple-choice questions for each chapter, divided into subsections that reflect the organization of the text. An effort has been made to create questions that cover content, worldview/values, and actions. Although we hope that instructors will find the multiple-choice questions useful, we also recognize that short answers and essays offer students more opportunity to synthesize and express ideas independently.

Appendixes. Appendix A contains concept maps for each chapter. Appendix B contains addresses of sources for audiovisual aids referenced in the Multisensory Learning section of each chapter. Appendix C contains information about computer software. Appendix D is a questionnaire that you can give your students to assess their environmental knowledge and feelings. Appendix E is a list of the review questions at the end of each chapter. Each question number is followed by the page number(s) of the textbook where the answer can be found. In the same Appendix suggested answers to the critical thinking questions have been included. Appendix F includes suggested discussion topics or questions that incorporate animations and interactions from the Interactive Concepts in Environmental Science CD-ROM. The questions and discussions topics are designed to encourage students to use the CD-ROM.

ACKNOWLEDGMENTS

Thanks to Richard Clements, David Cotter, Jane Heinze-Fry, and Gene Heinze-Fry for their work on prior editions of the *Instructor's Manual*. Most of the questions, activities, projects, and suggestions for term paper topics are built from prior editions.

Thanks to the following people who have contributed to the prior editions: Walter H. Corson of Global Tomorrow Coalition (audiovisual aids) and Gerald O. Barney of the Institute for 21st Century Studies (computer software programs).

Thanks to Marilyn Lary and Barbara Howerton for their support and contributions during the revision of this manual.

SECTION I

TEACHING RESOURCES

CHAPTER 1
ENVIRONMENTAL PROBLEMS, THEIR CAUSES, AND SUSTAINABILITY

THINKING

<u>Concept Map</u>

For an overview of the concepts of this chapter, see Appendix A, Maps 1A and 1B in the back of this manual. You might want to take this opportunity to look at the overview map for the whole textbook in the front cover of the text and see where this chapter fits in. The maps available in the Appendix are just one way of looking at the concepts. Instructors and students are encouraged to produce their own conceptual hierarchies and draw their own connections.

<u>Goals</u>

See bulleted list of questions on p. 2 of text.

<u>Objectives</u>

1. Define *earth capital*. Distinguish between living off of principal and living off of interest. Analyze which of these behaviors humans are currently illustrating. Evaluate the possibility of continuing to live in our current style. Define *sustainable society*.

2. Draw an exponential growth curve. Distinguish between exponential growth and linear growth. Describe what has happened to the length of the doubling time over the course of human history.

3. Describe economic growth and the wealth gap over the course of time. Distinguish between *developed* countries and *developing* countries.

4. Distinguish between the following terms: nonrenewable, renewable, and potentially renewable resources; reuse and recycle; point source of pollution and nonpoint source of pollution; degradable, slowly degradable, and nondegradable pollutants.

5. Define *biological diversity*. Briefly describe its three components. Analyze the relationship between biodiversity and human life. Describe the "tragedy of the commons."

6. Define *sustainable yield*. Describe the relationship between sustainable yield and environmental degradation.

7. Distinguish between pollution prevention and pollution cleanup. Evaluate the effectiveness of these two approaches in decreasing pollution. List seven root causes of environmental problems.

8. Describe a simple model and a more complex model of relationships among population, resource use, technology, environmental degradation, and pollution. Evaluate which model is most useful to you. Assess which model would be most useful in explaining relationships to young children and which more closely resembles reality.

9. Briefly describe hunter-gatherer societies, focusing on division of labor and power, the relationship of humans to nature, and the impact of their societies on the environment.

10. Describe early forms of agriculture. Describe changes that occurred in human population distribution, employment, and relationships between societies as the Agricultural Revolution unfolded.

11. Briefly describe the Industrial Revolution, focusing on changes in energy consumption. Describe relationships between energy consumption and the production and consumption of material goods. List the benefits that are distributed to most citizens of industrial societies.

12. Compare hunter-gatherer societies, agricultural societies, and industrial societies, focusing on division of labor and power, the relationship of population to food supply, the relationship of humans to nature, the use of resources (energy and materials) per person, and the environmental impacts. Project how a sustainable-earth society would fit into this analysis.

13. Analyze the amount of time over the course of history that has been used to bring about cultural changes. Include a comparison of the length of time to bring about the Agricultural Revolution and the length of time to bring about the Industrial Revolution. Project an amount of time to bring about a cultural change to an earth-wise society. Suggest modern capabilities that might enable this change to occur.

Key Terms (Terms are listed in the same font style as they appear in the text.)

exponential growth (p. 1)
environment (p. 2)
ecology (p. 2)
environmental science (p. 2)
ecologists (p. 2)
environmental scientists (p. 2)
conservation biologists (p. 2)
environmentalists (p. 2)
preservationists (p. 2)
conservationists (p. 2)
restorationists (p. 2)
solar capital (p. 2)
natural resources (capital) (p. 2)
solar energy (p. 2)
environmentally sustainable society (p. 3)
living sustainably (p. 3)
economic growth (p. 4)
gross national product (GNP) (p. 5)
gross domestic product (GDP) (p. 5)
gross world product (p. 5)
per capita GNP (p. 5)
economic development (p. 5)
developed countries (p. 6)
developing countries (p. 6)
poverty (p. 6)
resource (p. 7)
perpetual resource (p. 7)
renewable resource (p. 7)
sustainable yield (p. 7)
environmental degradation (p. 7)
common-property resources (p. 7)

free-access resources (p. 7)
tragedy of the commons (p. 7)
per capita ecological footprint (p. 8)
nonrenewable resources (p. 8)
energy resources (p. 8)
metallic mineral resources (p. 8)
nonmetallic mineral resources (p. 8)
economically depleted (p. 8)
recycling (p. 8)
reuse (p. 8)
pollution (p. 9)
point sources (p. 9)
nonpoint sources (p. 9)
pollution prevention (p. 9)
input pollution control (p. 9)
pollution cleanup (p. 9)
output pollution control (p. 9)
hunter-gatherers (p. 12)
agricultural revolution (p. 12)
slash-and-burn cultivation (p. 12)
shifting cultivation (p. 12)
sustainable cultivation (p.12)
industrial revolution (p. 13)
globalization (p. 14)
information and
    globalization revolution (p. 14)
frontier environmental worldview (p. 14)
technological optimists (p. 16)
environmental pessimists (p.16)
environmentally sustainable economic
    development (p. 16)

<u>Outline</u>

Exponential demands and exponential waste do not equal exponential resources.
   A. For environmental sustainability, mankind must satisfy his basic needs and must neither deplete nor degrade earth's natural resources.
   B. Population growth, economic growth and development, poverty, and globalization must be controlled to sustain the environment.
   C. Pollution must be decreased and other environmental problems must be addressed now, especially by the industrialized nations.
   D. Cultural changes, the agricultural, industrial information and global revolutions have all affected the environment.
   E. What shall we do?

1-1 Living more sustainably
   A. Natural resources and/or natural capital form the cornerstone of resource sustainability.
   B. Different environmental professionals--be they ecologists, conservation biologists, environmentalists, preservationists, restorationists, or environmental scientists--are concerned with environmental sustainability.

1-2 Population growth

1-3 Economic growth, economic development, poverty, and globalization
Economic growth and development must consider sustainability of the environment, not production of wealth, for the future of the planet. Widespread poverty in developing nations requires developed nations to use less of the planet's resources.

1-4 Resources
Perpetual and Renewal resources must be examined in light of economic needs.
   A. Tragedy of the commons
   B. Ecological footprints
   C. Nonrenewable resources

1-5 Pollution
Pollution threats to environments
   A. Point and nonpoint sources
   B. Environmental impacts of pollutants

1-6 Environmental and resource problems: Causes and connections
Problems in the environment and problems with resources
   A. Air and water pollution, biodiversity depletion
   B. Waste production, food supply issues

1-7 Cultural changes and sustainability
Cultural Changes' Influence on the Environment
   A. Agricultural Revolution
   B. Industrial Revolution
   C. Information and Globalization Revolution
   D. Environmental History has covered four separate eras.
       1. Tribal era (before 1600)
       2. Frontier era (1607-1890)
       3. Early Conservation era (1832-1870)
       4. Federal Government/private citizen influential era (1870--   )

1-8 Is our present course sustainable?
The environmental sustainability revolution has changing emphases.

A. It is better to prevent pollution than to clean it up.
B. It is better to prevent/reduce waste production than to dispose of it.
C. Protecting species' environments is the most effective action.
D. More efficient and less wasteful use must be made of resources
E. Decreased birth rates will stabilize world populations.
F. Natural capital must be protected with the world's living off its biological interest, not the capital itself.

Summary

1. Natural resources are earth's natural materials and processes that sustain all species. An environmentally sustainable society satisfies the basic needs of people for food, clean air, and clean water without depleting or degrading natural resources.

2. The world's population is currently increasing exponentially at a rate of 1.26% per year.

3. Economic growth is the increase in the capacity of a country to provide goods and services to people. Economic development is the improvement of living standards by economic growth. Poverty is the lack of ability to meet basic needs for food, shelter, and clothing. Harmful environmental effects of poverty include depletion and degradation of local forests, soil, grasslands, wildlife, and water resources.

4. Earth's resources are perpetual if they are renewed continuously, renewable if they can be replenished fairly rapidly through natural processes and non-renewable. Resources are depleted or degraded when supply use exceeds the replacement rate.

5. Principal types of pollution include point source and non-point source pollution. Ways of dealing with pollution include pollution prevention, or input pollution control, and pollution cleanup, or output pollution control.

6. The environmental impact of a population on a specific area depends on the number of people, the average use of resources per person, and the harmful environmental effects of this population.

7. Hunter-gatherer communities exploited their environment to survive but their impact was limited because of the small numbers of individuals and migration. Advanced forms of agricultural societies had adverse effects on the environment through soil erosion and livestock overgrazing. Industrialized society lead to increased air and water pollution, increased waste production, groundwater and biodiversity depletion, and habitat depletion.

8. Presently we are affecting negatively the earth's supports system at an accelerating rate. We can live sustainably through pollution prevention, waste prevention, species protection, and environmental restoration.

Multiple Choice Questions

See Instructor's Manual, Section II, p. 147.

More Depth: Conceptual Term Paper Topics

1. Population. UN population projections.

2. Poverty. Definition; roots; worldwide distribution; possibilities to alter the current situation.

3. Technology. Research, development, and distribution of new technologies in the United States.

4. State of the world. Bibliography of current resources summarizing the state of the world; most important areas of concern.

5. Pollution and environmental degradation. Report on one form of pollution or environmental degradation, and describe its existence in different countries or choose one incident as a case study.

6. Time for cultural change. The change process and how the rate of cultural change has accelerated; the rate of change of the earth's processes (such as erosion and movement of tectonic plates); the rate of evolutionary change of organisms; the rate of human adaptation in the past and what it is likely to be in the future.

7. Cultural differences. Cultural views of the human-environment relationship; attitudes toward nature; distribution of labor, power, and wealth; relationships between the sexes; social structure; and political style; cultural views that offer a sustainable-Earth worldview.

8. Environmental impacts of the cultural revolutions. Energy consumption and use of materials throughout history.

More Breadth: Interdisciplinary Activities and Projects

1. As a class project, "adopt" a less developed country. Assign teams of students to investigate various aspects of the nation's physical, population, economic, social, political, and other characteristics as well as lifestyle and life quality. Allocate class time for periodic brief reports and discussions of research results.

2. Find and share with the class songs, essays, poems, paintings, and literary passages that are strongly pro- or anti-technology.

3. As a class exercise, make lists of the beneficial and harmful consequences that have resulted from America's adoption of automobile technology.

4. As a class project or extra-credit exercise, contact the local Department of Transportation (DOT) and find out if they offer an Adopt-A-Highway program. Adopt a stretch of highway and have the students pick up the litter. Students can keep tallies of the different types of litter collected (metal cans, snack food wrappers, etc.) and prepare a pie chart and report to submit to the DOT.

5. Find and share with the class songs, folklore, literary passages, and art works that reflect U.S. land-use values and ethics as they have evolved from the frontier era to the present. Be sure to include Native American works. What can be discerned about the relationship of humans to nature in different cultures through their expressions of art?

6. Invite an anthropologist to visit your class to discuss the similarities and contrasts between hunter-gatherer societies and industrial societies. What can the study of hunter-gatherer societies teach that will be useful in the future?

7. Ask a psychologist and/or sociologist to address your class on the subject of human aggression, with particular emphasis on methods that have been or could be used to reduce its injurious effects and channel competitive energies into productive areas. Discuss the balance of competition and cooperation in different societies. Have each student give an example of competition and cooperation in his or her life and in the school. Discuss the benefits and drawbacks of each style. Suggest what the relationship of competition and cooperation might be in a sustainable-Earth society.

Multisensory Learning: Audiovisuals

Affluenza. 1997. 56 min. BFF
Biodiversity. 1994. NG
Economies and the Relation to Social Change and Our Lifestyles. 2001. 50 mins, BFF
Lost Generations. 2000 24 min. BFF
Our Fragile Earth. 22 min. VP
Pollution: World at Risk. 1989. 25 min, NG
Positive Action for the Environment. 1990 24 min., 1990. RCO
State of the Planet. BBC
Sustainable Futures. 338 min. VP
Wild Islands. 180 mins. PBS *The Living Earth;* 1991; 25 min.; NG.
Our Planet Earth; a collection of astronauts' recollections as they viewed Earth from space; BFF.
The Island: Will We Save Our Planet Earth?; 14 min.; a National Geographic Film that increases
    awareness of environmental problems; NG.
The Blue Planet; Earth, life, and space; 26 min.; CBS.
Turning the Toxic Tide environmental vs jobs issues; seven videos; major environmental issues facing the
    planet; BFF.
The Environmental Revolution from *Race to Save the Planet;* 1990; 60 min.; relationship of humans to their
    environment over time; ACPB.
Voices of the Land; 1991; 20 min.; correlations between the destruction of sacred land and destruction of
    the human spirit; BFF.

Listings include year of release and length of film where available. See Appendix B for suppliers.

ATTITUDES/VALUES

Assessment

Ask your students the following questions:

1. Is the world overpopulated? Have you experienced countries which you felt to be overpopulated?
    Have you seen videos of countries which you felt to be overpopulated?

2. Is the country in which you live overpopulated? What factors contribute to your feelings?

3. Is your local community overpopulated? What do you feel are the costs and benefits of the population
    size of your community?

4. Do you favor slowing the growth rate of the human population?

5. Do you favor slowing the growth rate of the country in which you live?

6. Do you favor growth management of the community in which you live?

7. Do you feel that the size of the human population is one of the top environmental issues?

8. How many children do you plan to have?

9. Do you believe that any person should be able to have as many children as they want?

10. Do you think the rate of resource consumption is too high?

11. Do you consume too many resources?

12. Do you think it's important to change your consumption patterns?

13. How do you feel toward past cultural revolutions?

14. Do you think it's time for another cultural revolution? What factors contribute to your feelings?

15. Do you feel our current cultural stage can continue indefinitely?

16. What kinds of changes do you think would improve the quality of life on Earth?

17. What kinds of changes are you willing to make to improve your own quality of life?

18. What kinds of changes do you think industrialized countries might make to improve the quality of life?

More Depth: Discussion and Term Paper Topics

1. What is quality of life?

2. What is the history of conflict among pollution control, environmental degradation, and employment in the United States? Possible cases of interest include the automobile industry and fuel efficiency standards, and the spotted owl and the logging industry.

3. Is the United States overpopulated? Explore people overpopulation and consumption overpopulation.

4. Is bigger better or is small beautiful? Explore Schumacher's philosophy.

5. What is the "good life"?

6. Do you feel a part of or apart from nature?

7. Do you think technology can solve our environmental problems?

8. Do you think human ingenuity and substitution for materials that are being used up quickly can create a good life for the earth's people?

9. When poor economic growth accompanies growing population growth, poverty increases. How does the use or misuse of natural/renewal resources affect poverty? How does this poverty affect the environment? How can the use of common property affect resources?

10. Why does a U. S. citizen's "ecological footprint" cover so much more area than that of someone in a developing country?

11. Describe some technological resources which compromise the environment and describe others which are environmentally beneficial/not harmful.

(Also, see text, Critical Thinking, p. 17)

PARTICIPATION

More Depth: Action-oriented Term Paper Topics

1. Computer modeling methods. *Limits to Growth* by Meadows and Meadows; today's global climate models.

2. National. National efforts to address environmental needs; *Blueprint for the Environment.*

3. Global. Global attempts to address the environment and the economy; the UN document *Our Common Future*; the Earth Summit at Rio de Janeiro in 1992.

SKILLS

Environmental Problem-Solving Skills: Projects

1. As a class exercise, compute the cost of a hamburger, a movie ticket, a single-family home, and/or other commodities 30 years in the future, assuming a steady inflation rate of 5% (or the current inflation rate).

2. As a class exercise, compile a list of resources that are considered important today but were not recognized as resources 100 years ago. What are some things that have ceased to be significant resources during the last 50 years? What resources of the present will probably be of little value 50 years from now?

3. Have the class make a list of changes in your community's environment that have occurred over the last 10 years. Have them vote on which changes they considered desirable and which undesirable. Discuss the changes on which there is least consensus about desirability. Clarify the differences in values that underlie differences in students' responses.

4. Have students assume roles as futurists. Have them describe life as they predict it will be in the year 2010.

Laboratory Skills

(none)

Computer Skills

International Futures Simulation (IFS)
   -Provides a framework for evaluating the widely different public statements made about the workings of the global development system and about probable global futures.
   -CONDUIT, The University of Iowa, Oakdale Campus, Iowa City, Iowa 52242

World Economic Model (WEM)
   -Offers a consistent quantitative framework for carrying out prospective analysis and policy design exercises in the area of international economic relations.
   -Dr. A.R. Gigengack, World Model Project, State University of Groningen, P.O. Box 800, 9700 AV Groningen, The Netherlands

*SimEarth
   -To modify, manage, and nurture a planet from creation, through the formation of life, to the development of technology; based on the Gaia theory.
   -Maxis, 2 Theatre Square, #230, Orinda, CA 94563 (510-254-9700)

*Balance of the Planet
   -Role play the "High Commissioner of the Environment" by levying taxes and granting subsidies to solve a variety of global environmental problems.
   -Accolade, 550 W. Winchester Blvd., Suite 200, San Jose, CA 95128 (800-245-7744)

CHAPTER 2
ENVIRONMENTAL ECONOMICS, POLITICS, AND WORLDVIEWS

THINKING

Concept Map

See Appendix A, Maps 2, 3, and 4.

Goals

See bulleted list of questions on p. 20 of text.

Objectives

1. Distinguish among the concepts in the following sets of terms: *natural resources, manufactured capital, human capital; centrally planned economy, market economy, mixed economic system.* Describe one difference between an economic and an environmental conceptual model of how the earth works.

2. Define *gross national product* (GNP). Evaluate the commonly held belief that GNP is an indicator of a country's well-being. Describe at least two alternative indicators that take social and environmental factors into account. Evaluate the accuracy of these indicators.

3. Define *externalities.* Give one example of an external cost and one example of an external benefit. Describe measures that can be taken to move toward full-cost pricing.

4. Evaluate the use of cost-benefit analysis. Define *discount rate.* Use your understanding of discount rate as you describe the pros and cons of using cost-benefit analysis.

5. List seven strategies that can be used to modify a pure market system to improve environmental quality and reduce resource waste. List advantages and disadvantages of each tool.

6. Predict likely consequences for a society whose goal is zero pollution. Draw a figure illustrating how to find the optimal level of pollution. Distinguish between pollution control and pollution prevention strategies.

7. Evaluate the potential impacts of global free trade.

8. Define *poverty.* Compare a trickle-down and sustainable development approaches to poverty.

9. List twelve ways to move toward earth-sustaining economies.

10. Summarize what individuals can do to influence public policy. List three types of environmental leadership. Assess which style best fits you. List three particular applications of environmental leadership that might be of interest to you.

11. Distinguish between mainstream and grass-roots environmental groups. List four key components of the anti-environmental movement. Summarize their key strategies. Analyze the "takings" issue. Briefly describe the wise-use movement.

12. Concept map a broad definition of "security." Summarize the results of the 1992 Rio Earth Summit.

13. Describe the relationship between actions and worldview. Explain how cultural changes take place.

14. Compare the human-centered environmental worldviews with the life-centered and earth-centered environmental worldviews. Focus on differences in beliefs about the relationship of humans to nature, resource availability, human capability (especially through science and technology), and human-to-human relationships through economics and politics, and views about the success of the human species.

15. Summarize the key pieces of a sustainability proposal.

16. Summarize earth ethics. Include ethical statements regarding ecosystems, species, cultures, and individual responsibilities.

17. List eight steps that would help emphasize earth education. List four questions that help to establish ecological identity. Elaborate on the common traps that lead to inaction.

18. Briefly describe the Earth-Wisdom (Environmental) Revolution. Describe the mini-revolutions within an Earth-wisdom Revolution.

Key Terms (Terms are listed in the same font style as they appear in the text.)

economy (p. 20)
economic decisions (p. 20)
economic resources (p. 20)
natural resources (capital) (p. 20)
human resources (p. 20)
financial resources (p. 20)
manufactured resources (p. 20)
pure command economic system (p. 20)
pure market economic system (p. 20)
pure competition (p. 20)
capitalist market economic systems (p. 20)
global free trade (p. 20)
conventional economists (p. 21)
ecological economists (p. 22)
environmentally sustainable economic development (p. 22)
gross national income (p. 22)
gross domestic product (GDP) (p. 22)
environmental indicators (p. 23)
genuine progress indicator (GPI) (p. 23)
internal costs (p. 24)
external benefit (p. 24)
external cost (p. 24)
internalizing external costs (p. 24)
full cost (p. 24)
breakeven point (p. 25)
optimum level of pollution (p. 25)
market forces (p. 26)
economic incentives (p. 26)
economic disincentives (p. 26)
green taxes (p. 26)
effluent fees (p. 26)
user fees (p. 26)
resistance-to-change management era (p. 27)

innovation management era (p. 28)
poverty (p. 28)
microlending (p. 29)
politics (p. 30)
democracy (p. 30)
constitutional democracy (p.30)
special-interest groups (p. 30)
profit-making organizations (p. 30)
nonprofit, nongovernment organizations (*NGOs*) (p. 31)
humility principle (p. 31)
reversibility principle (p. 31)
precautionary principle (p. 31)
prevention principle (p. 31)
integrative principle (p. 31)
environmental justice principle (p. 31)
environmental justice (p. 31)
leadership (p. 32)
policy (p. 32)
laws (p. 32)
regulations (p. 32)
funding (p. 32)
green job market (p. 32)
policy life cycle (p. 33)
mainstream groups (p. 34)
grassroots environmental groups (p. 34)
microscale experiments (p. 35)
anti-environmental movement (p.35)
military security (p. 36)
economic security (p. 36)
environmental worldviews (p. 36)
environmental ethics (p. 36)
individual-centered (atomistic) (p. 36)
earth-centered (holistic) (p. 36)

human-centered (anthropomorphic) (p. 37)
life-centered (biocentric) (p. 37)
planetary management worldview (p. 37)
instrumental value (p. 37)
no-problem school (p. 38)
free-market school (p. 38)
responsible planetary
      management school (p. 38)
spaceship-earth school (p. 38)
stewardship school (p. 38)
inherent value (p. 38)
intrinsic value (p. 38)
environmental wisdom worldview (p.39)
Aldo Leopold (p. 39)
land ethics (p. 39)
ecological identity (p. 40)

voluntary simplicity (p. 40)
principle of enoughness (p. 40)
forced simplicity (p. 41)
law of progressive simplification (p. 41)
gloom-and-doom pessimism (p. 41)
blind technological optimism (p. 41)
fatalism (p. 41)
extrapolation to infinity (p. 41)
paralysis by analysis (p. 41)
environmental revolution (p. 42)
efficiency revolution (p. 42)
pollution prevention revolution (p. 42)
sufficiency revolution (p. 42)
demographic revolution (p. 42)
economic and political revolution (p. 42)

Outline

Mankind cannot sustain himself; we are dependent on the goodness of the Earth.
   A. Our economic systems (natural, human, financial, and manufactured) must be integrated with a commitment to sustain our environment to guarantee mankind a future.
   B. Realistic economic controls in full-cost pricing, in pollutant regulation, in responses to market forces, and in appropriate world-wide resource utilization must be implemented to improve environmental quality, to reduce poverty, and to create sustainable development.
   C. Environmental policy change must be embraced by governments and individuals, in homes and in workplaces, throughout the world—particularly the industrialized world—to reclaim the health of this planet.
   D. Global environmental efforts must become human-centered and life-centered in order to produce a sustainable future.

2-1 Economic systems and environmental problems
   A. Major types of economic systems: pure command and free-market systems
   B. Six rules help for maximizing company's success in a capitalist market system.
      1. No competition and monopolistic control of market prices
      2. Unrestricted free trade
      3. Support market advantage for one company over its competitors
      4. Cover dangers posed by products of the company
      5. Charge for the costs of harm to people and the environment
      6. Be concerned foremost with producing the greatest profit
   C. Government intervention in market economic systems greatly influences the system outcomes.
      1. Control of monopolies and dominance of the market
      2. Control price or demand of particular items/services
   D. The conventional view of economic activity and the ecological view of economic activity view environmental integrity in different ways.

2-2 Monitoring economic and environmental progress
   A. Differences in GNI and GDP
   B. Environmental compromise and economic justice

2-3 Solutions: Using economics to improve environmental quality
   Environmental quality may be improved through economic measures.
   A. Internal costs, external costs and full-cost pricing
   B. Regulations, market forces, and economic incentives
   C. Economic disincentives, taxes, and environmental management

2-4 Reducing poverty to improve environmental quality and human well-being
Environmental quality and human well-being are interlinked and influenced by the
poverty.

2-5 Making the transition to more environmentally sustainable economies
The world must shift to more environmentally sustainable economies.

2-6 Politics and environmental policy
The challenge for sustaining the environment is in political will.
A. Representative politics and social change
B. Long-range plans for future generations
C. Principles for environmental decisions:
    1. Humility, reversibility and precautionary principles
    2. Prevention, integrative and environmental justice principles

2-7 Case study: Environmental policy in the United States
Individual actions and environmental leadership commitments are necessary to affect environmental
policy and change:
A. Campaign finance reform
B. Leadership: environmental policy, law, and enforcement of the law
C. Interaction with local, existing systems with mainstream and grassroots environmental groups

2-8 Global environmental policy
Global, environmental security may be seen from two different bases:
A. A human-centered environmental worldview, atomistic or holistic
B. A life-centered environmental worldview

2-9 Human centered environmental wordviews
The components of environmental literacy and environmental worldviews to allow us to live more
sustainability are:
A. A respect/reverence for life
B. To understand the earth and use that understanding to protect our planet
C. To seek environmental wisdom and apply it
D. To understand and evaluate our environmental worldview throughout our lives
E. To learn to evaluate the beneficial and harmful consequences of our individual life-styles
F. To determine to make the world a better place and act

2-10 Life-centered environmental wordviews
Life-centered worldview people embrace the following beliefs:
A. Earth-centered worldview
B. We are responsible for the future

2-11 Solutions: Living more sustainably
Environmental sustainability must become a way of life.
A. Environmental sustainability requires reverence for all life, an effort to learn all that we can about
    the earth, that we become seekers of environmental wisdom, and continuously evaluate our
    worldview while working to make the world a better place.
B. Components necessary to save our planet follow:
    1. Efficiency revolution: no waste
    2. A solar-hydrogen revolution: solar energy
    3. Pollution prevention revolution: less waste
    4. Biodiversity protection revolution: protect life
    5. Sufficiency revolution: enough resources for all
    6. Demographic revolution: balance in populations
    7. Economic and political revolution: environment sustainability

Summary

1. The two types of economic systems are command and market. They are methods to choose what goods or services to produce, how to produce them, how much to produce them, and how to distribute them to people.

2. Economic and environmental progress are monitored through the gross national income (GNI), gross domestic product (GDP), and per capita GNI and GDP indicators.

3. We can use economics to control pollution and manage resources with the internalization of external costs through economic incentives and economic disincentives.

4. Poverty can be reduced by forgiving dept to developing countries, through increase of nonmilitary government and private aid, and by stabilizing populations.

5. Principles of shifting to more environmentally sustainable economies include rewarding earth sustaining behavior, penalizing earth degrading behavior, use of full-cost pricing, and reduction of poverty.

6. Environmental policy in the US is made through: persuasion of lawmakers that an environmental problem exists, influence on how the laws are written, finding funds to implement and enforce each law, drawing up regulations for implementing each law by the appropriate government department, and the enforcement of these regulations.

7. The planetary management worldview is the human centered environmental worldview that guides most industrial societies. Variations include the no-problem school, the free-market school, the responsible planetary management school, the spaceship school, and the stewardship school.

8. Life-centered and earth-centered worldviews include environmental wisdom worldview, species centered, biosphere centered, and ecosystem centered.

Multiple Choice Questions

See Instructor's Manual, Section II, p. 156.

More Depth: Conceptual Term Paper Topics

1. Traditional versus sustainable-Earth economics. Hazel Henderson's views of converting the economic pie into a layer cake (by adding social and environmental measures of well-being and worth); GNP, NEW, ISEW, and other economic indicators; pollution control as a growth industry; a U.S. energy policy.

2. Economic and political aspects of poverty. The sharing ethic and enlightened self-interest; land reform; the World Bank and development projects; debt-for-nature swaps; technology transfer.

3. Green groups. Germany's Green Party; Earth First!; Greenpeace; the Environmental Defense Fund; the Natural Resources Defense Council; Earth Day; Public Interest Research Groups (PIRGs); Sierra Club; the Nature Conservancy; the National Wildlife Association.

More Breadth: Interdisciplinary Activities and Projects

1. Will people refrain from polluting excessively if they understand that such behavior is socially and ecologically irresponsible? Discuss this question with your class and make a list of the various reasons

people might have for ignoring moral persuasion and preaching. If possible, invite a social psychologist to address your class on the subject of attitude-behavior consistency and motivation.

2. Ask industrial and environmental lobbyists to visit the class and discuss their goals, methods, and problems.

Multisensory Learning: Audiovisuals

Heroes of the Earth; 1993; 45 min.; people who are fighting to protect the environment: the Goldman Environmental Prize winners; VP.

It Needs Political Decisions from *Race to Save the Planet;* 1990; 60 min; explores power and limitations of politics in protecting the environment; ACPB.

Now or Never from *Race to Save the Planet;* 1990; 60 min; individual action; ACPB.

Earth First: The Struggle for the Australian Rainforest; 1990; 58 min.; everyday people who stirred the conscience of a nation through their risk-taking actions; VP.

Environment Under Fire: Ecology and Politics in Central America; 1988; 28 min.; threats to Central America's environment and potential solutions; VP.

Energy and Morality; 33 min.; complex relationships among energy use, economics, and ethics; BFF.

Banking on Disaster (road in Amazonia). 78 mins., 1988. BFF

Borderline Cases. 65 mins., 1997. BFF

The Climate Puzzle (The Blue Planet series). 1986 ACPB

Concerto for the Earth. 16 min., 1992. BFF

Cry at the End of the 20th Century. 45 min. VP

The God Squad. 57 mins., 2001 BFF (politics & environmental policy)

Paying the Price. 27 mins., 2002 BFF

Rain Forest. 1991. NG.

Secrets of Silicon Valley. 60 mins., 2001. BFF

See Appendix B for suppliers.

ATTITUDES/VALUES

Assessment

1. Do you believe that individuals and countries should have the right to consume as many resources as they can afford?

2. Do you believe that the most important nation is the one that can command and use the largest fraction of the world's resources to promote its own economic growth?

3. Do you believe that the more we produce and consume, the better off we are?

4. Do you believe that humans have a duty to subdue wild nature to provide food, shelter, and other resources for people and to provide jobs and income through increased economic growth?

5. Do you believe that resources are essentially unlimited because of our ability to develop technologies to make them available or to find substitutes?

6. Do you believe that environmental improvement will result in a net loss, a net gain, or no change in the total number of jobs in your country? In your community?

7. Do you believe that environmental improvement will result in a net loss, a net gain, or no change in the total number of jobs in your country? In your community?

8. Would you be in favor of improving the air or water quality in your community if this meant a net loss of local jobs?

9. Would you be in favor of improving the air or water quality in your community if this meant that you lost your job?

10. Would you favor requiring that the market cost of any product or service include all estimated present and future environmental costs?

11. Do you favor debt-for-nature swaps in which poor countries would be forgiven most of their debts to rich countries, in exchange for protecting specified wild areas of their country from harmful and unsustainable forms of development?

12. Have you ever had an opportunity to be a leader? What leadership style do you find most comfortable?

13. Have you met a legislator who worked on environmental policy? How did you feel about the experience?

14. Have you met a grassroots environmental activist? How did you feel about the experience?

15. Do you feel the government can play a responsible role in establishing a sustainable relationship between humans and their environment?

16. Do you feel global environmental security is necessary for national security?

17. Would you support a 10% increase in income taxes if you knew this revenue would be used to improve environmental quality?

More Depth: Discussion and Term Paper Topics

1. What priorities should guide the design of a measure of sustainable economic welfare?

2. Are the best things in life not things? What are the basic material requirements for survival with dignity and security?

3. How useful is cost-benefit analysis?

4. Is global free trade a good thing?

5. What is the best way to address poverty?

(Also, see text, Critical Thinking, p. 44)

PARTICIPATION

More Depth: Action-oriented Term Paper Topics

1. Individual. Exercising environmental ethics as a consumer and as a voter; strategies for being an agent of change; Mahatma Gandhi; Martin Luther King, Jr.

2. Environmental group strategies. Active interference with environmentally damaging activities: tree hugging and painting baby seals; lobbying; letters campaigning for and against particular legislation; buying land for conservation.

3. National government methods to control pollution. Pollution prevention vs. pollution control; pollution rights; taxes; payments and incentives for pollution control; environmental legislation (such as the National Environmental Policy Act of 1969); the Environmental Protection Agency; the "regulatory takings" issue; the wise-use movement; strategies of the anti-environmental movement.

4. Global. The UN Environment Program (UNEP); 1992 Rio Earth Summit.

SKILLS

<u>Environmental Problem-Solving Skills: Projects</u>

1. Have your class survey the economic growth that has taken place recently in your state or community. Make lists of the positive and negative consequences associated with this growth; then discuss the implications for human well-being and future life quality. Should growth in your state or community be redirected? If so, specifically how? Invite a professional planner to discuss this issue with your class.

2. As a class exercise, explore the agencies in your community or state that are responsible for recruiting new industries. What are their goals and methods? Compare these values and methods with sustainable-Earth values and methods.

3. Have your class design an indicator of sustainable economic welfare that can be applied to individual communities to monitor change.

4. Have your students make a list of the employers whose payrolls are very important to the economic health of your community. How would a transition to a sustainable-Earth economy affect the employment structure of your community?

5. As a class exercise, conduct a school or community poll to find out if people are willing to pay for pollution control. Have the entire class participate in the design of a brief opinion poll. The questions should be designed to find out what kinds of environmental qualities people want to see preserved and what they are willing to give up (in monetary or other terms) to ensure that these qualities are protected. Try to standardize the procedure and get as many respondents as practical. Analyze the results and discuss them in class.

6. As a class exercise, develop the basic elements of a federal budget for next year that includes realistic levels of spending for environmental quality management. Have students decide on a list of priorities for pollution control.

7. As a class exercise, use the *Congressional Record* (or equivalent state documents) to follow the progress of various pollution, land-use, energy, population, or other environmentally related bills. If possible, have your institution join an environmental network, such as Econet, that will allow students to access information about environmental legislation, the members of relevant congressional committees, and background material to understand different environmental issues.

8. Does the United States have a sustainable-Earth president ? Have students evaluate the current administration's performance from the point of view of sustainability. They should use specific references and examples. Have students locate resources (such as documents prepared by the League of Conservation Voters) that report the voting records of members of Congress on environmental legislation. Using those resources, have students evaluate representatives from the locations where they live. Have them evaluate how important their findings are in forming an opinion about their elected officials.

9. As a class project, identify a local environmental issue early in the semester or term and follow the actions of environmental groups addressing that issue. What strategies and tactics are used, and with what effects?

Laboratory Skills

(none)

Computer Skills

Dynamic Synthesis of Basic Macroeconomic Theory (DSBMT)
 -Provides, in a single model, a synthesis of the major theoretical macroeconomic models used by economists to provide advice on the management of the economies of nations and thereby reduce disagreement among economists on economic policy.
 -System Dynamics Group, Sloan School of Management, Massachusetts Institute of Technology, 50 Memorial Dr., Cambridge, MA 02139

Environmental Assessment System (EASY)
 -Provides a flexible decision support system for political decisions involving multiple decision makers and complex issues, such as the environment.
 -R. Janssen and W. Hafkamp, Institute for Environment and Energy, Free University, P.O. Box 7161, 1007 Amsterdam, The Netherlands

CHAPTER 3
SCIENCE, SYSTEMS, MATTER, AND ENERGY

THINKING

Concept Map

See Appendix A, Maps 5a, 5b, and 6.

Goals

See the bulleted list of questions on p. 47 of text.

Objectives

1. Briefly describe how science works. State the questions science tries to answer. Summarize scientific methods.

2. Distinguish between science and technology; frontier science and consensus science.

3. Define *environmental science*. Describe two problems that arise when science is used to address environmental problems. Define *model*. Explain the conditions under which mathematical models are particularly useful to environmental science.

4. Draw a simple, generalized system. Include accumulations, flows, and feedback loops. Distinguish between positive and negative feedback loops. Give examples of each.

5. Define *matter*. Distinguish between forms of matter and quality of matter. State the law of conservation of matter. Discuss the properties of pollutants.

6. Define *energy*. Distinguish between forms of energy and quality of energy.

7. Distinguish among physical, chemical and nuclear changes. Distinguish between nuclear fission and nuclear fusion.

8. State the first and second laws of energy.

9. Describe the implications of the laws of matter and energy for a long-term sustainable-Earth society.

10. Distinguish among high-waste, matter-recycling, and low-waste societies.

Key Terms (Terms are listed in the same font style as they appear in the text.)

science (p. 47)
scientific data (p. 47)
scientific hypothesis (p. 47)
model (p. 47)
scientific theory (p. 47)
scientific law (p. 48)
natural law (p. 48)
scientific methods (p. 48)
variables (factors) (p. 48)
controlled experiment (p. 48)
single-variable analysis (p. 48)
experimental group (p. 48)

control group (p. 48)
multivariable analysis (p. 48)
frontier science (p. 49)
consensus science (p. 49)
system (p. 49)
inputs (p. 49)
flows (throughputs) (p. 49)
stores (storage areas) (p. 49)
outputs (p. 49)
mathematical model (p. 49)
feedback loop (p. 49)
positive feedback loop (p. 49)

Cutting a tree will someday make you treeless; and eventually, you will be homeless.
   A. The environment is a set of complex systems that support life as we know it.
   B. The building blocks of matter and energy support our complex environment and are weakened by pollutants, nuclear changes, and resource depletion.
   C. A sustainable economy must protect resources and make resources use more efficient.

3-1 The nature of science
   Basing their research on scientific hypotheses, scientists ask questions to explain how the world works.
   A. Scientific Theory vs. Scientific Law
   B. Scientific methods
   C. Frontier science vs. consensus science
   D. Environmental science's limits

3-2 Models and behavior of systems
   Interacting, environmental systems include three key components (matter, energy or information) which function as inputs, flows and/or storage areas and outputs.
   A. Systems change: feedback loops, time delays
   B. Influence of synergy
   C. Law of conservation of problems

3-3 Matter: Forms, structure, and quality
   The two chemical forms of matter are elements and compounds which are found together in mixtures.
   A. Characteristics of atoms, ions, and molecules
   B. Organic and inorganic compounds' influence on matter quality and efficiency

3-4 Energy: Forms and quality
   Energy can be either kinetic or potential, high-quality or low-quality.

3-5 Physical and chemical changes and the law of conservation of matter
   No physical or chemical change can create or destroy matter.
   A. Physical and chemical changes and the law of conservation of matter
   B. Example of change: pollutants

3-6 Nuclear changes
   Nuclear change occurs in three types: natural radioactive decay, nuclear fission, and nuclear fusion.
   A. Radioactive isotopes and gamma rays
   B. Effects of ionizing radiation

3-7 Two laws governing energy changes
   The first and second laws of energy explain that when energy is changed, less usable energy is the result.
   A. Mechanical, electrical, and chemical energy and their results
   B. Energy efficiency

3-8 Connections: Matter and energy change laws and environmental problems
   A 'high-throughput/high-waste economy' operates in the advanced industrialized countries of today, compromising the environment for the entire world.

Summary

1. Science is an effort to discover order in nature and make predictions on what will happen in nature. Scientists use the scientific method to formulate hypotheses or tentative explanations of their observations in nature.

2. Key components of most complex systems include inputs from the environment, throughputs, and outputs to the environment.

3. The basic forms of matter are elements and compounds. Matter is made of 115 known chemical elements. Matter quality is a measure of usefulness of specific types of matter.

4. The major forms of energy include kinetic and potential energy. Energy quality is a measure of the ability of the energy's source to perform work.

5. Physical changes of matter do not involve changes of their chemical composition. Chemical changes or chemical reactions involve alterations of the chemical nature of matter. Physical and chemical changes are governed by the law of conservation of matter.

6. The three main types of nuclear changes include the natural radioactive decay of the nucleus, nuclear fusion, and nuclear fission.

7. The two laws of thermodynamics governing energy changes are the law of conservation of energy and the law according to which we can never recycle high quality energy.

8. Through human activities high quality energy and matter resources are converted to low quality heat and waste materials added to the environment.

Multiple Choice Questions

See Instructor's Manual, Section II, p. 167.

More Depth: Conceptual Term Paper Topics

1. The universe. Total amounts of matter and energy in the universe; the big bang theory of the origin of the universe; the role of entropy in the destiny of the universe.

2. Low-energy lifestyles. Individual case studies such as Amory Lovins and national case studies such as Sweden.

3. Nature's cycles and economics. Recycling attempts in the United States; bottlenecks that inhibit recycling; strategies that successfully enhance recycling efforts.

More Breadth: Interdisciplinary Activities and Projects

1. Ask a physics professor or physics lab instructor to visit your class and, by using simple experiments, demonstrate the matter and energy laws.

2. As a class exercise, try to inventory the types of environmental disorders that are created in order to maintain a classroom environment—the lighting, space heating and cooling, electricity for projectors, and other facilities, equipment, and services.

3. Invite a medical technician to speak to your class on the beneficial uses of ionizing radiation. What controls are employed to limit the risks associated with the use of radioisotopes for diagnostic and treatment procedures?

Multisensory Learning: Audiovisuals

Climate Puzzle (Planet Earth series). 1986 ACPB
Turning Down the Heat. 46 mins, 2000. BFF

Science and the Third World; 1994; 23 min.; challenge to science to develop solutions for third-world fecal contamination of drinking water, large-scale deforestation, and inefficient agricultural methods; FHS.

See Appendix B for suppliers.

ATTITUDES/VALUES

Assessment

1. Do you feel a part of the flow of energy from the sun?

2. Do you feel you play a role in nature's cycles?

3. How do you feel when your home is air-conditioned? heated?

4. How do you feel when you turn on a light? the television? your CD player?

5. How do you feel on a sunny day? a cloudy day?

6. What right do you have to use of the earth's material resources? Are there any limits to your rights? What are they?

7. What rights do you have to the earth's energy resources? Are there any limits to your rights? What are they?

8. Do you believe that cycles of matter and energy flow from the sun have anything to do with your lifestyle? with your country's policies?

More Depth: Discussion and Term Paper Topics

1. An evaluation of the positive and negative contributions of nuclear technologies. Nuclear weapons in World War II and the cold war; radioisotopes in research and medical technology; nuclear power plants.

2. How much are you willing to pay in the short run to receive economic and environmental benefits in the long run? Explore costs and payback times of energy-efficient appliances, energy-saving light bulbs, and weather stripping.

3. Can we get something for nothing? Explore the attempts of advertising to convince the public that we can indeed get something for nothing. Explore attempts to create perpetual motion machines. Explore the history of the *free lunch* concept.

4. Is convenience more important than sustainability? Explore the influence of U.S. frontier origins on the throwaway mentality.

(Also, see text, Critical Thinking, p. 62)

PARTICIPATION

More Depth: Action-oriented Term Paper Topics

1. Individual. Actions that improve energy efficiency and reduce consumption of materials.

2. Community. Enhance recycling efforts: curbside pick up versus recycling center drop-offs; high-tech versus low-tech sorting of materials; Osage, Iowa, a case study in community energy efficiency.

3. National energy policy. Evaluation of the current national energy policy proposals in light of the laws of energy and long-term economic, environmental, and national-security interests.

SKILLS

<u>Environmental Problem-Solving Skills: Projects</u>

1. A human body at rest yields heat at about the same rate as a 100-watt incandescent light bulb. As a class exercise, calculate the heat production of the student body of your school, the U.S. population, and the global population. Where does the heat come from? Where does it go?

2. As a class exercise, conduct a survey of the students at your school to determine their degree of awareness and understanding of the three basic matter and energy laws. Discuss the results in the context of the need for low-entropy lifestyles and sustainable-Earth societies.

<u>Laboratory Skills</u>

(none)

<u>Computer Skills</u>

<u>(none)</u>

CHAPTER 4
ECOSYSTEMS: COMPONENTS, ENERGY FLOW, AND MATTER CYCLING

THINKING

<u>Concept Map</u>

See Appendix A, Maps 7 and 8.

<u>Goals</u>

See bulleted list of questions on p. 65 of text.

<u>Objectives</u>

1. List six characteristics of life. Distinguish between *sexual reproduction* and *asexual reproduction*. Briefly describe a mechanism for evolution.

2. List and briefly describe four layers or spheres of the earth. Compare the flow of matter and the flow of energy through the biosphere.

3. Define *biome*. Explain the major cause of the distribution of biomes on the Earth. Define biological diversity and distinguish among three types of biodiversity. Distinguish between *population and species; wild species and domestic species; biome and aquatic life zone.*

4. Distinguish between *abiotic* and *biotic* components of ecosystems. Describe how organisms are classified by how they get their nutrients. Be sure to distinguish between the following sets of terms: *producer and consumer; autotroph and heterotroph; photosynthesis and chemosynthesis, aerobic respiration and anaerobic respiration; herbivore, carnivore, omnivore and detritivore.*

5. Explain the concept of *tolerance*. Define *limiting factor*. Give one example of a limiting factor in an ecosystem.

6. Apply the second law of energy to food chains and pyramids of energy, which describe energy flow in ecosystems. Briefly describe two other ecological pyramids and indicate if their shape is always a pyramid.

7. Discuss *productivity*, its importance and factors which influence it. Give examples of areas of high, moderate, and low productivity and give reasons for their respective productivities.

8. Apply the law of conservation of matter to biogeochemical cycles, which describe the flow of matter through ecosystems. Briefly describe the following cycles: carbon, nitrogen, phosphorous, sulfur. Summarize the major ways that humans affect each cycle.

9. Briefly describe the hydrologic cycle. Distinguish among the following: *evaporation, transpiration, condensation, precipitation, infiltration, percolation, runoff.*

10. What are *ecosystem services*, and how are they important to human life?

Key Terms (Terms are listed in the same font style as they appear in the text.)

ecology (p. 65)
organism (p. 65)
cell (p. 65)
eukaryotic (p. 65)
organelles (p. 65)
prokaryotic (p. 65)
microorganisms (p. 66)
species (p. 66)
asexual reproduction (p. 66)
sexual reproduction (p. 66)
population (p. 66)
genetic diversity (p. 66)
habitat (p. 66)
community (p. 68)
biological community (p. 68)
ecosystem (p. 68)
biosphere (p. 68)
atmosphere (p. 68)
troposphere (p. 68)
stratosphere (p. 68)
hydrosphere (p. 68)
lithosphere (p. 68)
biosphere (p. 68)
photosynthesis (p. 69)
visible light (p. 69)
infrared radiation (p. 69)
ultraviolet radiation (p. 69)
natural greenhouse effect (p. 70)
biomes (p. 70)
climate (p. 70)
aquatic life zone (p. 70)
freshwater life zones (p. 70)
ocean or *marine life zones* (p. 70)
abiotic (p. 70)
biotic (p. 70)
range of tolerance (p. 72)
optimum level or *range* (p. 72)
law of tolerance (p. 72)
limiting factor (p. 73)
limiting factor principle (p. 73)
dissolved oxygen content (p. 73)
salinity (p. 73)
producers (p.73)
autotrophs (p. 73)
phytoplankton (p. 73)
photosynthesis (p. 73)
chemosynthesis (p. 73)
consumers (p. 73)
heterotrophs (p. 73)
detritivores (p. 73)
detritus (p. 73)
omnivores (p. 73)
decomposers (p. 73)

aerobic respiration (p. 73)
anaerobic respiration (p. 73)
fermentation (p. 73)
matter recycling (p. 73)
one-way energy flow (p. 73)
biological diversity (p. 74)
biodiversity (p. 74)
genetic diversity (p. 74)
species diversity (p. 74)
ecological diversity (p. 74)
functional diversity (p. 74)
human cultural diversity (p. 74)
food chain (p. 76)
trophic level (p. 76)
food web (p. 76)
biomass (p. 76)
ecological efficiency (p. 76)
pyramid of energy flow (p. 76)
gross primary productivity (GPP) (p. 79)
net primary productivity (NPP) (p. 79)
nutrient (p. 81)
nutrient cycles (p. 81)
biogeochemical cycles (p. 81)
hydrologic cycle (p. 81)
water cycle (p. 81)
evaporation (p. 81)
transpiration (p. 81)
condensation (p. 81)
precipitation (p. 81)
infiltration (p. 81)
percolation (p. 81)
aquifer (p. 81)
runoff (p. 81)
surface runoff (p. 81)
carbon cycle (p. 82)
natural greenhouse effect (p. 84)
global warming (p. 84)
nitrogen cycle (p. 84)
nitrogen fixation (p. 84)
Rhizobium (p. 85)
nodules (p. 85)
nitrification (p. 85)
nitrite ions (NO_2^-) (p. 85)
nitrate ions (NO_3^-) (p. 85)
assimilation (p. 85)
ammonia (NH_3) (p. 85)
ammonium ions (NH_4^+) (p. 85)
ammonification (p. 85)
denitrification (p. 85)
acid deposition (p. 85)
acid rain (p. 85)
phosphorus cycle (p. 85)
phosphate ion (PO_4^-) (p. 85)

sulfur cycle (p. 86)
sulfate (SO_4^{2-}) (p. 86)
hydrogen sulfide (H_2S) (p. 86)
sulfur dioxide (SO_2) (p. 86)
field research (p. 87)
remote sensing (p. 87)

geographic information systems (GISs) (p. 87)
laboratory research (p. 87)
systems analysis (p. 88)
ecosystem services (p. 89)
sustainability (p. 89)

Outline

Ants, flies, mosquitoes, and cockroaches all form living biological communities, necessary components of an ecosystem.
    A. The earth's life-support systems maintain entire ecosystems.
    B. Eco-systems, influenced by physical and chemical components, support bio-diversity while connecting food webs and energy flows.
        1. Law of tolerance
        2. Producing or consuming organisms
        3. Biodiversity's importance
        4. Food webs and matter cycling
    C. Biogeochemical cycles affect the biosphere as well as the earth's ecosystems
    D. What are the connections between ecosystems and sustainability?

4-1 The nature of ecology
Ecology studies the interaction of organisms with each other and with their non-living environment.
    A. Eukaryotic and prokaryotic organisms are classified into species which reproduce sexually and asexually.
    B. Populations and their habitats form biological communities which eventually establish an ecosystem.

4-2 Connections: The earth's life-support systems
The earth's life-support systems are protected by several layers which help sustain life through energy from the sun, cycling of matter, and gravity

4-3 Ecosystem concepts and components
Biotic and abiotic components make up ecosystems which are distinguishable by their chemical and physical characteristics.
    A. Biomes and aquatic life systems
    B. Physical and chemical environments
        1. Range of tolerance and law of tolerance
        2. Limiting factor(s)
    C. Ecosystem biological components
        1. Producers/autotrophs
        2. Consumers/heterotrophs
    D. Biodiversity: genetic, species, ecological, functional

4-4 Connections: Food webs and energy flow in ecosystems
Ecosystem connections support and enhance food webs and energy flow.
    A. Food chains and food webs
    B. Energy flow in an ecosystem

4-5 Primary productivity of ecosystems

4-6 Connections: Matter cycling in ecosystems
Nutrient cycles composed of various carbon, oxygen, nitrogen, phosphorus, and hydrologic cycles are cycled through the non-living environment.
    A. The biosphere and nutrient cycles
    B. Human activities and the nutrient cycles

4-7 How do ecologists learn about ecosystems
Knowledge about ecosystems is acquired through field research, laboratory research and system analysis.

4-8 Connections: Ecosystem services and sustainability
The two basic principles of ecosystem sustainability are renewable solar energy and recycling of chemical nutrients.

<u>Summary</u>

1. Ecology is the study of the interactions between organisms and their environment.

2. The basic processes that keep organisms alive include the one-way flow of high quality energy, the cycling of matter, and gravity.

3. The two major components of an ecosystem are the biotic and abiotic. The biotic components include all living organisms and the abiotic are represented by all chemical and physical factors present within an ecosystem.

4. Energy flow through an ecosystem is characterized by an ecological efficiency that varies from 5% to 20%.

5. The main components of an ecosystem are linked by matter recycling. There is very little matter wasted in natural ecosystems.

6. Scientists study ecosystems through field and laboratory research. In field research the scientists observe and measure various parameters of the ecosystems. In the laboratory they study models of ecosystems.

7. Ecosystems services support life on the earth and define the quality of human life. The ecosystem sustainability is characterized by two basic principles. Ecosystems use renewable solar energy, and they recycle chemical nutrient needed by the biotic components for survival.

<u>Multiple Choice Questions</u>

See Instructor's Manual, Section II, p. 177.

<u>More Depth: Conceptual Term Paper Topics</u>

1. Cycles of matter. Particular cycles of matter, clarifying chemical changes throughout the cycle; the processes of photosynthesis and respiration and how they connect autotrophic and heterotrophic organisms.

2. Energy flow. Energy flow in a particular ecosystem; relationships among species in a particular ecosystem; comparison of the life of a specialist with that of a generalist.

3. Humans trying to work with ecosystems. Composting; organic gardening; land reclamation; rebuilding degraded lands; tree-planting projects.

<u>More Breadth: Interdisciplinary Activities and Projects</u>

1. Organize a class trip to a natural area such as a forest, grassland, or estuary to observe the elements of ecosystem structure and function. Arrange for an ecologist or naturalist to provide interpretive services.

2. Bring a self-sustaining terrarium or aquarium to class and explain the structure and function of this conceptually tidy ecosystem. Discuss the various things that can upset the balance of the ecosystem and describe what would happen if light, food, oxygen, or space were manipulated experimentally.

3. Find works of literature, art, and music that show human attachment to and destruction of natural ecosystems.

Multisensory Learning: Audiovisuals

Principles of Ecology; 1994; 23 min.; humans connected to nature, Gaia, and urban life; FHS.
Arctic Wildlife Refuge: a wilderness in peril. 15 min., WS
Clean Water. FHS
Creatures of the Sun. 24 min., 1998. BFF
Dams, Debates, and Development. 60 mins., 1994. WBG
Inside-Outside. 26 min., 1998. BFF
Partnership. 26 min., 1998. BFF
A Plague Upon the Land. 24 mins., 1983. WBG
Where the Bay (of Fundy) Becomes the Sea. 30 min., 1986 BFF

See Appendix B for suppliers.

ATTITUDES/VALUES

Assessment

1. Do you feel you are part of an ecosystem? What niche do you fill?

2. Do you hold any particular feelings for producers? consumers? decomposers?

3. Do you feel there will always be enough matter and energy for the survival of all individuals of all species? Will the carrying capacity of the Earth be expanded by new technologies? Will nature be able to continually absorb "waste-products" from human societies?

4. How do you feel you think of a coyote eating a rabbit? How do you feel when you think of humans eating hamburgers?

5. Do you feel any responsibility to protect natural ecosystems? Would you support the preservation of representative ecosystems? If so, on what basis?

More Depth: Discussion and Term Paper Topics

1. Should we eat lower on the food chain?

2. Should we rely more on perpetual sources of energy?

3. What do nature's cycles of matter suggest about landfills, incinerators, reducing consumption, and recycling?

(Also, see text, Critical Thinking, p. 90.)

PARTICIPATION

More Depth: Action-oriented Term Paper Topics

1. Field and laboratory methods used in ecological research. Measuring net primary productivity and respiration rates; analyzing for particular chemicals in the air, water, and soil; studying relationships among species; population studies; computer modeling of ecological interrelationships.

SKILLS

Environmental Problem-Solving Skills: Projects

1. As a class exercise, have each student list the kinds and amounts of food he or she has consumed in the past 24 hours. Aggregate the results and compare them on a per capita basis with similar statistics derived from studies of dietary composition and adequacy in food-deficient nations. How many people with a vegetarian diet could subsist on the equivalent food value of the meat consumed by your class?

2. Have the students debate the argument that eating lower on the food chain is socially and ecologically more responsible, cheaper, and healthier. Also, look at the long-term picture: will eating low on the food chain sustain an exponentially growing human population indefinitely?

3. Define an ecosystem to study on campus. As a class project, analyze the abiotic and biotic components of the ecosystem. Draw webs and construct pyramids to show the relationships among species in the ecosystem. Project what might happen if pesticides were used in the ecosystem, if parts of the ecosystem were cleared for development, or if a coal-burning power plant were located upwind.

Laboratory Skills

Laboratory Manual for Miller's Living in the Environment and Environmental Science, Lab 1: Introduction to the Compound Microscope; Lab 2: Biological Classification; Lab 3: The Plankton Community.

Computer Skills

SimEarth

CHAPTER 5
EVOLUTION AND BIODIVERSITY: ORIGINS, NICHES, AND ADAPTATION

THINKING

Concept Map

See Appendix A, Map 9.

Goals

See bulleted list of questions on p. 93 of text.

Objectives

1. List the five kingdoms of life. Distinguish between annual and perennial plants. Distinguish between vertebrates and invertebrates.

2. Summarize chemical and biological evolution. Explain the importance of mutations and natural selection to adaptation and differential reproduction. Define coevolution. Summarize the roles played by mass extinctions and adaptive radiations in the evolutionary process.

3. Define *niche*. Distinguish among the following sets of terms: specialist, generalist; fundamental niche, realized niche. Differentiate between *niche* and *habitat*.

4. Describe connections among mutations, adaptations, differential reproduction, and biological evolution. List and describe three possible outcomes of natural selection.

5. List four limits of adaptation to change. Summarize three common misconceptions about evolution.

6. Describe biodiversity in terms of speciation and extinction.

7. Summarize how humans have tinkered with evolutionary processes; nature's lessons that can be adopted as principles for more sustainable lifestyles; and ways that humans can restore and rehabilitate ecosystems.

Key Terms (Terms are listed in the same font style as they appear in the text.)

biological evolution (p. 93)
chemical evolution (p. 93)
fossils (p. 93)
biological evolution (p. 93)
populations (p. 95)
theory of evolution (p. 95)
microevolution (p. 95)
macroevolution (p. 95)
genetic variability (p. 95)
chromosomes (p. 95)
nucleotides (p. 95)
gene pool (p. 95)
alleles (p. 95)
mutation (p. 95)
natural selection (p. 95)

differential reproduction (p. 95)
adaptation (p. 95)
adaptive trait (p. 95)
directional natural selection (p. 95)
stabilizing natural selection (p. 96)
diversifying natural selection (p. 96)
coevolution (p. 96)
ecological niche (niche) (p. 96)
habitat (p. 96)
fundamental niche (p. 96)
realized niche (p. 98)
generalist species (p. 98)
specialist species (p. 98)
speciation (p. 100)
geographic isolation (p. 100)

reproductive isolation (p. 100)
divergence (p. 100)
divergent evolution (p. 100)
extinction (p. 100)
background extinction (p. 102)

mass extinction (p. 102)
mass depletion (p. 102)
adaptive radiations (p. 102)
biodiversity (p. 103)

Outline

Earth, the 'just-right' planet, must maintain certain environmental conditions to survive.
    A. Evolution and adaptation have changed life on earth, influencing each and every organism.
    B. Genetic variability, through mutations, occurs in the three types of natural selection: directional, stabilizing, and diversifying natural selection.
    C. Ecological niches and adaptation influence each ecosystem.
    D. Species evolve, become extinct and create biodiverse environments.

5-1 Origins of life
How did life emerge and survive on earth?

5-2 Evolution and adaptation
Evolution and adaptation have been the basis of earth's survival.
    A. Chemical and biological evolution
    B. Theory of evolution: microevolution and macroevolution
    C. Types of natural selection
    D. Artificial selection
    E. Co-evolution

5-3 Ecological niches and adaptation
What is an ecological niche, and how do adaptations affect the fundamental and realized niches?
    A. Generalist species-broad niches
    B. Specialist species-narrow niches
    C. Limits on Adaptation

5-4 Speciation, extinction, and biodiversity
The two phases of speciation, geographic isolation and reproductive isolation, may produce two species from an original one specie.
    A. Species extinction: background and mass extinction
    B. Speciation, extinction and biodiversity

Summary

1.   Organisms convert solar energy to chemical energy; chemicals are involved in specific cycles; and various species have evolved and are adapted in various environmental conditions.

2.   Evolution is the driving force of adaptation of organisms to their environmental conditions.

3.   Adaptive traits enable organisms to reproduce and survive under adverse environmental conditions through the mechanisms of natural selection.

4.   The ecological niche of an organism describes its functional role within a specific ecosystem, and it involves all the factors that affect its survival and reproductive success.

5.   Speciation and extinction define a measure of biodiversity seeing as the massive gene pool of our planet.

Multiple Choice Questions

See Instructor's Manual, Section II, p. 190.

More Depth: Conceptual Term Paper Topics

1. Evolution. The theory of evolution. Supporting and detracting evidence. Fossils; embryological homologies, structural homologies; biochemical evidence; DNA evidence. Contrast the views of slow, gradual change and relatively rapid (punctuated) change.

2. Biological Evolution: endosymbiont hypothesis; Gaia hypothesis; extinctions and radiations; natural selection and genetic drift; adaptations and their limits; gradualism and punctuated equilibrium.

3. Diversity of species: choose a kingdom.

4. Genetic engineering: how humans are changing the course of evolution.

More Breadth: Interdisciplinary Activities and Projects

1. As a class exercise, evaluate the diversity of your community using criteria such as ethnic, racial, religious, and socioeconomic groups; lifestyles; and industries, landscape features, and landscape forms. What elements of diversity have proved troublesome? What additional elements of diversity would improve your community?

2. Invite an evolutionary biologist to your class. Ask about evidence for different parts of the theory of evolution, including the endosymbiont hypothesis. Ask about the Gaia hypothesis.

3. Arrange a field trip providing opportunities to compare and contrast ecosystems of several different types, including some damaged or stressed by human activities. Invite an ecologist or biologist along to identify and discuss specific examples of species adaptation to environmental conditions. Do the boundaries between different kinds of ecosystems tend to be sharply delineated? Can you identify factors that limit the growth of certain species?

Multisensory Learning: Audiovisuals

Continental Drift: Legacy of Fire; 1998; 50 min.; geologists explore the Pacific Rim with earthquakes, volcanoes, and rich mineral deposits, all clues to continental drift; FHS.
Death of the Dinosaurs; 1998; 50 min.; exploration of a theory that a series of volcanic eruptions lead to the demise of the dinosaurs; FHS.
Dawn of Man. 300 min. (2 parts). BBC America
Death of the Dinosaurs. 50 min., 1998. FHS
Evolution series 8 hours, 2001. PBS
Great Gene Robbert: genetic diversity crisis. 26 min., 1988. BFF
Natural Connections. 46 mins., 2000. BFF
Origins of Human Kind (Web video). PBS (free access)
Shape of Life (animal evolution). 8 parts. PBS
Nature's Numbers: Assessing Species Extinction; 1998; 47 min.; scientists attempting to quantify loss of species; FHS.
Oxygen: The Poison Gas; 1998; 50 min.; the origins of bacteria-generated oxygen in the atmosphere viewed in light of current human-generated atmospheric emissions; FHS.

See Appendix B for suppliers.

ATTITUDES/VALUES

Assessment

1. Do you think that biodiversity is an ecosystem service? Explain.

2. Do you think you have a responsibility to sustain biodiversity?

3. Do you think evolution of species has occurred? If so, how?

4. Do you think species have a right to struggle to survive without human interference?

More Depth: Discussion and Term Paper Topics

1. To what extent should humans take evolution into their own hands?

2. Should there be limits on genetic engineering?

3. How does the change that humans create through cultural evolution compare to the process of evolution by natural selection?

(Also, see text, Critical Thinking, p. 104)

PARTICIPATION

More Depth: Action-oriented Term Paper Topics

1. Scientific methods: genetic engineering; DNA analysis.

SKILLS

Environmental Problem-Solving Skills: Projects

1. As a class, consider the crops that provide the majority of our food. Brainstorm a list of "designer genes" that would improve those crops for human consumption. Reflect on how genetic engineering alters the relationship between humans and evolution. Consider the power and the limits of that relationship.

Laboratory Skills

Replicate some of Oparin's experiments adding energy to atmospheric gases that probably existed before the formation of organic molecules.

Computer Skills

-Evolution: *Sim Earth*

CHAPTER 6
CLIMATE, TERRESTRIAL BIODIVERSITY, AND AQUATIC BIODIVERSITY

THINKING

Concept Map

See Appendix A, Maps 10 and 11.

Goals

See bulleted list of questions on p. 107 of text.

Objectives

1. Distinguish between weather and climate. List and briefly describe seven factors that determine patterns of global air circulation.

2. Describe how climate affects the distribution of plant life on Earth. Compare the climate and adaptations of plants and animals in deserts, grasslands, and forests. Be sure to distinguish among the three major kinds of forests.

3. Evaluate the significance of the ecological contributions of the oceans. Distinguish between coastal zones and open sea. List and compare the four principal zones of an ocean.

4. Distinguish between coastal and inland wetlands. Describe the ecological functions performed by wetlands. Describe environmental problems associated with coastal and inland wetlands.

5. List and compare the four zones of a lake. Distinguish among oligotrophic, eutrophic, and mesotrophic lakes. Distinguish among the three zones of a freshwater stream.

Key Terms (Terms are listed in the same font style as they appear in the text.)

troposphere (p. 107)
weather (p. 107)
climate (p. 107)
average temperature (p. 107)
average precipitation (p. 107)
uneven heating (p. 107)
seasonal changes (p. 108)
upwelling (p. 109)
El Niño – Southern Oscillation (*ENSO*) (p. 109)
La Niña (p. 109)
greenhouse gasses (p. 110)
greenhouse effect (p. 111)
water vapor (p. 111)
ozone layer (p. 111)
thermal cap (p. 112)
microclimates (p. 112)
rain shadow effect (p. 112)
biomes (p. 112)
latitude (p. 113)
altitude (p. 113)

succulent plants (p. 116)
broadleaf evergreen plants (p. 120)
coniferous evergreen plants (p. 114)
desert (p. 115)
tropical deserts (p. 115)
temperate deserts (p. 115)
cold deserts (p. 115)
semidesert (p. 116)
grasslands (p. 116)
topical grasslands (p. 116)
savanna (p. 116)
grazing (p. 116)
browsing (p. 116)
temperate grassland (p.118)
tall-grass prairies (p. 118)
short-grass prairies (p. 118)
pampas (p. 118)
veldt (p. 118)
steppes (p. 118)
polar grasslands (p. 118)

Outline

    A. Over a period of time weather patterns determine the climate of a particular area.

    B. Land areas with particular characteristics adapted to climate are called biomes: deserts, mountains, aquatic environments, for example.

    C. Individual biome sustainability must be maintained to support both terrestrial and aquatic biodiversity.

6-1 Weather and climate: A brief introduction

    A. Short-term properties in earth's inner atmosphere, the troposphere, at a particular time and place are weather.

    B. The general pattern of weather over time constitutes climate.

        1. Factors in air circulation patterns

        2. Effect of ocean currents on climate

6-2 Biomes: Climate and life on land

    A. Biomes are land areas that support characteristic types of ecological communities adapted to regional climates.

B.   The climate and vegetation of biomes vary with changes in latitude and altitude.

6-3 Desert and grassland biomes
A.   There are three major types of desert: tropical, temperate, and cold deserts.
B.   Grasslands, also, are divided into three major types: tropical, temperate, and polar/tundra.
1.   Savannas, tall-grass prairies and short-grass prairies
2.   Polar grasslands/arctic tundra and permafrost

6-4 Forest and mountain biomes
A.   Moderate to high annual precipitation and average temperatures support the growth of forests.
B.   Plants and animals of tropical rainforests are usually very abundant.
C.   Temperate deciduous forests contain oak, hickory, maple, poplar, and sycamore trees.
D.   Most boreal forests contain a few species of coniferous evergreen trees.
E.   Mountains may be 'islands of biodiversity'.
1.   Human impact on forests
2.   Human impact on mountains

6-5 Aquatic environments: Types and characteristics
A.   Marine zones and freshwater zones are the major zones of aquatic life.
1.   Aquatic life zone organisms
2.   Layers of aquatic life zones
B.   Nutrient availability influences the kind and amount of marine life.

6-6 Saltwater life zones
A.   The earth is an ocean planet whose coastal zone is much affected by humans.
B.   Different areas of the coastal zone contain different biomes: estuaries, coastal wetlands and intertidal zones.
C.   In addition to beauty, coral reefs provide both ecological and economic advantages.
D.   Biological zones of the open sea are the euphotic zone, the bathyal zone, and the abyssal zone.
E.   Human degradation of marine systems is extensive.

6-7 Freshwater life zones
A.   Freshwater life zones are divided into either lentic bodies of fresh water or lotic bodies of flowing water.
B.   The four zones of lakes are the littoral zone, the limnetic zone, the profundal zone and the benthic zone.
1.   Oligotrophic lake
2.   Eutrophic lake
C.   Water, which is not absorbed into the ground and does not evaporate is called surface water; when it goes into a stream it is called runoff.
D.   As water flows down from the mountains, it passes through three different aquatic zones: the source zone, the transition zone, and the floodplain zone.
E.   Freshwater inland wetlands are from coastal areas and covered with fresh water all or much of the time.
F.   What are the impacts of humans on freshwater systems?

6-8 Sustainability of aquatic life zones
A.   Aquatic life zones constantly purify and replenish themselves; but they do not work if overloaded with pollutants, overfishing, and human carelessness.
B.   Everything in the earth's terrestrial and aquatic systems is interconnected.

Summary

1. The key factors that determine the earth's weather and climate include the uneven heating of the earth's surface, the seasonal changes in temperature and precipitation, and the rotation of the earth on its axis.

2. Climate determines where the various biomes are found on earth through differences in average temperature and precipitation determined by the global air circulation patterns.

3. Major types of desert include tropical, temperate, cold deserts, and semideserts. The human impacts on deserts involve soil destruction, and salinization, depletion of underground water, land disturbance and pollution, and storage of toxic waste.

4. Major types of grasslands are the tropical, temperate, and cold (tundra). The human impacts of grasslands are the conversion of cropland and subsequent release of massive amounts of carbon dioxide into the atmosphere, overgrazing, and the damage to the tundra by oil production and pollution.

5. Major types of forests are the tropical, temperate, and polar (boreal). The human impacts on forests include clearing, degradation, and conversion to less biodiverse tree plantations.

6. Major types of saltwater aquatic life zones include estuaries, coastlines, coral reefs, coastal marshes, mangrove swamps, and oceans. Human impacts include loss of coastal wetlands, mangroves, and coral reefs, beach erosion, and ocean bottom degradation.

7. Major types of fresh water aquatic life zones include lakes, ponds, streams, rivers, and inland wetlands. Human impacts include alteration and destruction of habitats through draining, damming, building levees, and dredging canals.

Multiple Choice Questions

See Instructor's Manual, Section II, p. 196.

More Depth: Conceptual Term Paper Topics

1. Long- and short-term climate change, effects of changing climate on composition and distribution of ecosystems.

2. Plant and animal adaptations to different biomes. Desert plants and animals; plants and animals of the tundra; mountain microclimates and vertically zoned vegetation; organisms of the Amazon.

3. Fragile ecosystems. Deserts; tropical forests; tundra.

More Breadth: Interdisciplinary Activities and Projects

1. Ask students to bring to class and share examples of art, music, poetry, and other creative expressions of human thoughts and feelings about Earth's deserts, grasslands, forests, and oceans. Lead a class discussion on the subject of how human culture has been shaped to an important degree by the environmental conditions of each major biome.

Multisensory Learning: Audiovisuals

Fragile Ecosystems; 1994; 23 min.; marshes, soils, the atmosphere; FHS.
Ecology of the Southern Seas; 1994; 23 min.; corals, mollusks, and hurricanes; FHS.

The Desert; 1994; 23 min.; adaptations; FHS.
Estuary; 12 min.; use of underwater microphotography; BFF.
The Intertidal Zone; 17 min.; ecology of the intertidal and pollution effects on food chains; BFF.
Aliens from Planet Earth, 2000. TVE
America's Prairie. 53 mins., 1998 FHS
Assessing Our Planets Health. 1990. FHS
Australia's Great Barrier Reef. 60 mins. NG
Coral Reef Adventure. 42 min., NWF
Coral Reefs: vanishing treasures. 22 min., OCE
Desert Biomes. 2002. FHS
Forest Environments: Mesic forest types. 28 mins., 2000. FHS
Global Warming and Climate Change. 58 min., 1996. WBG
Grasslands Biomes. 2002. FHS
Great North (arctic ecosystem). 40 min., ATA
Is There a Crisis? Biodiversity in decline. 2000. FHS
The Living Landscape (Australian ecosystem series). GF
Killer Wave: power of the Tsunami. NG
Once and Future Planet. 24 mins., 1990 BFF
Rainforest. 60 mins. NG
Rainforest: the puzzle of diversity. 25 min., 1995. FHS
Secrets of the Bay (San Francisco Bay). 28 min. VP
Understanding Oceans. 53 mins., 1996 FHS
Wild Weather. 50 min (4 pts.), 2002. BBC

See Appendix B for suppliers.

ATTITUDES/VALUES

Assessment

1.   Do you feel that the development of your community is related to the climate of the area?

2.   Are you aware of mountains or bodies of water in your area that affect local climate conditions?

3.   Have you visited a variety of types of ecosystems? If so, where do you feel most at home?

More Depth: Discussion and Term Paper Topics

1.   Human influence on good and bad ozone.

2.   What is life like at hydrothermal vents in the deep ocean?

3.   Should we retreat from the beach? Should houses built on barrier beaches have access to insurance?

(Also, see text, Critical Thinking, p. 138)

PARTICIPATION

More Depth: Action-oriented Term Paper Topics

1.   The Montreal Protocol; Kyoto Protocol.

2.   Wetlands protection.

3.   Prevention of beach erosion.

4.   Coastal cleanup strategies.

SKILLS

Environmental Problem-Solving Skills: Projects

1. What soil types and significantly different microclimates exist in your locale? As a class project, inventory these elements of diversity and relate them to observable differences in the distribution of vegetation, animal life, agricultural activities, and other phenomena.

2. Are inland wetlands being drained and filled in your locale? Is there a nearby stream or river being subjected to excessive levels of pollution? Are there ponds and lakes in your vicinity suffering from cultural eutrophication? Do you live where spartina marshes or estuaries are suffering from human-induced stresses? Is it feasible for you and your class to "adopt" one of these disturbed ecosystems and help restore it to health?

3. Arrange a debate on the problems and alternatives of coastal zone management. Debate the proposition that we should severely restrict engineering approaches to beach stabilization and adopt a "retreat from the beach" strategy, emphasizing the preservation of coastal ecosystems and the ecosystem services they provide.

Laboratory Skills

(none)

Computer Skills

-Prof. John D. Sterman, Sloan School of Management, Massachusetts Institute of Technology, 50 Memorial Dr., Cambridge, MA 02139 (Ask about Limits to Growth Model)

-Earth Explorer, Claris Corporation. Contact: Richard Finlayson, Product Marketing Manager, Apple Home Learning Solutions, 5201 Patrick Henry Dr. MS: C-21, Santa Clara, CA   95054 (408) 987-3084 (voice); 408-987-3084 (fax)

CHAPTER 7
COMMUNITY ECOLOGY: STRUCTURE, SPECIES INTERACTIONS, SUCCESSION, AND SUSTAINABILITY

THINKING

<u>Concept Map</u>

See Appendix A, Map 12.

<u>Goals</u>

See bulleted list of questions on p. 141 of text.

<u>Objectives</u>

1. Summarize the theory of island biogeography. Imagine two islands of two different sizes and distances from the mainland. Predict which would show the greatest species diversity. Defend your position.

2. List characteristics and examples of *native species, exotic species, indicator species,* and *keystone species.*

3. Describe the following relationships between species: *interspecific competition* including *interference competition, exploitation competition,* and *resource partitioning; predation* and *parasitism; commensalism* and *mutualism.* Summarize how competition and cooperation enable species to define their realized niche in the ecosystem.

4. Distinguish among the following species interactions and give one example of each: *interspecific competition, predation,* and *symbiosis.* Distinguish between *interference competition* and *exploitation competition.* Summarize the competitive exclusion principle. List two strategies species use to reduce competition.

5. List two strategies that predators use to capture their prey. List at least five strategies that prey use to defend themselves against predators.

6. Distinguish among three forms of symbiotic relationships and give one example of each: *parasitism, mutualism, and commensalism.*

7. Define *succession.* Distinguish between *primary* and *secondary succession.* List four categories of successional species and give one example of each. List three factors that affect how succession occurs.

8. Summarize contributions of disturbances (such as fire) to your understanding of succession. Evaluate the intermediate disturbance hypothesis. Support your conclusions with examples from your own experience if possible. Summarize how chaos theory contributes to your understanding of succession.

9. Distinguish among the following types of stability and give an example of an ecosystem which exemplifies each: inertia, constancy, resilience. Evaluate the interaction of stability and diversity.

Key Terms (Terms are listed in the same font style as they appear in the text.)

structure (p. 141)
spatial distribution (p. 141)
physical appearance (p. 141)
species diversity (*richness*) (p. 141)
species abundance (p. 141)
niche structure (p141)
vegetation patches (p. 141)
ecotones (p. 141)
edge effects (p. 141)
degree of isolation (p. 142)
species equilibrium model (p. 142)
theory of island biogeography (p. 142)
native species (p. 143)
nonnative species (p. 143)
exotic species (p. 143)
alien species (p. 143)
indicator species (p. 144)
keystone species (p. 145)
habitat modifications (p. 145)
top predator (p. 145)
intraspecific competition (p.146)
interspecific competition (p.147)
resource partitioning (p. 147)
predation (p. 147)
predator-prey relationship (p. 147)
pursuit (p. 147)
ambush (p. 147)
camouflage (p. 148)
chemical warfare (p. 148)
warning coloration (p. 149)
mimicry (p. 149)

parasitism (p. 150)
parasite (p. 150)
host (p. 150)
mutualism (p. 150)
pollination (p. 150)
nutritional mutualism (p. 150)
lichens (p. 150)
commensalism (p. 151)
epiphytes (p. 151)
ecological succession (p. 152)
primary succession (p. 152)
secondary succession (p. 152)
soil (p. 152)
pioneer species (p. 152)
early successional plant species (p. 153)
midsuccessional plant species (p. 153)
late successional plant species (p. 153)
disturbance (p. 154)
intermediate disturbance hypothesis (p. 154)
climax community (p. 154)
balance of nature (p. 154)
biotic change (p. 154)
mature community (p. 154)
vegetation patches (p. 154)
inertia (p. 155)
persistence (p. 155)
constancy (p. 155)
resilience (p. 155)
stability (p. 155)
diversity (p. 155)
precautionary principle (p. 155)

Outline

Flying foxes and fruit, who would have thought it?
    A. Community structure and diverse species help define an ecosystem.
    B. Different species' interaction with and influence on their environments
        are not completely clear.
        1. Species competition and predation
        2. Species parasitism, mutualism, and commensalisms
    C. Ecological communities are constantly changing, establishing communities, responding to disturbances, and seeking stability.
    D. For the continuing survival of man's environment, we should remember the adage: "First, do no harm."

7-1 Community structure and species diversity
    A. The four characteristics of 'community structure' are physical appearance, species diversity, species abundance, and niche structure.
    B. Communities differ in physical appearance and the distribution of their animal and plant populations.
        1. Within an ecosystem: mosaic of vegetation patches
        2. At the boundaries: edge effects

C. Factors which affect the diversity of species in an ecosystem are:
1. Latitude in terrestrial communities
2. Depth in aquatic systems
3. Pollution in aquatic systems
D. Two factors affect the diversity of species in an isolated ecosystem.
1. Species equilibrium model/theory of island biogeography
2. Island's distance from mainland

7-2 General types of species
A. The four types of ecological roles of a species are the native, the nonnative, the indicator, or the keystone.
1. Indicator species: vanishing amphibians
2. Keystone species and their roles

7-3 Species interactions: Competition and predation
A. The basic types of interactions among species are interspecific competition, predation, parasitism, mutualism, and commensalisms.
1. Intraspecific and interspecific competition
2. Resource partitioning
3. Predator-prey relationships
B. Defensive methods
1. Camouflage and chemical warfare
2. Warming coloration, mimicry
3. Behavioral strategies

7-4 Species interactions: Parasitism, mutualism, and commensalism
A. Species interactions provide positive and negative benefits for both interacting parties.
B. The specific types of interactions are parasitism, mutualism, and commensalisms.

7-5 Ecological succession: Communities in transition
A. Biotic communities may either gradually establish a community on 'nearly lifeless ground' or establish a biotic community in an area which already has an established community.
1. Primary succession = pioneer species + plant species
2. Secondary succession
B. Disturbances in an ecosystem's environment can cause an ecological succession to revert.
C. An ecological succession's progress cannot be predicted.

7-6 Ecological stability and sustainability
A. A stable and sustained ecosystem is influenced by Inertia, constancy, and resilience.
B. Since ecosystems are always changing, it is not possible to predict the necessary creatures or numbers that would sustain a particular ecosystem.
C. The 'precautionary principle' suggests that we should be careful of our environments and environmental resources; we have no sure knowledge of their inter-connectivity nor of their long-term importance.

Summary

1. The number of species in a community is determined by latitude in terrestrial systems, and depth and pollution in aquatic systems.

2. According to their ecological roles within an ecosystem, species are classified as native, nonnative, indicator, and keystone species.

3. Interspecific interactions include competition for resources, predation, parasitism, mutualism, and commensalism. Intraspecific interactions are represented by competition for resources.

4. Communities and ecosystems change in response to environmental change. The change of ecosystem species composition is known as ecological succession.

5. High species diversity increases the stability of an ecosystem since there are more ways to respond to environmental stressors.

Multiple Choice Questions

See Instructor's Manual, Section II, p. 209.

More Depth: Conceptual Term Paper Topics

1. Niche: relationships among species in a particular ecosystem, pick-a-predator, resource partitioning vs. direct competition strategies.

2. Unusual niches: write a case study of a particular alien species, indicator species, or keystone species.

3. Competition and predation: important features of natural selection, the competitive exclusion principle.

4. Making peace in natural ecosystems: resource partitioning, symbiotic relationships.

5. Ecological succession: the role of humans in succession, the role of fires and chaos in determining succession.

6. The theory and application of island biogeography.

7. Nature's response to human activities. Succession on deserted farmlands; succession after fire; dilution of pollution by streams; species migration; a closer look at homeostatic systems; population crashes; pioneer species; problems with crop monocultures.

More Breadth: Interdisciplinary Activities and Projects

1. Arrange a field trip providing opportunities to compare and contrast ecosystems of several different types, including some damaged or stressed by human activities. Invite an ecologist or biologist along to identify and discuss specific examples of species adaptation to environmental conditions. Do the boundaries between different kinds of ecosystems tend to be sharply delineated? Can you identify factors that limit the growth of certain species?

2. Organize a class field trip to systematically investigate the ecological niches for plant and animal life existing in a landscape significantly modified by human activities. If possible, arrange to travel along a gradient that will take you from farmland to suburbs to city to central business district. (A simplified version of this exercise could be done by walking around campus.)

3. Organize a local field trip for the class to examine recently disturbed areas for evidence of resilience.

4. Organize a class trip to a natural area such as a forest, grassland, or estuary to observe a variety of species interactions. Arrange for an ecologist or a naturalist to provide interpretive services.

5. Organize a class trip to an abandoned field, coastal dune, rock outcrop, or other disturbed are and observe the various aspects of ecological succession. If possible, visit and compare two areas that have experienced different types of disturbance.

Multisensory Learning: Audiovisuals

Creatures of the Deep. 60 mins., SA [Scientific American Frontier series] PBS
Living Edens: Denali. 60 mins., PBS.

See Appendix B for suppliers.

ATTITUDES/VALUES

Assessment

1. Do you have any particular feelings toward relationships demonstrated in ecosystems? Competition? Predation? Commensalism? Parasitism? Mutualism?

2. Have you ever suffered from environmental stress? If so, were you able to respond to the stress? Please describe.

3. Is there evidence of environmental stress in your community?

4. Is there evidence of ecosystem responses to stress in your community?

5. How do you feel when you see an ecosystem under stress?

6. Do you feel you have a right to create environmental stress? Are there limits to your rights? If so, what are they?

7. Do you feel you have a responsibility to protect natural ecosystems?

8. Has your local ecosystem been invaded by a nonnative species? If so, how did you feel about the invasion?

More Depth: Discussion and Term Paper Topics

1. To what extent should we disrupt and simplify natural ecosystems for our food, clothing, shelter, and energy needs and wants?

2. Do predators fulfill a valuable ecological function or should their numbers be reduced?

3. What lessons for human societies can be drawn from a study of species interactions in ecosystems?

4. How should we manage predator populations?

5. What can be done to decrease the incidence and impacts of invasions of nonnative species?

6. What is the wisest strategy to handle fires in natural ecosystems?

7. What are the most appropriate applications of the theory of island biogeography?

(Also, see text, Critical Thinking, p. 158)

PARTICIPATION

More Depth: Action-oriented Term Paper Topics

1. Field methods of ecological research. Relationships among species; computer modeling of ecological interrelationships.

2. Regional. Restoration of degraded ecosystems such as Lake Erie; coastal zone management.

SKILLS

<u>Environmental Problem-Solving Skills: Projects</u>

1. As a class exercise, systematically study a modern freeway or interstate highway and trace its impact on the surrounding land in terms of succession, diversity, and stability.

<u>Laboratory Skills</u>

Laboratory Manual for Miller's Living in the Environment and Environmental Science. Lab 4: Ecological Succession.

<u>Computer Skills</u>

-Evolution: *Sim Earth*

CHAPTER 8
POPULATION DYNAMICS, CARRYING CAPACITY, AND CONSERVATION BIOLOGY

THINKING

Concept Map

See Appendix A, Map 13.

Goals

See bulleted list of questions on p. 161 of text.

Objectives

1. Compare the abiotic and biotic factors that contribute to population growth (biotic potential) with the abiotic and biotic factors that limit population growth (environmental resistance).

2. Define *carrying capacity*. Describe how carrying capacity affects exponential growth. Distinguish the concepts within each of the following sets of terms: *stable, irruptive,* and *cyclic* population change curves; *r-strategist* and *K-strategist; Type I, Type II* and *Type III* survivorship curves.

3. Summarize how humans affect natural ecosystems. List six key features of living systems. Describe implications these features carry for human lifestyles. State the first law of human ecology and describe its implications for human interactions with the environment.

Key Terms (Terms are listed in the same font style as they appear in the text.)

size (p. 161)
density (p. 161)
dispersion (p. 161)
age distribution (p. 161)
population dynamics (p. 161)
biotic potential (p. 161)
intrinsic rate of increase (r) (p. 161)
environmental resistance (p. 161)
carrying capacity (K) (p. 161)
minimum viable population (MVP) (p. 162)
exponential growth (p. 162)
logistic growth (p. 162)
overshoots (p. 163)
reproductive time lag (p. 163)
dieback (crash) (p. 163)
density-independent population controls (p. 164)
density-dependent population controls (p. 164)
population fluctuations (p. 164)
stable (p. 164)
irruptive (p. 164)

irregular (p. 164)
cyclic (p. 164)
predator-prey cycles (p. 165)
top-down control (p. 165)
bottom-up control (p. 165)
asexual reproduction (p. 165)
sexual reproduction (p. 165)
r-selected species (p. 166)
opportunists (p. 166)
competitor (p. 166)
K-selected species (p. 166)
life expectancies (p. 167)
survivorship curve (p. 167)
late loss (p. 167)
early loss (p. 167)
constant loss (p. 167)
life table (p. 167)
conservation biology (p. 168)

What will the extinction of the Southern sea otter mean?
- A. Population dynamics, composed of size, density, dispersion and age distribution, describe responses to environmental stress and changing conditions.
- B. Changes in population are governed by birth, deaths, immigration, and emigration.

8-1 Population dynamics and carrying capacity
- A. The major characteristics of a population are size, density, dispersion, and age distribution.
- B. Four variables affect population size: births, death, immigration, and emigration.
    1. Carrying capacity = biotic potential + environmental resistance
    2. Minimum viable population
- C. Types of population growth: exponential and logistic
- D. Population density affects population growth.
- E. The four types of population fluctuations are stable, irruptive, irregular, and cyclic.

8-2 Connections: The role of predation in controlling population size
- A. Cyclic changes in predator-prey species have been explained by the theories: the top-down control hypothesis and the bottom-up control hypothesis.
- B. Predation can provide a top-down control system.

8-3 Reproductive patterns and survival
- A. Sexual and asexual reproduction are used to continue a species.
- B. Sexual reproductive advantages
- C. Types of reproductive patterns: opportunist and competitor
- D. Survivorship curves

8-4 Conservation biology: Sustaining wildlife populations
Conservation biology's basic principles are that biodiversity is necessary.
- A. Humans should not disrupt ecological processes or hasten any species' extinction.
- B. Intact ecosystems must be sustained.

8-5 Humans impacts on ecosystems: Learning from nature
Humans have undermined natural ecosystems:
- A. Fragmented, degraded wildlife habitats
- B. Simplified natural ecosystems
- C. Compromised a growing percentage of the earth's primary productivity
- D. Inadvertent strengthening of pest species and harmful bacteria
- E. Elimination of predators
- F. Introduction of new/nonnative species
- G. Overharvested renewable resources
- H. Interfered with chemical cycling and energy flows
- I. Ecological guidelines
    1. Man is dependent on the earth.
    2. Everything is inter-connected.
    3. Every single thing has side effects.
    4. Sustainability must be based on the earth's biological income.

Summary

1. The population size of species in a place is affected by the biotic potential and the environmental resistance.

2. Two hypotheses are proposed about the role of predators in controlling population size, the top-down control and the bottom-up control.

3. Reproductive patterns that enhance the survival of different species include r-selected or opportunistic and K-selected or competitor species, depending on their position on the growth curve and the characteristics of the reproductive patterns.

4. Conservation biology is a multidisciplinary field of science that employs the best scientific methodology to preserve species and ecosystems.

5. Major human impacts on ecosystems include the fragmentation and degradation of wildlife habitats, the simplification of natural ecosystems, the use, waste, or destruction of primary productivity, the strengthening of pests and pathogens, the invasion of exotic species, and the elimination of predators.

6. The ecological lessons on living sustainably include the fact that we are all dependent on solar energy, everything in connected with everything else, we can never do just one thing, and we can sustain a civilization that lives off the biological income of our earth without depleting the natural capital.

Multiple Choice Questions

See Instructor's Manual, Section II, p. 217.

More Depth: Conceptual Term Paper Topics

1. Population fluctuations in different species. K-selected vs. r-selected species: advantages and disadvantages of each.

2. Preservation of ecological integrity: the role of conservation biology.

3. Rehabilitation and restoration of ecosystems: success stories.

More Breadth: Interdisciplinary Activities and Projects

1. Have your class secure a large jar or glass container and equip it with a ventilated (finely perforated or meshed) top. Place a male and a female fruit fly in it, together with a plentiful supply of food. Set the jar aside and monitor the fly population as the days pass. Why does the population increase slowly at first and then very rapidly? What causes the inevitable population collapse? Why do all of the flies, rather than just the "surplus" population, die?

2. Visit ecosystems in your area that are being restored or managed. Investigate and draw a model of the multiple forces that allow this restoration/management to take place.

Multisensory Learning: Audiovisuals

Future in the Cradle. 22 min., 1997. VP

See Appendix B for suppliers.

ATTITUDES/VALUES

Assessment

1. Have you ever observed fluctuations in populations of species? What were your explanations for the fluctuations?

2. Do you feel that you have the right to manipulate the populations of other species? If so, under what circumstances?

3. Do you feel that you have a right to create environmental stress? Are there limits to your rights? If so, what are they?

4. Do you feel that rehabilitation and restoration of ecosystems are important investments of time and money?

5. Do you feel that ecosystems should be actively managed by humans, or should systems be allowed to change and evolve naturally?

6. Do you feel that you have a responsibility to protect natural ecosystems? Why or why not?

7. Do you feel that new technologies will be able to help natural ecosystems survive stresses under which they are placed?

More Depth: Discussion and Term Paper Topics

1. To what extent should we disrupt and simplify natural ecosystems for our food, clothing, shelter, and energy wants and needs?

2. Should our goal for the human population be to reach the Earth's carrying capacity?

(Also, see text, Critical Thinking, p. 171)

PARTICIPATION

More Depth: Action-oriented Term Paper Topics

1. Scientific methods. Carrying capacity analysis.

2. Regional. Restoration of degraded ecosystems, ecosystem management, restoration vs. rehabilitation.

SKILLS

Environmental Problem-Solving Skills: Projects

1. Identify an ecosystem in your community that has been stressed by human tinkering. Analyze the factors that affect the health of the ecosystem. Design a plan to restore of rehabilitate the ecosystem.

2. Visit a wildlife management are in your region. Describe the strategies used to maintain populations of wildlife. Describe how a conservation biologist would approach the ecosystem in a different way than a wildlife manager.

Laboratory Skills

(none)

Computer Skills

Sim Earth

CHAPTER 9
ENVIRONMENTAL GEOLOGY: PROCESSES, MINERALS, AND SOILS

THINKING

Concept Map

See Appendix A, Map 14.

Goals

See bulleted list of questions on p. 174 of text.

Objectives

1. Briefly describe the layers of the Earth's interior. Describe the internal and external Earth processes responsible for forming Earth's landscape. Be sure to distinguish three different tectonic plate boundaries and the geologic features often found at each. Explain how this knowledge is significant for understanding mineral deposits and evolution.

2. List and define three broad classes of rock. Briefly describe the rock cycle and indicate interrelationships among these classes.

3. Distinguish between surface and subsurface mining. Briefly describe three types of surface mining.

4. Distinguish between mineral resources and mineral reserves. Draw a hypothetical depletion curve. Project how this curve would be affected by the following changes in assumptions: (a) recycling of the resource is increased, (b) discoveries of new deposits of the resource are made, (c) prices rise sharply, (d) a substitute for the resource is found.

5. Evaluate the statement: "Prices of minerals determine the supply and demand of minerals." Assess the possibility of increasing mineral resource supplies through finding new deposits, improving technology of mining low-grade ore, getting minerals from the ocean, and finding substitutes.

6. Summarize the environmental impacts of extracting, processing, and using mineral resources. Evaluate the impact of the U.S. 1872 Mining Law. List seven proposals to reform the U.S. 1872 Mining Law.

7. Describe how earthquakes are caused. Describe how the severity of earthquakes is measured. Describe how losses can be reduced. Describe what causes a volcano. Describe how prediction of volcanic activity has improved.

8. Define soil horizon. Briefly describe six soil layers. Using Figure 9-18 on p. 191 in the text, compare soil profiles of five important soil types.

9. Describe a *fertile soil*. In doing so, be sure to refer to soil texture, porosity, loam, and acidity.

10. Describe the problems of soil erosion and desertification. Describe both world and U.S. situations and explain why most people are unaware of this problem. 11. Describe the problems of salinization and waterlogging of soils and how they can be controlled.

11. Define soil conservation. List nine ways to approach the problem of soil erosion. Be sure to distinguish between conventional-tillage and conservation-tillage farming. Describe a plan to maintain soil fertility. Be sure to distinguish between organic and inorganic fertilizers.

<u>Key Terms</u> (Terms are listed in the same font style as they appear in the text.)

geology (p. 174)
core (p. 174)
mantle (p. 174)
asthenosphere (p. 174)
crust (p. 174)
continental crust (p. 174)
oceanic crust (p. 174)
tectonic plates (p. 175)
lithosphere (p. 175)
plate tectonics (p. 175)
continental drift (p. 175)
divergent plate boundaries (p. 175)
convergent plate boundaries (p. 175)
subduction zone (p. 175)
trench (p. 175)
transform faults (p. 175)
external processes (p. 175)
erosion (p. 175)
weathering (p. 175)
mechanical weathering (p. 175)
frost wedging (p. 175)
chemical weathering (p. 177)
mineral (p. 177)
rock (p. 177)
igneous rock (p. 177)
sedimentary rock (p. 177)
metamorphic rock (p. 177)
rock cycle (p. 177)
mineral resource (p. 178)
nonrenewable resources (p. 178)
metallic mineral resources (p. 178)
energy resources (p. 178)
nonmetallic mineral resources (p. 178)
ore (p. 178)
identified resources (p. 178)
undiscovered resources (p. 178)
reserves (p. 178)
other resources (p. 178)
surface mining (p. 179)
subsurface mining (p. 179)
overburden (p. 179)
spoil (p. 179)
open-pit mining (p. 180)
dredging (p. 180)
area strip mining (p. 180)
spoil banks (p. 180)
contour strip mining (p. 180)
highwall (p. 180)
mountaintop removal (p. 180)
acid mine drainage (p. 180)
ore mineral (p. 180)
gangue (p. 180)
tailings (p. 180)

smelting (p. 180)
grade (p. 181)
economically depleted (p. 183)
depletion time (p. 183)
reserve-to-production ratio (p. 183)
General Mining Law of 1872 (p. 184)
hardrock minerals (p. 184)
patenting (p. 184)
materials revolution (p. 186)
fault (p. 186)
earthquake (p. 186)
focus (p. 186)
epicenter (p. 186)
magnitude (p. 186)
aftershocks (p. 186)
foreshocks (p. 187)
primary effects of earthquakes (p. 187)
secondary effects of earthquakes (p. 187)
tsunamis (p. 187)
volcano (p. 187)
magma (p. 187)
ejecta (p. 187)
Mount St. Helens (p. 188)
Mount Pinatubo (p. 188)
soil (p. 188)
soil horizons (p. 188)
soil profile (p. 188)
surface-litter layer (p. 188)
O-horizon (p. 188)
topsoil layer (p. 188)
A-horizon (p. 188)
humus (p. 188)
B-horizon (p. 188)
subsoil (p. 188)
C-horizon (p. 188)
parent material (p. 188)
bedrock (p 188)
infiltration (p. 189)
clay (p. 189)
silt (p. 189)
sand (p. 189)
gravel (p. 189)
soil texture (p. 189)
loams (p. 189)
soil porosity (p. 189)
soil permeability (p. 190)
soil structure (p. 190)
pH (p. 190)
soil erosion (p. 193)
Natural Resources Conservation Service (p. 194)
desertification (p. 194)
salinization (p. 196)
waterlogging (p. 196)

soil conservation (p. 196)
conventional-tillage farming (p. 197)
conservation-tillage farming (p. 197)
minimum-tillage farming (p. 197)
no-till farming (p. 197)
terracing (p. 197)
contour farming (p. 197)
strip cropping (p. 197)
alley cropping (p. 197)
agroforestry (p. 197)

gully reclamation (p. 197)
windbreaks (p. 197)
shelterbelts (p. 197)
land classification (p. 197)
organic fertilizer (p. 199)
commercial inorganic fertilizer (p. 199)
animal manure (p. 199)
green manure (p. 199)
compost (p. 199)
crop rotation (p. 199)

Outline

The lessons from the Dust Bowl of the Great Plains in the 1930s must never be forgotten.
A. Geologic processes both inside and on the earth's surface continually 'remake' our planet.
B. Igneous, sedimentary, and metamorphic rock are changed from one type to another in the rock cycle.
C. Various methods are used to identify, remove, and process mineral resources.
D. We mine mineral resources because of their economic value, but we must also evaluate the environmental consequences.
E. Various stresses in the earth will produce earthquakes and volcanoes.
F. Soil characteristics vary and influence its suitability for agriculture; soil erosion and desertification undermine the health of the earth and its residents.
G. Methods to prevent soil erosion and increase soil fertility are required for the future.

9-1 Geologic processes
A. The earth's structure is divided into the core, the mantle.
B. The continental crust, as well as the oceanic crust, compose the outer surface.

9-2 Internal and external earth processes
A. The earth's geologic processes—plate tectonics, erosion and weathering—cause changes in the earth.
B. Plate tectonics is the theory which explains movement in the earth's plates.
C. Mechanical and chemical weathering contribute to erosion.

9-3 Minerals, rocks, and the rock cycle
A. The rock cycle, using physical and chemical conditions, changes igneous, sedimentary, and metamorphic rock.
B. Nonrenewable mineral resources include metallic minerals, nonmetallic minerals, and energy resources.

9-4 Finding, removing, and processing nonrenewable mineral resources
A. Aerial photos and satellite images can reveal possible mineral deposits.
B. Other methods for finding minerals include radiation-measuring equipment, magnetometers, gravimeters, deep well drilling, seismic surveys, and chemical analysis.
C. Surface mining, area strip mining, open-pit mining, and contour strip mining are all used to retrieve minerals.
D. Mining has serious environmental impacts.
   1. Scarring/disruption of land surface
   2. Toxin-laced mining wastes
   3. Toxic chemicals in the air
   4. Pollution from smelting

9-5 Supplies of mineral resources
  A. Depletion of mineral resources is a serious problem for today's world.
    1. Economics and mineral use
    2. Mining public lands
    3. *"in situ"* mining
  B. Substitutes for mineral resources

9-6 Natural hazards: Earthquakes and volcanic eruptions
  A. Stress within the earth can produce earthquakes and volcanoes.
  B. Some solutions to lessen the damage of both is available.

9-7 Soil resources: Formation and types
  A. Soil is composed of several distinct layers.
  B. Different sizes and type of mineral particles determine the soil texture: Clay, silt, sand, and gravel.
    1. Soil porosity
    2. Soil permeability
    3. Soil structure

9-8 Soil Erosion
  A. Flowing water and wind cause soil erosion which produces the loss of soil fertility and a lessening of ability to hold water and sediment.
  B. Soil erosion is an internationally very serious occurrence.
  C. Desertification, also, robs the land of its productive potential.
  D. Irrigation can produce crops but the salinization of the land undercuts its growing potential. Waterlogging is not a good response to this.

9-9 Solutions: Soil conservation
  A. Traditional soil conservation methods have been used for many years to protect the soil.
    1. Conventional-tillage farming
    2. Conservation-tillage farming
  B. Newer soil conservation methods have been developed.
    1. Contour farming
    2. Strip cropping
    3. Alley cropping
    4. Shelterbelts/windbreaks
    5. Gully reclamation
    6. Land classification
  C. Organic and commercial inorganic fertilizers can be used to maintain and restore soil fertility.

<u>Summary</u>

1. Major geological processes that occur within the earth are known as internal processes, and they build up the surface of the earth. Geological processes that occur on the surface of the earth include erosion and weathering.

2. Rocks are large, natural, continuous parts of the earth's crust. There are three major types of rocks: igneous, sedimentary, and metamorphic. Rocks are affected by changes of physical and chemical conditions that change them overtime from one type to another through the rock cycle.

3. Aerial photography, satellite imagery, drilling, gravimetry, and seismic surveys are used to locate mineral resources. Mineral resource extraction methods include surface and subsurface mining. Surface mining types are open-pit, contour strip mining, and mountain removal.

4. Mineral resources that can be reused and recycled have a longer depletion time compared to those that cannot be reused or recycled and there is no increase in reserves discovery.

5. The hazards from earthquakes relate to shaking and vertical and horizontal displacement of ground, affecting buildings, dams, bridges, freeway overpasses, and pipelines. Secondary hazards are rockslides, fires, and flooding. The hazards from volcanoes are related to the effects of liquid lava, ejecta, and gases.

6. Soils are complex mixtures of eroded rock, mineral nutrients, decaying organic matter, water, air, and microscopic decomposers. Soils are formed through rock weathering, deposit of sediment , and decomposition of organic materials.

7. Soil erosion is the movement of soil components between two places. Methods that prevent soil erosion include conservation-tillage and contour farming, strip and alley cropping, use of windbreaks, and gully reclamation.

Multiple Choice Questions

See Instructor's Manual, Section II, p. 223.

More Depth: Conceptual Term Paper Topics

1. Geologic processes. Plate tectonics; plate formation.

2. Resource demands. The commodities market; aluminum industry in the United States; steel alloys; industrial use of chromium and other strategic minerals.

3. Mining processes. Manganese-rich nodule mining methods; Frasch process sulfur mining; improved technology for mining low-grade ore.

4. Mining and the environment. Modern surface mining reclamation methods; surface mining and the acid runoff problem; smelting and air pollution problems.

5. Increasing resource supply. History of resource substitution; Landsat technology and mineral resources; extracting minerals from seawater.

6. Soil. The web of life in the soil; soil formation and pioneer ecological succession; soils of your locale.

7. Human impact on the soil. Overgrazing and desertification; acid deposition as a threat to soil quality; sediment: how serious a water pollutant?

More Breadth: Interdisciplinary Activities and Projects

1. Invite an economic geologist to your class to discuss state-of-the-art technology for exploration and development of metal and nonfuel minerals.

2. Are any surface mining operations taking place in your vicinity? If so, arrange for a spokesperson to explain how the mining company complies with the specifications of the Surface Mining Control and Reclamation Act.

3. Invite a Soil Conservation Service representative to your class to discuss local soil conservation problems and erosion-control methods.

4. Take a class field trip to several farms or ranches in your locale that offer you the opportunity to contrast excellent soil management practices with poor ones.

5. As a class exercise, discuss the economic, political, social, and environmental consequences that might ensue if the fertile soils of the Great Plains and the Corn Belt were ruined by human-accelerated soil erosion.

6. With your class, visit several construction sites in your locale. Look for evidence of human-accelerated soil erosion and methods or practices employed to minimize it.

7. Have your students find poems, songs, or paintings that express intense human feelings about the land and soil of working farms or ranches. Discuss these feelings in the context of modern large-scale commercial agriculture or agribusiness.

8. Ask an experienced practitioner of organic farming or gardening to visit the class and describe methods used to preserve the soil and maintain its fertility without using inorganic fertilizers and chemical poisons.

Multisensory Learning: Audiovisuals

Geological Processes
Living Glaciers. 30 mins. FHS
Quake Hunters. 1998. FHS
Nature's Fury. 60 mins. NG
Understanding Volcanoes. 46 mins., 1994. FHS

Minerals
Mines and Minerals; 1994; 23 min.; mineral exploration, extraction, and shaping; FHS.

Soils
The Living Soil: the value of humus. 20 mins, 1991. FHS

See Appendix B for suppliers.

ATTITUDES/VALUES

Assessment

1. What types of geological formations are found in your area?

2. Where is the nearest tectonic plate junction to your area? What type of junction? What are the likely geological processes to occur at that junction?

3. How do you feel when you see the results of a volcano, flood, or earthquake on the news?

4. Do you feel that human behavior should be modified by knowledge of geology? If so, how?

5. Would you support policies which discourage human development in areas where natural hazards are most likely to occur? If so, please specify.

6. Do you think new technologies will enable us to reduce the effects of natural disasters on humans?

7. How do you feel as a member of the human species when you consider the full span of geological time?

8. What soil type is most common in your area?

9. What are the most common soil problems in your area?

10. What feelings do you have toward the soil?

11. Do you feel humans have a right to use the soil in any way they choose? If not, what are the limits?

12. Do you feel nature can take care of any harm humans bring the soil?

13. Do you feel new technologies will solve any problems humans create with the soil?

14. Do you feel humans have a responsibility to protect the quality and fertility of the soil? If so, what steps do you think should be taken to protect the soil?

More Depth: Discussion and Term Paper Topics

1.   Should mineral-rich but under explored Antarctica be opened to mineral exploration and development without delay?

2.   Should seabed mineral deposits such as manganese-rich nodules be declared an ecosphere resource to which landlocked less-developed nations may rightfully stake a fair share claim?

3.   Should we build in earthquake zones?

4.   Do you have an attachment to any particular piece of land? Explore the roots of your attachment. Is the land protected from erosion and other forms of land degradation?

5.   Do you think land-use management and zoning are good practices? Why or why not?

6.   Is the rapid deterioration of agricultural soils in the United States a sufficiently serious problem to warrant strict federal laws with heavy fines for farmers or ranchers failing to employ wise soil conservation methods? Arrange a class debate on this issue.

7.   What impact have the Dust Bowl, Hugh Bennett, and the Soil Conservation Service had on this country?

(Also, see text, Critical Thinking, p. 201)

PARTICIPATION

More Depth: Action-oriented Term Paper Topics

1.   Individuals. Soil testing methods and procedures; what individuals can do to prevent soil erosion and nutrient depletion on their own property; agricultural practices that restore nutrients and prevent erosion; composting; no-tillage farming; crop rotation; windbreaks; forestry practices that minimize erosion; ranching management that minimizes erosion.

2.   City/Regional. Land-use planning and zoning; urban soil management problems; the Soil Conservation Service.

SKILLS

Environmental Problem-Solving Skills: Projects

1.   As a class exercise, identify the minimum metal and mineral resources required to support human life at an acceptable level of quality. (Decide for yourself what acceptable life quality is.) What is the present and anticipated supply of these resources? Which essential element of the mix is least

dependable in future supply? Write comprehensive and internally consistent scenarios describing what life would be like without this resource (or an affordable substitute).

2. Have your students consult recent issues of the *Wall Street Journal, Forbes, Fortune,* and other reputable sources of commodities information and forecasts. Note the metal and nonfuel mineral resources that are in the news because of supply and demand problems. Are the concerns and opinions expressed in market publications reflected adequately in the print and broadcast media reporting that is oriented to the public?

3. As a class, conduct a school and community survey to assess people's beliefs about and attitudes toward America's reliance on foreign sources for various strategic materials.

4. As a class exercise, assign appropriate roles and research assignments to students (or teams of students) and stage mock negotiations among several less-developed nations seeking to establish a cartel for controlling the supply and price of the vitally important industrial commodity X. Assume that the cartel is successful and stage additional mock negotiations between the cartel and more-developed nations whose economies are suffering grievously for want of affordable supplies of commodity X.

5. As a class exercise, have your students create a soil management plan (illustrated by sketches, drawings, or photographs) for a hypothetical badly eroded farm.

6. Visit the town planning office with your class. See if there is a land-use plan for the town. Are there zoning laws that prevent the development of certain areas, such as prime farmland and wetlands? Why or why not?

7. Take a field trip around the community with your class. See if you can identify any sloped areas that are eroding significantly. Try to discern if the land erosion is resulting in sediment pollution in surface waters. Investigate if anything is being done about it. Draw up a plan that would prevent further erosion. Share it with people who might be interested in implementing the plan.

Laboratory Skills

Laboratory Manual for Miller's Living in the Environment and Environmental Science. Lab 15: Introduction to the Arthropods; Lab 16: Soil Diversity.

Computer Skills

(none)

CHAPTER 10
RISK, TOXICOLOGY, AND HUMAN HEALTH

THINKING

Concept Map

See Appendix A, Map 15.

Goals

See bulleted list of questions on p. 204 of text.

Objectives

1. List four classes of common hazards and give two examples of each. List seven cultural hazards in order of most to least hazardous.

2. Define *toxicology*. List three types of studies which contribute to our knowledge of toxicology. Distinguish between *acute and chronic effects; bioaccumulation and biomagnification.*

3. Draw a dose-response curve and explain how it can be used. Draw graphs of two hypothetical dose-response curves: no threshold and threshold. Explain which model is used most often and why.

4. Define epidemiology. Summarize limits of toxicological research. Describe the actions humans can take to ameliorate the limits of toxicological research.

5. List five principal types of chemical hazards and give two examples of each.

6. Distinguish between transmissible and nontransmissible diseases. Explain which occurs most in developing countries and which occurs most in developed countries. Relate an epidemiologic transition to a demographic transition.

7. Describe how the hazards of smoking and sexually transmitted diseases could be reduced in the United States. List diet changes which can help prevent cancer.

8. Define *risk analysis*. Summarize its limitations. Compare technology reliability to human reliability. Distinguish between *risk-benefit analysis* and *risk assessment*. List seven questions risk assessors might ask.

9. List six questions asked by risk managers. List seven cases in which the public generally perceives that a technology or product has a greater risk than the risk estimated by experts.

Key Terms (Terms are listed in the same font style as they appear in the text.)

risk (p. 204)
hazard (p. 204)
probability (p. 204)
risk assessment (p. 204)
risk management (p. 204)
comparative risk analysis (p. 204)
cultural hazards (p. 204)
chemical hazards (p. 204)

physical hazards (p. 204)
biological hazards (p. 204)
toxicity (p. 204)
dosage (p. 204)
water-soluble toxins (p. 204)
oil (fat)-soluble toxins (p. 204)
persistence (p. 204)
bioaccumulation (p. 204)

biomagnification (p. 204)
chemical interactions (p. 205)
antagonistic interactions (p. 205)
synergistic interaction (p. 205)
response (p. 205)
acute effect (p. 205)
chronic effect (p. 205)
poison (p. 206)
median lethal dose (LD$_{50}$) (p. 206)
case reports (p. 206)
laboratory investigations (p. 206)
epidemiology (p. 207)
dose-response curve (p. 207)
controlled experiments (p. 207)
test group (p. 207)
control group (p. 207)
nonthreshold dose-response model (p. 207)
threshold dose-response model (p. 207)
toxic chemicals (p. 208)
hazardous chemicals (p. 208)
mutagens (p. 208)
teratogens (p. 208)
carcinogens (p. 208)
metastasis (p. 208)
immune system (p. 208)
nervous system (p. 208)
neurotoxins (p. 208)
endocrine system (p. 208)
hormones (p. 208)
hormonally active agents (HAAs) (p. 208)
endocrine disrupters (p. 208)
hormone mimics (p. 208)

hormone blockers (p. 208)
thyroid disrupters (p. 208)
precautionary principle (p. 209)
nontransmissible disease (p. 210)
transmissible disease (p. 210)
pathogens (p. 210)
vectors (p. 210)
bacterium (p. 210)
virus (p. 210)
acute respiratory infections (p. 211)
acquired immune deficiency syndrome (AIDS) (p. 211)
diarrheal diseases (p. 211)
tuberculosis (p. 211)
malaria (p. 211)
measles (p. 211)
hepatitis B (p. 211)
epidemiological transition (p. 211)
influenza (flu) (p. 213)
Ebola (p. 213)
rabies (p. 213)
vaccines (p. 213)
Plasmodium (p. 213)
Anopheles mosquito (p. 213)
risk analysis (p. 215)
risk assessment (p. 215)
risk communication (p. 215)
comparative risk analysis (p. 215)
benefit-cost analysis (p. 219)
alternative assessment (p. 219)
risk management (p. 219)

Outline

Between 1950 and 2002, smoking has killed more than twice the number of people killed in all 20th century wars.
    A. Risk assessment and risk management processes express suffering in terms of probability. There are cultural hazards, chemical hazards, biological hazards and physical hazards.
    B. Several factors' determine the harmfulness of a substance.
    C. Toxicity in the environment has far-flung implications for the entire planet.
    D. The three types of toxic agents are: mutagens, teratogens, and carcinogens.
    E. Transmissible diseases are threats to the entire world.
        1. Infectious diseases
        2. Viral diseases
    F. Risk analysis identifies hazards, assesses associated risks, identifies options, makes decision about the risks, and informs the public.

10-1 Risk, probability, and hazards
    A. Risk is defined as a probability—the likelihood of suffering harm from some type of hazard.
    B. The major types of hazards people face are cultural hazards, chemical hazards, physical hazards, and biological hazards.

10-2 Toxicology
    A. Several factors influence the toxicity of a substance: does, solubility, persistence, bioaccumulation, biomagnification, and chemical interaction.

B. "Any synthetic or natural chemical (even water) can be harmful if ingested in a large enough quantity."
C. Case reports and epidemiological studies are used to estimate toxicity.
   1. Physicians' case reports
   2. Epidemiological studies
   3. Laboratory experiments with dose-response curve applications

10-3 Chemical hazards
   A. Toxic chemicals, those fatal to more than 50% of test animals, may be of three types: mutagens, teratogens, or carcinogens.
   B. The body's immune, nervous, and endocrine systems are compromised by toxic chemicals in the environment.
   C. Human-made chemicals, endocrine disrupters, appear to disrupt human's immune functions.
   D. Very few everyday chemicals have been evaluated for toxicity, so we know almost nothing about their effects.

10-4 Biological hazards: Disease in developed and developing countries
   A. Because of the interconnectedness of life today, transmittable diseases are of special concern.
   B. Infectious agents that spread transmissible diseases are called pathogens.
      1. Infectious disease kills one in four people.
      2. Some infectious bacteria have genetic immunity to antibiotics.
      3. Many disease-carrying species are immune to pesticides.
   C. The world faces a rise in the incidence of infectious bacterial diseases.
      1. Adaptability of bacteria
      2. Increasing spread of bacteria worldwide
      3. Overuse of antibiotics
      4. Overuse of pesticides
      5. Use of antibiotics in animal production
   D. Viral diseases also present threats to human health, especially AIDS.
      1. Drugs kill host cells.
      2. Vaccine development is lengthy and expensive.
      3. Most dangerous viral disease—malaria.
   E. Reducing the incidence of infectious disease is possible.
      1. Immunizations
      2. Oral rehydration therapy
      3. Disinfect water

10-5 Risk analysis
   A. Risk analysis includes risk assessment, comparative risk analysis, risk management, and risk communication.
      1. Statistical probabilities and epidemiological studies for estimating risk
      2. Models for estimating risk
   B. Today's major risks are poverty and lifestyles' influences.
   C. Technological systems' risk is computed by the following factors—system reliability = technology reliability x human reliability.
   D. The results of risk analysis must be evaluated while some advocate that a more useful emphasis would be on alternative assessment instead of risk assessment.
   E. Risk management considers these questions.
      1. Reliability of the risk analysis for each risk
      2. Priority of each risk
      3. Degree of risk acceptability
      4. Cost of risks' being moved to an acceptable level
      5. Greatest benefit for the least expense
      6. Procedures for monitoring and enforcing the risk management plan and communicating with the public

F.   Perceptions of risk are at great variance to the reality of those risks.
     1.   Risk of immediate hazards and non-daily ones
     2.   Public perception of hazards
          a.   New/complex conditions—riskier
          b.   Involuntary risks—riskier
          c.   Unnecessary risks—riskier
          d.   Single, catastrophic accident—riskier
          e.   Risks' unfairly distributed to specific groups

Summary

1.   Major types of hazards faced by humans include cultural, physical, chemical, and biological hazards.

2.   Toxicology is the scientific field that measures the degree of harm a hazardous agent can cause. Scientists measure toxicity based on dosage, solubility, persistence, bioaccumulation, biomagnification, and chemical interactions.

3.   Chemical hazards include agents that are flammable or explosive, damage or irritate lungs or skin, interrupt oxygen uptake, and cause allergies. Three major types of toxic chemicals include mutagens, teratogens, and carcinogens.

4.   The types of disease threatening people in developing countries are primarily infectious diseases of childhood while those threatening people in developed countries tend to be chronic diseases of adults, such as heart disease, stroke, cancer, and respiratory conditions.

5.   Risk analysis identifies hazards, evaluates related risks (risk assessment), ranks risks (comparative risk analysis), determines alternative solutions, makes decisions about reducing risks (risk management), and informs decision makers about risks (risk communication).

Multiple Choice Questions

See Instructor's Manual, Section II, p. 241.

More Depth: Conceptual Term Paper Topics

1.   Environmental risks. Brown lung disease and the textile industry; black lung disease and the coal mining industry; asbestos as a carcinogen.

2.   Lifestyle risks. Health effects from secondary smoke; the rising lung cancer rate for women.

3.   Transmissible disease risks. History of infectious disease control; vaccines and immunology; how smallpox was eradicated; waterborne diseases of the developing countries; the history of malaria; schistosomiasis; cholera; tuberculosis; AIDS.

More Breadth: Interdisciplinary Activities and Projects

1.   Have local public health officials discuss with your class the types and frequency of diseases in the local area and describe efforts for disease control.

2.   Invite a spokesperson for the American Cancer Society to address your class on the subject of "nonsmokers' rights." What specific things can a person do to minimize his or her passive exposure to cigarette smoke? What are the limits of smokers' rights to pollute air that nonsmokers cannot avoid breathing? Review the changes in attitudes and behaviors that people in the United States have shown toward smoking over the last 10 years.

3. Ask a nutritionist to discuss problems with the typical U.S. diet and how to make changes recommended by the National Academy of Sciences and the American Heart Association.

4. Assign several students to visit a store that specializes in organically grown and "natural" foods. Have them describe the advertising claims made on behalf of natural foods.

Multisensory Learning: Audiovisuals

Noise, Radioactive, and Electromagnetic Pollution; 1994; 23 min.; controversy; FHS.
Acid Assault: acid rain and the environment. 20 mins., 1991. FHS.
The Cost of Living (AIDS). 24 min., 2000. BFF
Drumbeat for Mother Earth. 54 min., 2000. BFF
It Can't Happen Here: improper waste handling… 30 min. CF
Our Fragile Earth: recycling. 16 min. VP
Up Close and Toxic. 52 min., 2003. BFF

See Appendix B for suppliers.

ATTITUDES/VALUES

Assessment

1. What kinds of risks do you take every day?

2. What kinds of risks from the natural environment occur in your area?

3. What kinds of risks are you exposed to each day over which you have no control?

4. Do you feel that societal risks should be distributed equally among all citizens?

5. Should people who choose unhealthy lifestyles be covered by national health insurance?

More Depth: Discussion and Term Paper Topics

1. When do smokers' rights infringe on nonsmokers' rights?

2. Should we continue government subsidies of the tobacco industry?

3. Pros and cons of risk-benefit analysis

(Also see text, Critical Thinking, p. 220)

PARTICIPATION

More Depth: Action-oriented Term Paper Topics

1. Individual lifestyle changes that cut risks. Quitting smoking; changing to a low-risk diet; steps to prevent breast cancer; preventive medicine.

2. Groups spreading the word about risks. the American Cancer Society; the American Lung Association; the American Heart Association.

3. National. The National Centers for Disease Control; Occupational Safety and Health Administration (OSHA); U.S. efforts to export tobacco products; the tobacco lobby; the Food and Drug Administration; new ingredient labels for food.

4. International. Sweden's antismoking campaign.

SKILLS

Environmental Problem-Solving Skills: Projects

1. Have your students obtain mortality and morbidity data for people living in poor and affluent sections of your community to determine the frequency and types of illness. Compare results with national statistics and attempt to explain any significant local differences.

2. What occupational health hazards are prevalent in your community? What is being done to protect workers from these on-the-job hazards? Have some students investigate this subject and report the results to the class.

Laboratory Skills

(none)

Computer Skills

Waterborne Toxic Risk Assessment Model (WTRISK)
-Estimates the risks of adverse human health effects from substances emitted into the air, surface water, soil, and groundwater from sources such as coal-fired power plants.
-Manager, Software and Publications Distribution, Electric Power Research Institute, 3412 Hillview Ave., P.O. Box 10412, Palo Alto, CA 94303

CHAPTER 11
THE HUMAN POPULATION: GROWTH AND DISTRIBUTION

THINKING

Concept Map

See Appendix A, Map 16.

Goals

See bulleted list of questions on p. 223 of text.

Objectives

1. Define *birth rate, death rate, emigration rate,* and *immigration rate.* Write an equation to mathematically describe the relationship between these rates and the rate of population change.

2. Define *fertility rate.* Describe how fertility rate affects population growth. List at least five factors that affect birth rate and five factors that affect death rate.

3. Compare rates of population growth in developed and developing countries. Explain the differences you find. Briefly describe the state of teenage pregnancy in the United States.

4. Using population age structure diagrams, explain how the age structure of a country creates population growth momentum. Summarize social impacts resulting from declining populations.

5. List five approaches to slowing human population growth. List the four stages of the demographic transition. Briefly describe the controversies that surround controlling population size through controlling migration and family planning.

6. Summarize India and China's experiences. Describe the three major shifts in population distribution in U.S. history.

7. List seven resource and environmental problems faced by urban areas. Briefly describe the process of ecological land-use planning.

8. Evaluate the costs and benefits of the automobile on U.S. society. List three alternative forms of transportation to the car, and evaluate the costs and benefits of each.

9. Describe your conception of a sustainable urban environment.

Key Terms (Terms are listed in the same font style as they appear in the text.)

births (p. 223)
deaths (p. 223)
migration (p. 223)
population change (p. 223)
zero population growth (ZPG) (p. 223)
birth rate (p. 223)
crude birth rate (p. 223)
death rate (p. 223)
crude death rate (p. 223)

replacement-level fertility (p. 224)
total fertility rate (TFR) (p. 224)
life expectancy (p. 227)
infant mortality rate (p. 227)
age structure (p. 229)
prereproductive (p. 229)
reproductive (p. 229)
postreproductive (p. 229)
baby boom (p. 230)

baby bust generation (generation X) (p. 230)
echo-boom generation (p. 231)
optimum sustainable population (p. 232)
cultural carrying capacity (p. 232)
demographic transition (p. 233)
preindustrial stage (p. 233)
transitional stage (p. 233)
industrial stage (p. 233)
postindustrial stage (p. 233)
demographic trap (p. 233)
family planning (p. 234)
urban (metropolitan) area (p. 238)
rural area (p. 238)
degree of urbanization (p. 238)
urban growth (p. 238)
push factors (p. 238)
pull factors (p. 239)
megacities (p. 239)

megalopolis (p. 239)
squatter settlements (p. 239)
shantytowns (p. 239)
urban sprawl (p. 241)
urban heat island (p. 244)
compact cities (p. 245)
motor scooters (p. 246)
bicycles (p. 246)
mass transit rail systems (p. 247)
rapid rail systems (p. 247)
buses (p. 247)
land-use planning (p. 247)
property taxes (p. 247)
zoning (p. 248)
smart growth (p. 248)
ecocity (p. 248)
green city (p. 248)

Outline

A. Birth, deaths, and migration affect population change, as do fertility rates.
B. Population age structure affects population growth and can be used to make economic projections.
C. Identifying an 'optimum sustainable population' for the earth is a difficult mission, influenced by economics and cultural factors.
D. Population growth and population distribution patterns are significant for environmental protection throughout the world.
E. As more of the world's people live in urban areas, urban problems become more wide-spread.
    1. Poverty
    2. Pollution
    3. Lack of employment
    4. Limited water and sewage treatment
    5. Aging infrastructures
    6. Urban sprawl
F. Urbanization creates environmental disadvantages.
    1. Destruction of land areas
    2. Produce no food
    3. Sustain no trees and their result contributions
    4. Poor/old/badly developed water supplies
    5. Pollution: air/water/noise
    6. Health problems: diseases, injuries, densities
G. Transportation systems are more effective and more economical in urban areas.
    1. Motor vehicles
    2. Mass transit and buses
H. Land-use planning has historically advocated increased population growth and economic development.

11-1 Factors affecting human population size
    A. Global population is affected by fertility rate and births, by death, and by migration.
        1. Replacement-level fertility and total fertility rate
        2. Factors affecting birth and fertility rates
            a. Economic needs
            b. Expense of children
            c. Pension support
            d. Urbanization

The Human Population: Growth and Distribution

  e. Opportunities for women

  f. Infant mortality rate

  g. Average age at marriage for women

  h. Availability of abortion and birth control methods

 3. Factors affecting the decline in death rates

  a. Increased food supply and distribution

  b. Better nutrition

  c. Medical and public health technical improvements

  d. Sanitation and personal hygienic improvement

  e. Safer water supplies

 4. Health expectancy indicators

  a. Life expectancy

  b. Infant mortality rate influences

   i. Inadequate health care

   ii. Malnutrition

   iii. Insufficient food

   iv. High incidence of infectious disease

11-2 Population age structure

Population age structure explains the continual increase in a people's population.

 A. Prereproductive and reproductive ages

 B. Population age structure as population projector

  1. Baby boom generation

  2. Baby bust generation

  3. Baby echo generation

 C. Rapid population decline and results

  1. Rise in health care for older people

  2. Labor shortages

  3. Increased demand for public services

11-3 Solutions: Influencing population size

 A Migration

 B. Reduction of birth rate

  1. Define the optimum sustainable population

  2. Define the earth's cultural carrying capacity

  3. Influence of economic development on birth rates

   a. Four stages of demographic transition

   b. Demographic trap

  4. Family planning influences

  5. Family planning improvements

 C. Economic rewards and penalties

11-4 Case studies: Slowing population growth in India and China

11-5 Cutting global population growth: A new vision

The United Nations is encouraging the world to stabilize its population growth.

 A. Goals of health care improvement, increased reproductive health, and services

 B. Eradicate poverty and reduce unsustainable patterns of production and consumption

 C. Provide education and economic opportunity to women and girls

 D. Implement national population policies

11-6 Population distribution: Urbanization and urban growth

 A. Urban and rural growth influences include

  1. Push-pull factors of poverty, famine, war, decline in agricultural jobs, and lack of land

        2. Urbanization patterns
           a. More and more urban residents
           b. Growth of megacities/megapolies
           c. Developing countries' urban growth
           d. Developed countries' urban growth
           e. More urbanization, more poverty
   B. Urban problems
        1. Poverty
        2. Pollution
        3. Aging infrastructure
        4. Urban sprawl

11-7 Urban resources and environmental problems

Urbanization produces economic development, scientific and technical innovation, and centralizes work and services, but the environment often suffers.
   A. Environmental advantage: recycling, preserving biodiversity
   B. Environmental disadvantages
        1. Use many resources and produce high waste
        2. Croplands, wetlands, and wildlife habitat destruction
        3. Little vegetation; compromised water supplies
        4. Infectious disease and pollution
        5. Heat islands; problems of crowded people

11-8 Transportation and urban development

Land availability and transportation affect urban development.
   A. Individual and mass transportation
   B. Automobile based cities' effects
        1. Many auto deaths
        2. Air pollution
        3. Urban sprawl and congestion
   C. Methods for reducing automobile use
        1. User pays fees
        2. Alternative transportation
           a. Scooters and bicycles
           b. Mass transit rail systems and rapid rail systems
           c. Bus systems

11-9 Making urban areas more livable and sustainable

To improve urban areas' sustainability and livability different methods can be used.
   A. Land use planning vs. ecological land use planning
   B. Smart growth
   C. Ecocity or green cities
   D. Model city: Curitita, Brazil

<u>Summary</u>

1. Birth and immigration rates affect the population size positively, while deaths and emigration affect the population negatively.

2. Population age structure affects population size. Age structures with many individuals below the age 15 tend to indicate momentum in population growth.

3. Population growth can be slowed by birth reduction and facilitated through demographic transition, family planning, empowering women, and economic rewards or penalties.

4. India had a moderate success in slowing population growth due to poor planning, bureaucratic inefficiency, the low status of women, poverty, and lack of administrative support. China succeeded in controlling population growth through the most extensive, intrusive, and strict program in the world.

5. Population growth may be reduced through access to family planning services, improvement of health care, development of national population policies, improvement of the status of women, increased access to education, increased involvement of males in child rearing, eradication of poverty, and elimination of unsustainable production and consumption.

6. Urban growth depends on natural growth and immigration. Urban areas develop influence by push factors (poverty, lack of land to grow food, declining agriculture, famine, war) and pull factors (jobs, entertainment, better life, freedom of religious, racial, and apolitical conflicts).

7. Major problems in urban areas include contamination of water and air, noise pollution, traffic congestion, increased flooding, increased energy use and waste, increased greenhouse gas emissions, and increased global warming.

8. Cheap gas, expanse of land, and networks of highways produce urban sprawling with negative effects. Alternative forms of transportation are energy efficient, reduce air pollution, require less resources to manufacture, and some are quiet and reduce car congestions in cities.

9. Cities can be made more sustainable and desirable places to live by finding solutions to problems that are cheap, simple, fast, innovative, and fun, and by establishing government that is honest, accountable, and open to public scrutiny.

Multiple Choice Questions

See Instructor's Manual, Section II, p. 255.

More Depth: Conceptual Term Paper Topics

1. Population growth. A case study of Mexico, China, India, Kenya; the geography of global population distribution; infant mortality trends and issues; illegal immigration into the United States; marriage age trends; fertility trends and the women's rights movement; factors influencing family size preferences; Earth's carrying capacity; developing countries trapped in phase two of the demographic transition; the World Bank and family planning; economics of fertility control technology in the United States; economic costs of childrearing in the United States.

2. Environmental impacts of population. Air pollution in urban areas; land degradation from urban sprawl; deforestation and desertification in developing countries.

3. Population control. Case studies: India, China, Japan.

4. Urbanization, transportation, and land-use planning. Rural to urban migration patterns; the Sun Belt shift; central city lifestyles; mass transit systems: BART, METRO; case study in sustainable living: Davis, California; green spaces; building self-sufficient cities.

More Breadth: Interdisciplinary Activities and Projects

1. Invite a public health official or nutritionist to your class to explain the factors involved in the decline in the global death rate over the past century and the decline in the infant mortality rate in the United States. Why is the latter rate higher in the United States than in many other developed nations?

2. U.S. immigration policy had become a volatile political issue by the 1980s. Arrange a debate on this subject. Debate the proposition that the United States should enact and strictly enforce legislation that holds legal immigration to levels consistent with the achievement of ZPG within a few generations.

3. Ask your students to share with the class poems, short stories, songs, paintings, collages, photographic displays, slide talks, or other works expressing their feelings about population issues and problems.

4. Are there family planning clinics in your community that provide contraceptives and birth control counseling? Invite a family planning worker to visit your class and discuss the birth control aspects of family planning.

5. As a class project, investigate the fate of agricultural land in your city's vicinity. Is anything being done to prevent prime agricultural land from being overtaken by urban sprawl?

Multisensory Learning: Audiovisuals

The Population Reference Bureau rents through the mail over 50 video tapes, films, and slide/tape programs on population dynamics, the environment, and related topics. For a free list, send a self-addressed, stamped envelope to the Population Reference Bureau. PRB.

Mega-Cities: Innovation for Urban Life; 1996; 56 min.; innovative solutions to urban problems; VP.
The Heartbeat of America; 1993; 87 min.; environmental and economic impacts of the automobile on American society; VP.
World Population; 1990; 7 min.; a depiction of human population growth from 1 A.D. and projected to 2020; VP.
Seeds of Progress; 28 min.; Mexican rural development; WBP.
The Neighborhood of Coehlos; 28 min.; urban development program in Brazil; WBP.
Dandora; 20 min.; urban development in Nairobi; WBP.
Cities (Reinventing the World series). 60 mins., 2000. BFF
Decade of Decision. 14 min., 1994. BFF
Developing Stories. Series 2 211 mins., 1994. BFF
The Neighborhood of Coehlos. 28 min, 1982. WBP
Not the Numbers Game. 60 mins., 1997. BFF (women & population problems)

See Appendix B for suppliers.

ATTITUDES/VALUES

Assessment

1. Do you feel the size of the human population is an important environmental issue?

2. Do you feel consumption by the human population is an important environmental issue?

3. Do you feel that humans have the right to have as many children as they want? Are there any limits on this right? If so, what are they?

4. Do you feel that there should be a national population policy? What steps would you support?

5. Do you feel that teen pregnancy is a problem?

6. Do you feel that women's roles are important in addressing population size?

7. What are your feelings toward birth control? Population control?

8. Do you feel that the Earth will be able to sustain the projected increases in human population growth?

9. How do you feel when you see skyscrapers? clover-leaf highways? parks? greenspaces?

10. Are you familiar with mass transit possibilities in an urban center in your area?

11. Are you familiar with zoning procedures in an urban center in your area?

12. How do you feel toward urban sprawl? urban renewal?

13. Do you feel that some forms of urban growth are more desirable than others? Which ones?

14. Are there any limits to urban growth? What are they?

15. What efforts do you support to make cities more sustainable environments?

More Depth: Discussion and Term Paper Topics

1. Do you think the United States needs a population policy? Should the federal government stop subsidizing large families?

2. Evaluate U.S. immigration policy.

3. Do you think the United States should play a global leadership role in promoting stabilization of the world's human population?

4. Would you rather be a baby boomer or a baby buster?

(also, see text, Critical Thinking, p. 252)

PARTICIPATION

More Depth: Action-oriented Term Paper Topics

1. Individual. Decisions individuals make about family size and urban conditions and ways individuals can influence government agencies and non-government institutions concerned with population.

2. Regional. Urban renewal programs; mass transit systems.

3. National. Zero Population Growth during the 1980s; ZPG analysis of the U.S. way of taxing.

4. Global. The UN International Conference on Population; UN Family Planning Association; International Planned Parenthood Federation.

SKILLS

Environmental Problem-Solving Skills: Projects

1. Survey the marriage and childbearing intentions of your female students. Find out at what age students' mothers married and the number of children each had. Tally the results and compare them with recent trends in marriage age and total fertility.

2. Survey your students to obtain age or lifespan information about their grandparents. Compare the results with the average life expectancy in the United States in the year 1900 (46 for men and 48 for women). Invite your students to discuss major implications of these findings.

3.   As a class, research the environmental impact of the growing populations of the developing countries and developed countries. Find data comparing the impact of children from developed countries and developing countries. Collect data comparing population growth in developed countries and developing countries. Project the responsibilities for environmental degradation by future human populations from developed countries and developing countries . Collect data on the birth control policies of representative developed countries and developing countries. Hold a brainstorming session about strategies to control the human population. See if a consensus can be formed about appropriate strategies for limiting environmental damage of human populations.

4.   Have your students analyze the political platforms of the major political parties in the United States. What positions do they take on the birth of American children and birth control? What positions do they take on the influence of the United States in global population growth patterns? To what extent does debate on population policy revolve around right to life, desired pregnancies, and quality of life for the children who are born?

Laboratory Skills

Laboratory Manual for Miller's Living in the Environment and Environmental Science. Lab 5: Exponential Growth; Lab 6: Population Control.

Computer Skills

Microcomputer Programs for Demographic Analysis (MCPDA)
    - Performs a wide range of tests and analyses on demographic data.
    - Institute for Resource Development, Westinghouse, P.O. Box 866, Columbia, MD 21044
DYNPLAN
    -Calculates the effects that specific health-care interventions and family-planning measures can be expected to have on the demography of a nation.
    -Stan Berstein, Department of Population and International Health, School of Public Health, University of Michigan, Ann Arbor, MI 48109

CHAPTER 12
AIR AND AIR POLLUTION

THINKING

Concept Map

See Appendix A, Map 17.

Goals

See bulleted list of questions on p. 256 of text.

Objectives

1. List and briefly describe the layers of the atmosphere. Compare the function of ozone in the troposphere with the function of ozone in the stratosphere. List three ways humans interact with the earth's gaseous nutrient cycles.

2. List eight classes of outdoor air pollutants. Distinguish between a primary pollutant and a secondary pollutant. Distinguish between stationary and mobile sources of pollution.

3. Distinguish between photochemical smog and industrial smog. Describe a thermal inversion and conditions under which it is most likely to occur.

4. Define *acid deposition*. List four effects of acid deposition. Summarize how serious acid deposition is in the United States.

5. Assess the significance of the problem of indoor air pollution. List the four most dangerous indoor air pollutants.

6. Using the Figure 12-14 on p. 269, list three potential sources of indoor air pollution where you live. Describe the best ways to deal with asbestos and radon.

7. Summarize air pollution effects on human health, plants, aquatic life, and materials.

8. Summarize the Clean Air Act. List six ways to strengthen the Clean Air Act. Summarize the concept of "emissions trading." Evaluate the pros and cons of this strategy. Evaluate the effectiveness of pollution prevention vs. pollution cleanup strategies.

9. Evaluate alternatives to gasoline. Determines which alternatives look best to you.

10. Summarize California's South Coast Air Quality Management Plan. Describe an integrated approach to protect the atmosphere.

Key Terms (Terms are listed in the same font style as they appear in the text.)

atmosphere (p. 256)
troposphere (p. 256)
stratosphere (p. 256)
air pollution (p. 256)
stationary sources (p. 257)
mobile sources (p. 257)
primary pollutants (p. 258)

secondary pollutants (p. 258)
criteria air pollutants (p. 259)
photochemical reaction (p. 260)
photochemical smog (p. 260)
photochemical ozone (p. 260)
industrial smog (p. 261)
temperature inversion (p. 262)

Outline

Lichens and canaries warn us of toxic air.
  A. The innermost layer of the earth's air, the troposphere, contains most of the polluted air.
      1. Outdoor air pollution comes primarily from burning fossil fuels and from motor vehicles—brown-air smog and gray-air smog.
      2. Temperature inversions prolong the influence of air pollutants.
      3. Acid deposition is also a pollutant resulting from industrial processes.
  B. Indoor air pollution has the most serious health effects; things like radon, formaldehyde, pesticides, etc.
      1. Respiratory systems help to protect you from the effects of air pollutants, but air pollution is still deadly, claiming about 1.8 million people each year.
      2. Laws help to lessen air pollution but need to be strengthened.
          a. Market factors
          b. Coal-burning facilities
          c. Motor vehicle pollution
          d. Ultrafine particles

12-1 The atmosphere
  A. The earth's air is composed of three layers: the atmosphere, the troposphere, and the stratosphere.

12-2 Outdoor air pollution
  A. The major types and sources of air pollution are carbon oxides, sulfur oxides, nitrogen oxides, volatile organic compounds, photochemical oxidants, radioactive substances, and suspended particulate matter.
  B. Both primary pollutants and secondary pollutants have deleterious effects on people and the environment.

12-3 Photochemical and industrial smog
  A. Photochemical or brown-air smog is air pollution formed by sunlight.
  B. Industrial or gray-air smog contains sulfur gases and suspended solid particles.
  C. Natural factors like rain and snow or salty sea spray help reduce/decrease air pollution; wind also clears pollutants from the air.
  D. Urban buildings, hills and mountains, and high temperatures all contribute to the development of photochemical smog.
  E. Temperature inversion often holds pollutants near the earth.
      1. Subsidence temperature inversion
      2. Radiation temperature inversion

12-4 Regional outdoor air pollution from acid deposition
  A. Pollutants produced by industrial operations are carried by the wind and form nitric acid vapor, sulfuric acid droplets, and sulfate and nitrate salts.
      1. Wet deposition: acid rain, snow, fog, cloud vapor
      2. Acid deposition: acid rain

B. Acid deposition develops in areas downwind from coal-burning power plants, smelters, factories and/or in urban areas with many cars.
C. Acid deposition's effects on any ecosystem include respiratory diseases, leaching of toxic metals from water pipes, and damages to outdoor buildings, metal, etc.
D. Acid deposition's effects on aquatic systems are overwhelming: fish populations are destroyed by it.
E. Acid deposition's effects on plants and soils are caused by the chemical interactions in forest and crop soils. Leaves and tree needles are directly damaged; calcium and magnesium salts are leached from the soil; metals, which are toxic to plants and animals, are released into the soil.

12-5 Indoor air pollution
A. Indoor air pollutants often put people's health at serious risk because so much time is spent indoors.
   1. Fine particles contain toxins and metals.
   2. Pesticide concentrations
   3. Traffic-produced pollution
B. Most dangerous indoor pollutants are cigarette smoke, formaldehyde, radioactive radon, and fine/ultrafine particles.
   1. Formaldehyde symptoms: breathing problems, dizziness, rash, headaches, sore throat, sinus, eye irritation, nausea
   2. Radon exposure: radiation particles in tissue

12-6 Effects of air pollution on living organisms and materials
A. Nose hairs, mucus in your respiratory tract lining, sneezing, and coughing all help protect respiratory systems.
B. Cilia in respiratory tract trap pollutants.
C. Diseases exacerbated by air pollutants are asthma, lung cancer, chronic bronchitis, and emphysema.
D. Plant health is undermined by air pollution, though it may take years for the damage to surface.
E. Ozone reduces U. S. food production by as much as 10%.

12-7 Solutions: Preventing and reducing air pollution
A. EPA has established national ambient air quality standards (NAAQS).
B. Clean Air Act has reduced the amount of air pollution in the U. S.
C. Problems with air pollution laws in the U. S.
   1. Prevention is more important than clean-up of polluted air.
   2. Fuel-efficiency standards for automobiles have not been increased.
   3. Emissions from two-cycle engines have not been regulated.
   4. Clean Air Act does not reduce emissions of carbon dioxide and other greenhouse gases.
D. The marketplace can help reduce pollution.
   1. Allow emissions trading
   2. Emission trading does not pressure older utilities to clean up.
E. Air pollution from coal-burning facilities needs to be decreased.
   1. Outdoor air pollution: disperse/dilute pollutants and remove particulate pollutants; use low-sulfur coal
   2. Older coal burning facilities: upgrade equipment hope undermined by Bush administration
F. Air pollution from motor vehicles
   1. Mass transit; bicycling and walking
   2. Less polluting engines and fuels
   3. Improve fuel efficiency
   4. Restrict driving
   5. Take older cars off the road
   6. Tax write-offs for low-polluting vehicles

G. Reducing indoor air pollution
    1. Cover ceiling tiles and AC ducts' lining
    2. Ban smoking
    3. Stricter standards for formaldehyde emissions
    4. Prevent radon infiltration
    5. Use cleaner substances (cleansers, paint, etc.)

Summary

1. The layers of the atmosphere are the troposphere, stratosphere, mesosphere, and thermosphere.

2. Major classes of air pollutants include carbon, sulfur, and nitrogen oxides, volatile organic compounds, suspended particulate matter, photochemical oxidants, radioactive substances, and hazardous chemicals that can cause health problems such as cancer, birth defects, and nervous system problems. Primary sources of these pollutants include cars, industry, and natural phenomena such as volcanic eruptions.

3. The two types of smog are the photochemical and the industrial or gray-air smog.

4. Acid deposition includes wet deposition of acidic rain, snow, fog, and cloud vapor with pH less than 5.6, and dry deposition of acidic particles. The solution to this problem is prevention that reduces emissions of acidic nitrogen and sulfur oxides, and particulates.

5. Harmful effects of air pollution include various respiratory diseases, premature deaths, damage to plants and materials such as buildings, cars, statues, etc.

6. We can reduce air pollution through prevention and cleanup, including burning low sulfur coal, shifting to less polluting fuels, removal of pollutants after combustion, use of mass transit or alternative transportation, improving fuel efficiency, and tax incentives.

Multiple Choice Questions

See Instructor's Manual, Section II, p. 274.

More Depth: Conceptual Term Paper Topics

1. Atmosphere. Air pollution meteorology as an applied science.

2. Outdoor air pollution. The geographic distribution of air quality problems; air pollution and major ecosystem disruption; fine particulates as a health hazard; Donora, Pennsylvania air pollution disaster; reducing urban heat island effects.

3. Indoor air pollution. Radon gas; sources, health effects, and control measures for indoor air pollution.

4. Acid deposition. Tall smokestacks and acid deposition; acid deposition in the northeastern United States; Germany's waldsterben; liming lakes; acid deposition and freshwater ecosystems.

More Breadth: Interdisciplinary Activities and Projects

1. Visit the chemistry department or invite a chemistry professor to visit your class to discuss measurement of air and water pollution. Have the professor show you instruments for measuring air and water pollutants in the parts per million or lower range and explain the difficulty of making accurate and reproducible measurements of such low concentrations.

2. As a class exercise, interview farmers, foresters, and wildlife experts in your area to determine whether they know of any plant, fish, or animal damage from air pollution. Is acid deposition a problem in your locale? If so, what is the extent of the damage? Is anything being done about it?

3. Have a doctor or health official visit your class to explain and illustrate the various types of lung disease and damage that can result from air pollution. If possible, have the expert show you specimens (or photographs) of lung tissue from a young child, an urban dweller, a rural dweller, a smoker, a nonsmoker, and from patients suffering from lung cancer, emphysema, and chronic bronchitis.

4. Have an epidemiologist visit the class to present available evidence on relationships between air pollution and human health.

5. Have someone knowledgeable about automobile engine design visit your class and discuss some of the problems associated with designing engines that pollute less and deliver better fuel economy.

6. Have a meteorologist visit your class to discuss the weather and climate patterns of your locale. Find out if there are any atmospheric patterns in your area that aid or hinder air pollution effects.

Multisensory Learning: Audiovisuals

The Search for Clean Air; 1994; 57 min.; ecological and health effects of polluted air and issues to correct the problems; FHS.

Do You Really Want to Live This Way? from *Race to Save the Planet;* 1990; 60 min.; air and water pollution caused by western lifestyles; ACPB.

Our Planet Earth; 23 min.; from space, shows how pollution travels through the atmosphere; BFF.

Acid Rain; 20 min.;geological and meteorological interactions; sources and potential solutions; FHS.

Air Pollution: Outdoor; 16 min.; burning fuel and the status of research into new and cleaner fuels and combustion methods; FHS.

Air Pollution: Indoor; 13 min.; the problem; FHS.

The Air We Breathe. 49 mins., 1997. BFF

Cities. 50 min., 2000. BFF

Down/Downstream. 59 min., 1988. BFF

Emissions and Emotions. 30 mins., 1992. BFF.

Nowhere to Hide. 28 min, VP. (banned footage of Iraq bombing)

PCBs and the Food Chain (Fragile Planet series), FHS.

Poison in the Rockies. 56 min, 1990. BFF

Noise Pollution; 26 min.; FHS.

See Appendix B for suppliers.

ATTITUDES/VALUES

Assessment

1. What is blowing in the wind in your community? How does the wind make you feel?

2. Do you feel that the development of your community is related to the climate of the area? Are there any connections you have experienced?

3. Are you aware of mountains or bodies of water in your area that affects local climate conditions?

4. Do humans have a right to use the atmosphere in any way they wish? Do you see limits to freedom of choice? If so, what determines those limits?

5. Do you feel that humans have the power to alter Earth's climate? Do you feel that humans can responsibly control their impact on the atmosphere?

6. Have you ever breathed pristine air? How did it feel?

7. Have you ever breathed highly polluted air? How did it feel?

8. Do humans have a right to breathe clean air?

9. Do you take steps to improve the indoor air quality of your living space?

10. Are you willing to drive your car less to create less air pollution?

11. Do you support strong emissions standards on automobiles and power plants?

More Depth: Discussion and Term Paper Topics

1. How much air pollution should we tolerate?

2. What are you willing to do to prevent acid rain from defacing statues and historical monuments?

3. How much responsibility for clean air should areas upwind carry for areas downwind?

4. How much do Americans value clean air in their homes?

(Also, see text, Critical Thinking, p. 279)

PARTICIPATION

More Depth: Action-oriented Term Paper Topics

1. Methods of assessing and cleaning up air pollution. Scientific methods for measuring indoor and outdoor air pollutants; methods for measuring automobile emissions; stack scrubber technology; catalytic converters and their problems; electric automobiles.

2. Cities. The Pittsburgh air pollution cleanup; air pollution cleanup in Los Angeles.

3. National. The Clean Air Act amendments; the EPA's record on enforcement of the Clean Air Acts.

4. International. The London air pollution cleanup; air pollution in Eastern Europe; joint responsibility of Canada and the United States for acid deposition in the Great Lakes region.

SKILLS

Environmental Problem-Solving Skills: Projects

1. Have students survey corrosion and damage to buildings and statues that result from air pollution in your area. Try to estimate the total cost per year for replacement, repair, cleaning, and painting. Who pays for this?

2. Have your class make a community-wide survey of particulate fallout and plot the results on a map of your area. Obtain some small, open-top boxes–all the same size. Use masking tape to stick a clean piece of white typing paper in the bottom of each box. Place the boxes at various locations for a period of 24 hours and compare the relative darkness on the paper. Does the particulate fallout vary with height? (Try some rooftops.) Compare your map with any official air pollution monitor locations or test spots. Do the official monitors give a realistic picture? See if you can trace the major causes in heavy fallout areas. You can vary the experiment by using a strip of exposed masking tape to collect the solids and then observe or count them under a microscope.

3. Have your class use a local map to determine the distance from your classroom or school to mountains, hills, tall buildings, towers, and other recognizable landmarks at varying distances. Each day for several weeks estimate visibility by noting which of these landmarks you can see. Note whether the weather is rainy, cloudy, or hazy in order to determine if poor visibility is due primarily to weather conditions or to air pollution. Try to compare your results with official records (if available).

4. As a class project, test the vital capacity of the lungs of each member of the class. Your vital capacity is the total volume of air you can exhale in one breath. Low vital capacity indicates that only a small fraction of the volume of a person's lungs is being used for breathing and obtaining oxygen. It can also lead to an enlarged heart because the heart must work harder to pump blood through the lungs. Test lung capacity as a function of age and sex, and on track team members, smokers and nonsmokers, urban and rural dwellers, and people with asthma, bronchitis, and emphysema. A portable vital-capacity tester can easily be made by inserting a two-hole stopper in a gallon jug. Put a short glass tube with a 6-inch piece of rubber tubing attached through one hole and a long glass tube that almost reaches the bottom of the jug through the other hole. Attach a 15- to 24-inch rubber tube to this glass tube. Fill the jug half to two-thirds full of water. Fix the stopper tightly, take a deep breath, blow into the short rubber tube to force the water out of the jug and into another jug or container, and measure the water in the second jug. Run several trials and get an average for each person tested.

5. Ask your students to conduct a class or school survey to see what percentage of the respondents (a) can identify the major pollutants from automobiles, (b) know what air pollution devices are on their cars, (c) have their engines tuned on a regular basis, and (d) would be willing to pay extra for more effective air pollution control devices (including the maximum they would pay).

Laboratory Skills

Laboratory Manual for Miller's Living in the Environment and Environmental Science. Lab 12: The Human Respiratory System; Lab 13: Air Pollution; Lab 14: Thermal Inversion; Lab 17: Noise Pollution.

Computer Skills

Acid Deposition (ADEPT) Model
    -Analyzes alternative strategies for dealing with the problem of acid deposition.
    -Manager, Software and Publications Distribution, Electric Power Research Institute, 3412 Hillview Ave., P.O. Box 10412, Palo Alto, CA 94303

User's Network for Applied Modeling of Air Pollution (UNAMAP)
    -Provides tools to analyze the implications for air quality of a wide variety of possible development projects and programs and for assessing alternative air-pollution control regulations
    -Computer Products, National Technical Information Service, 5285 Port Royal Rd., Springfield, VA 22161

CHAPTER 13
CLIMATE CHANGE AND OZONE LOSS

THINKING

Concept Map

See Appendix A, Map 18.

Goals

See bulleted list of questions on p. 281 of text.

Objectives

1. Summarize consensus views of the scientific community about climate change. Describe patterns of timing of past glacial and interglacial periods. Indicate which type of period we are now enjoying.

2. List the four greenhouse gases that humans contribute to the atmosphere. Using Figure 13-4 on p. 283, construct a table which succinctly compares these gases for % contribution to human-caused greenhouse gases, main sources, length of time gas remains in the atmosphere, and relative strength of the gas per molecule compared to carbon dioxide.

3. Describe the change in global temperature since 1860.

4. Describe how future changes in climate are projected. List five uncertainties that determine the correspondence between projections of climate models and their fit to the real world. List four projections made from major climate models. List seven factors that may amplify or dampen the effects of global warming.

5. Briefly describe how global warming might affect agriculture, water supplies, forests, biodiversity, sea level, weather extremes, human health, and human refugees.

6. Evaluate the need to respond to the threat of global warming. List three strategies that could help prevent global warming. List three "technofixes" for global warming and consider the pros and cons of each. List three ways to prepare for global warming.

7. Briefly describe what is happening to ozone in the stratosphere. Evaluate the positions taken over the existence of ozone depletion. Describe what is causing changes in the ozone levels, what the likely effects of this change will be, and how this change can be prevented.

8. List two technofixes for ozone loss.

Key Terms (Terms are listed in the same font style as they appear in the text.)

global cooling (p. 281)
global warming (p. 281)
greenhouse effect (p. 282)
greenhouse gases (p. 282)
global warming (p. 283)
enhanced greenhouse effect (p. 284)
global circulation models (GCMs) (p. 285)
albedo (p. 287)

aerosols (p. 289)
soot (p. 289)
precautionary strategy (p. 292)
no-regrets strategy (p. 292)
Kyoto Protocol (p. 295)
ultraviolet (UV) radiation (p. 296)
chlorofluorocarbon (CFC) (p. 297)
halons (p. 298)

methyl bromide (p. 298)
carbon tetrachloride (p. 298)
methyl chloroform (p. 298)
hydrogen chloride (p. 298)

ozone hole (p. 298)
ozone thinning (p. 301)
Montreal Protocol (p. 301)

Outline

Earth's climate has changed in the past and continues to do so.
  A. How have the temperature and climate of earth changed in the past?
  B. The climate and temperature change has many affects on human beings.
  C. Implications of global warming are, as yet, unknown.
  D. Short-term and long-term temperature change will influence life on earth.
  E. Mathematical models are being used to predict climate change.
  F. Changing climatic conditions will affect man, and man's environmental damage will affect the climate.

13-1 Past climate change and the natural greenhouse effect
  A. Earth's climate is always changing; sometimes in a seemingly cyclical manner, but always with patterns of global cooling and warming.
  B. Water vapor and carbon dioxide are the two greenhouse gases with the largest concentrations.

13-2 Climate change and human activities
  A. Three human activities have released greenhouse gases into the troposphere.
  B. Global warming/global climate instability has been encouraged by the concentration of carbon dioxide, rising temperatures of the atmosphere, and use of fossil fuel.

13-3 Projecting future changes in the earth's climate
  A. Earth's future climatic changes are projected by mathematical models.
  B. Predications are that earth's surface temperature will continue to increase.
  C. Emissions of carbon dioxide, methane, and nitrous oxide will continue to increase.
  D. Global sea level and global temperatures are expected to rise.

13-4 Factors affecting changes in the earth's average temperature
  A. Several changes may affect the earth's temperatures.
      1. Solar output
      2. Earth's reflectivity
      3. Oceans' storing of carbon dioxide and heat, and carbon dioxide's effect on photosynthesis
      4. Changing ocean currents
      5. Changing sea levels
      6. Changes in cloud cover and in air pollution

13-5 Some possible effects of a warmer world
  A. The positive and negative effects of a warmer climate will depend on the location and the rapidity of the temperature change.
  B. Effects could include dying forests, shifting of climate belts, expanding wildlife ranges, rising sea levels, and concomitant loss of estuaries and coral reefs.

13-6 Solutions: Dealing with the threat of climate change
  A. There are four approaches to the threat of climate change.
      1. Do nothing.
      2. Undertake more research.
      3. Act now to reduce risks.
      4. Undertake key actions now to reduce warming.
  B. Reduce greenhouse gases' entering the atmosphere.
      1. Limit carbon dioxide entering the atmosphere.
      2. Reduce the release of carbon dioxide and nitrous oxide into soil.

13-7 What is being done to reduce greenhouse gas emissions?
  A. Kyoto treaty
  B. We should prepare for the effects of global warming and climate change.

13-8 Ozone depletion in the stratosphere
  A. Causes of ozone depletion
    1. Chlorofluorocarbons
    2. Methyl bromide
    3. Hydrogen chloride
    4. Carbon tetrachloride
    5. Methyl chloroform
    6. n-propyl bromide
    7. Hexachlorobutadiene
  B. Ozone thinning is a better description of the phenomenon.
  C. UV-sensitive plants and animals cannot adapt quickly.
  D. Skin cancers
    1. Malignant carcinoma
    2. Squamous cell carcinoma
    3. Basal cell carcinoma
    4. Melanoma

13-9 Solutions: Protecting the ozone layer
  A. Montreal Protocol
  B. Copenhagen Protocol

Summary

1. The earth's average surface temperature and climate has changed in the past. The changes include prolonged periods of global cooling and global warming.

2. In the future there will be increased emissions of carbon dioxide, methane, and nitrogen oxide leading to increased natural greenhouse effects.

3. Factors influencing changes of earth's average surface temperature include changes in the solar output, the earth's reflectivity, the ability of oceans to store carbon dioxide, the ocean currents, the average sea level, cloud cover, and air pollution.

4. Possible effects from a warmer earth include shifts in plant-growing areas, crop yields, and pests, extinction of some species, loss of habitats, prolonged heat waves and droughts, increased flooding, changes in water supplies, decreased water quality, changes in forest composition, increased fires, rising sea levels, beach erosion, contamination of aquifers, spread of tropical diseases into temperate zones, increased respiratory diseases and allergies, increased deaths, and migration.

5. To prevent global warming we should limit fossil fuel use, shift from coal to natural gas use, place energy efficient technologies in developing countries, improve energy efficiency, shift to renewable energy sources, reduce deforestation, use sustainable agriculture, limit urban sprawl, reduce poverty, and slow population growth.

6. Human activities that cause ozone depletion include emissions of chlorofluorocarbons, methyl bromide, hydrogen chloride, carbon tetrachloride, methyl chloroform, and others. We should care about the ozone depletion because it causes sunburns, cataracts, skin cancers, immune suppression, reduced crop yields, reduced seafood supplies, decreased forest productivity, increased acid deposition, increased photochemical smog, and global warming.

7. To slow and eventually eliminate depletion of the ozone layer, we must ban use of all the chemicals that cause it.

Multiple Choice Questions

See Instructor's Manual, Section II, p. 287.

More Depth: Conceptual Term Paper Topics

1. Climate patterns. El Niño-Southern Oscillation; weather control and modification; paleogeography; evidence from bubbles in Arctic ice; the ice ages; the Gulf Stream; upwellings; thermal inversions.

2. Greenhouse effect. Greenhouse gases; global warming and our coastlines; global warming and the incidence of severe storms; deforestation and global warming; climate and biodiversity; rates of global climate change and adaptation; global warming and agriculture.

3. Ozone loss. Health effects of increased ultraviolet radiation; distinguishing tropospheric and stratospheric ozone; CFCs: uses and control of production.

More Breadth: Interdisciplinary Activities and Projects

1. Invite an atmospheric scientist (preferably a climatologist) to address your class on the subject of regional and global climatic change and why it is so difficult to forecast climate several years or decades into the future. What progress has been made in the development and testing of very large computerized models of global climate?

2. Visit a first-class weather station.

3. Have local emergency officials explain to your class the precautions that have to be taken in adverse weather conditions.

4. Have experts in various fields present their views on the impact that global warming will have on their arenas: for example, how will it affect farming, forestry, coastal zone management, and town planning?

Multisensory Learning: Audiovisuals

Ozone: Cancer of the Sky; 1994; 40 min.; causes of ozone depletion, seriousness of the threat, extent of the damage, and what can be done; VP.
Only One Atmosphere from *Race to Save the Planet;* 1990; 60 min.; the environmental challenge of potential global warming; ACPB.
Greenhouse Crisis—The American Response; the Union of Concerned Scientists look at the interactions of energy consumption, greenhouse effect, and global warming; VP.
Greenhouse Earth. 2001. FHS
Heat Is On: the effects of global warming. 26 mins., FHS.
Silent Sentinels & the Perils of Plectropomus. 2000, BFF.
Turning Down the Heat. 46 mins., 2000. BFF
Winds of Change: global warming and extinction. 20 mins., 1991. FHS
Global Warming; 26 min.; FHS.
Danger Ahead: Is There No Way Out; 26 min.; responding to global warming; FHS.
Alterations in the Atmosphere; 18 min.; pollutants implicated in climate changes; FHS.
Drought and Flood: Two Faces of One Coin; 18 min.; potential effects of global warming; FHS.
Prophets and Loss; 1990; 60 min.; environmental thinkers discuss climate change; VP.
Once and Future Planet; 23 min.; industry, lifestyle, and the Earth's atmosphere; BFF.
Hole in the Sky; 1994; 52 min.; evidence of continuing ozone depletion in the stratosphere; FHS.
Assault on the Ozone Layer; 18 min.; global connections in destruction of the ozone layer; FHS.

See Appendix B for suppliers.

ATTITUDES/VALUES

Assessment

1. How do you feel when you consider the possibility of global climate change?

2. Do you feel that the environment will be able to absorb any of the changes that human cultures bring about?

3. Do you feel that new technologies will be able to modify any harmful effects that humans bring about in the environment?

4. Do you feel that humans have a responsibility to ameliorate the causes of global climate change? If so, what steps are you willing to take to slow the rate of global climate change?

5. Have you ever experienced a severe sunburn?

6. How would you feel carrying a protective umbrella for life?

7. Do you feel that humans have a responsibility to ameliorate the causes of ozone depletion? If so, what steps are you willing to take to slow the rate of global climate change?

More Depth: Discussion and Term Paper Topics

1. Do humans have a commitment to future generations? If so, how much?

2. How much are humans willing to spend for energy efficiency in the short term to receive long-term economic payoffs and help slow potential global warming?

3. Would humans rather prevent global warming or adapt to global warming as it happens?

(Also, see text, Critical Thinking, p. 303)

PARTICIPATION

More Depth: Action-oriented Term Paper Topics

1. Individual. Improving energy efficiency; recycling CFCs from appliances.

2. Global: Montreal Protocol; 1992 Earth Summit in Rio; International Atomic Energy Agency

SKILLS

Environmental Problem-Solving Skills: Projects

1. Develop students' awareness of the effect of temperature by working out the following:

    Heating degree days or cooling degree days (variation of daily mean in your locale from 65 degrees F.)

    Growing degree days for several crops (taking the base temperature for a given crop and comparing it to the daily mean in your locale)

Temperature and humidity index using the formula:

$$\text{THI} = T - 0.53 \, (1 - \text{RH}) \, (T - 14)$$

where THI = temperature and humidity index
  T = temperature
  RH = relative humidity

Weather stress index (mean apparent temperatures averaged over 40 years compared to mean apparent temperature for a particular day)

2. As a class project, carefully prepare a questionnaire to investigate what people know about global warming (causes and potential effects), attitudes toward potential global warming, and actions (if any) they are willing to take to ameliorate rapid global climate change. Administer the questionnaire to a variety of citizens, deciding upon a sampling strategy in advance. Summarize your results in appropriate tables, graphs, charts, and written descriptions. What conclusions can be drawn from your results? Who might be interested in receiving a copy of your work?

<u>Laboratory Skills</u>

(none)

<u>Computer Skills</u>

Long-Term Global Energy-Carbon Dioxide Model
  -Makes long-term global projections concerning energy utilization and carbon dioxide emissions from the energy sector.
  -Thomas A. Boden, Oak Ridge National Laboratory, P.O. Box X, Carbon Dioxide Information Analysis Center, Building 2001, Oak Ridge, TN 37831

Atmospheric Greenhouse Model (AGM)
  -Analyzes the consequences for the global climate of various scenarios regarding the production of carbon dioxide from fossil fuel combustion.
  -Prof. L. D. D. Harvey, Department of Geography, University of Toronto, 100 St. George Street, Toronto, Ontario M5S 1A1, Canada

Nuclear Crash: The U.S. Economy After Small Nuclear Attacks
  -Studies nuclear bottleneck attacks on the United States and especially the time required for the U.S. economy to recover from such attacks.
  -Prof. Kosta Tsipis, Program in Science and Technology for International Security, Massachusetts Institute of Technology, 20A-011, Cambridge, MA 02139

CHAPTER 14
WATER RESOURCES AND WATER POLLUTION

THINKING

Concept Map

See Appendix A, Maps 19 and 20.

Goals

See bulleted list of questions on p. 306 of text.

Objectives

1. List seven physical properties that make water unique.

2. Briefly describe Earth's water supply. Compare amounts of salt water and fresh water. Compare amounts of frozen fresh water and water available for human use. Define *watershed* and *groundwater*.

3. List four causes of water scarcity and five methods to increase water supply. Explain how watershed transfer projects illustrate the principle that you can never do just one thing. State four ways to prevent unnecessary water waste.

4. Define floodplain. Describe the significance of the problem of flooding. List four ways to reduce the problem of flooding. Evaluate the water supply problems of your locality. Do you have too much, not enough, or just right?

5. List nine common types of water pollutants and give one example of each. Distinguish between point and nonpoint sources of pollution.

6. Briefly explain the differences among streams, lakes, groundwater, and oceans that vary in their vulnerability to pollution. Draw an oxygen sag curve to illustrate what happens to dissolved oxygen levels in streams below points where degradable oxygen-demanding wastes are added.

7. Define *cultural eutrophication*. List three ways to reduce cultural eutrophication. Compare the effectiveness of pollution control and pollution prevention strategies. Describe a groundwater protection plan.

8. Describe at least three strategies to reduce nonpoint-source pollution. Briefly describe the Clean Water Act. State five ways it could be strengthened.

9. Briefly describe and distinguish among primary, secondary, and advanced sewage treatment. Summarize one natural approach to water purification. Describe how drinking water is protected and purified.

10. Summarize an integrated water pollution control plan. List three things individuals can do to maintain water supply and quality.

Key Terms (Terms are listed in the same font style as they appear in the text.)

hydrogen bonds (p. 306)   **reliable runoff** (p. 307)
hydrologic cycle (p. 307)   **watershed** (p. 307)
surface runoff (p. 307)   **drainage basin** (p. 307)

Outline

Water, Water....not enough anywhere!
    A. Various characteristics of water make it unique in its support of life.
    B. Fresh water, partly available both as surface runoff and groundwater, is being withdrawn faster than it is being replenished.
    C. Water must be managed more carefully and wasteful practices must be changed, or the world will have even more inadequate supplies.

14-1 Water's importance and unique properties
    A. We all need large amounts of water to provide food, shelter, etc.
        1. Characteristics
          a. Liquid form is spread all over the earth.
          b. Water temperature changes slowly and, thereby, is protective of living things.
          c. Much heat is necessary to evaporate water.
        2. Chemical properties
          a. Strong hydrogen bonds; maintains balance between acids and basics in cells.
          b. Filters out ultraviolet radiation and dissolves many compounds.
          c. It adheres to a solid and expands when it freezes.
    B. We waste and pollute water.

14-2 Supply, renewal and use of water resources
   A. Only 0.014% of the world's fresh water is easily available for use.
       1. The hydrologic cycle collects, purifies, recycles, and distributes water.
       2. Water availability between the *haves* and *have nots* is not equitable.
   B. Various types of water provide access—surface water, reliable runoff, watersheds, and groundwater—and add up to humans using about 55% of reliable surface water runoff.
   C. Throughout the world, 69% of water is used for irrigation and industry uses 23%.

14-3 Too little water: Problems and solutions
   A. Freshwater shortages are caused by a dry climate, drought, desiccation, and water stress.
   B. Freshwater supplies can be increased by building dams and reservoirs, reducing water waste and using less water.
   C. Dams and reservoirs have advantages and disadvantages.
       2. China's Three Gorges Dam project
       3. Aral Sea Disaster
       4. California Water Transfer Project
   D. Indiscriminate withdrawing groundwater from aquifers is one of the most serious water issues throughout the world.
   E. Desalination is not an efficient method to produce more water.
       1. Process is expensive.
       2. Concentrate brine from desalination must be disposed of.

14-4 Reducing water waste
   A. Reducing water waste is necessary as water becomes scarcer.
   B. Reducing water waste in various activities must be implemented: irrigation, industry, business, among individuals, as quickly as possible.

14-5 Too much water: Problems and solutions
   A. Human activities that increase flooding: remove water-absorbing vegetation, draining wetlands, living on floodplains, paving and building, deforestation.
   B. To reduce flood risks, we can channel streams, build levees, build dams, identify and manage flood-prone areas, and maintain/restore wetlands.

14-6 Types, effects, and sources of water pollution
   A. The major categories of water pollutants are: infectious agents, oxygen-demanding wastes, inorganic chemicals, organic chemicals, plant nutrients, radioactive materials, and heat.
   B. How much money would produce a safe world-wide water supply?

14-7 Pollution of freshwater streams, lakes, and groundwater
   A. Water pollution of streams in the U. S. is currently under control.
   B. Lakes/reservoirs are more vulnerable to pollution than streams because they may have stratified layers and they have little flow.
       1. Cultural eutrophication
       2. Groundwater pollution

14-8 Ocean pollution
   A. As the oceans are absorbing our pollutants, coastal areas are greatly undermined.
       1. Human sewage and agricultural waste
       2. Dredge spoils
       3. Crude and refine petroleum effects on ocean ecosystems
           a. Death of aquatic organism
           b. Oil 'globs' on marine animals = death
           c. Oil smothering of bottom-dwelling creatures
           d. Long-term effects
   B. Cleaning up oil spills entails mechanical, chemical, fire, and natural methods.

14-9 Solutions: Preventing and reducing surface water pollution
    A. Water pollution from nonpoint sources can be reduced.
        1. Slow release fertilizers
        2. Buffer zones between cultivation and surface waters
        3. Biological control of pests, instead of chemical control
    B. Some water pollution from point sources can be controlled by market forces.
        1. Discharge trading policy
        2. Responses to the Clean Water Act of 1972
        3. Hogs, poultry, and cattle production plants
        4. Wetland degradation
        5. Wastewater treatment
            a. Mechanical process which separates primary sewage
            b. Biological process used in secondary sewage
            c. Advanced sewage treatment: chemical and physical processes: bleaching, disinfection, chlorination
            d. Sewage sludge
        6. Methods to improve sewage treatment
            a. Prevent toxic/hazardous waste's reaching sewage plants
            b. Purify by using ecological treatment systems: wastewater
            c. Garden system
            d. Use wetlands
        7. Drinking water concerns
            a. Purification
            b. Quality

14-10 Solutions: Achieving a more sustainable water future
    A. Water sustainability demands several factors.
        1. More efficient irrigation
        2. Use water-saving technologies
        3. Improve/integrate management of water basis and groundwater
        4. Integrate policies for water management and air pollution reduction

Summary

1. Water's unique properties include the hydrogen bonds, high specific heat, evaporative cooling, being the universal solvent, ionization into hydrogen ions and hydroxyl ions, high surface tension, adhesion, cohesion, and highest density at 4 °C.

2. The amount of fresh water available to us represents 55% of the world's runoff of surface water. Of this, we use 35% while 20% is left to the streams for transportation of goods, dilution of pollution, and to sustain fisheries and wildlife.

3. Freshwater shortages are caused by dry climate, droughts, desiccation, and water stress. Solutions for this problem include building dams and reservoirs, transport of freshwater between locations, withdrawing of groundwater, and desalination.

4. Flooding is caused by heavy rain or melting of snow within a short time. To reduce flood damage or the risk of flooding we must avoid building on floodplains, removing water-absorbing vegetation, or draining wetlands.

5. Water pollutants include infectious agents from human or animal wastes, oxygen-demanding wastes from sewage, paper mills, and food processing, inorganic chemicals from surface runoff, industrial effluents, and household cleaners, organic chemicals from oil, plastics, pesticides, and detergents, sediment from erosion, and thermal pollution from power plant cooling.

6. The adverse effects of water pollution include degradation of water quality; skin cancer; crippling spine and neck damage; nervous system, kidney, liver, and reproductive defects; acceleration of metal corrosion; dissolved oxygen depletion; eutrophication; fish kills; and genetic mutations.

7. Water pollution problems in streams, lakes, and groundwater relate to chemical and biological pollutants with the greater problems being cultural eutrophication.

8. Water pollution of oceans relates to nitrogen oxide from industry and cars, heavy metals from effluents, toxic sediment, sewage, runoff of pesticides, manure, and fertilizers, and red tides from excess nitrogen.

9. Reduction or prevention of water pollution can be achieved through reduction of use of toxic pollutants, banning of ocean dumping of sludge, protection of sensitive areas from oil drilling and oil transport, regulation of coastal development, and regulation of sewage treatment.

10. To achieve a sustainable use of water resources, we must not deplete aquifers, and we must preserve ecological health of aquatic environments, preserve water quality, use watershed management and surface water use management, prevent water waste, and slow population growth.

Multiple Choice Questions

See Instructor's Manual, Section II, p. 295.

More Depth: Conceptual Term Paper Topics

1. Water pollution. Animal feedlot wastes; electric power plants and thermal pollution; waterborne disease-causing agents and their control; waterborne disease problems in developing countries; pesticides; deep-well disposal and groundwater contamination; sanitary landfills and groundwater contamination; hazardous storage and disposal problems; *Exxon Valdez* oil spill; leaking underground gasoline tanks; salinity problems in irrigated areas.

2. Case studies in water pollution. The fight to save Lake Erie; Lake Baikal; James River kepone spill; Chesapeake Bay; ocean dumping in the New York Bight.

3. Water supply. Drought history of the African Sahel; trickle irrigation; urban construction and aquifer recharge problems; water diversion projects in China and India; groundwater hydrology: research needs; the Ogallala Aquifer; groundwater use and land subsidence in central Florida.

More Breadth: Interdisciplinary Activities and Projects

1. Ask your class to determine the local agricultural and industrial uses of water. Is irrigation used widely? What is the source of irrigation water? What water conservation practices are used by local government, industry, and agriculture?

2. Ask your students to bring to class and share paintings, photographs, poems, songs, or other expressions of intense human feelings about water as a life-sustaining and precious substance.

3. Invite a local, state, or federal water pollution control official to discuss water pollution control methods, progress, and problems with your class.

4. Visit a sewage treatment plant with your class. Find out what level of sewage treatment is used in your community. What is the volume of effluent discharged? If effluent is discharged into a river or stream, is the water subsequently used for drinking water supply? Are there bodies of water in your locale unfit for fishing or swimming because of inadequately treated sewage effluent? If so, is anything being done to correct the problem?

Multisensory Learning: Audiovisuals

 Ocean Resources; 1994; 23 min.; oyster farming, chemicals in seaweed, sea organisms as natural
     resources; FHS.
The Water Cycle; 1993; 28 min.; questions about the proper use of water as a limited natural resource; VP.
Drinking Water: Quality on Tap; 1991; 25 min.; how the source of water, the supply, the treatment, and the
     delivery systems work together to provide quality drinking water; VP.
Downwind/ Downstream: Threats to the Mountains and Waters of the American West; 58 min.; water
     quality and mining operations; BFF.
Natural Waste Water Treatment; 1987; 29 min.; use of marsh plants in decentralized sewage treatment in
     Germany, Switzerland, and the Netherlands; BFF.
No Dam Good; BFF.
Pointless Pollution: America's Water Crisis; 28 min.; nonpoint source pollution; BFF.
The Wasting of a Wetland; 23 min.; industry, agriculture, population growth, and the Everglades; BFF.
Estuary; 12 min.; closeup of wetlands and waterways; BFF.
Fighting Pollution; 1994; 23 min.; water and sewage treatment, vacuum pyrolysis for recycling of wastes
     such as tires; FHS.
Testing the Waters; 57 min.; BFF.
The Ocean Planet: The Death of the Mississippi; 23 min.; FHS.
Black Triangle. 52 mins., 1991. Filmakers
Blue Planet. 6.66 hrs. (4 videos) BBC [also available in DVD]
Underwater, Out of Sight. 15 mins., VP
Water: a celebration. 1993. NG
We All Live Downstream. 30 mins., VP
When the Spill Hit Homer (Valdez oil spill). 27 mins., VP
Troubled Waters: Plastics in the Marine Environment; 57 min.; BFF.

See Appendix B for suppliers.

ATTITUDES/VALUES

Assessment

1. Do you consume too much water? Does your community consume too much water?

2. Do you feel your community is doing enough to provide water? Do you feel other strategies should be
    tried?

3. Are you confident that your community has an adequate water supply for the needs of the community
    for the next decade? Do you feel other strategies should be tried?

4. What are your feelings toward increasing water supply through building dams?

5. What are your feelings toward increasing water supply through more withdrawal of groundwater?

6. Do you favor metering water use and charging water consumers the full cost of proving fresh water?

7. Do you favor increasing the price of irrigation water to reflect its true cost and encourage conservation
    among farmers?

8. Do you favor local ordinances that conserve water (such as the low-use toilet requirement for new
    housing)?

9. Would you support sharp increases in monthly water bills for all homes, buildings and industries to
    discourage water waste?

More Depth: Discussion and Term Paper Topics

1. How responsible are upstream communities for ensuring that high-quality water is delivered to downstream communities?

2. What role has water supply played in wars between countries in the last decade?

3. What are human attitudes toward cleanliness of water resources?

4. Is the public ready for water recycling?

(Also, see text, Critical Thinking, p. 345)

PARTICIPATION

More Depth: Action-oriented Term Paper Topics

1. Scientific methods of analyzing water. Groundwater pollution testing and monitoring; water quality testing, such as with Hach kits.

2. Individuals acting to conserve water and prevent water pollution. New uses for residential "gray" water; water-saving showers, faucets, and toilets.

3. State. The California Water Plan.

4. National. The Safe Drinking Water Act of 1974; protection of groundwater; the Clean Water Act; problems in enforcing water quality standards; the role of the Environmental Protection Agency in water quality management; the Toxic Substances Control Act; the National Eutrophication Survey; the Coastal Barrier Resources Act; water-rights battles in the West.

5. Global. UN Conference on the Law of the Sea.

SKILLS

Environmental Problem-Solving Skills: Projects

1. Have your students explore community water resources. Where does your town get its water? What is the average daily use in summer? In winter? What are the major uses in your area? (List the ten biggest users.) How much does your class use?

2. Have students pick out finished products in your classroom or home and, beginning with the raw materials, trace the use of water in giving you the final product.

3. If a dam has been constructed or is being built in your area, visit the site with your class. Ask students to find pictures of the area and its water control problems before the dam was built, evaluate whether the dam should have been built, and substantiate their claims. Were there alternatives to dam construction? What is the expected lifetime of the dam?

4. Have your class identify the present or potential sources of contaminants in your community's drinking water supply. If surface water from a river or lake is used, how and to what degree is it being polluted before it is withdrawn for your use? If groundwater is used, is the aquifer subject to contamination by leaking sanitary landfills, improperly functioning septic tanks, uncontained hazardous wastes, or other sources of pollution? (Ask a public health and/or environmental official to discuss these problems with your class.)

5. Ask your students to explore the principal sources of industrial water pollution in your community. What specific types of chemicals are removed in the treatment of these industrial wastes? How is this accomplished?

6. With your class, take a field trip to the nearest lake, river, or stream, preferably with a biologist. Note its smell, appearance, taste (if safe), flow, and ecological characteristics. How have these changed over the past 20 years? What plants and animals do you find living in or near the water? What are their functions? If possible, measure oxygen content, temperature, and pH. Use the library to determine what types of fish and other plant and aquatic life might exist under these conditions. What shifts would happen if acidity, dissolved oxygen, or temperature were individually or collectively increased? Decreased? What might happen if acidity decreased and temperature increased? Try to visit other sites upstream and downstream from your town to compare water quality. Which sites did you prefer? Why?

7. With your class, visit the nearest reservoir, pond, or lake and try to find evidence of natural eutrophication and human-induced eutrophication. How deep is the body of water? How does depth and water quality vary throughout the year? How old is the body of water? What factors appear to limit growth of organisms in the body of water? What might the normal life span of the body of water be? Its actual life span? If possible, get a chemist or biologist to help you gather physical data (pH, salinity, turbidity, algae counts, species diversity, depth of bottom sediments) to establish the stage of succession. Try to find people who have lived near the body of water for a number of years and ask them to describe changes they have observed.

Laboratory Skills

Laboratory Manual for Miller's Living in the Environment and Environmental Science. Lab 7: The Bacteria: Representatives of Kingdom Monera; Lab 8: Water Quality Testing I: The Coliform Test; Lab 9: Water Quality Testing II: Dissolved Oxygen and Biochemical Oxygen Demand; Lab 10: Water Quality Testing III: phyla 11: Wastewater Treatment.

Computer Skills

Water Supply Simulation Model (WSSM)
    -Evaluates the physical and economic characteristics of a water supply system.
    -U.S. Environmental Protection Agency, Office of Research and Development, Water Engineering Research Laboratory, ATTN: Dr. James A. Goodrich, Environmental Scientist, Systems and Cost Evaluation Staff, Drinking Water Research Division, Cincinnati, OH 45268

CHAPTER 15
SOLID AND HAZARDOUS WASTE

THINKING

Concept Map

See Appendix A, Map 21.

Goals

See bulleted list of questions on p. 348 of text.

Objectives

1. State the quantity of the world's solid wastes that is produced by the United States. State the percentage of solid waste produced in the United States that is municipal solid waste. Define *hazardous waste*. State the percentage of hazardous waste that is not regulated. List seven substances that are "linguistically detoxified."

2. Compare waste management and pollution prevention approaches to solid and hazardous waste. List the priorities for dealing with material use and solid waste. List priorities in dealing with hazardous waste. List seven ways to reduce waste and pollution. List four goals of an ecoindustrial revolution.

3. List reuse strategies for refillable containers and grocery bags. Define *compost*.

4. Distinguish between *closed-loop recycling* and *open-loop recycling*; centralized recycling of mixed solid waste and a source-separation approach.

5. List the three most important obstacles to recycling in the United States and suggest ways to overcome them. Summarize lessons to be learned from Germany's experience with tough packaging laws. Summarize the U.S. experience with recycling aluminum, wastepaper, and plastics.

6. Summarize Denmark's experience with detoxification of hazardous waste. Assess the pros and cons of incineration of hazardous and solid wastes.

7. Describe a modern sanitary landfill. Summarize the benefits and drawbacks of burying solid wastes in sanitary landfills. Summarize the benefits and drawbacks of deep-well disposal of hazardous wastes. Summarize the status of export of wastes. Summarize the causes, effects, and ways to deal with lead, dioxins, and chlorine.

8. Name and briefly describe two U.S. hazardous-waste laws. Describe how Superfund has been subverted and how its enforcement can be improved.

9. Summarize the goals of the ecojustice movement. List four ways to make a transition to a low-waste society.

Key Terms (Terms are listed in the same font style as they appear in the text.)

solid waste (p. 348)
municipal solid waste (p. 348)
electronic waste (p. 349)
garbage (p. 349)
hazardous waste (p. 349)

waste management (p. 350)
pollution (waste) prevention (p. 351)
high-waste approach (p. 351)
low-waste approach (p. 351)
trash taxes (p. 353)

<u>Outline</u>

Pollution and its effects never end.
    A. Solid waste and hazardous wastes are proportionately more of a problem in the United States than in any other country.
    B. Low-waste societies practice waste management and waste prevention.
    C. Societies increase resource productivity through cleaner production and selling services, not things.
    D. Resources may be reused and recycled. If not, they may be detoxified, burned, or exported.
    E. Regulations in the U. S. and throughout the world can govern hazardous waste disposal but becoming a low-waste society is preferable.

15-1 Wasting resources
    A. The United States' less than 5% of the world population produces 33% of the world's solid waste.
        1. Solid waste in a wasteful society
        2. Municipal waste
        3. Electronic waste: fastest-growing kind
    B. Hazardous waste meets one or more of the following criteria:
        1. Contains toxic, carcinogenic, mutagenic, or teratogenic compound at unacceptable levels
        2. Easily catches fire
        3. Can explode or release toxic fumes
        4. Can corrode metal containers
    C. Hazardous warning: Union Carbide plant in Bhopal, India

15-2 Producing less waste and pollution
    A. Methods to deal with solid and hazardous waste
        1. High-waste approach
        2. Low-waste approach: characterized by reduction, reuse, recycling, and redesign
    B. Methods to reduce waste and pollution
        1. Consume less
        2. 'Redesign manufacturing process to use less material and less energy.'
        3. 'Redesign manufacturing processes to produce less waste and pollution.'
        4. Develop products that are easy to recycle, reuse, repair, remanufacture, or compost.
        5. Design products to last

6. Eliminate unnecessary packaging
7. Implement trash taxes

15-3 Solutions: Cleaner production and selling services instead of things
    A. Apply nature's methods of sustainability to manufacturing processes.
    B. Industries interact in resource exchange webs.
    C. *Service Flow or product stewardship economy* is characterized by:
        1. Using a minimum amount of materials
        2. Lasts as long as possible
        3. Easy to Maintain, repair, reuse, recycle, remanufacture
        4. Provides services, not things

15-4 Reuse
    A. Reuse is a method for reducing waste.
    B. Reuse reduces energy use and extends resource supplies.

15-5 Recycling
    A. The two types of recycling are closed-loop recycling and downcycling.
    B. Solid waste recycling and composting: is either worth it?
        1. Wastepaper
        2. Plastics
    C. Four factors hinder recycling.
        1. Failure to implement full-cost pricing
        2. Subsidies for extracting resources, not for recycling or reusing
        3. Low landfill costs to consumers
        4. No large, steady market for recycled items

15-6 Detoxifying, burning, burying, and exporting wastes
    A. Bioremediation and phytoremediation
    B. Plasma torch to detoxify
    C. Incinerating wastes
    D. Land disposal: solid and hazardous wastes
    E. Basel Convention on Hazardous Waste

15-7 Case studies: lead, mercury, chlorine and dioxins
    A. Lead and mercury are especially threats to children.
    B. Chlorine and dioxins are highly toxic to people and the environment.

15-8 Hazardous waste regulation in the United States.
    A. Both the Resource Conservation and Recovery Act and the Superfund Act were supported to deal with hazardous wastes.
    B. Brownfields are contaminated industrial/commercial sites.

15-9 Solutions: Achieving a low-waste society
    A. Most citizens support a no wastes in anybody's backyard or a 'not on planet earth' philosophy.
    B. The POP Treaty was ratified in 2000.
    C. Transitioning to a low-waste society

Summary

1. Solid waste is any discarded and unwanted material that is not liquid or gas. The greater portion (98.5%) of solid waste comes from mining, oil and gas production, agriculture, sewage, and industrial activities. The remaining 1.5% is municipal solid waste.

2. Hazardous waste is any discarded solid or liquid material that is one or more of 39 toxic, carcinogenic, mutagenic, or teratogenic compounds, catches fire easily, is reactive or unstable enough to explode or release toxic fumes, or is capable of corroding metals.

3. To reduce, reuse, or recycle solid waste, we should use waste management or pollution prevention. For hazardous wastes, we produce less waste, convert to less hazardous waste, or put in perpetual storage.

4. Recycling paper includes removing the ink, glue, and coating and reusing the pulp for press new paper. In 2000, the United States recycled 49% of wastepaper. Recycling plastics is difficult because it cannot be separated from other waste, recovered resins do not yield significant volume of reusable material, the cost of making new plastic is lower.

5. The advantages of burning wastes include reduction of trash volume, minimizing the need for landfills, and lowering water pollution. The disadvantages include high cost, air pollution, producing toxic ash, and encouraging waste production.

6. The advantages of burying wastes include safety, wastes can be retrieved, ease of application, and low cost. Disadvantages include leaks and spills, existing fractures or earthquakes can cause waste escape, and encouraging waste production.

7. We can prevent lead poisoning through reduced use of leaded gasoline and waste incineration and by banning lead solder, glazing, and candles containing lead. Mercury pollution can be prevented by reducing waste incineration, removing mercury from coal, and using natural gas in the place of coal.

8. The United States regulate hazardous waste through the 1976 *Resource Conservation and Recovery Act* that was amended in 1984.

Multiple Choice Questions

See Instructor's Manual, Section II, p. 315.

More Depth: Conceptual Term Paper Topics

1. Solid waste. Sanitary landfill space shortages; Virginia Beach's Mt. Trashmore; *Mobro*, the garbage barge; plastics in the environment.

2. Hazardous waste. Definitions: what is included and what is excluded; household hazardous wastes and alternatives; lead; dioxin.

More Breadth: Interdisciplinary Activities and Projects

1. Visit a community recycling center and observe its operations. If no recycling program for household waste is available in your vicinity, why not lobby for one or set one up as a class project?

2. Does your state require refundable deposits on all beer and soft-drink containers? If so, investigate the extent to which the program is living up to expectations. If not, invite spokespersons for both sides of the issue to debate the matter for the benefit of your class.

3. Invite a city or county official responsible for solid waste disposal to discuss related economic, political, and logistical problems. Ask about possible plans for future improvements in collection and resource recovery plants.

4. Invite public health officials to address your class on the subject of hazardous waste risks to public health in your community.

5. Invite a toxicologist to visit your class and discuss the problem of metal toxicity.

Multisensory Learning: Audiovisuals

Solid Waste

Waste Disposal; 1994; 23 min.; household recycling, medical wastes, animal wastes; FHS.
Solid Solutions: Rural America Confronts the Waste Crisis; 1994; 30 min.; how smaller and poorer
    communities are creating strategies to deal with waste; VP.
Waste Not, Want Not from *Race to Save the Planet;* 1990; 60 min.; potential solutions to waste problems;
    ACPB.
Competitive Edge (i. e. waste audits). 7 min., 1989. RCO
Hot Potato. 11 mins., 1990. BFF
Human Waste. 52 mins., 1993. FL
Solid Solutions: rural America confronts the waste crisis. 30 mins., 1994. VP
Waste. 29 mins., 1985. BFF
The Disposable Society; 26 min.; solid waste; FHS.
Down in the Dumps; 26 min.; running out of landfill space and a look at alternatives; FHS.

Recycling

Canon: a clean earth. 6 min., 1992. RCO
Care and Be Careful (recycling glass). 1994. RCO
Garbage Into Gold. 25 min., 1995. RCO
Greening Business. 45 mins., 1994. BFF
No Spare Parts. 22 mins., 1991. BFF

Incineration

Warren County's Incinerator: the wrong model for N. J. 40 min., 1991. RCO
Europeans Mobilizing Against Trash Incineration; 1990; VAP.
The Rush to Burn; 1989; 35 min.; examines incineration; VP.
Restoring the Environment; 26 min.; incineration of hazardous wastes; FHS.

Hazardous Waste

Drugs and Poisons; 1994; 23 min.; drugs the human body, toxics and the biosphere; FHS.
Witness to the Future: The Legacy of "Silent Spring" & A Call for Environmental Action; 1996; 50 min.;
    citizens to activists in Hanford, WA, San Joaquin Valley, Cancer Alley, LA; VP.
Times Beach, Missouri; 1994; 57 min.; residents of a small town learn their community has been
    extensively contaminated with dioxin; VP.
Can Buildings Make You Sick? 60 mins., 1995. FL
Fate of Earth (Blue Planet). 1986. A/CPB
Ships of Shame. 54 mins., 2001. FL
In Our Own Backyard: The First Love Canal; 1982; 59 min.; BFF.
Toxic Racism; 1994; 60 min.; grassroots movement to prevent toxic waste dumping and industrial pollution
    of poor and minority neighborhoods.
Sowing the Seeds of Disaster; 26 min.; biotechnology to produce pollutant-eating organisms and frost-
    resistant plant strains as well as a consideration of dangers of introduction of nonnatural substances into
    our ecosystem; FHS.
The Toxic Goldrush; 26 min.; growth of the waste clean-up industry; FHS.
PCBs in the Food Chain; 18 min.; how marine pollution moves through the food chain from plankton
    through dolphins; FHS.
Poisonous Currents of Air and Sea; 18 min.; focus on PCBs moving globally; FHS.

See Appendix B for suppliers.

ATTITUDES/VALUES

<u>Assessment</u>

1. Have you visited a landfill? How did you feel during your visit?

2. Have you visited an incinerator? How did you feel during your visit?

3. Have you visited a recycling center? How did you feel during your visit?

4. Do you feel that natural ecosystems will be able to continue to absorb the wastes from human activities?

5. Do you feel that new technologies will be able to eliminate our current solid waste problems?

6. Do you feel that solid waste issues are one of the top three environmental concerns?

7. Are you willing to separate your trash, carry reusable shopping bags, and purchase products with reduced packaging?

8. Are you willing to make purchases based on lifetime cost of items rather than just the initial cost?

9. Would you favor a nationwide law requiring a 25¢ refundable deposit on all bottles and cans to encourage their recycling or reuse?

10. Would you support a law requiring everyone to separate their trash into paper, bottles, aluminum cans, steel cans, and glass for recycling and to separate all food and yard wastes for composting?

11. Would you support a law that bans all throwaway bottles, cans, and plastic containers and requires that all beverage and food containers be reusable (refillable)?

12. Would you support a law requiring that at least 60% of all municipal solid waste be recycled, reused, or composted?

13. Would you support a law banning the construction of any incinerators or landfills for disposal of hazardous or solid waste until at least 60% of all municipal solid waste is recycled, reused, or composted and the production of industrial hazardous waste has been reduced by 60%?

14. Have you ever visited a landfill or incinerator that handles hazardous waste? How did you feel?

15. Should industries and other producers of hazardous waste be allowed to inject such waste into deep underground wells?

16. Would you support a law banning the emission of any hazardous chemicals into the environment, with the understanding that many products you use now would cost more and some would no longer be made?

17. Would you support a law banning the export of any hazardous wastes and pesticides, medicines, or other chemicals banned in your country to any other country? Would you also support a law banning export of such wastes from one part of a country to another so that each community is responsible for the waste it produces?

More Depth: Discussion and Term Paper Topics

1. Trace the roots of the throwaway mentality.

2. Should disposable goods and built-in obsolescence be discouraged by legislation and economic means (such as taxes)?

3. Should urban incinerators be encouraged as an alternative to sanitary landfills?

4. Should we redefine hazardous wastes?

(Also, see text, Critical Thinking, p. 375)

PARTICIPATION

More Depth: Action-oriented Term Paper Topics

1. Recycle, reuse, reduce, rethink. Garage sales; source separation of household wastes; appliances built to last; what consumers can do about excessive packaging; recycling centers; resource recovery plants: the Saugus model.

2. City/County. Municipal resource recovery plants; recycling industrial wastes; scrap yards; anti-litter campaigns; incinerators; sanitary landfills.

3. State. Bottle bills.

4. National. The 1976 Resource Conservation and Recovery Act; EPA's Superfund program.

5. International. Recycling programs in Sweden and Switzerland; Germany's tough packaging law.

SKILLS

Environmental Problem-Solving Skills: Projects

1. If possible, take a class field trip to an open dump, a sanitary landfill, a secured landfill, and an incinerator. Observe problems associated with each approach to waste management.

2. Encourage your students to find out how your school and community dispose of wastes. Are recycling centers available? Are they conveniently located? What materials do they accept? Do any local factories or other industries accept wastes for recycling? How much is recycled? Would a source separation program be feasible?

3. Have students who live at home maintain a record of solid wastes discarded by their families in the course of one week. What percentage of this material could actually be recycled?

4. As a class, survey excess packaging in various products at local supermarkets. (Ask permission first; many supermarket managers are cooperative, but some are not.) Make up ecological ratings for each category based on the concept that packages inside of packages are very undesirable. Write manufacturers about the results of your findings. See if store managers would make your results available to customers at an environmental education stand or bulletin board.

5. Is classic lead poisoning a serious health problem in your community? Have your students consult with public health officials and find out what has been done to make people aware of potential hazards and to reduce the likelihood of dangerous exposure. Are there houses and other buildings in your community with flaking lead-based paint?

<u>Laboratory Skills</u>

Laboratory Manual for Miller's Living in the Environment and Environmental Science. Lab 20: Solid
    Waste Prevention and Management.

<u>Computer Skills</u>

(none)

CHAPTER 16
FOOD RESOURCES

THINKING

Concept Map

See Appendix A, Maps 22 and 23.

Goals

See bulleted list of questions on p. 378 of text.

Objectives

1. Using Figure 16-2 on p. 379, list four types of agriculture. Compare the inputs of land, labor, capital, and fossil-fuel energy of these systems. Evaluate the green revolution. What were its successes? Its failures? Describe four interplanting strategies. Summarize major consequences of eating meat.

2. Describe the trends in world food production since 1950. Summarize food distribution problems. Define *malnutrition* and *undernutrition*. Indicate how many people on Earth suffer from these problems. List six steps proposed by UNICEF, which would help address these problems.

3. From what nutritional malady do people in developed countries suffer? Describe the health implications and what steps can be taken to alleviate the problem.

4. List twelve environmental effects of agriculture.

5. Describe the possibilities of increasing world food production by increasing crop yields, cultivating more land, using unconventional foods and perennial crops, and growing more food in urban areas. Briefly describe the role of location, soil, insects, water, and loss of genetic diversity as limiting factors of food production.

6. Describe trends in the world fish catch since 1950. Assess the potential for increasing the annual fish catch. Evaluate the potential of fish farming and fish ranching for increasing fish production.

7. Assess the pros and cons of agricultural subsidies and international food relief. Describe strategies that you feel would be most sustainable.

8. Define pesticide and list five types of pesticides. Distinguish between broad-spectrum and narrow-spectrum agents.

9. Make a case for using pesticides. List three encouraging developments in pesticide production. List five characteristics of the ideal pesticide.

10. Describe the consequences of relying heavily on pesticides. Summarize threats to wildlife and the human population.

11. List and briefly describe seven alternative pest management strategies.

12. Define *integrated pest management*. Analyze the pros and cons of using IPM.

13. Name three steps individuals can take to control pests in an environmentally sound way.

14. Describe a sustainable agricultural system. List twelve steps that could be taken to move toward more sustainable agriculture.

15. List three things individuals can do to move society toward more sustainable agriculture.

<u>Key Terms</u> (Terms are listed in the same font style as they appear in the text.)

croplands (p. 378)
rangelands (p. 378)
oceanic fisheries (p. 378)
net primary productivity (p. 378)
wheat (p. 378)
rice (p. 378)
corn (p. 378)
annuals (p. 378)
monoculture (p. 378)
polyculture (p. 378)
industrialized agriculture (p. 378)
high-input agriculture (p. 378)
plantation agriculture (p. 379)
traditional agriculture (p. 379)
traditional subsistence agriculture (p. 379)
traditional intensive agriculture (p. 379)
green revolution (p. 380)
multiple cropping (p. 380)
first green revolution (p. 380)
second green revolution (p. 380)
agribusiness (p. 380)
interplanting (p. 382)
polyvarietal cultivation (p. 382)
intercropping (p. 382)
agroforestry (p. 382)
alley cropping (p. 382)
polyculture (p. 382)
macronutrients (p. 382)
micronutrients (p. 383)
undernutrition (p. 383)
malnutrition (p. 384)
overnutrition (p. 386)
gene revolutions (p. 387)
genetic engineering (p. 388)
gene splicing (p. 388)
**genetically modified
        organisms (GMOs)** (p. 388)
advanced tissue culture techniques (p. 388)
genetically modified food (GMF) (p. 388)
microlivestock (p. 390)
rangeland (p. 391)
grazing (p. 391)
browsing (p. 391)
pastures (p. 391)

metabolic reserve (p. 391)
feedlots (p. 391)
overgrazing (p. 392)
undergrazing (p. 392)
range condition (p. 392)
rangeland management (p. 393)
fisheries (p. 393)
riparian zones (p. 393)
sustainable yield (p. 395)
overfishing (p. 395)
commercial extinction (p. 395)
bycatch (p. 395)
aquaculture (p. 396)
fish farming (p. 396)
fish ranching (p. 396)
pest (p. 399)
natural enemies (p. 399)
opportunistic species (p. 399)
pesticides (p. 399)
biocides (p. 399)
insecticides (p. 399)
herbicide (p. 399)
fungicide (p. 399)
nematocide (p. 399)
rodenticide (p. 399)
broad-spectrum agents (p. 400)
selective (narrow-spectrum) agents (p. 400)
Rachel Carson (p. 400)
genetic resistance (p. 401)
tolerance level (p. 402)
cultivation practices (p. 404)
genetic engineering (p. 404)
biological pest control (p. 404)
insect birth control (p. 404)
sex attractants (p. 404)
pheromones (p. 404)
hormones (p. 405)
food irradiation (p. 405)
integrated pest management (IPM) (p. 405)
sustainable agriculture (p. 405)
low-input agriculture (p. 406)

Outline

Polyculture helps to use the environmental aspects of a particular growing environment to mimic the environment's natural growing conditions.
   A. Three systems have historically supplied our food: the croplands, the rangelands, and the oceanic fisheries systems.
   B. The various types of agriculture—plantation, traditional subsistence, and traditional intensive—have all been influenced by the green revolution.
   C. Even though food production has increased worldwide, people still do not have sufficient food nor sufficient nutrients.
   D. Efforts to increase crop production, increase meat availability, and grow fisheries must all work to stabilize and maintain the world's environment.
   E. Governmental assistance to farmers, widespread use of chemical pesticides, and agricultural processes that undermine the world's eco-systems must all be assessed to describe sustainable agricultural policies.

16-1 How is food produced?
   A. Future food production may be limited by environmental degradation, pollution, scarce water, overgrazing, and overfishing, etc.
   B. Various types of agriculture supply food.
       1. Plantation agriculture
       2. Traditional subsistence agriculture
       3. Traditional intensive agriculture

16-2 Producing food by green revolution and traditional techniques
   A. The green revolution was characterized by monocultures of high-yield crops, use of fertilizers, pesticides, and water to increase yield.
   B. Second green revolution, since 1967, uses fast-growing dwarf varieties of rice and wheat.
   C. Food production in the U. S. has risen steadily because of industrialized farming; however, traditional agriculture is more efficient in energy costs.

16-3 Food production, nutrition, and environmental effects
   A. Food production has increased throughout the world but people continue to be malnourished.
       1. One in six people in developing countries suffer from being either undernourished or malnourished.
       2. Nutrition-related deaths of children could be prevented with $5-10.00/year for each child.
       3. The program in #2 above would immunize children, encourage breast-feeding, prevent dehydration, prevent blindness with vitamin A dosage, provide family planning services, and increase health education for women.
   B. Deficiencies in micronutrients (Vitamin A, Iron, Iodine) undermine people's health all over the world, even in developed countries.
   C. Agriculture produces harmful effects on the environment.
       1. Soil degradation: erosion, desertification, salinization, waterlogging
       2. Water deficits and droughts; global warming; loss of wild species

16-4 Increasing world crop production
   A. To continue to increase food production, the world will have to improve its crossbreeding; genetic engineering is one aspect of this.
   B. There are reservations and resistance to genetically modified foods.
   C. Increased yields in the green revolutions as well as in the gene revolutions have been affected by the following:
       1. There is the need for more fertilizer and water.
       2. Amounts of water and genetic crops = expensive for developing countries
       3. Grain yields' increases are slow.
       4. As soil and environment are degraded, crop yields decrease.

5. Loss of biodiversity limits raw materials.
6. Projected yields may be overestimated.
D. Other efforts to produce more food have included introducing little known/little used foods: the winged bean, insects (microlivestock) as food.
E. Irrigation of land might be expanded, as well as cultivating more; but all choices have disadvantages.

16-5 Producing more meat
A. Rangeland and pastureland supplies grazing and browsing areas for animals.
B. While rangeland grazing is most often used to produce meat animals, feedlots are also used. Feedlots are harmful for the environment.
1. Air and water pollution
2. Nitrates from wastes
3. Increased pressure on grain supply
4. Endangers wildlife species
C. Many conflicting values exist in producing meat and in making it available equitably.
1. Health of rangeland: overgrazing, undergrazing
2. Management of rangelands

16-6 Catching and raising more fish and shellfish
A. Fisheries are the world's third major food-producing system.
1. Commercial fishing (producing 55% of the commercial catch) is dominated by ocean harvesting methods.
2. Aquaculture accounts for about 33% of the catch while inland freshwater fishing covers 12%.
B. The amount of commercial fish being caught is not increasing measurably.
1. Overfishing effects
2. Habitat degradation results
3. Effects of government subsidizing fishing
C. Fish farming and fish ranching comprise the industry of *aquaculture*.
1. Advantages and disadvantages
2. Fisheries sustainability

16-7 Government agricultural policy
A. Governmental assistance to farmers is controversial.
1. Food prices kept low.
2. Give farmers subsidies.
3. Let market drive prices.
B. Effects of these actions on the poor must be eliminated/controlled.

16-8 Protecting food resources: using conventional chemical pesticides to control pests
A. Pesticides are used to control competing species.
B. Pesticides save human lives, increase food supplies, lower food costs, and increase farmers' profits. The chemical pesticides work effectively and more cheaply. They are generally safe.
C. Their use also accelerates genetic resistance to pesticides, kill natural predators/parasites that provide population control, do not stay in one location, and harm wildlife.
D. Pesticide use, regulations, and success in the U. S.

16-9 Protecting food resources: alternatives to conventional chemical pesticides
A. Alternative pest control methods include cultivation practices, genetic engineering, biological pest control, insect birth control, sex attractants, hormones that disrupt normal life cycles, food irradiation.
B. Controls are developed that address different pests' place in an ecological system: integrated pest management.

16-10 Solutions: More sustainable agriculture
A. To reduce hunger-malnutrition as well as reduce the harmful environmental effects of agriculture, we must slow population growth, reduce poverty, and develop low-input agricultural systems.
B. Low-input agriculture/organic farming requires several factors.
1. Soil not fertilized with sewage sludge/fertilizers.
2. Use no chemical insecticides.
3. Do not plant genetically engineered crops nor raise such livestock.
4. Animals are raised to exercise, move, and with no growth hormones/antibiotics.
5. Irradiation cannot be used on the food.
C. More sustainable agriculture can be found through
1. Increased research
2. Sustainable agricultural demonstration projects,
3. Increase low-input agriculture aid to developing countries, and establish training programs in this type of agriculture.

Summary

1. The world's food is produced through industrialized or high input agriculture such as plantation agriculture and traditional subsistence and intensive agriculture.

2. Green revolution has resulted in the increase of global food production through developing and planting monocultures, producing high yields through the use of fertilizers, pesticides, and water, and increasing number of crops through multiple cropping.

3. Traditional agriculture raises crops through interplanting, polyvarietal cultivation, intercropping, agroforestry or alley cropping, and polyculture.

4. World grain production has tripled and the capita food production has increased in most places. Despite this, malnutrition is a very serious problem in many places on the globe.

5. Environmental effects of food production include soil erosion, desertification, salinization, water-logging, water deficits and droughts, loss of wildlife, and global warming.

6. Increasing crop yields has been achieved through genetic engineering, motivating people to try new foods, irrigating and cultivating more land, and growing more food in urban areas. To increase production of meat, we need to use sustainable rangeland management. Aquaculture appears to be the method to increase fish and shellfish availability.

7. Government policies represent three approaches and include keeping food prices artificially low, giving farmers subsidies to increase food production, or eliminating controls and subsidies and allowing the farmers to respond to market demands.

8. Pesticides are chemicals used to kill organisms we consider undesirable. The advantages of using pesticides include the fact that they save lives, increase food supplies, lower food cost, increase profit for farmers, and work fast. The disadvantages include the acceleration of pest resistance to pesticides and pesticides dispersing widely, harming wildlife, and threatening human lives.

9. Alternatives to pesticides include genetic engineering of pest resistant crop strains, insect birth control, use of pheromones, spraying hot water, and food irradiation.

10. To shift to more sustainable agricultural systems we must increase research, set up demonstration models for farmers to see, increase agricultural aid to developing countries, and establish training problems in sustainable agriculture for farmers and government officials.

Multiple Choice Questions

See Instructor's Manual, Section II, p. 324.

More Depth: Conceptual Term Paper Topics

1. Agricultural systems. Inorganic fertilizers; history of development of one crop or livestock species; green revolution; crops with designer genes; politics of American agriculture; feedlot beef cattle production in the Corn Belt; range livestock production in the American West; urban growth and the loss of prime cropland; modern food storage and transportation; comparisons of environmental impacts of traditional and industrial agricultural practices.

2. Hunger and food distribution. History of great famines; malnutrition and learning; the geography of malnutrition.

3. Fishing. Overfishing; aquaculture; the Peruvian anchovy story.

4. Pesticides. Pesticides as hazardous waste; pesticide hazards to agricultural workers; chlorinated hydrocarbons; organophosphates and carbonates; pyrethroids and rotenoids; biological amplification of persistent pesticides; DDT and malaria control; Agent Orange; the Bhopal accident; pesticide residues in foods; pesticide runoff as a threat to agriculture.

5. Pesticide alternatives. Integrated pest management; food irradiation; genetic control by sterilization: the screwworm fly; pheromones.

More Breadth: Interdisciplinary Activities and Projects

1. Have your students locate and bring to class photographs, paintings, or history passages describing the effects of hunger and starvation.

2. Ask students to find and bring to class photographs, songs, paintings, and literature reflecting human feelings for fishermen, whalers, and farmers.

3. Invite an agricultural economist to your class to discuss shifts in the United States from farming to agribusiness and the historical role of subsidies in agriculture.

4. Invite a representative from the United States Department of Agriculture (or some other informed source) to your class to discuss how U.S. political decisions such as emergency foreign aid and global trade affect U.S. farmers.

5. Invite a county agricultural agent to your class to discuss local agricultural problems and opportunities. What major changes in agricultural practices are likely to occur in the coming decades? With what consequences? What types of farming activities are carried on in your locale? What is the balance between large and small farms? What are the major products? How much of the produce is used in local areas? How much is shipped out and where does it go?

6. Invite an organic farmer or experienced organic gardener to address your class on the subject of alternatives to energy-intensive agriculture. If possible, arrange a field trip to investigate organic farming practices.

7. Invite a county agricultural agent to address your class on the subject of pesticide use and abuse in your locale. Try to determine what factors, including government programs, combine to keep farmers on the pesticide treadmill.

Multisensory Learning: Audiovisuals

Quantity of Food

Genetic Time Bomb; 1994; 50 min.; looks at the importance of maintaining biodiversity for new
    agricultural developments; profiles the growing worldwide network of "seed savers."; VP.
Save the Earth—Feed the World from *Race to Save the Planet;* 1990; 60 min.; intensive and traditional
    farming techniques; ACPB.
Circle of Plenty. 28 min., 1987. BFF
Close to Nature. 24 mins.   BFF
Dig IT!: biointensive sustainable mini-farming. 90 min., EA
Food: devising a sustainable food system. 49 mins., 2000. BFF
Fragile Harvest. 49 mins., 1987. BFF

Quality of Food/Natural Foods

Diet for a New America; 1991; 60 min.; food choices, personal health, and the planet's health; VP.
Diet for a Small Planet. 28 min., 1974. BFF
Growing Pains: world hunger & social justice. 26 mins., 1988. BFF

Agricultural Practices

Fueling the Future: Hot Wiring America's Farms; 1988; 58 min.; examines impacts of energy-intensive
    farming and explores efficient alternatives; VP.
Sowing for Need or Sowing for Greed?; 56 min.; impacts of modern agricultural methods exported to
    developing countries; BFF.
Circle of Plenty. 28 mins., 1987. BFF
Farmers of Gaho. 21 mins., 1998. BFF
Field of Genes. 44 min., 1998. BFF
Fistful of Rice. 27 mins., 2002. BFF
Food (sustainable food system). 49 min., 2000. BFF
Food for Tought. 28 mins., 1990. BFF
Hungry for Profit. 85 mins., RV
On American soil. 28 min., 1985. BFF
Slow Food: sustainable agriculture and responsible eating. 30 min., 1997.

Fish

Empty Oceans, Empty Nets. 55 min., 2003. BFF
Fish Farming in Amazonia. 13 min., 1989. BFF
The Perils of Plectropomus. 56 min., 2000. BFF
Where Have All the Dolphins Gone?; 1989; 48 min.; failure of U.S. government laws to protect marine
    mammals; VP.

Pesticides

Natural Enemies; 1994; 14 min.; controlling pests with natural enemies; FHS.
For Export Only: pesticides. 57 mins., RV
Hormone Imposters. 47 mins., 1997. BFF
Playing with Poisons. 46 mins., 2002. BFF
Times Beach, Missouri. 57 mins., VP
Toxic Secrets: 'invert' ingredients in pesticides. 1998 [PDF file—free] NCAP
Toxin that Won't Die. 28 mins., 2001. FL
Wheel of Hormones. 49 min, FL
Putting Aside Pesticides; 26 min.; long-term effects of pesticides and a look at alternatives; FHS.

See Appendix B for suppliers.

ATTITUDES/VALUES

<u>Assessment</u>

1. Have you ever fasted? If so, how did it feel?

2. Do you feel everyone has a right to a healthy diet?

3. Do you favor greatly increased foreign aid to poor countries to help them reduce poverty, to improve environmental quality, and to develop sustainable use of their own resources?

4. Do you favor a more equitable distribution of the world's resources and wealth to greatly reduce the current wide gap between the rich and the poor, even if this means less for you?

5. Have you ever eaten food grown with fertilizers and pesticides? How did it taste?

6. Have you ever eaten organically grown food? How did it taste?

7. Are you aware of places to obtain organically grown food in your area?

8. Do you prefer perfect looking fruits and vegetables grown with pesticides to slightly blemished fruits and vegetables grown without pesticides?

9. Do you favor regulation of pesticides exported from the United States?

<u>More Depth: Discussion and Term Paper Topics</u>

1. What is the best way to manage food distribution for foreign aid?

2. Is using lifeboat ethics the best way to decide who gets to eat?

3. Aldo Leopold's land ethic.

4. Evaluate pesticide advertising. What does it tell? What doesn't it tell?

5. Which do you prefer: unblemished fruits and vegetables that may contain pesticide residues or blemished fruits and vegetables without pesticide residues?

6. Rachel Carson's *Silent Spring*.

7. Which is better: a broad-spectrum or a narrow-spectrum pesticide?

(Also, see text, Critical Thinking, p. 409)

PARTICIPATION

<u>More Depth: Action-oriented Term Paper Topics</u>

1. Individuals: sustainable agriculture. Organic home gardening; neglected edible plants; composting; crop rotation; organic fertilizers; windbreaks.

2. Cities. Land-use planning and zoning.

3. Global. UN food conferences; 1982 UN Conference on the Law of the Sea; agricultural training and research centers in the developing countries.

4. Individual. Safe disposal of household pesticides; homeowner strategies and tactics to reduce pesticide use.

5. National regulation. Federal Insecticide, Fungicide, and Rodenticide Act.

6. Global. International sales of U.S.-produced pesticides whose use is banned in the United States; General Agreement on Tariffs and Trade (GATT) and its implications for U.S. regulations regarding pesticide levels in American foods.

SKILLS

Environmental Problem-Solving Skills: Projects

1. As a class, plan a daily menu for a family of four receiving minimum welfare payments (consult local welfare agencies for current payment levels and use current food prices). Ask your students how they would like subsisting solely on this diet.

2. As a class exercise, determine what percentage of your diet–as individuals and as a group–consists of meat. What are some ecological implications of this amount of meat in the diet? What are the health implications? What are the alternatives?

3. Arrange a class debate on the proposition that food-exporting nations should use population control and resource development as criteria to determine which of the food-importing nations will receive top priority. Conduct a mock triage and follow it with mock appeals hearings for denied nations.

4. With the help of a chemist or other appropriate consultant, have your students evaluate the ingredients, uses, and warning labels of a representative sample of pesticides sold for home and garden applications. Are the instructions for use, storage, and disposal adequate? How much additional information should be supplied to further reduce the likelihood of harm to people and wildlife?

5. Are people generally aware of and concerned about the hazards of using pesticides on a large-scale, long-term basis? As a class project, conduct a survey of students or consumers to address these and related questions. What do the results imply for the role that education should play in dealing with pesticide-related problems?

6. Have your students interview the college landscaping staff about which pesticides, if any, they use on campus. What tradeoffs did they consider when deciding to use those pesticides?

Laboratory Skills

(none)

Computer Skills

Computerized System for Agricultural and Population Planning Assistance and Training (CAPPA)
-Facilitates use of a multisectoral scenario approach to agricultural planning.
-Chief, Development Policy Training and Research Service, Policy Analysis Division, Food and Agriculture Organization of the United Nations, Via delle Terme di Caracalla, 00100, Rome, Italy

Standard National (Agricultural) Model (SNM)
-Analyzes the consequences of domestic or international policy changes for a nation's domestic food situation.
-Director, Food and Agriculture Program, International Institute for Applied Systems Analysis, Schloss Laxenburg, A-2361, Laxenburg, Austria

CHAPTER 17
SUSTAINING BIODIVERSITY: THE ECOSYSTEM APPROACH

THINKING

Concept Map

See Appendix A, Maps 24 and 25.

Goals

See bulleted list of questions on p. 412 of text.

Objectives

1. Define conservation biology and ecological integrity. List four ethical principles that guide conservation biology.

2. List five types of public lands in the United States. Explain the mission and principles of management of each.

3. Distinguish between old-growth and second-growth forests. Briefly describe the commercial and ecological significance of forests.

4. Distinguish between the goals of even-aged management and uneven-aged management. List five types of tree harvesting, indicating which type of management they are most likely to be used for.

5. Summarize the best current strategies for protecting forests from pathogens and insects, fires, air pollution, and climate change. Distinguish between industrial forestry and sustainable forestry.

6. Summarize the current state of old-growth forests in the United States and Canada. List ten steps that would help reform federal forest management.

7. Describe the current state of tropical forests. Describe the significance of tropical forests in terms of both ecosystems and indigenous cultures. List three underlying causes and seven direct causes of tropical forest destruction. List five ways to preserve the tropical rain forests.

8. Describe the fuelwood crisis and how it could be approached.

9. Briefly describe U.S. rangelands, national parks, and wilderness areas. Give one problem of each area and explain how that problem might be managed better.

10. Explain the principles that guide the establishment of nature reserves. Describe the best way to implement a nature preserve.

11. Discuss the issues involved in protecting the marine environment.

12. Describe ecological restoration and discuss way it might be done.

Key Terms (Terms are listed in the same font style as they appear in the text.)

public lands (p. 414)   *National Resource Lands* (p. 414)
multiple-use lands (p. 414)   Bureau of Land Management (BLM) (p. 414)
National Forest System (p. 414)   *moderately restricted-use lands* (p. 414)

<u>Outline</u>

Biodiversity must be protected for mankind to survive.
    A.   Man's impact on the earth has been devastating, leading to biological degradation on a massive scale.
    B.   Public lands throughout the world are logical places to begin managing resources—forests, parks, nature reserves, etc. and attempting to rehabilitate and restore ecosystems.
    C.   Terrestrial and aquatic systems need pro-active, sustainable management in order to reclaim the health of the planet.

17-1 Human impacts on biodiversity
    A.   Human activities have affected biodiversity all over the planet.
        1.   Degradation of land
        2.   Destruction of forests and wetlands
        3.   Eradication of numerous fish and terrestrial species
    B.   We must reduce the loss of biodiversity.

17-2 Land use in the world and in the United States.
    A.   The federal government manages about 35% of American land.
        1.   Multiple-use lands: National Forest System and National Resource Lands
        2.   Moderately restricted-use lands: National Wildlife Refuges
        3.   Restricted-use lands: National Park System
    B.   There is much controversy over the use of U. S. public lands.

17-3 Managing and sustaining forests
    A.   There are three types of forests: old-growth, second-growth forests, and tree plantations.

B. Forests are managed to grow wood that is used for different purposes.
1. Even-aged management
2. Uneven-aged management
C. Trees are harvested with different methods: selective cutting, shelterwood cutting, seed-tree cutting, and clear-cutting.
D. The world's forests are being compromised by over-cutting, deforestation, and degradation.
E. The earth's ecological services have never been appreciated; they cannot continue effectively under current conditions.
F. Forest sustainability is now a critical need.
1. Scientific Certification Systems attempt to guard the health of forests.
2. Preserving biodiversity and banning imported timber will reduce the impact of disease and insects on forests.
3. Forest fires and logging must be controlled/eliminated to help sustain the forests.

17-4 Forest resources and management in the United States
A. Forests are critical to the land's ecosystems.
1. Forests cover up to 33% of U. S. land systems.
2. Forests house more than 80% of this country's wild animals.
B. U. S. forests in 2002
1. More forests than in 1920
2. Large areas have been protected.
C. Our national forests provide economic, ecological, and recreational benefits for everyone.
D. Managing the U.S.'s national forests is an effort to maintain the principle of 'sustained yield' while using the forests for a variety of things: timber, grazing, watershed protection, wildlife habitat, etc.
E. Tree-free paper is being produced from the kenaf plant.

17-5 Tropical Deforestation
A. Tropical forests worldwide are being decimated hourly.
B. Tropical forests provide critical ecological services, as well as important economic ones.
C. The beautifully versatile Neem tree reforests land, grows well in poor soil and dry areas, and contains natural pesticides which kill some insect species, while its leaves' and seeds' extracts fight bacterial, viral, and fungal infections. The oil acts as a spermicide.
D. Interconnections among population growth, poverty, and government hasten and encourage forest deforestation.
E. Forests are logged, overgrazed by ranchers, burned by settlers, and eroded away from lack of concern or greed.
F. Various methods can be used to reduce deforestation and degradation of tropical forests.
1. Small-scale sustainable agriculture and forestry
2. Strip-cutting
3. Debt-for-nature swap
4. Conservation easement
5. Conservation concession
6. Identify timber produced by sustainable methods

17-6 Managing and sustaining National Parks
A. Threats against parks come from local people, loggers, miners, poachers, and politicians.
B. Park services need money to maintain themselves, provide services, and protect plants and wildlife.
C. Parks need restricted areas or recovery periods when people may not be in the parks.
D. Parks need protection from people, their ignorance, their waste and garbage, and their numbers.
E. Park management may be improved by improving biodiversity, by undertaking research to use parks as living laboratories, by implementing science-based management practices, and by educating the public.

17-7 Establishing, designing, and managing nature reserves
  A. Increase and preserve biodiversity through a worldwide network of protected areas.
  B. Costa Rica's vision can be modeled by other countries to guard their own natural ecosystems.
  C. The following principles should be used to establish and manage nature reserves.
      1. Ecosystems are in an ever-changing non-equilibrium state.
      2. The greatest diversity of species occurs when ecosystems have fairly frequent and moderate disturbances.
      3. Reserves are habitat islands in a sea of developed-fragmented land.
  D. The Man and the Biosphere Programme advocates establishing one biosphere reserve in each of the earth's biogeographical zones.
      1. Its three zones must contain a core area, a second buffer zone, and a third transition zone.
      2. Wilderness areas should also be established: areas that are left to evolve and change, untouched by man.
          a. To experience nature's beauty and see natural biodiversity
          b. To enhance mental and physical health
      3. The U. S. has very little wilderness area designated or protected.

17-8 Protecting and sustaining aquatic systems
  A. We know little about the planet's aquatic systems.
  B. The three general patterns of marine biodiversity are below.
      1. Greatest marine diversity found: coral reefs, deep-sea floor
      2. Coastal areas support the greatest biodiversity.
      3. Biodiversity—greater in bottom of the ocean
  C. Protection and sustainability of marine systems require that we:
      1. Establish protected areas.
      2. Use integrated coastal managerial practices.
      3. Prevent and regulate ocean pollution.
      4. Protect species which are endangered and threatened.
  D. International agreements and protection of marine sanctuaries
      1. United Nations Law of the Sea
      2. United Nations Environment Program: 350 biosphere reserves
      3. New Zealand, Australia, Belize, the Galapagos Island, the Caribbean, and the U. S. "no take" marine reserves
      4. National Center for Ecological Analysis and Synthesis report—marine reserves are good for fish growth and biodiversity.
      5. World Conservation Union—establish marine protected areas all around the world.
  E. Implement integrated coastal management.
  F. Wetlands are in danger of disappearing completely.

17-9 Ecological restoration
  A. We can speed up repairs to ecological systems by restoring a habitat or ecosystem to its predegraded state; by rehabilitating some of the ecosystem's species and functions; by replacing a degraded system with another type of ecosystem; and by creating artificial ecosystems.
  B. To restore or rehabilitate habitats and/or ecosystems, follow four basic steps.
      1. Identify the cause of the degradation.
      2. Eliminate/reduce the causative factors.
      3. Protect the area from additional degradation and from fires.
      4. Monitor restoration efforts, evaluate successes, and modify rehabilitative strategies as restoration moves forward.
  C. Restoration of a Costa Rican tropical dry forest
  D. Individuals must press governments to be ecologically sensitive, to commit money to restoration/rehabilitation projects, and ultimately to prevent ecosystem damage, rather than fixing it.

Summary

1. Effects of human activities on earth's biodiversity include degradation and destruction of natural ecosystems, alteration of natural chemical cycles and energy flows, changes in numbers and distribution of species, and pollution of air, water, and soil.

2. Only 27% of the earth's surface is undisturbed by human activity, excluding areas of rock, ice, desert, and steep mountain. In the United States, public lands are classified as multiple-use lands, moderately restricted-use lands, and restricted-use lands.

3. Forest resources are important because they support energy flow and chemical cycling; reduce soil erosion; absorb, release, and purify water; purify air; influence climate; store carbon; and provide wildlife habitats.

4. There are two forest management systems: the even-aged management or industrial forestry, and the uneven-aged management.

5. Tropical deforestation is a very serious problem. We can help sustain tropical forests through prevention and restoration. Prevention can be achieved through protection of endangered areas, education of settlers on sustainable agriculture and forestry, removal of subsidies that encourage unsustainable forest use, certification of sustainably grown timber, reduction of illegal cutting, reduction of poverty, and slowing of population growth. Restoration can be achieved through reforestation rehabilitation of degraded areas and concentration of farming and ranching in past cleared areas.

6. National parks face threats from people looking for wood, cropland, game animals, loggers, miners, and poachers. Popularity and invasion by exotic species are also a threat. We can manage them through addition of new parkland near threatened parks, buying of private lands in the parks, locating visitor parking outside the parks, increasing funds for maintenance and repairs, surveying the wildlife, and encouraging volunteerism.

7. Conservation biologists recommend the strict protection of at least 20% of the earth's land surface by establishing reserves. Two social principles should be used: inclusion of the local people in the establishment, management, and protection of the reserves and creation of user-friendly reserves.

8. We can protect and sustain aquatic systems through establishing protected areas, using integrated coastal management, regulating and preventing pollution, and protecting species.

9. Ecological restoration is returning a degraded habitat or ecosystem to a state close to its original condition. The steps to this end include identification of the causes of the degradation, elimination of these causes, protection of the area from further damage, and monitoring of the restoration efforts.

Multiple Choice Questions

See Instructor's Manual, Section II, p. 339.

More Depth: Conceptual Term Paper Topics

1. Tropical rain forests. U.S. imports and tropical deforestation.

2. Multiple-use and moderate-use public lands in the United States. Bureau of Land Management policies and programs in the arid West; the U.S. Forest Service; Gifford Pinchot and the forest conservation movement; sustainable forestry's answer to clear-cutting; the role of fire in forestry management; the Sagebrush Rebellion.

3. U.S. restricted-use lands. The National Parks System; the National Wilderness System.

4. Wilderness preservation in developing countries.

More Breadth: Interdisciplinary Activities and Projects

1. Invite a National Park Service or state official to your class to discuss park problems and future management plans.

2. As a class field trip, visit a forest managed for pulp and paper production or industrial timbering. What specific methods are used to maximize economic returns and to curb ecosystem damage? Contrast the appearance of commercial forestland and relatively undisturbed forestland. Which do you like best? Why?

Multisensory Learning: Audiovisuals

Ecosystems

Forests; 1994; 23 min.; intricate ecological connections, photosynthesis, global weather, and threats; FHS.
Preserving Forests; 1994; 23 min.; using forest management and science to preserve forests; FHS.
The Florida Everglades; 1994; 23 min.; ecological connections and drainage systems; FHS.
The Resources of the Forest; 1994; 23 min.; wood products, maple syrup, paper; FHS.
Logging Siberia; 1992; 28 min.; logging in the Siberian taiga forest around Lake Baikal; VP.
Battle for the Trees; 1993; 57 min.; documents clearcutting of the largest remaining temperate rainforest in North America; VP.
Rain Forests: Proving Their Worth; 1990; 30 min.; new movement to market sustainably-collected forest products; VP.
Biodiversity: the diversity of life. 42 min., 1992. BFF
Empty Oceans, empty nests. 60 min, PBS
Forests, Biodiversity, and You. 10 min., 2000. BFF
Gaia, the living planet. 45 min,, 1989. BFF
Lake of the Sky (Lake Tahoe), 15 min., 1993. USDA
Last Stand of the Tallgrass Prairie. 60 min., PBS
The Tropical Rain Forest; 28 min.; ecosystem focus on rich biodiversity adapted to heavy rainfall; FHS.
Preserving the Rain Forest; 24 min.; from indigenous cultures to forest depletion through shifting agriculture and technological efficiency; case study of controlled agriculture and industrial activity in a natural reserve in the Ivory Coast; FHS.

National Parks

To Protect Mother Earth (Broken Treaty II); 1989; 60 min.; the Shoshones struggle to save their ancestral lands from strip mining, nuclear tests, and oil drilling; CPr.
Antarctica; 1987; 26 min.; Antarctica: wilderness, garbage dump, ozone hole; FHS.
Antarctica on the Edge: impending ecologicaldoom. 1997. FHS
America's National Parks. 180 min, EV
Discovering Yosemite. 45 min., F-H
El Dorado. 56 min., 1998. USDA
Everglades & South Florida National Parks. 56 min, F-H
The Last Solitude. 38 min., 1992. USDA
Living Edens, The Yellowstone. 60 min., PBS
Our National Parks. 80 min., PBS

See Appendix B for suppliers.

ATTITUDES/VALUES

Assessment

1. What wildlife is most common in your area?

2. Where are the nearest locations in your area to go to observe wildlife?

3. What are your feelings toward wildlife species? What relationship between humans and wildlife do you find most desirable?

4. Do you feel that humans have the right to relate to other species in any way they wish? If not, what limits do you see on human behavior toward other species?

5. Do you use products that come from the tropical forest? Do the products you use result in destruction of forest or continued sustainable use of the forest?

6. How do you feel when you see pictures of the destruction of ancient forests?

7. Do you feel we can continue to find substitutes for losses we suffer when ancient forests are destroyed?

8. Do you feel nature can continue to replenish forests at any rate humans choose to harvest the forests?

9. How do you feel when you see pictures of unemployed loggers unable to support their families?

10. Do you feel it is right to destroy cultures that live sustainably in the tropical rain forests? If not, what steps do you support to protect these cultures?

11. What steps do you feel should be taken to support human cultures and wildlife species in ways that create sustainable societies?

12. Have you ever visited a mine? How did you feel about the mine? What benefits do you enjoy as a result of mining activity?

13. Have you ever visited rangeland? How did you feel about the land? What benefits do you enjoy as a result of cattle grazing?

14. Have you ever visited a national forest? How did you feel about the forest? What benefits do you enjoy as a result of lumbering activity?

15. Have you ever visited a wilderness area? How did you feel about the wilderness? What benefits do you enjoy as a result of protection of wilderness areas?

16. Would you support classifying a much larger proportion of the public lands (such as parks, forests, and rangeland) in your country as wilderness and making such land unavailable for timber cutting, livestock grazing, mining, hunting, fishing, motorized vehicles, or any type of human structure?

More Depth: Discussion and Term Paper Topics

1. Alaska's value: wilderness or oil supply?

2. Should fires be allowed to burn in forests on public lands?

3. Should products that result in destruction of tropical forests be banned in the United States?

4. Should mining be allowed in national wildlife refuges?

5. Should parts of the wilderness areas be set aside for wildlife only?

(Also, see text, Critical Thinking, p. 445)

PARTICIPATION

More Depth: Action-oriented Term Paper Topics

1. Individuals. Recycling wastepaper: obstacles and overcoming them.

2. Groups. The Nature Conservancy; the Wilderness Society; reducing the pressure of people on the national parks.

3. National laws. The Alaskan Land-Use Bill; the Endangered American Wilderness Act of 1978; the Wild and Scenic Rivers Act of 1968; the 1974 and 1976 Forest Reserves Management Acts.

4. Global. The UN World Heritage Trust; debt-for-nature swaps; solar cookers and the world firewood crisis.

SKILLS

Environmental Problem-Solving Skills: Projects

1. As a class project, compile a list of commodities for sale in your community whose production or harvesting contributes to the destructive exploitation of tropical forests. Are vendors and consumers aware of the consequences? Do they care about the consequences?

2. If there are rangelands in your locale, try to schedule a class visit to examples of well- and poorly managed grazing lands. Compare the quantity and quality of vegetation present.

3. If possible, visit a national park or wilderness area. Assess its current problems and analyze plans to address those problems.

Laboratory Skills

(none)

Computer Skills

The Rainforest; 1994; 60 min. of video clips, more than 400 photographs, maps, narration, animated sequences, and plant and animal guides; runs on PC and Mac with CD-ROM capability; RE Media, San Diego, 619-486-5030.

Range, Livestock, and Wildlife
   -Helps decision makers understand and evaluate policy alternatives for rangeland management.

   -Paul Faeth, World Resources Institute/International Institute for Environment and Development, 1709 New York Avenue, N.W., 7th Floor, Washington, D.C. 20006

BIOCUT
   -Assesses the economic viability of alternative designs and management strategies for wood energy plantations.
   -National Technical Information Service, U.S. Dept. of Commerce, 5285 Port Royal Rd., Springfield, VA 22161

CHAPTER 18
SUSTAINING BIODIVERSITY: THE SPECIES

THINKING

Concept Map

See Appendix A, Map 26.

Goals

See bulleted list of questions on p. 449 of text.

Objectives

1. Describe the economic, medical, aesthetic, ecological, and ethical significance of wild species. Define bioethics. Distinguish between *intrinsic value* and *instrumental value.*

2. Distinguish between *background (natural) rate of extinction and mass extinction.* Evaluate if an extinction crisis currently exists. Distinguish between endangered species and threatened species. Give three examples of each.

3. List nine characteristics that make species extinction prone.

4. Describe how species become extinct. List and describe eight ways that humans accelerate the extinction rate.

5. List and briefly describe three approaches to protect wild species from extinction. State one advantage particular to the ecosystem approach.

6. Summarize protection offered to wild species by CITES and the Endangered Species Act. List five steps, which would strengthen the Endangered Species Act. Describe one way to decide which species to save.

7. Describe how wildlife populations can be managed by manipulating successional stage of the habitat.

8. Describe how fish and game populations are managed in order to sustain the population. Analyze the lessons to be learned from the decline of the whaling industry.

9. List three ways individuals can help maintain wild species and preserve biodiversity.

Key Terms (Terms are listed in the same font style as they appear in the text.)

local extinction (p. 449)
ecological extinction (p. 449)
biological extinction (p. 449)
endangered species (p. 449)
threatened species (p. 449)
vulnerable species (p. 449)
adaptive radiations (P. 452)
extinction spasm (p. 452)
species-area relationship (p. 452)
theory of island biogeography (p. 452)

instrumental value (p. 454)
intrinsic value (p. 454)
ecotourism (p. 454)
ecological services (p. 454)
economical services (p. 454)
genetic information (p. 454)
endemic species (p. 455)
habitat islands (p. 455)
habitat fragmentation (p. 455)
nonnative species (p. 457)

Outline

Human beings are causing the extinction of 2–20 wild species per day.
- A. The three types of species extinction are local extinction, ecological extinction, and biological extinction.
- B. Human activities contribute greatly to species extinction rates.
  1. Extinction rates will increase with increased population.
  2. Areas rich in biodiversity have higher extinction rates.
  3. Potential species colonization sites for new species are being degraded, undermined, and destroyed daily.
- C. Wild species and ecosystems are useful to us and deserve to exist.
  1. Ecological services and economic services
  2. Genetic information
  3. Recreational pleasure
- D. Habitat loss and degradation threatens worldwide species.
  1. Loss and fragmentation
  2. Harm from nonnative species: deliberate and accidental
- E. Hunting and poaching threats are compromising many already endangered species.
  1. Exotic plants and animals
  2. Bushmeat; whales
- F. Additional threats increase the likelihood of plant and animal extinctions.
  1. Species competing with man
  2. Exotic species and decorative plants
  3. Climate change (precipitous/not) and pollution
- G. Protecting wild species has been approached in several ways.
  1. Bioinformatics
  2. International treaties (example: Endangered Species Act)
  3. Zoos and aquariums
- H. Wildlife management has two aims: to support wildlife habitats for the benefit of the wildlife and for the benefit of man.

18-1 Species extinction
- A. Local extinction describes a species that has disappeared from a particular area.
- B. When a species has been so depleted that it can no longer play its ecological role, it is called ecological extinction.
- C. When a species is found nowhere on earth, there is biological extinction.
- D. Endangered species are those that could become extinct because there are so few individual survivors.

E. Declining numbers that threaten the species extinction describe a threatened/vulnerable species.
F. Bats—because they reproduce slowly and live in places that can be blocked/isolated—are vulnerable to extinction.
   1. Bats, as keystone species, maintain plant biodiversity and help to regenerate large parts of tropical forest.
   2. In truth, bats are non-aggressive mammals that are man's allies.
G. 99% of all species are now extinct.
   1. Such massive extinction has been/is caused by background extinction, mass extinctions, and mass depletions.
      a. Adaptive radiations can rebuild biological diversity, but the rebuilding takes millions of years.
      b. We know little about which species have been lost and little about those still surviving.
   2. Several methods are used to estimate the rates of extinction.
      a. In a *species-area relationship*, the number of species present is compared with the size of the area.
      b. Observations are made to identify species diversity changes at different latitudes.
      c. Scientists use models to estimate probable extinction, models such as the theory of island biogeography previously discussed. Models are also used to estimate the minimum area of suitable habitat needed to support a population's survival for a specific time period.
   3. Human activities increase extinction rates between 1,000–10,000 times more than during the pre-human period.
   4. Extinction rates are likely to increase.
      a. Population rates and resource use are increasing.
      b. Biologically rich areas' extinction loss is greater than other areas.

18-2 Why should we care about species extinction?
A. Species extinction is important because 5 million years are required to rebuild the biodiversity that humans have destroyed during the 20th century.
   1. Biodiversity has instrumental value to humans.
      a. These values are ecological services, genetic information, and recreational pleasure.
      b. Eco-tourism generates thousands more dollars from living animals than one receives from dead ones.
B. Ecotourism should provide income to local people and should not cause ecological damage.

18-3 Extinction threats from habitat loss and degradation
A. One of the greatest threats to wild species is habitat loss, degradation, and fragmentation.
   1. Deforestation of tropical forests, coral reef and wetlands destruction, plowing of grasslands, and pollution of aquatic systems are major players in species elimination.
   2. Temperate biomes suffer more than tropical biomes from habitat disturbance, degradation, and fragmentation.
   3. Endemic species on islands are especially vulnerable.
   4. Habitat fragmentation has three consequences.
      a. Decreases the sustainable population size for many species
      b. Increases its edge area
      c. Limits the ability of some species to colonize new areas
   5. Habitat fragmentation is especially possible for species that are:
      a. Rare
      b. Need to roam over large area
      c. Have low reproductive capacity

18-4 Extinction threats from nonnative species
A. Nonnative species cause considerable plant and animal extinction.
   1. Cause damages and absorb much pest control funds

2. Threaten native endangered species
3. Cause most fish extinctions—68% in the U.S. in the last century
   B. Deliberately introduced nonnative species are difficult to control.
      1. Have no natural predators/competitors, parasites/pathogens
      2. Trigger ecological disruptions
   C. Different threats from different introduced species: kudzu, Argentina Fire ant, European wild boars, Asian tiger mosquito
   D. The best defense is the prevention of nonnative species establishing themselves in foreign habitats.
      1. Define vulnerable ecosystems and characteristics that allow species to invade.
      2. Inspect imported goods.
      3. Ban transfer of harmful invader species from one country to another.
      4. Replace ship ballast water with sale water at sea.

18-5 Extinction threats from hunting and poaching
   A. Commercial hunting and poaching are widespread, as is international trade in wild plants and animals.
      1. Live animals and animal parts
      2. Whales and whaling demands

18-6 Other extinction threats
   A. Animals which compete with humans for food: parakeet, elephants, prairie dogs
   B. Exotic pets and decorative plants comprise a huge, profitable business.
   C. Increasingly rapid climate change can threaten ecosystem life.
   D. Pollution and the use of pesticides threaten all plants, animals, and humans.

18-7 Protecting wild species from depletion and extinction: the research and legal approach
   A. Bioinformatics—the science of managing, analyzing, and communicating biological information—is needed to protect biodiversity.
   B. International treaties can help protect wildlife and plants.
      1. Convention on International Trade in Endangered Species
      2. Convention on Biological Diversity
      3. Lacey Act of 1900 (U.S.)
      4. Endangered Species Act of 1973 (of 1982, 1988)
         a. 33% of U.S. species are at risk of extinction.
         b. 15% of U.S. species are at high risk.
         c. 125 designated critical habitats—established
         d. Laws need more power and enforcement.
   C. Private landowners can be encouraged to protect endangered species.
      1. ESA advocates undermining actions for landowners.
         a. Safe harbor agreements (1999)
         b. Voluntary candidate conservation agreements (1999)
      2. Protective measures in habitat conservation plans are not always to the benefit of endangered species.
      3. There are both positive and negative evaluations of the success of the Endangered Species Act.
   D. Are we to protect all endangered and threatened species? How might our efforts be effective, no matter which ones we protect?

18-8 Protecting wild species from depletion and extinction: the sanctuary approach
   A. The success of the National Wildlife Refuge System, since 1903, has led to a call for more such refuges—these for protecting plants.
      1. Many refuges are being degraded by pollutants and invasive species.
      2. Invasions of nonnative species are doing immense damage to refuges each day.
   B. Many more gene banks need to be developed.
   C. Botanical gardens and farms for endangered/threatened species can be used to preserve species.

18-9 Zoos and aquariums use various methods to protect endangered animals.
   A. Egg pulling involves acquiring wild eggs and hatching them in zoos or research centers.
   B. Wild individuals of critically endangered species are captured and bred in captivity.
   C. Additional techniques for increasing captive species populations are artificial insemination, surrogate mother through embryo transfer, incubation, cross-fostering, and genetic cloning.
   D. Reintroduction of endangered species into natural habitats most often fail.
      1. Suitable habitats unavailable
      2. Inability of individuals to survive in the wild
      3. Renewed overhunting/capture

18-10 Wildlife management
   A. Wildlife management manipulated wildlife populations and habitats for both species and human benefit.
   B. Steps of wildlife management practice area:
      1. Controversial choice of animals to be managed
      2. Develop management plan, based on ecological succession principles and wildlife population dynamics
         a. Understanding of habitat needs for each specie
         b. Estimate the maximum sustained yield of a population
         c. Be aware of potential hunters, success rates, and regulation to prevent over-hunting
      3. Be sensitive to budget constraints and political pressure
   C. Different issues about sports hunting must be considered.
      1. Laws to identify hunting periods and hunting limits
      2. Economic benefit of hunting to those living near hunting areas
      3. Population control argument: deer, elk, cormorants, etc.
      4. Recreational issues and resulting taxes
      5. Ethics of hunting
   D. Habitats for migrating water birds must be maintained, especially along the 15 major flyway routes.
      1. Management efforts
         a. Regulate hunting
         b. Protect existing habitats
         c. Develop new habitats
      2. Waterfowl refuges of Ducks Unlimited, the Audubon Society, and the Nature Conservancy
      3. Migratory Bird Hunting and Conservation Stamp Act (1934)

Summary

1. Humans are affecting the extinction crisis through the increase of the human population and through elimination, degradation, and simplification of many biologically diverse environments.

2. We should care about species extinction based on the intrinsic value of biodiversity according to which every species has the right to exist regardless of its usefulness to humans.

3. Human activities that endanger wildlife include habitat loss and degradation, introduction of nonnative species, hunting, poaching, and pollution.

4. We can prevent extinctions through protecting endangered and threatened species, strengthening the endangered species act, encouraging private landowners to protect endangered species, and establishing wildlife refuges.

5. Managing game animals more sustainably involves manipulating wildlife populations and their habitat for their welfare and human benefit.

Multiple Choice Questions

See Instructor's Manual, Section II, p. 352.

More Depth: Conceptual Term Paper Topics

1. Significance of wildlife. Medicines derived from plants and animals; commercial products from wildlife; aesthetic and recreational significance of wildlife; ecological significance of wildlife.

2. Endangered and threatened wildlife. Tropical deforestation and species extinction; the international trade in endangered species and exotic pets; lead poisoning in waterfowl and the American bald eagle; Florida's alien species problem; the California condor; the Florida manatee; the blue whale.

3. Protecting wildlife. Gene banks; zoos and captive breeding programs; habitat management; artificial reef-building materials and methods.

More Breadth: Interdisciplinary Activities and Projects

1. Are there zoos, aquariums, botanical gardens, or arboretums in your locale operating programs designed to increase the populations of endangered species? If so, invite a spokesperson to explain one or more of these programs to your class.

2. Ask your students to bring to class and share paintings, sketches, poetry, songs, and other artistic creations depicting the beauty and wonders of wildlife.

3. Have a game warden address your class about management of populations of fish and animals that are hunted for sport.

Multisensory Learning: Audiovisuals

Biodiversity

Remnants of Eden from *Race to Save the Planet;* 1990; 60 min.; growing human populations and biodiversity; ACPB.
America's Endangered Species. 60 min., 1997. NG
Biodiversity for Forests and Farms. 28 min., 1996. CUMS
Challenge of the Seas. V.1. 52 min., 2001. NG
Forests, Biodiversity and You. 10 min., 2000. BFF
Lifesense. 175 min. (2 videos) BBC
Plant Biodiversity. (3 min video stream) @ libraryvideo.com

Wildlife Conservation Strategies

America's Endangered Species. 60 min., 1997. NG
America's National Wildlife Refuge System. 22 min. VT
        Online streaming video: http://video.fws.gov
Aquatic Conservation Challenges (National Fish Hatchery). 22 min., 1999. VT
Arctic Kingdom: life at the edge. NG
Challenge of the Seas. V.1 52 min., 2001.
Conservation videos online: @ video.fws.gov
Conserving America series. 60 min. each, 3 titles. LV
Equilibrium in a Mountain Habitat. FHS

Individual Wildlife Species

African Wildlife; 60 min.; CBS.

Where Have All the Dolphins Gone?; 1991; 58 min.; VP.
Black Tailed Prairie Dogs. NWF
Cheetahs: in the land of the tiger. 60 min., 1992. [available from Amazon]
Elephant. 60 min., 1989. NG
Fish in the Web of Life. 22 min., 1993. VT
The Great White Bear. NG
Great White Shark. 50 min. BBC
The Grizzlies. NG
Last Chance for the Pacific Salmon. 2 pts. 60 min., 1996. ENC
Orca: killer whale or gentle giant. 26 min., VP
Sea Turtles: ancient nomads. 60 min., 1988. NA+
Super Croc. NG
Tigers. NWF

See Appendix B for suppliers.

ATTITUDES/VALUES

Assessment

1. Do you believe that humans have a duty to subdue wild nature to provide food, shelter, and other resources for people and to provide jobs and income through increased economic growth?

2. Do you believe that every living species has a right to exist, or at least struggle to exist, simply because it exists?

3. Do you believe that we have an obligation to leave Earth for future generations of humans and other species in as good a shape as we found it, if not better? Did past generations do this for you?

More Depth: Discussion and Term Paper Topics

1. Should animals be used for medical research? As sources of organs for surgical implants in humans? As sources of food, fur, fat, oils, and other commercially valuable products?

2. Are extremist tactics by Greenpeace and Earth First! Necessary or justifiable?

3. Should sport hunting be used as a wildlife management tool?

4. Should limits be placed on genetic engineering for economic, aesthetic, ecosystem services, or other purposes?

5. Ancient forests: Is it only the spotted owl that is at stake?

(Also, see text, Critical Thinking, p. 476)

PARTICIPATION

More Depth: Action-oriented Term Paper Topics

1. Scientific methods for estimating wildlife populations and successional stage of ecosystems.

2. Groups. Ducks Unlimited; the National Wildlife Federation; the Audubon Society; Greenpeace; Earth First!

3. National. America's National Wildlife Refuge System.

4. Global. The World Wildlife Fund.

SKILLS

Environmental Problem-Solving Skills: Projects

1. Compile a list of the wildlife species in your locale that have been officially designated as threatened or endangered. As a class project, find out what specific actions are being taken to assist these species.

2. As a class, examine and evaluate the goals of the World Conservation Strategy. Develop objectives that could help implement the goals that are agreed upon by the class.

Laboratory Skills

(none)

Computer Skills

Biological and Conservation Data (BCD) System
   -Provides an inexpensive, effective tool to inventory, rank, protect, and maintain endangered species.
   -The Nature Conservancy, Data Systems Divisions, 1815 North Lynn Street, Rosslyn, VA 22209

*Audubon Wildlife Adventures
   -Explore wildlife conservation issues of grizzlies and whales using scientific information, state-of-the-art graphics, computerized data bases, and on-line guidebooks.
   -Advanced Ideas, Inc., 591 Redwood Highway, #2325, Mill Valley, CA 94941 (415-388-2430)

*Wildways: Understanding Wildlife Conservation
   -Emphasizes the need for wildlife conservation through integration of biology, geology, and sociology in sections on Earth and life, basic necessities of life, importance of wildlife, population ecology, community ecology, extinction, wildlife management, and citizen action.
   -Opportunities in Science, Inc., P.O. Box 1176, Bemidji, MI 56601 (218-751-1110)

CHAPTER 19
NONRENEWABLE ENERGY RESOURCES

THINKING

Concept Map

See Appendix A, Map 27.

Goals

See bulleted list of questions on p. 479 of text.

Objectives

1. Distinguish among primary, secondary, and tertiary oil recovery. List the advantages and disadvantages of using conventional oil, oil from oil shale, and oil from tar sands to heat space and water, produce electricity, and propel vehicles.

2. Distinguish among natural gas, liquefied petroleum gas, and liquefied natural gas. List the advantages and disadvantages of using natural gas as an energy source.

3. List and describe three types of coal. Indicate which is preferred for burning and which is most available. List advantages and disadvantages of using coal as a fuel source.

4. List two ways to convert coal to synfuels. List advantages and disadvantages of synfuels.

5. Briefly describe the components of a conventional nuclear reactor. List advantages and disadvantages of using conventional nuclear fission to create electricity. Be sure to include aspects of the whole nuclear fuel cycle, including disposal of radioactive wastes, safety and decommissioning of nuclear power plants, and the potential for proliferation of nuclear weapons. Briefly describe options for dealing with low-level radioactive waste, high-level radioactive waste, and worn out nuclear power plants.

6. Describe the potential use of breeder nuclear fission and nuclear fusion as energy sources.

7. List three ways that U.S. citizens can contribute to a more sustainable-energy future.

Key Terms (Terms are listed in the same font style as they appear in the text.)

solar energy (p. 479)
commercial energy (p. 479)
non-renewable energy (p. 479)
biomass (p. 480)
renewable energy (p. 480)
net energy (p. 481)
net energy ratio (p. 481)
petroleum (p. 483)
crude oil (p. 483)
heavy crude oil (p. 483)
refinery (p. 483)
petrochemicals (p. 483)
reserves (p. 483)
Organization of Petroleum
    Exporting Countries (OPEC) (p. 483)

oil shale (p. 488)
kerogen (p. 488)
shale oil (p. 488)
tar sand (p. 488)
bitumen (p. 488)
natural gas (p. 489)
conventional natural gas (p. 489)
unconventional natural gas (p. 489)
methane hydrate (p. 489)
liquefied petroleum gas (LPG) (p. 489)
liquefied natural gas (LNG) (p. 489)
combined-cycle natural gas systems (p. 490)
coal (p. 490)
area strip mining (p. 491)
contour strip mining (p. 491)

fluidized-bed combustion (p. 492)
synthetic natural gas (SNG) (p. 492)
coal gasification (p. 492)
coal liquefaction (p. 492)
synfuels (p. 493
light-water reactors (LWRs) (p. 493)
core (p. 493)
uranium oxide fuel (p. 493)
control rods (p. 493)
moderator (p. 493)

coolant (p. 493)
Atomic Energy Commission (p. 494)
Nuclear Regulatory Commission (NRC) (p. 496)
low-level radioactive waste (p. 497)
high-level radioactive waste (p. 498)
advanced light-water reactors (ALWRs) (p. 502)
passive safety features (p. 502)
breeder nuclear fission reactors (p. 502)
nuclear fusion (p. 502)

<u>Outline</u>

Major nuclear disasters, like the one at Chernobyl, affect the entire planet.
  A. Most renewable energy is being used by the industrialized countries, with the overwhelming amount being used by the U.S. alone.
  B. Renewable energy resources must be developed and substituted for the nonrenewable energy being used today.
    1. Projections of characteristics of each possible energy resource
      a. Short and long-term availability
      b. Net energy yield of each energy resource
      c. Costs of development, transition, and use
      d. Types and amounts of research, subsidies, and tax breaks provided to develop
      e. Resources affect on national and global economic and military security
      f. Resources vulnerability to terrorism
      g. Harmful environment and/or health issues related to each energy source
    2. Net energy and its calculations
      a. First law of thermodynamics
      b. Second law of thermodynamics
  C. Present-day energy sources include oil, natural gas, coal, and nuclear energy.
    1. Oil supplies, oil consumption, and oil damages
    2. Natural gas—limited supplies
    3. Coal—plentiful and fairly inexpensive to use
      a. Environmental and health damages
      b. Property damage
    4. Nuclear energy
      a. Production process
      b. History of development
      c. Safety issues in nuclear plants and in storage methods
    5. Nuclear energy and nuclear weapons
    6. Alternative nuclear methods

19-1 Evaluating Energy Resources
  A. The two available energy sources are solar energy and that produced by extracting and burning nonrenewable mineral sources.
  B. Most industrial countries use nonrenewable energy resources today.
  C. In developing countries, biomass (fuelwood and charcoal) is the main fuel source.
  D. Energy resources for the 21st century pose huge decisions and problems.
    1. Possibility of solar-hydrogen energy age
    2. Amount of energy from new sources will be available in 15 years, and in 50 years?
    3. Identify net energy yields from various sources
    4. Cost of developing, phasing in, and using energy sources
    5. Type of research, subsidies, and tax breaks to support the sources
    6. Energy resources' influence on nation, global economic, and military security

        7. Energy sources' vulnerability to terrorism
        8. Effects of extracting, transporting, and using the energy resources on the health of the earth
            and its beings
    E. Net energy equals the usable amount of high-quality energy.
        1. Net energy = first law of thermodynamics + the second law of thermodynamics + energy
            unnecessarily wasted in handling useful energy
        2. 'Nuclear fuel cycle uses energy and costs money.'

19-2 Oil
    A. High temperatures and pressures for millions of years convert dead organic matter to oil.
        1. Different extraction methods bring the oil to the surface of land or water.
        2. Crude oil is distilled to produce petro-chemicals.
    B. 78% of crude oil reserves are in the eleven OPEC countries.
        1. The U.S. is the most oil-dependent country and cannot supply its own needs.
        2. Estimates are that most oil supplies will be depleted within 75–90 years.
    C. U.S. oil drilling in the Arctic National Wildlife Refuge will produce limited oil supplies and
        threaten the environment of the refuge.
    D. Between 1905 and 2080, the so-called Age of Oil, oil reserves throughout the world will have
        been depleted.
    E. The energy economy must shift from a carbon-based to a hydrogen-based energy economy.
        1. Possible use of oil shale
        2. Possible use of tar sand

19-3 Natural Gas
    A. Conventional natural gas is found above most crude oil reservoirs; unconventional natural gas is
        alone in underground sources.
    B. Natural gas reserves are limited and little gas reserves are located in industrialized countries.
    C. Natural gas is projected to be a transition fuel between oil supplies and solar-hydrogen energy.

19-4 Coal
    A. Intense heat and pressure over millions of years transformed buried plant remains into coal, a solid
        fossil fuel.
        1. Coal is extracted from mines by area strip mining and by contour strip mining.
        2. The U.S. has 62% of the world's coal deposits and uses more coal than any other country; it,
            however, is a 'dirty' fuel.
            a. Produces serious environmental problems
            b. Difficult and expensive to transport
        3. Use of coal is expected to decrease in coming years because:
            a. High carbon dioxide emissions
            b. Harmful effect on the environment and on health
            c. Less environmentally harmful methods for producing electricity
    B. By coal gasification or coal liquefaction, coal's form can be changed into gaseous or liquid fuels.

19-5 Nuclear energy
    A. Nuclear energy is produced by a nuclear fission chain reaction, controlled by the reactor of a
        nuclear power plant.
        1. Light water reactors produce most of the nuclear-generated electricity in the world. The parts
            of a reactor are given below.
            a. Core contains fuel rods packed with fuel pellets
            b. Enriched uranium oxide fuel
            c. Control rods to absorb neutrons
            d. Moderator which keeps the fission process moving
            e. Coolant which removes heat and produces steam
            f. Containment vessel to hold radioactive materials
            g. Water-filled pools/dry casts for storing highly radio-active spent fuel rods

2. Additional issues in generating nuclear power are the storage of radioactive materials and isotopes produced in both the closed and open fuel cycles.
3. The three reasons for developing nuclear power plants were:
   a. Promise of lower cost power
   b. Government absorbed about ¼ the cost of commercial reactors
   c. Nuclear industry and utilities were protected from liability issues
C. Nuclear energy production and use have not continued to grow.
   1. Construction costs have far exceeded projections.
   2. Operating costs and malfunctions have exceeded expectations.
   3. Nuclear energy plants have been mismanaged.
   4. Safety concerns from the public and stricter governmental safety regulations have increased.
   5. The economic feasibility, as well as vulnerability to terrorist attack, has also raised questions.
D. Although nuclear energy's environmental and health impacts are much less troubling than those of coal energy, its expensive cost and low energy yield, the threat of major accidents, and the long-term storage problem for radioactive wastes are not positive for continuing development of nuclear energy.
   1. Lack of safety for nuclear plant personnel, for radioactive fall-out in case of an accident, and for terrorist threats all point to the public's lack of faith in the security of nuclear plants.
   2. Low-level radioactive waste varies in its half-life but must be contained between 100–200,000 years.
   3. Spent-fuel pools, poorly protected and holding spent fuel rods, are vulnerable places waiting for a tragedy. They represent high-level radioactive waste.
E. Storage of high-level radioactive waste has still not been solved.
   1. Storage choices: deep underground, send into space, bury under arctic ice, dump into deep ocean, bury in mud in deep-ocean floor, change into less harmful isotopes
   2. Example: Yucca Mountain waste site
F. There are radioactive sites throughout the world.
   1. Soviet Union: Chernobyl, Mayak, Lake Karachay
   2. Nuclear plants' decommissioning
G. Nuclear weapons and 'dirty bombs' threaten the entire planet and nuclear power itself still has not been accepted as the best choice to produce energy.
   1. Feasibility of nuclear fission
   2. Feasibility of nuclear fusion
      a. Practical and economic advantages
      b. Still in the laboratory

Summary

1. Alternative energy sources are evaluated based on the availability of each source in the future, the source's energy yield, cost to develop and use this source, the extent of subsidies needed, effects on national and global economic and military security, and environmental effects.

2. The advantages of oil include supply for the next 90 years, low cost, high net energy yield, easy transportation, low land use, well-developed technology, and efficient system of distribution. Disadvantages include need for a substitute discovery within the next 50 years; low price encourages waste, air pollution, and water pollution.

3. The advantages of natural gas include plentiful supplies, high net energy yield, low cost, less air pollution than oil, moderate environmental impact, and easy transport. Disadvantages include the fact that it is a nonrenewable resource, release of carbon dioxide when burned, leaks, and requirement of pipelines.

4. The advantages of coal include plentiful supplies, high net energy yield, low cost, well-developed technology, and air pollution can be managed with appropriate technology. Disadvantages include

very high environmental impact, land disturbance, air and water pollution, threat to human health, high carbon dioxide emissions, and release of radioactive particles and mercury.

5. The advantages of nuclear power include large fuel supply, low environmental impact, low carbon dioxide emissions, moderate land disruption and use, low risk of accidents. Disadvantages include high cost, low net energy yield, high environmental impact in case of accident, catastrophic accidents, long-term storage of radioactive waste, and nuclear weapons.

Multiple Choice Questions

See Instructor's Manual, Section II, p. 365.

More Depth: Conceptual Term Paper Topics

1. Oil and natural gas. Oil prices and economic development in the developing countries; enhanced oil-recovery techniques; shale oil extraction; petrochemicals; heavy oils from Athabascan tar sands; Alaska's Prudhoe Bay gas deposits.

2. Coal. Low-sulfur coal reserves in the United States; geographic distribution of coal-burning power plants in the United States; fluidized-bed combustion; the U.S. Synthetic Fuels Corporation.

3. Nuclear fission. Centralized energy planning in France; genetic damage to A-bomb survivors; Three Mile Island; Chernobyl; how nuclear fuel assemblies are made; radioactive tailings as a health hazard; geologic repositories for high-level radioactive wastes; commercial low-level nuclear waste dump sites; storing high-level liquid wastes; geographic distribution of nuclear power plants in the United States; keeping weapons-grade nuclear materials "out of the wrong hands"; nuclear reprocessing plants.

4. Breeder nuclear fission and nuclear fusion.

More Breadth: Interdisciplinary Activities and Projects

1. Arrange a class excursion to a coal-burning power plant in your vicinity. Have a company spokesperson explain the electricity generating process and the design and operating features of equipment and systems that control air pollution emissions and reduce thermal water pollution.

2. If there is a nuclear power plant operating in your vicinity, schedule a guided tour for your class.

3. If there is a nuclear power plant operating in your vicinity, invite a spokesperson from your local emergency disaster preparedness agency to present a guest lecture explaining the emergency evacuation plan for this facility.

Multisensory Learning: Audiovisuals

General

Conservation for a Sustainable Society. 1993. RCO
Nuclear

Nuclear Technology; 1994; 23 min.; fission and fusion, food irradiation; FHS.
Three Mile Island Revisited; 1993; 30 min.; challenges the claims of the nuclear industry and government that "no one died" from the core meltdown in 1979; evidence of cancer deaths and birth defects is presented; VP.
Nuclear Bombs in Our Future; 1994; 28 min.; the spread of nuclear weapons; political motivations of countries seeking nuclear weapons; VP.
Deafsmith: A Nuclear Folktale; 1990; 43 min.; citizens' attempts to defend the land from nuclear pollution; VP.

Chernobyl: Chronicle of Difficult Weeks; 1986; 54 min.; directed by Vladimir Shevchenko, two weeks to three months after the incident; VP.
Cherynobyl: chronicle of difficult weeks. 54 min., 1986. VP
Children of Chernobyl. 52 min., 1993. Filmakers
Four Corners—a National Sacrifice Area? 59 min., 1983. BFF
Nuclear Dynamite. 52 min., 2001. BFF
Question of Nuclear Power. 50 min., TV
The River That Harms; 1987; 45 min.; documentary of the largest radioactive waste spill in U.S. history and its impact on the Navajo Indians of New Mexico; VP.

Other Nonrenewable Energy Sources

Element One: hydrogen, the key to the sustainable energy revolution. 58 min., Filmakers
Fossil Fuels @ shnta.com. HSSR

See Appendix B for suppliers.

ATTITUDES/VALUES

Assessment

1. Do you favor requiring all cars to get at least 21 kilometers per liter (50 miles per gallon) and vans and light trucks to get at least 15 kilometers per liter (35 miles per gallon) of gasoline within the next ten years?

2. Would you favor much stricter, twice-a-year inspections of air pollution control equipment on motor vehicles and tough fines for not keeping these systems in good working order?

3. Would you favor a $2 tax on a gallon of gasoline and heating oil to help reduce wasteful consumption, extend oil supplies, reduce air pollution, delay projected global warming, and stimulate improvements in energy efficiency and the use of less harmful energy sources?

4. Would you vote for anyone proposing a program to add a $2 per gallon tax on gasoline and heating oil, assuming all other factors are the same?

5. Would you support laws requiring that all new homes and buildings meet high-energy efficiency standards for insulation, air infiltration, and heating and cooling systems?

6. Would you favor such a law for existing homes and buildings?

More Depth: Discussion and Term Paper Topics

1. Do you feel that the application process for nuclear power plants should be streamlined to limit citizen input?

2. Do you think emphasizing nuclear power and oil as the primary U.S. energy sources shows adequate concern for future generations?

3. Whistle-blowers. The Karen Silkwood story.

(Also, see text, Critical Thinking, p. 504)

PARTICIPATION

More Depth: Action-oriented Term Paper Topics

1. National. The Atomic Energy Commission (1946–1975); the Nuclear Regulatory Commission; the Energy Research and Development Administration (ERDA); the Nuclear Safety Analysis Center; the Institute of Nuclear Power Operations; the Price-Anderson Act.

SKILLS

Environmental Problem-Solving Skills: Projects

1. As a class exercise, (a) obtain cost estimates for the construction of a single large-scale synfuels plant and (b) calculate how many soft path energy facilities or systems of various types (such as solar water heaters, biogas digesters, and photovoltaic devices) could be installed with an equivalent amount of money.

2. As a class exercise, make a list of the geopolitical responsibilities and costs incurred by the United States in association with maintaining an uninterrupted supply of affordably priced oil from foreign sources.

3. A new power plant must be built in your community, but it remains to be decided whether it will be a fossil fuel or a nuclear plant. As a class exercise, set up a mock public hearing to present the arguments for both sides. Make specific role assignments so that prepared statements will accurately reflect varying points of view such as those of contractors, environmentalists, project engineers, state energy officials, and concerned citizens.

Laboratory Skills

(none)

Computer Skills

ENERPLAN
    -Performs basic energy analysis for a nation, province, or community.
    -Mr. Nicky Beredjick, Director, National Resources and Energy Division, Department of Technical Cooperation for Development, United Nations, New York, NY 10017

Estimating Fossil Fuel Resources (EFFR)
    -Simulates the global exploitation of oil resources and evaluates alternative resource-estimation techniques.
    -Prof. John D. Sterman, Sloan School of Management, Massachusetts Institute of Technology, 50 Memorial Dr., Cambridge, MA 02139

CHAPTER 20
ENERGY EFFICIENCY AND RENEWABLE ENERGY

THINKING

<u>Concept Map</u>

See Appendix A, Map 28.

<u>Goals</u>

See bulleted list of questions on p. 507 of text.

<u>Objectives</u>

1. List the five key questions that must be asked about each energy alternative to evaluate energy resources.

2. List the advantages and disadvantages of improving energy efficiency so that we do more with less. Define *net energy*, *life-cycle cost*, and *cogeneration*. Describe energy efficiency improvements that could be made via megawatts, transportation, and heating and lighting of buildings.

3. List the advantages and disadvantages of using direct solar energy to heat buildings and water and to produce electricity. Distinguish between *passive solar heating systems* and *active solar heating systems*. Describe a photovoltaic cell.

4. List the advantages and disadvantages of using hydropower, tidal power, wave power, ocean thermal currents, and solar ponds to produce electricity.

5. List the advantages and disadvantages of using wind to produce electricity.

6. List the advantages and disadvantages of using biomass to heat space and water, produce electricity, and propel vehicles.

7. List the advantages and disadvantages of using hydrogen gas to heat space and water, produce electricity, and propel vehicles. Name the energy source that is needed to produce hydrogen to create a truly sustainable future.

8. List the advantages and disadvantages of using geothermal energy to produce electricity and heat space and water.

9. List three ways that individuals can move toward use of perpetual and renewable energy resources.

<u>Key Terms</u> (Terms are listed in the same font style as they appear in the text.)

energy efficiency (p. 507)
life-cycle cost (p. 508)
cogeneration (p. 510)
Corporate Average Fuel Economy
          (CAFÉ) Standards (p. 512)
superefficient cars (p. 512)
hybrid electric internal
         combustion engine (p. 512)
fuel cells (p. 513)

electric bicycles (p. 513)
superinsulated houses (p. 515)
straw-bale houses (p. 515)
passive solar heating system (p. 519)
active solar heating system (p. 519)
earth tubes (p. 520)
solar thermal systems (p. 521)
central receiver system (p. 521)
power tower (p. 521)

Outline

By combining solar power, wind power, and hydrogen power, the world may eliminate air pollution, moving into the solar-hydrogen revolution.
  A. Improved energy efficiency will yield benefits for all phases of human undertakings.
  B. There are advantages and disadvantages to all types of energy resources; availability of resources and politics will influence any transition to alternative energy sources.
    1. Net energy efficiency is improved by keeping the number of steps in energy conversion small and striving to obtain the highest possible energy efficiency for each step.
    2. Energy efficiency is improved through
      a. Wasting less heat
      b. Combining heat and power systems = cogeneration
      c. Increased fuel efficiency
      d. Developing hybrid vehicles and fuel-cell cars
      e. Building design—homes and offices—to save energy
      f. Developing and using energy-saving appliances
  C. Alternative energy sources must be available at reasonable price.
    1. Solar energy: solar thermal systems, solar cells
    2. Energy from moving water and heat stored in water
      a. Hydropower
      b. Tides, oceans, ponds
    3. Energy from wind
    4. Energy from biomass
  D. The solar-hydrogen revolution is necessary to provide energy resources for the world's future.
    1. Split water atom by electrolysis or thermolysis
    2. Reforming: separate hydrogen from carbon atoms
    3. Storage methods for hydrogen: compressed gas, liquid hydrogen, solid metal hydride compounds, and fuel cells
  E. Geothermal energy sources are contained in magma, hot dry-rock zones' molten rock, and warm-rock reservoir deposits.
  F. Decentralized micropower for producing energy will define energy provision for the future.

20-1 Importance of improving energy efficiency
  A. Energy efficiency is doing more with less and is increasing the total energy put into an energy conversion system, doing so without producing useless heat.

B. Almost 43% of commercial energy in the U.S. is wasted unnecessarily by machinery, equipment and poorly designed/insulated buildings.
   1. Need more energy-efficient devices: incandescent light bulb, internal combustion engine, nuclear power plants, coal burning plants
   2. Need net energy efficiency applications
C. The basic principles for saving energy are to minimize the steps in an energy conversion process and to obtain the highest energy efficiency in each step.

20-2 Ways to improve energy efficiency
  A. There are many methods to improve energy efficiency in buildings.
    1. Insulate a building thoroughly.
    2. Eliminate air leaks.
    3. Install an air-to-heat exchanger.
    4. Use 'waste' heat to re-distribute or to drive an absorption chiller.
    5. Combine heat and power (CHp) systems in cogeneration.
    6. Replace energy-wasting electric mothers with adjustable-speed drive motors.
    7. Switch to fluorescent lighting.
  B. Energy can be saved in transportation by increasing the fuel efficiency of motor vehicles.
    1. Instituted Corporate Average Fuel Economy standards
    2. Missed opportunities to increase motor vehicle fuel efficiency
    3. Energy-efficient motor vehicles
      a. Hybrid-electric internal combustion engine: Toyota, Honda, Nissan
      b. Diesel-hybrid busses
      c. Fuel-cell cars
    4. Electric bicycles and scooters—no pollution
  C. Buildings can be designed to save energy.
    1. Design features: solar energy, shade and cooling, focus lighting on desks, not rooms
    2. Superinsulation
      a. Compacted bales of straw
      b. Eco-roofs: insulate, absorb storm water, last
    3. Heating energy-efficiently
      a. Passive solar hearing
      b. Heat pumps in warm climates
      c. High-efficiency natural gas furnaces
    4. Reduce energy costs in homes
      a. Use low-emission windows
      b. Insulating jacket around water heater and tankless water heaters
      c. Closing leaky ducts
      d. Cut off appliances
    5. Set higher energy-efficiency standards
      a. In building codes
      b. Energy-efficient lights and appliances
      c. Incandescent light bulbs
    6. Reduce energy and paper use with Internet

20-3 Using solar energy to provide heat and electricity
  A. Using solar energy has many advantages for consumers.
    1. Saves money and reduces air pollution, dependence on foreign oil, and reduces carbon dioxide emissions
    2. Backup need is reduced; backup and storage devices are available
    3. Less land use than with coal energy; low land use with solar cells and window glass system
  B. Solar Heating Systems provide passive solar heating and active solar heating.
  C. Natural cooling of houses can reduce electrical demand.
    1. Superinsulation of buildings and windows
    2. Block out the sun with deciduous trees, window overhangs/awnings

3. Catch breezes, keep air moving
4. Earth tubes

D. Use solar thermal systems to collect radiant energy to use or to convert to electricity through several different methods.
   1. Central receiver system/power tower
   2. Solar thermal plant/distributed receiver system
   3. Parabolic dish collectors tracks sun along two axes
   4. Solar cookers

E. Sunlight in solar cells energizes, causing electrons to flow and produce an electrical current.
   1. Solar cells in roof shingles, glass walls, windows, etc.
   2. Banks of solar cells—electricity

20-4 Producing electricity from moving water and from heat stored in water

A. Hydropower plants produce electricity through three methods.
   1. Large-scale hydropower
   2. Small-scale hydropower
   3. Pumped-storage hydropower

B. Hydropower plants produce high net energy, are efficient, produce low-cost electricity, and provide water for irrigation.

C. Reservoirs may provide flood control and are useful for recreation.

D. But, hydropower plants cost a lot to construct, impact the environment in negative ways, emit major greenhouse gases, flood natural areas, uproot people, and decrease fishes and the natural flow of silt.

E. Large applications from tides, waves, and/or heat stored in water (saline solar ponds or freshwater solar ponds) are not feasible at this time.

20-5 Producing electricity from wind

A. Wind power is economically a very attractive power source; its viability extends from Western Europe to the U.S. to India and China.

B. Wind power produces high net energy, high efficiency, low electrical costs, no carbon dioxide, and is easily expandable. It requires steady winds and backup systems.

C. Wind power produces visual and, sometimes, noise pollution; may interfere with birds' movements, and requires lots of land when used to support farm needs.

20-6 Producing energy from biomass

A. Biomass, plant materials and animal wastes, may be burned directly for energy or converted into liquid biofuels.
   1. Biomass plantations produce fuel for burning—trees, shrubs, perennial grasses, and water hyacinths.
   2. Crop residues (husks, stalks, shells) and animal manure can be burned or converted to biofuel.
   3. Gaseous and liquid biofuels can be converted from some types of biomass.
      a. Biogas converted by biogas digesters into methane
      b. Ferment and distill sugar and grain crops = ethanol
      c. Wood, agricultural wastes, sewage sludge, etc = methanol

20-7 Solar-hydrogen revolution

A. The fuel of the future may be hydrogen gas, produced by combining hydrogen gas with oxygen in the air.
   1. Reduce air pollution
   2. Reduce global warming threat

B. Hydrogen production methods vary.
   1. Split water into gaseous hydrogen and oxygen
   2. Reforming: separate hydrogen from carbon atoms
   3. Gasification of coal

C. Problems with producing hydrogen for a fuel source
   1. Need energy to obtain/release the hydrogen
   2. Methods—gasification adds more CO_2 to the air
D. The solar-hydrogen revolution will be driven by inexpensive solar methods for decomposing water.
   1. Storing hydrogen: compressed gas tanks, convert to liquid hydrogen, form solid metal hydride compounds, absorb hydrogen on activated charcoal/graphite nanofibers, store it inside tiny glass microspheres.
   2. Fuel cells for storing hydrogen would be efficient, emit only water and heat, are reliable, and not susceptible to lightning, military, or terrorists. They can be large or small.

20-8 Geothermal energy
   A. Geothermal energy produced inside the earth comes in three forms: dry steam has no water; wet steam which is a mixture of water and steam, and hot water is trapped in fractured/porous rock in the earth's crust.
   B. Three other sources of geothermal energy are molten rock/magma; hot dry-rock zones where molten rock heats subsurface rock, and warm-rock reservoir deposits.

20-9 Entering the age of decentralized micropower
   A. Electricity production is predicted to decentralize in the coming years;
   B. Rather than the present central power plant systems, electricity will be generated from micropower systems.
   1. Micropower systems will be supported by micro-turbines, wind turbines, sterling engines, fuel cells, solar panels and solar roofs—all of which generate from 1–10,000 kilowatts of power.
   2. Advantages of decentralized systems include rapid factory production, fast installation, high-energy efficiency, low air pollution, useful anywhere, easily financed, etc.

20-10 Solutions: a sustainable energy strategy
   A. Energy alternatives for the future will likely include:
   1. A gradual shift from present macropower systems to smaller, decentralized micropower systems
   2. Combining improved energy efficiency and natural gas to transition to using a variety of small-scale, decentralized, locally available energy resources, which would be renewable
   3. Reducing the harmful effects of fossil fuel use as alternative energy sources are phased in
   B. To affect both short- and long-term use of energy sources, governments use three economic-political strategies.
   1. Sustain free market demands and influences with no governmental interference.
   2. Influence the use of specific energy sources by keeping energy prices artificially low.
   3. Inflate energy prices to discourage use.
   C. The many problems with fossil fuels have led some to recommend increased taxes on such fuels. The resulting taxes would be used to reduce income taxes, improve energy efficiency, encourage usage of renewable energy sources, and provide assistance to poor and low-income users.
   D. The transition to a more sustainable energy future is surely possible; the cost of NOT choosing such a transition is not acceptable.
   E. Transitioning to a sustainable energy future will be enhanced by our improving energy efficiency, developing more renewable energy sources, and reducing pollution and health risk.

<u>Summary</u>

1. The advantages of improving energy efficiency include benefits to the environment, people, and the economy through prolonged fossil fuel supplies, reduced oil imports, very high net energy yield, low cost, reduction of pollution, and improved local economies.

2. The advantages of solar energy include reduction of air pollution, reduction of dependence on oil, and low land use. Disadvantages include production of photocells results in release of toxic chemicals, life of systems is short, can damage deserts, need backup systems, and high cost.

3. The advantages of hydropower include high net energy yield, low cost electricity, long life span, no carbon dioxide emissions during operation, food control below dam, water for irrigation, and reservoir development. Disadvantages include high construction cost, high environmental impact, high carbon dioxide emissions from biomass decay, flooding of natural areas, conversion of land habitats to lake habitats, danger of dam collapsing, people relocations, limits fish populations below dam, and decrease flow of silt.

4. The advantages of wind power include high net energy yield and efficiency, low cost and environmental impact, no carbon dioxide emissions, and quick construction. Disadvantages include need for winds and backup systems, high land use, visual and noise pollution, interfering with bird migrations, and causing the death of birds of prey.

5. The advantages of biomass include large potential supplies, moderate costs, no net carbon dioxide increase, and can make use of agricultural, timber, and urban wastes. Disadvantages include nonrenewable resource, moderate to high environmental impact, low photosynthetic efficiency, soil erosion, water pollution, and loss of wildlife habitat.

6. The advantages of hydrogen gas include the fact that it can be produced from water, the low environmental impact, no carbon dioxide emissions, competitive price, ease of storage, safety, and high efficiency. Disadvantages include energy need to produce the fuel, negative energy yield, nonrenewable, high cost, and no fuel distribution system exists.

7. The advantages of geothermal energy include very high efficiency, low carbon dioxide emissions, low cost and land use, low land disturbance, and moderate environmental impact. Disadvantages include suitable sites are scarce, potential depletion, moderate to high air pollution, noise and odor, and high cost.

8. We can improve energy efficiency by increasing fuel efficiency standards, large tax credits for purchasing energy efficient cars, houses, and appliances, encouraging independent energy production, and increasing research and development.

Multiple Choice Questions

See Instructor's Manual, Section II, p. 377.

More Depth: Conceptual Term Paper Topics

1. Improving energy efficiency. Energy-efficient office buildings; earth-sheltered houses; retrofitting energy-wasting houses; superinsulation; earth tubes; evaporative coolers; energy-efficient appliances; compact fluorescent light bulbs; "smart" windows; superinsulated windows; roof-attachable solar cell rolls; the Albers Technologies air conditioner.

2. Solar technologies. The solar power tower; the Odeillo furnace; solar power satellites; photovoltaics; active solar systems; passive solar heating; microprocessors to control house temperatures.

3. Biomass. Modern wood stoves; biogases as a biomass fuel; biogas digesters in the developing countries; gasohol; methanol.

4. Wind. Wind farming in California; wind turbine designs.

5. Water power. Large-scale hydropower projects in the developing countries; rehabilitating small-scale hydroelectric plants in New England; wave power devices—a comparison of various approaches; ocean thermal energy conversion; solar ponds; the Bay of Fundy tidal power project.

6. Hydrogen gas: a versatile fuel of the future.

More Breadth: Interdisciplinary Activities and Projects

1. Ask an architect or contractor with experience in renewable energy resource systems to visit the class and discuss the practical aspects of designing, financing, and installing small-scale solar, wind, and biogas systems for individual residences, farms, businesses, or factories.

2. Find out if representatives from your local electrical utility offer customers energy audits of their homes. If so, ask them to come to your class and tell what they look for in homes and what seem to be the most frequent ways that customers can increase their energy efficiency.

3. Have your students find out if your institution's electrical utility has a conservation program. Does it have policies that encourage customers to purchase energy-efficient appliances and use energy-efficient light bulbs?

4. Organize a class field trip featuring guided tours of homes and/or other buildings that have solar heating systems. If possible, include examples of both passive and active systems and an earth-sheltered house.

Multisensory Learning: Audiovisuals

Element One: Hydrogen: Key to the Sustainable Energy Revolution; 1996; 60 min.; complete and up-to-date review of hydrogen technology; VP.
More for Less from *Race to Save the Planet;* 1990; 60 min.; ways to reduce fossil fuel consumption and improve energy efficiency; ACPB.
Green Energy; 26 min.; renewable energy alternatives with focus on biomass; FHS.
Energy Alternatives: Solar; 26 min.; FHS.
Energy Efficiency; 23 min.; meeting U.S. energy needs and energy standards; BFF.
Harness the Wind; 12 min.; history and potential of wind power; BFF.
Kilowatts from Cowpies: The Methane Option; 25 min.; BFF.
Energy Alternative. 30 mins., TV
Energy Alternative series (3 pts: 52 min. each) 1992, Filmakers
Energy Through Hydrogen. FCS
Prophets & Loss. 49 min., VP
Saving with Solar. EREC.
Solar Hydrogen Technology, FCS
Solar Water Pumping. 59 min., Pt
Solutions for the 21st Century. 28 min., VP

See Appendix B for suppliers.

ATTITUDES/VALUES

Assessment

1. What is the major energy source for heating your living space?

2. What is the major energy source for providing electricity to your living space?

3. How do you feel toward different energy sources?

4. What would be the best alternative energy source in your area?

5. Do you feel a responsibility to use energy wisely? What steps are you willing to take to reduce your energy consumption?

6. How do you feel toward decentralization of the power grid?

7. Do you favor policies which encourage energy conservation and more development of renewable and perpetual energy sources?

More Depth: Discussion and Term Paper Topics

1. Choose: free-flowing streams or a network of small-scale hydropower facilities?

2. Should millions of homeowners erect small wind turbines for electrical production?

3. Should building codes be required to include passive solar concepts?

(Also, see text, Critical Thinking, p. 537)

PARTICIPATION

More Depth: Action-oriented Term Paper Topics

1. Individual. Household energy savings.

2. Industry. The horizontal integration of large energy companies.

3. Policy. Government taxing and subsidizing policies and energy conservation; the National Audubon Society intermediate national energy strategy; an evaluation of the current administration's energy plan.

SKILLS

Environmental Problem-Solving Skills: Projects

1. As a class project, identify the major energy-related economic, political, environmental, and social problems in your community and state. What specific actions are being taken to alleviate these problems? Are these piecemeal efforts, or are they components of comprehensive and internally consistent energy plans?

2. Bring to a class recent issues of periodicals devoted exclusively to renewable energy industry reporting. As a class exercise, scan the contents of these periodicals to see what research and development is on the cutting edge of progress.

3. Have your students audit energy use and waste on your campus and in activities (such as commuting) associated with the operation of your campus. Are opportunities to conserve significant amounts of energy going unrecognized or ignored?

4. As a class project, conduct a survey of students at your school to determine what beliefs and attitudes they have regarding sustainable-Earth energy alternatives that entail a loss of convenience or additional expenditures of time and money on the part of energy users. Are young people today willing to significantly alter their lifestyles to use and waste less energy?

5. As a class project, develop a simple questionnaire or test that can be used to measure a person's knowledge about the efficiency of various energy conversion devices, appliances, and systems in common use. What is the "energy IQ" of the average student on your campus? To obtain a crude measure, administer the test to a random sample of students and analyze the results.

6. Have your students examine recent issues of weekly news magazines, local newspapers, and nationally recognized newspapers. How much space is devoted to energy-related reporting and analysis? What is the relative degree of emphasis placed on developing alternative energy sources and systems? Curbing energy waste? Lifestyle adjustments that reduce energy needs? How are energy-related topics and issue handled in the *Wall Street Journal* and *Fortune?* How does corporate advertising address energy topics and issues? In these and other ways, try to determine how thoroughly and accurately the public is being informed about matters of critical importance to the nation's energy future.

Laboratory Skills

Laboratory Manual for Miller's Living in the Environment and Environmental Science. Lab 19: Energy Conservation; Lab 18: Energy Alternatives.

Computer Skills

(none)

SECTION II

TEST BANK

CHAPTER 1
ENVIRONMENTAL PROBLEMS, THEIR CAUSES, AND SUSTAINABILITY

1-1   LIVING MORE SUSTAINABLY

1.   Most of the environmental problems we face are
      a.   increasing linearly.
      b.   decreasing linearly.
   * c.   increasing exponentially.
      d.   decreasing exponentially.
      e.   are not increasing or decreasing.

2.   Earth's capital includes all of the following *except*
      a.   wildlife.
      b.   nutrients
      c.   water.
      d.   soil.
   * e.   sunlight.

3.   A sustainable society
      a.   manages its economy and population size without doing irreparable environmental harm.
      b.   satisfies the needs of its people without depleting Earth capital.
      c.   protects the prospects of future generations of humans and other species.
   * d.   all of these answers.
      e.   none of these answers.

1-2   POPULATION GROWTH

4.   Exponential growth
      a.   remains constant.
      b.   starts out slowly and remains slow.
   * c.   starts out slowly then becomes very rapid.
      d.   starts rapidly and remains rapid.
      e.   starts rapidly and then slows.

5.   Linear growth
      a.   is characterized by a rapidly growing population.
   * b.   is demonstrated by the sequence 12, 13, 14, 15, 16.
      c.   is illustrated by the numbers 2, 4, 8, 16, 32.
      d.   is characterized by resource use and consumption.
      e.   is characterized by a slowly decreasing population.

6.   If the world's population grew by 2% in 1998 and continued at that rate, how long would it take the Earth's population to double?
      a.   20 years
      b.   25 years
      c.   30 years
   * d.   35 years
      e.   40 years

7.   Conservation International estimated that roughly _____% of the habitable area of the planet has been altered by human activities.
      a.   13
      b.   33
      c.   53
   * d.   73
      e.   93

1-3 ECONOMIC GROWTH, ECONOMIC DEVELOPMENT, POVERTY, AND GLOBALIZATION

8. Which of the following choices would make the statement *false?* Economic growth
    a. provides goods and services for people's final use.
    * b. is accomplished by minimizing the flow of matter and energy through an economy.
    c. is encouraged by population growth.
    d. is encouraged by increased consumption per capita.
    e. all of these answers.

9. The market value in current dollars of all goods and services produced within a country for final use during a year is the
    a. gross national product.
    b. gross world product..
    c. per capital GNP.
    d. per capita GDP.
    * e. gross domestic product

10. Developed countries
    * a. are highly industrialized.
    b. have a low GNP per person.
    c. are generally located in Asia.
    d. make up about 80% of the world's population.
    e. use about 12% of the world's natural resources.

11. Which of the following statements about developing countries is *true?*
    a. They are highly industrialized.
    b. They have high average GNPs per person.
    c. They include the United States, Germany, and Japan.
    * d. They have about 15% of the world's wealth and income.
    e. They have about 85% of the world's wealth and income.

12. About ___% of the world's human population lives in the developing countries.
    a. 20
    b. 40
    c. 60
    * d. 80
    e. 90

13. Since 1960, the gap between rich and poor, as measured by GNP per capita, has
    a. decreased, then increased since 1980.
    b. increased, then substantially decreased since 1980.
    * c. increased, then substantially increased since 1980.
    d. decreased, then substantially decreased since 1980.
    e. has remained constant since 1980.

1-4 RESOURCES

14. For something to be classified as a natural resource, it must
    * a. satisfy a human need or desire.
    b. be steadily renewed or replenished.
    c. be a form of matter.
    d. exist in great abundance.
    e. renewable.

15. Solar energy is a(n) _____ resource.
    a. renewable
    b. potentially renewable
    c. nonrenewable
    d. exhaustible
  * e. perpetual

16. All of the following are potentially renewable resources *except*
    a. groundwater
    b. trees in a forest
    c. fertile soil
  * d. oil
    e. animals

17. Which of the following terms includes the others?
    a. ecological diversity
    b. species diversity
  * c. biological diversity
    d. genetic diversity
    e. none of these answers.

18. Use of a natural resource based on sustainable yield applies to
  * a. potentially renewable resources.
    b. nonrenewable resources.
    c. perpetual resources.
    d. amenity resources.
    e. all of these answers.

19. Which of the following statements *best* illustrates the tragedy of the commons?
  * a. A factory pollutes a river as much as the law allows.
    b. Some levels of pollution are life threatening.
    c. Some activities harm the environment, but others do not.
    d. Irrigated cropland can be ruined by salinization.
    e. Cropland can decrease biodiversity.

20. Which of the following *best* describes the concept of environmental degradation?
    a. using solar power at a rapid rate
    b. using oil
    c. cutting trees for wood products
  * d. letting agricultural runoff cause oxygen depletion and fish kills downstream
    e. growing crops for food.

21. We can extend use of nonrenewable resources by
    a. increasing consumption of the resource.
    b. reusing energy resources where possible.
    c. putting used resources in a landfill.
  * d. finding substitutes for a resource.
    e. all of these answers.

22. Resources that are called nonrenewable
    a. are also called perpetual resources.
    b. are only resources that are alive.
    c. include soil, water and air.
    d. none of these answers.
  * e. are capable of economic depletion.

23. Nonrenewable resources include
    * a. energy resources.
    b. wildlife resources.
    c. soil resources.
    d. sunshine.
    e. soil.

24. Renewable resources include
    a. oil.
    b. minerals.
    c. copper ore.
    d. coal.
    * e. fertile soil.

25. Which of the following is an example of recycling?
    * a. collecting and remelting aluminum beer cans
    b. cleaning and refilling soft-drink bottles
    c. selling used clothing at a garage sale
    d. saving leftovers in a peanut butter jar.
    e. using household water to water a garden.

26. Reserves
    a. indicate limitless supplies of a resource.
    b. indicate established limits of a resource.
    * c. can be increased when new deposits are found.
    d. can be increased when prices fall.
    e. are resources that have been recycled.

27. New efforts to prevent the tragedy of the commons include
    a. using common-property resources at or above their sustainable yields.
    b. converting land from private to more public ownership.
    * c. moving from a *taxpayers pay* approach to a *users pay* approach.
    d. deregulation of industries that use common-property resources.
    e. increase public availability to resources.

1-5 POLLUTION

28. Pollution include(s)
    a. dumping detergents into streams, causing fish kills.
    b. spraying with DDT, lowering the eagle population.
    c. releasing gases from coal combustion, causing acid rain.
    * d. all of these answers.
    e. allowing fertilizers runoff from cropland.

29. Point sources of pollution
    a. enter ecosystems from dispersed and often hard-to-identify sources.
    b. include runoff of fertilizers and pesticides from farmlands and suburban lawns.
    * c. are cheaper and easier to identify than nonpoint sources.
    d. are more difficult to control than nonpoint sources.
    e. are always found in rural areas.

30. Nonpoint sources of pollution
    a. enter ecosystems from single identifiable sources.
    * b. are more difficult to control than point sources.
    c. include smokestacks and automobile exhaust pipes.
    d. are cheaper and easier to identify than point sources.
    e. are always found in rural areas.

31. Effects of pollution might include
    a. less diversity of stream life because of road salt runoff.
    b. acid rain-induced destruction of a statue in your city park.
    c. spread of disease from an open dump.
    * d. all of these answers.
    e. fish kills in lakes and streams.

32. You generally buy and eat microwave dinners. After dinner, cardboard tops and plastic trays remain. The *least* effective way to deal with this type of solid waste problem is to
    a. store leftovers in the plastic trays.
    * b. put all of the solid waste in the household trash to be taken to the landfill.
    c. donate the plastic containers to the local nursery schools to use with preschoolers.
    d. recycle the components.
    e. all of these are effective.

33. Pollution cleanup efforts can be ineffective because
    a. they often transfer pollutants from one part of the environment to another.
    b. once pollutants are dispersed, it costs too much to reduce them to acceptable levels.
    c. they can be overwhelmed by growth in population and consumption.
    * d. all of these answers.
    e. none of these answers.

34. Efforts to improve environmental quality in the United States are predominantly based upon _____ wastes and pollutants.
    a. reducing
    b. reusing
    c. recycling
    * d. cleaning up
    e. there are no efforts to improve environmental quality in the United States.

35. Pollution prevention and cleanup can be encouraged by
    a. regulations.
    b. taxes.
    c. subsidies.
    * d. all of these answers.
    e. education.

1-6   ENVIRONMENTAL AND RESOURCE PROBLEMS: CAUSES AND CONNECTIONS

36. Root causes of unsustainability include all of the following *except*
    a. wasteful use of resources.
    b. an urge to manage and dominate nature.
    c. rapid population growth.
    * d. inclusion of environmental and social costs in market prices.
    e. greed.

37. A very simple model of environmental degradation and pollution would include all of the following *except*
    a. number of people.
    b. amount of remaining resource available for use.
    c. average number of units of resources each person uses.
    d. amount of environmental degradation/pollution generated when each unit of resource is produced.
    * e. the climate in which the people live.

38. Two children in the United States have as much environmental impact as _____ children in the world's poorest countries.
    a. 5-10
    b. 10-20
    c. 50-100
  * d. 70-200
    e. 90-300

1-7 CULTURAL CHANGES AND SUSTAINABILITY

39. The species *Homo sapiens* has lived on earth about _____ years.
    a. 4,000
    b. 12,000
  * c. 60,000
    d. 160,000
    e. 250,000

40. Exponential growth over time is characteristic of
    a. human population growth.
    b. resource consumption.
    c. energy use per capita.
  * d. all of these answers.
    e. none of these answers.

41. Which of the following statements does *not* characterize human skills and relationships within hunter-gatherer societies?
    a. They lived in small groups of 50 or less.
    b. They depended on sun, fire, and muscle power for energy.
  * c. They had little knowledge about their natural surroundings.
    d. They gradually developed tools.
    e. They moved as needed to find food.

42. Which of the following statements does *not* characterize relationships between hunter-gatherers and the environment?
    a. They understood medicinal value of some plants.
    b. They exploited their environment for food and other resources.
    c. They were experts in survival and had a great understanding of nature.
  * d. They caused global environmental impacts.
    e. Resource usage per person was low.

43. Advanced hunter-gatherer societies did all of the following *except*
    a. make many kinds of tools and weapons.
    b. use fire to flush out animals and to stampede herds.
    c. use fire to convert forests into grasslands.
    d. live in small groups.
  * e. subdue and dominate most other forms of life.

44. The Agricultural Revolution is characterized by
    a. use of chemical pesticides.
  * b. cultivation of wild plants near settled communities.
    c. use of chemical fertilizers to improve soil fertility.
    d. use of diesel-powered farm equipment.
    e. use of genetically engineered crops.

45. Domestication of wild plants and animals occurred about ___ years ago.
    a. 5,000
  * b. 10,000
    c. 15,000
    d. 20,000
    e. 50,000

46. All of the following are characteristic of the first agricultural communities *except*
    a. slash-and-burn cultivation.
  * b. specialized farming of one crop.
    c. shifting cultivation.
    d. subsistence agriculture.
    e. abandon plots after several years.

47. Slash-and-burn cultivation
  * a. leaves ashes from burned vegetation, which add plant nutrients to the soil.
    b. contours and terraces the land.
    c. ultimately leads to desertification.
    d. rotates crops yearly.
    e. increases biodiversity.

48. Shifting cultivation
  * a. alternates planting periods with fallow periods.
    b. permanently depletes the soil nutrients.
    c. ultimately leads to desertification.
    d. can be eliminated in stable societies.
    e. contours and terraces the land.

49. Subsistence farmers
    a. use draft animals to pull plows.
    b. require large, flat fields in grassland areas.
  * c. grow only enough food to feed their families.
    d. tend to cause severe deforestation.
    e. grow only enough food to feed their community.

50. Which of the following human-resource relationships does *not* characterize a shift from hunter-gatherer to agricultural societies?
    a. Use of domesticated animals increased average energy use per person.
    b. Population increased with the increased food supply.
  * c. People used muscle, sun, and coal as energy sources.
    d. People began accumulating material goods.
    e. People began to cut down vast forests.

51. The Agricultural Revolution resulted in all of the following *except*
    a. urbanization.
    b. increased soil erosion.
    c. increased deforestation.
    d. salt buildup from irrigation.
  * e. protection of wild plants and animals.

52. The Industrial Revolution began in
    a. the United States.
    b. Japan.
  * c. England.
    d. France.
    e. Australia.

53. The Industrial Revolution started in the United States in the
   a. 1500s.
   b. 1600s.
   c. 1700s.
   * d. 1800s.
   e. 1900s

54. The Industrial Revolution is characterized by all of the following *except*
   a. increased average per capita energy consumption.
   b. increased ability to utilize Earth's resources.
   * c. increased social concern for workers.
   d. increased trade and distribution of goods.
   e. increased population growth.

55. Energy use during the Industrial Revolution
   a. was based primarily on wood.
   b. was based primarily on solar power.
   c. was based primarily on labor by human muscle.
   * d. shifted from potentially renewable to nonrenewable sources.
   e. all of these answers.

56. Benefits bestowed on most citizens of industrialized countries include all of the following *except*
   a. more affordable material goods.
   b. increase in average agricultural production per person.
   c. higher average life expectancy.
   * d. continued exponential growth of human population.
   e. lower infant mortality rates.

1-8   IS OUR PRESENT COURSE SUSTAINABLE?

57. All of the following are components of a multiple-factor model to account for environmental degradation and pollution *except*
   a. poverty.
   b. inappropriate application of technology.
   * c. realistic market prices.
   d. overconsumption.
   e. waste

58. Which of the following pieces of evidence is likely to form the basis of an economist's opinion?
   a. The human population is growing exponentially.
   b. The rate of crop yield increases is declining.
   * c. Increased urbanization protects biodiversity.
   d. Consensus science suggests that potential global climate change from human activities should be taken as a serious problem.
   e. all of these answers.

59. Which of the following pieces of evidence is likely to form the basis of an environmentalist's opinion?
   a. The rate of human population growth is declining.
   b. Food is more abundant and cheaper than at any other time in human history.
   c. Total forest area of the temperate zone region's industrialized countries increased during the 1980's.
   * d. Consensus science suggests that potential global climate change from human activities should be taken as a serious problem.
   e. all of these answers.

60. Which of the following statements about nonrenewable resources and solid wastes is *false*?
   a. Since 1950, proven supplies of virtually all nonrenewable fossil fuel and key mineral resources have increased significantly.
   b. Harmful environmental effects may limit use of nonrenewable resources in the future.
   c. In the U.S., recycling and composting of solid municipal waste increased from 7% to 25% from 1970 to 1996.
* d. 100% of solid waste could be reused, recycled, or composted.
   e. all of these answers are false.

61. Lester Brown predicts that the new environmental revolution will
   a. stabilize human population size.
   b. see a shift away from fossil fuels.
   c. be driven by restructuring the global economy.
* d. all of these answers.
   e. none of these answers.

62. Working with the earth implies
   a. sustaining biodiversity.
   b. taking no more than we need.
   c. slowing the rate of population growth and poverty.
* d. all of these answers.
   e. sustaining resources.

CHAPTER 2
ENVIRONMENTAL ECONOMICS, POLITICS, AND WORLDVIEWS

2-1 ECONOMIC SYSTEMS AND ENVIRONMENTAL PROBLEMS

1.   Which of the following categories includes the others?
     a.   human capital
     b.   natural resources
 *   c.   economic resources
     d.   manufactured capital
     e.   none of these answers.

2.   Which of the following is *not* classified as an economic resource?
 *   a.   time
     b.   labor
     c.   capital or intermediate goods
     d.   natural resources
     e.   human resources

3.   In a pure command (centralized planning) economic system, decisions are made by
     a.   the markets.
 *   b.   the government.
     c.   past customs and experience.
     d.   businesses.
     e.   individuals.

4.   Economic decisions in a pure capitalistic economy are made by
     a.   individuals.
     b.   the government.
     c.   past customs and experience.
     d.   the banks.
 *   e.   the markets.

5.   *Capitalistic system* is another name for
     a.   the traditional system.
     b.   the pure command system.
     c.   the pure government system.
     d.   the mixed economic system.
 *   e.   the pure market system.

6.   The pure market system is based on all of the following *except*
     a.   the flow of economic goods and money between households and businesses.
 *   b.   obligation to provide a safe workplace.
     c.   freedom of choice.
     d.   pure competition.
     e.   no government controls.

7.   In a pure capitalistic system, a company's only obligation is to
     a.   provide taxes to the government.
     b.   supply needed goods and services.
     c.   provide jobs and safe workplaces.
     d.   provide pensions for its workers.
 *   e.   produce the highest short-term profits for owners and stockholders.

8. If price, supply, and demand are the only factors involved, the demand and supply curves
    a. run parallel to each other.
    b. are reciprocals of each other.
*   c. intersect at the market equilibrium.
    d. are straight lines that run in opposite directions.
    e. none of these answers.

9. The *most* common economic system is
    a. the pure market economic system.
    b. the pure command economic system.
    c. socialism.
*   d. the mixed economic system.
    e. communism.

2-2 MONITORING ECONOMIC AND ENVIRONMENTAL PROGRESS

10. All of the following would be counted as part of the gross national product *except*
    a. a new car purchase.
    b. government purchases.
*   c. home health care.
    d. dental services.
    e. none of these answers.

11. The search for increased profits can be addressed by
    a. economic development.
    b. economic growth.
    c. ecologically sustainable development.
*   d. all of these answers.
    e. none of these answers.

12. GNP is generally accepted as a measure of
    a. the quality of life.
*   b. the status of economic progress.
    c. social welfare.
    d. the quality of the environment.
    e. all of these answers.

13. GNP does not measure the well being of a society because it does not include
    a. differences between beneficial and harmful services.
    b. how the resources are divided.
    c. subtraction of natural resource depletion and degradation.
*   d. all of these answers.
    e. none of these answers.

14. Which of the following is a characteristic of a useful environmental indicator?
    a. add to GDP and GNP those things, which deplete natural resources
    b. subtract from GDP and GNP those things, which enhance environmental quality
*   c. subtract from GDP and GNP those things, which deplete natural resources
    d. subtract the GNP from the GDP
    e. none of these answers.

2-3   SOLUTIONS: USING ECONOMICS TO IMPROVE ENVIRONMENTAL QUALITY

15. Which of the following is *not* an external cost of driving a domestic car?
   a. air pollution and litter
   * b. cost of manufacture
   c. highway accidents
   d. health costs
   e. all of these answers.

16. Full-cost pricing
   * a. requires government action.
   b. reduces final cost of goods.
   c. would result in redirecting economic growth and would drop the NEW.
   d. would make the market price higher than the true cost of a product or service.
   e. all of these answers.

17. Full-cost pricing
   * a. involves making the market price approach the true cost of an economic good.
   b. fails to include the cost of pollution.
   c. omits the costs of taxes.
   d. increases the chance for environmental degradation.
   e. all of these answers.

18. Full-cost pricing is difficult to implement for all of the following reasons *except*
   a. producers of harmful and wasteful products might go bankrupt.
   b. producers of harmful and wasteful products might lose subsidies.
   * c. it is difficult to externalize internal costs.
   d. it is difficult to place a price tag on external costs.
   e. all of these answers.

19. Which of the following statements is *false?*
   a. Benefit-cost analyses have a built-in bias against the future.
   b. Conservationists generally place a higher value on the future value of resources than economists do.
   * c. In benefit-cost analysis it is easy to determine who pays the costs and who gets the benefit.
   d. Many costs and benefits cannot be labeled with a price tag.
   e. none of these answers.

20. Which statement about benefit-cost analysis is *true?*
   * a. In benefit-cost analyses, the future value of a resource is usually discounted.
   b. Benefit-cost analyses clearly assess all the winners and losers in any situation.
   c. Benefit-cost analyses are based on well-established values.
   d. Benefit-cost analyses employ only objective criteria that can be easily assessed.
   e. all of these answers.

21. Benefit-cost estimates
   * a. analyze data to determine the most economically efficient course of action.
   b. provide bottom-line numbers.
   c. are not useful and should not be made.
   d. are objective assessments of the real costs of doing business.
   e. all of these answers.

22. For environmentalists, the discount rate is
   a. a social indicator.
   b. an environmental indicator.
   c. an economic indicator.
   * d. an ethical decision about responsibility to future generations.
   e. all of these answers.

23. Use of benefit-cost analysis is difficult because
    a. figures can be weighted to achieve the outcome desired by the proponents.
    b. a dollar figure cannot be placed on many things we value.
    c. they do not take who benefits and who is harmed into account.
 * d. all of these answers.
    e. none of these answers.

24. Which of the following would not be recommended as a means of avoiding possible abuses, which can result from benefit-cost analyses?
    a. Open the evaluations to public scrutiny.
    b. Show the estimated range of costs and benefits based on various sets of assumptions.
 * c. Use variable standards.
    d. Evaluate the reliability of all data inputs as high, medium, or low.
    e. all of these answers.

25. The pollution control approach, which does the least to internalize external costs, is
    a. tradable rights.
    b. withdrawing harmful subsidies.
 * c. subsidizing beneficial actions.
    d. green taxes and user fees.
    e. all of these answers.

26. Using tax dollars to subsidize businesses that install pollution control equipment is an example of
    a. marketing pollution rights.
    b. marketing resource use rights.
 * c. rewarding beneficial actions.
    d. making harmful actions illegal.
    e. all of these answers.

27. Selling the right to harvest timber up to a sustainable yield level would be an example of
    a. tradable rights.
    b. withdrawing harmful subsidies.
    c. subsidizing beneficial actions.
 * d. green taxes and user fees.
    e. all of these answers.

28. A pollution control strategy *least* likely to confer a disadvantage in the international marketplace is
    a. tradable rights.
    b. green taxes.
 * c. subsidizing beneficial actions.
    d. user fees.
    e. a and b only.

29. Administrative costs are highest for
 * a. regulation.
    b. withdrawing harmful subsidies.
    c. subsidizing beneficial actions.
    d. green taxes and user fees.
    e. none of these answers.

30. All of the following economic approaches contribute to government revenues *except*
 * a. pollution-prevention bonds.
    b. withdrawing harmful subsidies.
    c. user fees.
    d. green taxes and user fees.
    e. c and d only.

31. Which of the following things is the most important thing to keep in mind about economics and the environment?
    a. Benefit-cost analyses will answer our questions about options to choose.
    b. Businesses will voluntarily produce less pollution.
  * c. We need to achieve a balance between the costs of cleaning up pollution and the costs of a polluted environment.
    d. It's important not to hold up new chemical products by requiring them to be tested for environmental safeness before release into the marketplace.
    e. all of these answers.

32. For most pollutants, economists say our goal should *not* be zero pollution because
    a. it is too costly.
    b. everything we do produces some pollution.
    c. nature can handle some of the pollution.
  * d. all of these answers.
    e. none of these answers.

33. The graph of the cost of removing pollutants is
    a. an ascending straight line.
    b. a descending straight line.
    c. a horizontal line.
  * d. a J-shaped curve.
    e. a S-shaped curve.

2-4   REDUCING POVERTY TO IMPROVE ENVIRONMENTAL QUALITY AND HUMAN WELL-BEING

34. Poverty is usually defined as
    a. not being able to buy shoes.
  * b. not being able to meet one's basic economic needs.
    c. earning less than $100 per year.
    d. eating an unbalanced diet.
    e. all of these answers.

35. Currently, one in every _____ persons on the planet lives in poverty in a developing country.
    a. three
  * b. four
    c. five
    d. six
    e. seven

36. Since 1950, the gap between the rich and the poor has
    a. disappeared.
  * b. increased.
    c. stayed the same.
    d. decreased.
    e. stayed the same and then decreased.

37. Developed countries can help address poverty, thereby investing in global environmental and economic security, by all of the following methods *except*
    a. forgiving of the present debt owed by developing countries to developed countries in exchange for agreement by the governments of developing countries to increase expenditure for rural development, family planning, health care, education, land distribution, and protection of wilderness areas.
    *   b. insisting that developing countries stop ruining their natural resource base and that they pay off their debt to developed countries to establish their reliability and encourage more investment by developing countries in their economies.
    c. increasing nonmilitary aid given by developed countries to developing countries.
    d. lifting trade barriers that hinder the export of commodities from developing countries to developed countries.
    e. c and d only.

2-5 MAKING THE TRANSITION TO MORE ENVIRONMENTALLY SUSTAINABLE ECONOMIES

38. Humans can move toward creating restorative economies by all of the following *except*
    a. using full-cost accounting.
    b. using low discount rates.
    c. revoking charters of environmentally and socially irresponsible businesses.
    *   d. a primary commitment to economic growth.
    e. a and c only.

39. Paul Hawken would encourage all of the following *except*
    a. leave the world better than you found it.
    *   b. maintain the status quo.
    c. take no more than you need.
    d. do no harm.
    e. c and d only.

40. An earth-sustaining economy determines progress by all of the following factors *except*
    a. pollution prevention.
    b. the amount of recycling and reuse of nonrenewable materials.
    *   c. the bottom line.
    d. the sustainable use of renewable resources.
    e. b and d only.

41. Ways to ease the transition from the current economy to a sustainable-earth economy include all of the following *except*
    a. providing tax breaks to make it more profitable for companies to keep or hire more workers instead of automating.
    b. using incentives to encourage location of emerging industries in hard-hit communities and helping such areas diversify their economic base.
    c. providing income and retraining assistance for workers displaced from environmentally destructive businesses.
    *   d. changing as quickly as possible so that change is not dragged out.
    e. a and b only.

42.   The process by which individuals and groups try to influence the decisions and policies of governments is
       a.   economics.
       b.   resource management.
   *   c.   politics.
       d.   ethics.
       e.   all of these answers.

43.   Incremental rather than revolutionary change in constitutional democracies stems from
       a.   conflicting information from experts.
       b.   distribution of power among federal, state, and local authorities.
       c.   distribution of power among different branches of government.
   *   d.   all of these answers.
       e.   none of these answers.

44.   According to your text, history shows that significant change
       a.   is cyclical.
       b.   is exponentially decreasing.
   *   c.   is from the bottom up.
       d.   is from the top down.
       e.   all of these answers.

45.   Individuals influence and change government policies in constitutional democracies by all of the following *except*
       a.   whistle-blowing.
       b.   education and persuasion.
   *   c.   coup d'état.
       d.   participating in grass-roots activities.
       e.   b and d only.

46.   Effective environmental leadership
       a.   leads by working within the system.
       b.   leads by example.
       c.   leads by challenging the system.
   *   d.   all of these answers.
       e.   a and b only.

2-7   CASE STUDY: ENVIRONMENTAL POLICY IN THE UNITED STATES

47.   Environmental legislation in the United States
   *   a.   sets standards for pollution.
       b.   discourages resource conservation.
       c.   ignores evaluation of environmental impact before an activity is undertaken.
       d.   protects private rights at the expense of or species.
       e.   all of these answers.

48.   The National Environmental Policy Act requires
       a.   screening of new chemical substances to determine if they are a hazard.
       b.   protection of certain areas, resources, or species.
   *   c.   comprehensive evaluation of the environmental impact statement of an activity before it is undertaken.
       d.   encouragement of resource conservation.
       e.   all of these answers.

49. The Students Environmental Action Coalition has
    a. protected the redwood forests by chaining themselves to trees.
    b. written most of the new environmental legislation.
    c. swollen the record number of members of national environmental organizations.
  * d. given students skills in researching and developing strategies to make their campuses and communities more sustainable.
    e. all of these answers.

50. Students on college campuses have
    a. established a Green Cup competition among dorms to save energy and water.
    b. worked with faculty and administration to make environmental improvements on campus.
    c. established organic farms to supply food services with organic produce.
    d. a and c only.
  * e. all of these answers.

51. Of the following strategies the one *least* likely to be used by the anti-environmental forces is
    a. a SLAPP on individual environmental activists.
    b. weaken and intimidate activists.
  * c. a search for common ground.
    d. diversion of attention away from environmental issues.
    e. none of these answers.

52. Environmentalists would *least* expect anti-environmental forces to
    a. build up a good environmental image.
    b. exploit the limitations of science.
    c. influence the media and deny environmental problems exist.
  * d. collect and publish data about environmental issues.
    e. a and c only.

53. You would *least* expect an anti-environmental organization to
    a. encourage compensation for regulatory takings.
    b. utilize paralysis-by-analysis.
  * c. submit bills to improve energy efficiency and recycling.
    d. urge legislators not to fund environmental laws.
    e. b and d only.

54. In evaluating our positions on environmental issues, we need to
    a. distinguish between frontier and consensus science.
    b. apply the precautionary principle.
    c. apply critical thinking.
    d. b and c only.
  * e. all of these answers.

2-8   GLOBAL ENVIRONMENTAL POLICY

55. What was the general reaction by environmentalists to the 1992 Rio Earth Summit?

    a. great enthusiasm for the significant agreements made
    b. general approval for most of the results of the conference
  * c. disappointment because the agreements were neither binding nor funded
    d. it was a total waste of time
    e. a and b only.

2-9   HUMAN-CENTERED ENVIRONMENTAL WORLDVIEWS

56.   Planetary management worldviews include all of the following variations *except*
    a.   spaceship-Earth.
    b.   free-market school.
*   c.   ecocentrism.
    d.   stewardship.
    e.   none of these answers.

57.   The "no problem" variation of the planetary management worldview is based on the general belief that
    a.   pure capitalism should be used to make our economic decisions.
*   b.   better management and technology and more economic growth can fix our problems.
    c.   an ethical responsibility to "tend our garden" would improve most technological–economic growth worldviews.
    d.   a mixture of market-based competition, improved technology, and government intervention can solve our problems.
    e.   none of these answers.

58.   People calling for more stewardship generally believe that
    a.   pure capitalism should be used to make our economic decisions.
    b.   better science and technology can fix our problems.
*   c.   an ethical responsibility to "tend our garden" would improve most technological–economic growth worldviews.
    d.   a mixture of market-based competition, improved technology, and government intervention can solve our problems.
    e.   all of these answers.

59.   A spaceship-Earth strategy is often used by which of the following worldviews?
    a.   ecocentrism
    b.   free-market global economy with minimal government interference
*   c.   responsible planetary management
    d.   stewardship
    e.   all of these answers.

2-10   LIFE-CENTERED ENVIRONMENTAL WORLDVIEWS

60.   Species which have a right to life regardless of their usefulness to humans have
    a.   net worth.
    b.   dollar value.
    c.   aesthetic value.
*   d.   intrinsic value.
    e.   all of these answers.

61.   Which of the following beliefs does *not* characterize an environmental-wisdom worldview?
*   a.   Human ingenuity can fix any problems we face.
    b.   Earth has limited resources.
    c.   Some forms of economic growth are environmentally beneficial and some are not.
    d.   Earth has limited capability to absorb human pollutants.
    e.   none of these answers.

62. An environmental -wisdom worldview is characterized by all of the following *except*
    a. seeing the world as an integrated, interconnected, interdependent whole rather than as a fragmented collection of parts.
    b. seeing our most fundamental value as maintaining Earth's life-support systems.
  * c. believing that all types of economic growth are important for alleviating poverty.

    d. seeing the need for less competition and more cooperation in building relationships.
    e. b and d only.

63. Which of the following worldviews is *most* likely to support the view that most public property should be turned over to private ownership?
    a. ecocentrism
  * b. free-market global economy
    c. responsible planetary management
    d. stewardship
    e. c and d only.

2-11 SOLUTIONS: LIVING MORE SUSTAINABLY

64. Which question is Lester Brown *least* likely to ask in evaluating a sustainable development policy?
  * a. Does it give investors the best quarterly returns?
    b. Does it slow population growth?
    c. Does it increase tree cover?
    d. Does it reduce generation of carbon emissions and toxic wastes?
    e. none of these answers.

65. Until we can make reasonable estimates of the carrying capacity of the earth, the precautionary principle suggests that we
  * a. use material resources more efficiently.
    b. continue use of energy resources at current rates.
    c. live off Earth capital.
    d. increase population growth.
    e. all of these answers.

66. Which of the following positions *least* reflects a code of earth ethics?
    a. Preserve as much biodiversity as possible.
    b. Protect the habitats of earth's creatures.
    c. Protect human cultures from extinction.
  * d. Drive only animals which are harmful to humans to extinction.
    e. a and c only.

67. Earth education calls for educational systems to become more
    a. reductionistic.
    b. discipline oriented.
    c. back to basics.
  * d. interdisciplinary.
    e. all of these answers.

68. According to Mitchell Thomashow's view, all of the following questions are significant to establishing your "ecological identity" *except*
    a. What is my purpose and responsibility as a human being?
    b. How am I connected to the earth and other living things?
  * c. How can I use the system to supply all my needs and wants?
    d. Where do the things I consume come from?
    e. b and d only.

69. It is easier to live sustainably when you
    a. have a sense of place.
    b. live simply.
    c. seek wisdom instead of information.
    d. b and c only.
  * e. all of these answers.

70. All of the following are traps that block living sustainably *except*
    a. a faith in simple, easy answers.
    b. gloom-and-doom pessimism.
  * c. critical evaluation of experts and leaders.
    d. blind technological optimism.
    e. b and c only.

71. Which of the following positions is most likely to be helpful in responding to environmental problems?
    a. Humans are the root of all evil and can never make up for the harm they have done the planet.
    b. Most of the human population is composed of victims of a few powerful industries who are causing severe environmental degradation.
    c. Life is as good as it has ever been in the course of human history, and there really isn't much of a problem.
  * d. Individual knowledge, attitudes, and action can make a difference.
    e. all of these answers.

72. Within an Earth-Wisdom Revolution is found
    a. an efficiency revolution to conserve energy and matter.
    b. a sufficiency revolution in which the basic needs of all people are met.
    c. a pollution prevention revolution.
    d. b and c only.
  * e. all of these answers.

CHAPTER 3
SCIENCE, SYSTEMS, MATTER, AND ENERGY

3-1   THE NATURE OF SCIENCE

1.   Science
    a.   studies the past to predict the future.
    b.   attempts to discover order in nature to interpret the past.
    c.   is best-described as a collection of facts found through using scientific methods.
    d.   is supported by small amounts of evidence.
*   e.   uses data to formulate scientific laws.

2.   The type of model *least* likely to be used in environmental studies is a
    a.   mathematical model.
    b.   conceptual model.
    c.   graphic model.
*   d.   fashion model.
    e.   computer model.

3.   Discovering and formulating scientific laws requires
    a.   logic.
    b.   imagination.
    c.   use of scientific methods.
*   d.   all of these answers.
    e.   none of these answers.

4.   Which of the following statements does *not* describe the scientific enterprise?
    a.   Science is the acceptance of what works and the rejection of what does not.
*   b.   Once established, scientific theories are rarely challenged and continue to hold true into the future.
    c.   Advances in scientific knowledge are often based on vigorous disagreement, speculation, and controversy.
    d.   Scientific laws and theories are based on statistical probabilities, not certainties.
    e.   Science attempts to reduce the degree of uncertainty and lack of objectivity.

5.   Which of the following statements best describes the scientific enterprise?
    a.   There is one scientific method used to advance our understanding of science.
    b.   Intuition has no place in the scientific process.
    c.   Controlled experiments are the only way of advancing scientific understanding.
*   d.   Consensus science is more widely accepted by the scientific community than pioneer science.
    e.   Scientists use data to prove that their models, theories, and laws are absolutely true.

6.   Which of the choices makes the following statement *false?* Technology _____
    a.   is the creation of new products and processes.
    b.   is supposed to improve our quality of life.
*   c.   is the development of scientific laws and theories.
    d.   resulted in lasers and pollution control devices.
    e.   resulted in computers and cell phones.

7.   Environmental science integrates knowledge from the disciplines of
    a.   chemistry and physics.
    b.   ecology and demography.
    c.   economics and politics.
*   d.   all of these answers.
    e.   a and b only

3-2 MODELS AND BEHAVIOR OF SYSTEMS

8. Human mental models tend to be unreliable when
   a. there are few interacting variables.
   b. we attempt to extrapolate from many experiences to a general case.
   c. the consequences occur immediately following causal events.
   d. responses do not vary from one time to the next.
   * e. consequences of one event lead to other consequences.

9. Mathematical models are useful when
   a. controlled experiments are impossible.
   b. responses to causing events are highly variable.
   c. controlled experiments are too slow or expensive.
   d. there are many interacting variables.
   * e. all of these answers.

10. Mathematical models are tested by comparing the predictions with
    a. observations.
    b. experimental data.
    c. scientific laws and theories.
    d. predictions of mental models.
    * e. all of these answers.

11. In systems diagrams, inputs, accumulations, and outputs of matter, energy, or information are often represented by
    * a. circles or boxes.
    b. trapezoids.
    c. single arrows.
    d. dots.
    e. lines.

12. In systems diagrams, flows of matter, energy, or information are often represented by
    a. circles.
    b. triangles.
    * c. arrows.
    d. rectangles.
    e. lines.

13. A feedback loop
    a. affects the rate of change.
    b. may be positive or negative.
    c. has at least one storage area.
    * d. all of these answers.
    e. none of these answers.

14. A negative feedback loop keeping conditions stable is
    * a. homeostasis.
    b. a synergistic interaction.
    c. leverage.
    d. chaos.
    e. all of these answers.

3-3   MATTER: FORMS, STRUCTURE, AND QUALITY

15. Matter is anything that
 * a. has mass and occupies space.
   b. has the capacity to do work.
   c. can be changed in form.
   d. can produce change.
   e. moves mass.

16. All of the following are elements *except*
 * a. water.
   b. oxygen.
   c. nitrogen.
   d. hydrogen.
   e. carbon.

17. N_2 and O_2 are examples of
   a. compounds consisting of two different elements.
   b. elements consisting of a compound and an ion.
   c. molecules consisting of two elements of the same compound.
   d. molecules consisting of two atoms of different elements.
 * e. molecules consisting of two atoms of the same element.

18. The atomic number is the number of
   a. atoms in a molecule.
 * b. protons in an atom.
   c. nuclei in a molecule.
   d. electrons in an atom.
   e. protons and neutrons in an atom.

19. Protons, neutrons, and electrons are all
   a. forms of energy.
   b. equal in mass.
 * c. subatomic particles.
   d. negative ions.
   e. charged particles.

20. The atomic mass number is equal to the sum of the
   a. neutrons and isotopes.
   b. neutrons and electrons.
 * c. neutrons and protons.
   d. protons, neutrons, and electrons.
   e. protons only.

21. Isotopes differ from each other by their number of
   a. ions.
   b. protons.
   c. atoms.
 * d. neutrons.
   e. electrons.

22. All organic compounds are characterized by the presence of
 * a. carbon.
   b. hydrogen.
   c. oxygen.
   d. nitrogen.
   e. phosphorus.

23. Organic compounds include all of the following *except*
    a. chlorofluorocarbons.
    b. hydrocarbons.
    c. chlorinated hydrocarbons.
    d. carbohydrates.
    * e. carbon dioxide.

24. Which complex compound is correctly matched with its building block?
    * a. complex carbohydrates—simple sugars such as glucose
    b. nucleic acids—amino acids
    c. chromosomes—proteins
    d. proteins— simple sugars such as glucose
    e. proteins-nucleic acids

25. Which of the following sources of iron would be of the highest quality?
    a. iron deposits on the ocean floor
    b. a field of spinach
    * c. a large, scrap metal junkyard
    d. a one-half-mile deep deposit of iron ore
    e. none of these answers.

3-4   ENERGY: FORMS AND QUALITY

26. Energy can be formally defined as
    a. the random motion of molecules.
    * b. the ability to do work or produce heat transfer.
    c. a force that is exerted over some distance.
    d. the movement of molecules.
    e. the loss of matter.

27. Most forms of energy can be classified as either
    a. chemical or physical.
    b. kinetic or mechanical.
    c. potential or mechanical.
    d. chemical or kinetic.
    * e. potential or kinetic.

28. All of the following are examples of kinetic energy *except*
    a. a speeding bullet.
    * b. a stick of dynamite.
    c. a flow of electric current.
    d. a falling rock.
    e. flowing water.

29. An example of potential energy is
    a. electricity flowing through a wire.
    * b. the chemical energy in a candy bar.
    c. a bullet fired at high velocity.
    d. a leaf falling from a tree.
    e. water flowing.

30. Which of the following is an example of low-quality energy?
    a. electricity
    * b. heat in the ocean
    c. nuclei of uranium-235
    d. coal
    e. oil.

31. High-quality energy is needed to do all of the following *except*
   a. run electric lights.
   b. run electric motors.
   c. run electric appliances.
   * d. heat the White House.
   e. run automobiles.

32. Which of the following energy sources has the lowest quality?
   a. high-velocity water flow
   b. fuelwood
   c. food
   d. coal
   * e. dispersed geothermal energy

3-5 PHYSICAL AND CHEMICAL CHANGES AND THE LAW OF CONSERVATION OF MATTER

33. Which of the following statements is *not* an example of a physical change?
   a. Confetti is cut from pieces of paper.
   b. Water evaporates from a lake.
   c. Ice cubes are formed in the freezer.
   * d. A plant converts carbon dioxide into carbohydrate.
   e. a tree is cut down.

34. All of the following statements can be concluded from the law of conservation of matter *except*
   a. We can't throw anything away because there is no away.
   * b. We'll eventually run out of matter if we keep consuming it at current rates.
   c. There will always be pollution of some sort.
   d. Everything must go somewhere.
   e. We do not consume matter.

35. Earth is essentially a closed system for
   * a. matter.
   b. energy.
   c. matter and energy.
   d. neither matter nor energy.
   e. none of these answers.

36. In regard to matter, the earth
   a. might gain small amounts.
   b. might lose small amounts.
   c. has essentially all it will ever have.
   * d. all of these answers.
   e. none of these answers.

37. We can reduce our environmental impact through
   a. pollution containment.
   b. waste incineration.
   * c. more efficient use of resources.
   d. consuming more.
   e. burying waste.

38. Which of the following is *not* important in determining the damage produced by a pollutant?
    a. concentration
    b. persistence
    * c. origin
    d. chemical nature
    e. ability to be degraded.

39. Nondegradable pollutants include
    a. tin cans.
    b. detergent.
    * c. lead.
    d. human sewage.
    e. newspaper.

40. Which of the following is a degradable pollutant?
    * a. human sewage
    b. DDT
    c. aluminum cans
    d. lead
    e. mercury.

41. Which of the following is a persistent pollutant?
    * a. DDT
    b. plutonium
    c. lead
    d. mercury
    e. human sewage.

3-6 **NUCLEAR CHANGES**

42. Nuclear changes include
    a. nuclear fission.
    b. nuclear fusion.
    c. natural radioactive decay.
    * d. all of these answers.
    e. none of these answers.

43. Which of the following involves changes of mass into energy?
    a. chemical changes
    b. energy changes
    c. physical changes
    * d. nuclear changes
    e. all of theses answers.

44. Natural radioactive decay is best-described as a
    a. chemical change.
    b. physical change.
    * c. nuclear change.
    d. environmental change.
    e. molecular change.

45. All of the following are given off by natural radioactivity *except*
    a. alpha particles.
    * b. delta rays.
    c. gamma rays.
    d. beta particles.
    e. none of these answers.

46. The two most common types of ionizing particles emitted by radioactive isotopes are
    a. gamma and alpha particles.
    b. gamma and beta particles.
* c. alpha and beta particles.
    d. electrons and protons.
    e. neutrons and protons.

47. Which of the following statements is *true?*
    a. Exposure of a substance to alpha, beta, or gamma radiation makes it radioactive.
    b. All isotopes are radioactive.
* c. Radioactive isotopes give off radiation at a fixed rate.
    d. Only naturally occurring substances are radioactive.
    e. Radioactive isotopes give off radiation at variable rates.

48. To decay to what is considered to be a safe level, a sample of radioisotope should be stored in a safe enclosure for approximately _____ half-lives.
    a. 2
    b. 5
* c. 10
    d. 20
    e. 30

49. Nuclear fission is best-described as a
    a. chemical change.
    b. physical change.
    c. nuclear change with spontaneous release of fast-moving particles and/or high-energy radiation from unstable isotopes.
    d. molecular change.
* e. nuclear change with release of energy from splitting of isotopes with large mass numbers.

50. During a nuclear fission reaction, each fission releases two or three
    a. protons and energy.
    b. electrons and energy.
* c. neutrons and energy.
    d. protons, requiring the input of energy.
    e. neutrons, requiring the input of energy.

51. In conventional nuclear-fission reactors, the fuel is
    a. natural gas.
* b. uranium-235.
    c. alpha particles.
    d. beta particles.
    e. iodine-131

52. The explosion of an atomic bomb is best described as
    a. uncontrolled radioactive decay.
* b. uncontrolled nuclear fission.
    c. uncontrolled nuclear fusion.
    d. controlled nuclear fission.
    e. controlled nuclear fusion.

53. The generation of energy in a nuclear electric power plant comes from
    a. uncontrolled radioactive decay.
    b. uncontrolled nuclear fission.
    c. uncontrolled nuclear fusion.
* d. controlled nuclear fission.
    e. controlled nuclear fusion.

54. Nuclear fusion is best-described as a
    a. chemical change.
    b. physical change.
  * c. nuclear change with release of energy from combining two nuclei of isotopes of light elements.
    d. nuclear change with release of energy from splitting of isotopes with large mass numbers.
    e. molecular change.

55. Nuclear fusion requires temperatures of at least _____ degrees centigrade.
    a. 100
    b. 100 thousand
  * c. 100 million
    d. 100 billion
    e. 100 trillion.

56. Thermonuclear weapons get their energy from
    a. uncontrolled radioactive decay.
    b. uncontrolled nuclear fission.
  * c. uncontrolled nuclear fusion.
    d. controlled nuclear fission.
    e. controlled nuclear fusion.

57. Which of the following is a product of a fusion reaction?
    a. alpha particles
    b. deuterium
    c. tritium
    d. hydrogen
  * e. helium

3-7 TWO LAWS GOVERNING ENERGY CHANGES

58. Which of the following statements is *false?*
    a. Energy can be converted from one form to another.
  * b. Energy and matter can generally be converted into each other.
    c. Energy input always equals energy output.
    d. The laws of thermodynamics can be applied to living systems.
    e. Energy conversion results in higher quality energy.

59. The first law of energy tells us that
    a. doing work always creates heat.
    b. altering matter is the best source of energy.
    c. energy cannot be recycled.
  * d. it takes energy to get energy.
    e. energy cannot be converted.

60. Which of the following statements does *not* apply to the second law of energy?
    a. Energy conversion results in lower-quality energy.
  * b. Energy can be neither created nor destroyed.
    c. Energy conversion results in more-dispersed energy.
    d. Heat is usually given off from energy conversions.
    e. None of these answers.

61. Energy input is
    a. usually greater than energy output.
    b. always greater than energy output.
  * c. always equal to energy output.
    d. usually less than energy output.
    e. always less than energy output.

62.   The energy lost by a system is
      a.   usually found.
      b.   equal to the energy the system creates.
*   c.   converted to lower-quality energy.
      d.   returned to the system eventually.
      e.   converted to lower-quality energy.

63.   In an energy transformation, some of the energy usually ends up as
*   a.   heat energy that flows into the environment.
      b.   mechanical energy that performs useful work.
      c.   chemical energy that performs useful work.
      d.   electrical energy that performs useful work.
      e.   molecular energy that performs useful work.

64.   The matter and energy laws tell us that we can recycle
      a.   both matter and energy.
      b.   neither matter nor energy.
*   c.   matter but not energy.
      d.   energy but not matter.
      e.   none of these answers.

65.   The quality of the energy available after work is performed is _____the initial energy quality.
*   a.   lower than
      b.   equal to
      c.   higher than
      d.   equal to or higher than
      e.   equal to or lower than

66.   An example of the second energy law is
      a.   90% of the high-quality chemical energy in gasoline burned in automobiles is degraded to low-quality heat.
      b.   most of the chemical energy in the food we eat is given off as waste heat.
      c.   95% of the electrical energy flowing through an incandescent light bulb is given off as heat.
      d.   41% of energy in the United States is unavoidably wasted.
*   e.   all of these answers.

3-8   CONNECTIONS: MATTER AND ENERGY CHANGE LAWS AND ENVIRONMENTAL PROBLEMS

67.   A high-waste society sustains economic growth by
      a.   minimizing the rate of energy resource use.
      b.   minimizing the rate of energy and matter resource use.
      c.   maximizing the rate of energy resource use.
      d.   maximizing the rate of matter resource use.
*   e.   maximizing the rate of energy and matter resource use.

68.   Which of the following statements is the most logical way to cope with the problem of limitations imposed by the three basic physical laws governing matter?
*   a.   Use and waste less energy and matter.
      b.   Shift to nonpolluting nuclear fusion power.
      c.   Increase the output of low-quality heat.
      d.   Increase the input of high-quality energy.
      e.   all of these answers.

69. Which of the following statements about a matter-recycling society is *false?*
    a. The goal of a matter-recycling society is to allow economic growth to continue without depleting matter resources and without producing excessive pollution and environmental degradation.
    b. One limit of a matter-recycling society is dependence on high-quality energy to recycle materials.
    c. A matter-recycling society is limited by the environment's capacity to absorb and disperse waste heat and to dilute and degrade waste matter.
    * d. A matter-recycling society becomes independent of high-quality matter because materials can continue to be recycled indefinitely.
    e. none of these answers.

70. Low-waste societies would do all of the following *except*
    a. use energy more efficiently.
    b. shift to perpetual and renewable energy sources.
    c. recycle and reuse most matter that is now discarded.
    * d. create goods with a short life cycle to increase recycling.
    e. none of these answers.

CHAPTER 4
ECOSYSTEMS: COMPONENTS, ENERGY FLOW, AND MATTER CYCLING

4-1 THE NATURE OF ECOLOGY

1. Ecology is the study of how
   a. atoms make up the environment.
   b. humans affect the environment.
   * c. organisms interact with each other and their nonliving environment.
   d. energy runs the environment.
   e. evolution affects nature

2. What is the goal of ecology?
   a. To eliminate pollution.
   b. To eliminate environmental degradation.
   c. To trace flow of energy through the environment.
   * d. To learn about connections in nature.
   e. To study environmental issues .

3. A group of individuals of the same species occupying a given area at the same time is called a
   a. species.
   * b. population.
   c. community.
   d. genus.
   e. niche

4. The place where an organism lives is its
   a. niche.
   b. community.
   c. ecosystem.
   * d. habitat.
   e. home

5. A community of living organisms interacting with one another and the physical and chemical factors of their nonliving environment is called a(n)
   a. species.
   * b. ecosystem.
   c. population.
   d. lithosphere.
   e. community

6. Which of the following includes all of the others?
   a. species
   b. population
   c. community
   * d. biome
   e. ecosystem

7. The basic unit of life is the
   a. nucleotide.
   b. mitochondrion.
   * c. cell.
   d. tissue.
   e. DNA

8. You are a microbiologist. You observe a cell divide into two identical cells. You are most likely watching
    * a. asexual reproduction.
      b. photosynthesis.
      c. aerobic respiration.
      d. sexual reproduction.
      e. human reproduction

4-2 CONNECTIONS: THE EARTH'S LIFE-SUPPORT SYSTEMS

9. The thin, gaseous layer of air around the planet is called the
    * a. atmosphere.
      b. lithosphere.
      c. stratosphere.
      d. hydrosphere.
      e. troposphere

10. All physical forms of water (solid, liquid, and gas) make up the
      a. atmosphere.
      b. lithosphere.
      c. biosphere.
      d. troposphere.
    * e. hydrosphere.

11. Fossil fuels and minerals are found in the
      a. atmosphere.
    * b. lithosphere.
      c. biosphere.
      d. hydrosphere.
      e. troposphere

12. Submarines explore the
      a. atmosphere.
      b. lithosphere.
      c. biosphere.
    * d. hydrosphere.
      e. troposphere

13. Geologists find rock and soil samples in the
      a. atmosphere.
    * b. lithosphere.
      c. biosphere.
      d. hydrosphere.
      e. troposphere

14. Children fly kites in the
      a. stratosphere.
    * b. troposphere.
      c. biosphere.
      d. hydrosphere.
      e. lithosphere

15. Ecosphere is the same as
    a. atmosphere.
    b. lithosphere.
 * c. biosphere.
    d. hydrosphere.
    e. troposphere

16. Life on earth depends on the interaction of gravity and the
 * a. one-way flow of energy.
    b. cycling of energy.
    c. one-way flow of matter.
    d. the destruction of matter.
    e. the consumption of matter

17. Energy
    a. recycles through the ecosystem.
 * b. flows in only one direction.
    c. is used over and over again.
    d. tends to be concentrated by living organisms.
    e. flows in two directions.

18. The sun is composed primarily of
 * a. hydrogen.
    b. helium.
    c. heavy metals.
    d. ions.
    e. nitrogen

19. Which of the following statements is *false?*
    a. About one-quarter of the solar energy hitting the earth is immediately reflected back to space.
    b. A spectrum of electromagnetic radiation emanates from the sun.
 * c. About one-quarter of the solar energy hitting the earth warms the land and lower atmosphere, runs cycles of matter, and generates winds.
    d. Less than 1% of sunlight is captured via photosynthesis.
    e. none of these answers.

20. When incoming solar radiation is converted to heat, it is *least* likely to be trapped in the atmosphere by
    a. water vapor.
    b. carbon dioxide.
    c. methane.
 * d. nitrogen gas.
    e. methane

4-3   ECOSYSTEM CONCEPTS AND COMPONENTS

21. The primary factor determining the types and abundance of life in a particular land area is
 * a. climate.
    b. longitude.
    c. weather.
    d. soil.
    e. minerals.

22. All of the following are abiotic factors *except*
   a. light.
   * b. bacteria.
   c. pH.
   d. size of soil particles.
   e. water.

23. Which of the following statements is *false?*
   a. The existence, abundance, and distribution of a species in an ecosystem are determined by whether the levels of one or more physical or chemical factors fall within the range tolerated by a species.
   b. Organisms can adapt to slowly changing new conditions by acclimation.
   c. Too much or too little of any abiotic factor can limit or prevent growth of a population of a species in an ecosystem even if all other factors are at or near the optimum range of tolerance.
   * d. There is no such thing as too much fertilizer.
   e. none of these answers.

24. The factor *least* likely to limit growth of a population in a land ecosystem is
   * a. salinity.
   b. temperature.
   c. water.
   d. soil nutrients.
   e. sunlight.

25. In aquatic ecosystems, the factor *least* likely to limit growth of a population is
   a. salinity.
   b. temperature.
   c. sunlight.
   d. dissolved oxygen.
   * e. precipitation.

26. The most inclusive components of the biotic portion of an ecosystem are
   * a. producers, consumers, and decomposers.
   b. primary and secondary consumers.
   c. herbivores, carnivores, and omnivores.
   d. all nonliving chemicals or matter.
   e. none of these answers.

27. Autotrophs
   a. can live without heterotrophs.
   b. are know as producers.
   c. carry on photosynthesis.
   * d. all of these answers.
   e. none of these answers.

28. Photosynthesis
   a. converts glucose into energy and water.
   b. requires the combustion of carbon.
   c. produces carbon dioxide and oxygen gas.
   * d. yields glucose and oxygen gas as products.
   e. yields glucose and carbon dioxide as products.

29. The conversion of solar energy into chemical energy occurs in
    * a. photosynthesis.
    b. food chains.
    c. chemosynthesis.
    d. heterotrophic organisms.
    e. food webs.

30. Chemosynthesis could utilize _____ as an energy source.
    a. sunlight.
    b. carbon dioxide.
    * c. hydrogen sulfide.
    d. heat generated by radioactive decay in the earth's core.
    e. oxygen.

31. Organisms that feed on plants are called
    a. detritus feeders.
    b. omnivores.
    c. carnivores.
    * d. herbivores.
    e. decomposers.

32. Organisms that feed on both plants and animals are called
    a. detritus feeders.
    * b. omnivores.
    c. carnivores.
    d. herbivores.
    e. decomposers.

33. All of the following are consumers *except*
    a. herbivores.
    b. carnivores.
    c. omnivores.
    * d. producers.
    e. decomposers.

34. The organisms that are classified as primary consumers are the
    a. detritivores.
    b. omnivores.
    c. carnivores.
    d. decomposers.
    * e. herbivores.

35. Vultures, hyenas, and flies are all examples of
    a. detritivores.
    b. detritus feeders.
    c. decomposers.
    * d. scavengers.
    e. omnivores

36. In the field, you observe a lion chase, kill, and eat a gazelle. A vulture pecks away at the left over meat scraps. Crabs attack the remaining fragments. Finally, bacteria complete the breakdown and recycling of organic material. If you were to apply a general classification to the feeders, what would be the correct sequence?
    a. decomposer—>scavenger—>detritus feeder—>carnivore
    b. carnivore—>detritus feeder—>scavenger—>decomposer
  * c. carnivore—>scavenger—>detritus feeder—>decomposer
    d. carnivore—>scavenger—>decomposer—>detritus feeder
    e. scavenger→carnivore→detritus feeder→decomposer

37. Organisms that live off parts of dead organisms and cast-off fragments and wastes of living organisms are called
    a. detritivores.
    b. detritus feeders.
    c. decomposers.
  * d. scavengers.
    e. omnivores

38. Organisms that complete the final breakdown and recycling of organic materials from the remains or wastes of all organisms are called
    a. detritivores.
    b. detritus feeders.
  * c. decomposers.
    d. scavengers.
    e. omnivores

39. Carpenter ants, termites, earthworms, and wood beetles are all examples of
    a. detritivores.
  * b. detritus feeders.
    c. decomposers.
    d. scavengers.
    e. primary producers

40. If something is biodegradable, it
    a. can be broken down by autotrophs.
    b. can be broken down by heterotrophs.
    c. can be broken down by omnivores.
    d. cannot be broken down by any living processes.
  * e. can be broken down by decomposers.

41. Aerobic respiration requires
    a. glucose and carbon dioxide.
  * b. glucose and oxygen.
    c. oxygen and water.
    d. carbon dioxide and water.
    e. carbon dioxide and oxygen.

42. Anaerobic respiration may produce all of the following *except*
    a. methane gas.
    b. hydrogen sulfide.
  * c. carbon dioxide and water.
    d. ethyl alcohol.
    e. none of these answers.

43. The process that results in alcoholic beverages is
    a. aerobic respiration.
  * b. anaerobic respiration.
    c. photosynthesis.
    d. chemosynthesis.
    e. none of these answers.

44. An ecosystem can survive without
    a. producers.
  * b. consumers.
    c. decomposers.
    d. autotrophs.
    e. none of these answers.

45. Which term includes the others?
    a. species diversity
    b. genetic diversity
  * c. biological diversity
    d. ecological diversity
    e. functional diversity

4-4   CONNECTIONS: FOODS WEBS AND ENERGY FLOW IN ECOSYSTEMS

46. Complex feeding patterns for consumers in an ecosystem are called
  * a. food webs.
    b. food chains.
    c. trophic levels.
    d. pyramids of energy.
    e. trophic chains.

47. Most of the energy input in a food chain is
    a. in the form of heat.
    b. converted to biomass.
    c. recycled as it reaches the chain's end.
  * d. degraded to low-quality heat.
    e. converted to carbon dioxide.

48. The shorter the food chain the
  * a. smaller the loss of usable energy.
    b. fewer the number of organisms supported.
    c. lower the net primary productivity.
    d. smaller the gross primary productivity.
    e. all of these answers.

49. Which of the following statements is *false?*
  * a. There is considerable waste in functioning natural ecosystems.
    b. Food webs reflect the complexity of real ecosystems better than food chains.
    c. Producers belong to the first trophic level.
    d. Primary consumers are on a lower trophic level than secondary consumers.
    e. Tertiary consumers are on the highest trophic level.

50. Which of the following would be considered a tertiary consumer?
    a. phytoplankton
    b. zooplankton
  * c. osprey
    d. jellyfish
    e. sea slugs.

51. The amount of energy transferred from an organism on one trophic level to the next trophic level is about _____%.
    a. 1
  * b. 10
    c. 15
    d. 25
    e. 50

52. The "ironclad" ecological pyramid with no exceptions is the pyramid of
  * a. energy.
    b. biomass.
    c. numbers.
    d. herbivores.
    e. carnivores.

4-5   PRIMARY PRODUCTIVITY OF ECOSYSTEMS

53. Net primary productivity
    a. is the rate at which producers manufacture chemical energy through photosynthesis.
    b. is the rate at which producers use chemical energy through respiration.
    c. is the rate of photosynthesis plus the rate of respiration.
  * d. is usually reported as the energy output of a specified area of producers over a given time.
    e. none of these answers.

54. Which of the following ecosystems has the lowest productivity?
    a. savanna
    b. tropical rain forest
  * c. open ocean
    d. lakes and streams
    e. temperate forest

55. Which of the following ecosystems has the highest net primary productivity?
    a. agricultural land
    b. open ocean
    c. temperate forest
  * d. swamps and marshes
    e. lakes and streams

56. Which of the following statements is *false?*
    a. Biomass is the organic matter synthesized by producers.
    b. Energy pyramids show why a larger human population can be supported if people eat grains rather than animals.
  * c. Plants from swamps and marshes are a good alternative food for the growing human population.
    d. Clearing tropical forests rapidly depletes soil nutrients.
    e. none of these answers.

4-6   CONNECTIONS: MATTER CYCLING IN ECOSYSTEMS

57. All of the following are elements involved in major biogeochemical cycles *except*
    a. nitrogen.
  * b. calcium.
    c. sulfur.
    d. oxygen.
    e. water.

58. The hydrologic cycle refers to the movement of
    a. hydrogen.
    b. oxygen.
    c. nitrogen.
    d. hydrocarbons.
  * e. water.

59. Of the following water-cycle processes, the one working against gravity is
    a. percolation.
    b. infiltration.
    c. runoff.
  * d. transpiration.
    e. precipitation.

60. The hydrologic cycle is driven primarily by
  * a. solar energy and gravity.
    b. solar energy and the moon.
    c. solar energy and mechanical energy.
    d. mechanical and chemical energy.
    e. chemical energy and the moon.

61. The amount of water vapor found in a certain mass of air is the
    a. relative humidity.
  * b. absolute humidity.
    c. average humidity.
    d. air pressure.
    e. dew point.

62. Condensation nuclei form from all of the following *except*
    a. sea salt.
    b. soil dust.
  * c. carbon monoxide emitted from vehicles.
    d. volcanic ash.
    e. smoke.

63. Humans *strongly* affect the hydrologic cycle through all of the following *except*
    a. water withdrawal in heavily populated areas.
    b. clearing vegetation for agriculture.
    c. creating housing developments.
    d. paving roads and parking lots.
  * e. boiling water.

64. A key component of nature's thermostat is
    a. oxygen.
  * b. carbon dioxide.
    c. glucose.
    d. methane.
    e. nitrogen.

65. All of the following increase the amount of carbon dioxide in the atmosphere *except*
    a. respiration.
  * b. photosynthesis.
    c. combustion.
    d. decomposition.
    e. none of these answers.

66. Transfer of carbon among organisms depends primarily on
    a. fuel combustion and decomposition.
  * b. photosynthesis and cellular respiration.
    c. soil bacteria and precipitation.
    d. volcanic activity and organic decay.
    e. the rock cycle.

67. Of the following carbon-based compounds, which would have the slowest turnover rate?
  * a. calcium carbonate shells
    b. wood in a tree
    c. protein in a cow
    d. DNA in a bacterium
    e. fats in humans.

68. The two ways in which humans interfere with the carbon cycle are
    a. removal of forests and aerobic respiration.
    b. aerobic respiration and burning fossil fuels.
    c. respiration and photosynthesis.
  * d. burning fossil fuels and removal of forests.
    e. respiration and removal or forests.

69. The most common gas in the atmosphere is
  * a. nitrogen.
    b. carbon dioxide.
    c. oxygen.
    d. hydrogen.
    e. methane.

70. Nitrogen is a major component of all of the following *except*
    a. proteins.
    b. nitrites.
    c. ammonia.
    d. DNA
  * e. groundwater.

71. Nodules containing nitrogen-fixing bacteria would be expected to occur on the roots of
    a. pines.
    b. roses.
  * c. legumes.
    d. grasses.
    e. oak trees.

72. Nitrogen fixation is accomplished by
    a. legumes.
  * b. cyanobacteria.
    c. algae.
    d. protozoa.
    e. round worms.

73. The form of nitrogen most usable to plants is
    a. ammonia.
    b. nitrogen gas.
    c. proteins.
  * d. nitrates.
    e. methane.

74. Ammonium ions are converted to nitrite ions and nitrate ions through the process of
    * a. nitrification.
    b. nitrogen fixation.
    c. denitrification.
    d. assimilation.
    e. leaching.

75. Nitrogen gas is converted to nitrate through
    a. ammonification.
    * b. nitrogen fixation.
    c. denitrification.
    d. assimilation.
    e. leaching.

76. When organisms die, their nitrogenous organic compounds are converted to simpler inorganic compounds such as ammonia through the process of
    a. nitrification.
    * b. ammonification.
    c. denitrification.
    d. assimilation.
    e. leaching.

77. Inorganic nitrogen-containing ions are converted into organic molecules through
    a. nitrification.
    b. nitrogen fixation.
    c. denitrification.
    * d. assimilation.
    e. leaching.

78. Ammonia is converted to nitrate and finally to nitrogen gas through the process of
    a. nitrification.
    b. nitrogen fixation.
    c. leaching.
    d. ammonification.
    * e. denitrification.

79. Which of the following statements about human alteration of the nitrogen cycle is *false?*
    * a. Eating protein puts "dead ends" in the nitrogen cycle.
    b. Nitric oxide can be converted in the atmosphere to nitric acid, which contributes to acid deposition.
    c. Nitrous oxide, released by bacterial action on commercial inorganic fertilizers, is a heat-trapping gas.
    d. Nitrate and ammonium ions are depleted from the soil by harvesting nitrogen-rich crops.
    e. Irrigation of crops removes nitrogen from topsoil.

80. All of the following human behaviors substantially affect the nitrogen cycle in aquatic systems *except*
    * a. runoff from salt-treated icy highways.
    b. using nitrogen fertilizers.
    c. runoff from feedlots.
    d. adding sewage to aquatic systems.
    e. none of these answers.

81. Which one of the following is *not* one of the common phosphorous reservoirs in the ecosystem?
    a. water
    b. organisms
    * c. atmosphere
    d. rocks
    e. marine sediment

82. To which of the following cycles is guano an important component?
    * a. phosphorous
    b. carbon
    c. hydrologic
    d. sulfur
    e. water

83. All of the following are sources of phosphorous *except*
    a. inorganic fertilizer.
    b. runoff of animal wastes from feedlots.
    c. detergents.
    * d. acid rain.
    e. rocks.

84. The major plant nutrient most likely to be a limiting factor is
    * a. phosphorous.
    b. calcium.
    c. nitrogen.
    d. potassium.
    e. carbon.

85. The primary location of sulfur is the
    a. troposphere.
    b. stratosphere.
    c. atmosphere.
    d. hydrosphere.
    * e. lithosphere.

86. Humans intervene in the phosphorous cycle by
    a. mining large quantities of phosphate rock.
    b. using phosphate-based detergents.
    c. adding runoff of animal wastes from livestock feedlots to aquatic ecosystems.
    d. discharge of municipal sewage.
    * e. all of these answers.

87. Sulfur naturally enters the atmosphere from
    a. manufacturing plastic bottles.
    b. nuclear power plants.
    c. burning matches.
    * d. hydrogen sulfide from volcanoes.
    e. animal waste runoff

88. About _____ of all sulfur reaching the atmosphere comes from human activities.
    a. 1/2
    * b. 1/3
    c. 1/4
    d. 1/5
    e. 1/6

89. All of the following human activities intervene in the sulfur cycle except
    a. smelting sulfur compounds of metallic minerals into free metals.
    b. burning sulfur-containing oil.
    c. burning sulfur-containing coal.
 * d. burning sulfur-containing wood.
    e. refining sulfur-containing petroleum

4-7   HOW DO ECOLOGISTS LEARN ABOUT ECOSYSTEMS?

90. Which statement describes field research *least?*
    a. It has been used to develop most of our knowledge about ecosystems.
 * b. It is comparatively easy to set up controlled experiments.
    c. It is relatively time-consuming.
    d. It is relatively expensive.
    e. none of these answers.

91. Which statement *least* characterizes laboratory research?
    a. It allows measurement of model ecosystems and populations under controlled conditions.
    b. It is faster than similar field research.
    c. It is cheaper than similar field research.
 * d. It has been used to develop most of our knowledge about ecosystems.
    e. none of these answers.

92. Which statement *least* characterizes systems analysis as a research strategy?
 * a. It is usually carried out by an expert in the field.
    b. It has developed over the last twenty-five years.
    c. It can be applied to complex systems that cannot be adequately studied in the field or laboratory.
    d. It can simulate ecosystems.
    e. none of these answers.

4-8   CONNECTIONS: ECOSYSTEM SERVICES AND SUSTAINABILITY

93. The cycling of oxygen and carbon, the decomposition of dead organisms, and the food that we eat are examples of
    a. nonrenewable resources.
    b. biodiversity.
    c. renewable resources.
    d. entropy.
 * e. ecosystem services.

94. What are the two basic principles of ecosystem sustainability?
    a. Use fossil fuels for energy and reuse organic materials.
 * b. Use sunlight for energy and recycle nutrients.
    c. Use fossil fuels for energy and recycle nutrients.
    d. Use sunlight for energy and reuse organic materials.
    e. Use fossil fuel and sunlight energy.

CHAPTER 5
EVOLUTION AND BIODIVERSITY: ORIGINS, NICHES, AND ADAPTATION

5-1   ORIGINS OF LIFE

1.   Evidence for the evolution of life comes from
       a.   chemical experiments.
       b.   fossils.
       c.   chemical analysis of ancient rocks and core samples.
  *   d.   all of these answers.
       e.   DNA

2.   You are a fossil hunter. Which of the following are you least likely to find in a fossil?
       a.   bone
       b.   leaves
       c.   teeth
  *   d.   muscle
       e.   shells

3 .   The fossil record is incomplete because
       a.   not all fossils have been found.
       b.   some fossils have decomposed.
       c.   some life forms left no fossils.
  *   d.   all of these answers.
       e.   none of these answers.

5-2   EVOLUTION AND ADAPTATION

4.   A change in the genetic composition of a population over successive generations is called
       a.   emigration.
       b.   mutation.
       c.   natural selection.
  *   d.   evolution.
       e.   genetic drift.

5.   The term that describes small genetic changes that a population within a species experiences is
       a.   coevolution.
  *   b.   microevolution.
       c.   convergent evolution.
       d.   macroevolution.
       e.   genetic drift.

6.   The term used to describe the long-term, large-scale evolutionary changes among groups of species is
       a.   coevolution.
       b.   microevolution.
       c.   convergent evolution.
       d.   genetic drift.
  *   e.   macroevolution.

7.   A gene pool is
       a.   the collection of genes being used in the human genome project.
       b.   the genetic composition of an organism.
  *   c.   the genetic composition of a population.
       d.   the genetic composition of a community.
       e.   the genetic composition of an ecosystem.

8.   Mutations can be caused by
      a.   ultraviolet light.
      b.   X rays.
      c.   certain chemicals.
*   d.   all of these answers.
      e.   radioactivity.

9.   The change from a light to a dark color in the peppered moth was the result of
      a.   insecticides.
      b.   migration.
      c.   a change in predators.
      d.   an increase in ultraviolet radiation.
*   e.   industrial pollution.

10.   The changes in coloration within the population of peppered moths is an example of
      a.   coevolution.
*   b.   microevolution.
      c.   convergent evolution.
      d.   macroevolution.
      e.   none of these answers.

11.   Mutations are
      a.   always occurring in patterns.
      b.   very common events.
*   c.   a source of new genetic material.
      d.   always harmful.
      e.   all of these answers.

12.   You are an evolutionary biologist studying a population of bats in the rainforest of Brazil. Most of
      the population possesses moderate length wings, although some individuals have long wings and
      some individuals have short wings. Over the course of time, you notice that the frequency of
      moderate-length wings increases. You conclude that the most likely cause of this development is
*   a.   stabilizing natural selection.
      b.   directional natural selection.
      c.   diversifying natural selection.
      d.   coevolution.
      e.   continuous natural selection.

13.   As you study a population of fruit flies, you notice that pink eye color is the most common, although
      white eyes and red eyes are also present. Over the course of time and many generations, you notice
      that the proportion of individuals with pink eyes steadily increases. You conclude that this
      population is undergoing
      a.   continuous natural selection.
      b.   diversifying natural selection.
      c.   directional natural selection.
*   d.   stabilizing natural selection.
      e.   coevolution.

14.   In a population of cats, you notice there is considerable variation of length of fur. Over the course of
      time, you observe that there are many cats that exhibit very long fur and many with very short fur.
      However, there are few cats that exhibit an intermediate length of fur. You conclude that this
      population is undergoing
      a.   continuous natural selection.
      b.   discontinuous natural selection.
*   c.   diversifying natural selection.
      d.   directional natural selection.
      e.   coevolution.

15. You study fossils of giraffes. Although there appears to be considerable variability in lengths of necks, there appears to be a definite shift to longer necks over the course of time. You conclude that this species is undergoing
    a. continuous natural selection.
    b. discontinuous natural selection.
    c. diversifying natural selection.
 * d. directional natural selection.
    e. coevolution.

16. When natural selection results in a shift toward one end of a normal range of traits, an evolutionary biologist would credit
    a. continuous natural selection.
    b. discontinuous natural selection.
    c. diversifying natural selection.
 * d. directional natural selection.
    e. coevolution.

17. When natural selection results in a shift toward the average of a range of genetic expressions for a particular trait, an evolutionary biologist would credit
 * a. stabilizing natural selection.
    b. discontinuous natural selection.
    c. diversifying natural selection.
    d. directional natural selection.
    e. coevolution.

18. When natural selection shifts allelic frequencies toward the extremes of a range of genetic expressions for a particular trait, an evolutionary biologist would credit
    a. continuous natural selection.
    b. discontinuous natural selection.
 * c. diversifying natural selection.
    d. directional natural selection.
    e. coevolution.

19. Coevolution can involve the interaction of
    a. plants and herbivores.
    b. pollinators and flowers.
    c. parasites and hosts.
    d. plant roots and fungi.
 * e. all of these answers.

20. Which of the following is *false?* Coevolution
    a. occurs when interacting species exert selective pressures on each other.
    b. occurs between plants and the herbivores that eat them.
    c. may play a role in the evolution of camouflage.
 * d. leads to competitive relationships.
    e. all of these answers.

21. Over the course of time, the change in the gene pool of one species may lead to the change of the gene pool of another species. This process is called
 * a. coevolution.
    b. microevolution.
    c. convergent evolution.
    d. macroevolution.
    e. diversifying natural selection.

22.   An organism's niche is analogous to its
       a.   address.
    * b.   way of life.
       c.   food source.
       d.   trash dump.
       e.   all of these answers.

23.   An ecological niche includes all of the following *except*
       a.   the nutrient relationships with other species.
    * b.   the location where a species lives.
       c.   the types of resource requirements.
       d.   the range of tolerance to different physical and chemical conditions.
       e.   the types of competitors.

24.   Which of the following best describes an organism's habitat?
       a.   the nutrient relationships with other species.
    * b.   the location where a species lives.
       c.   the types of resource requirements.
       d.   the range of tolerance to different physical and chemical conditions.
       e.   the types of competitors.

25.   A species has the potential to survive successfully over a wide area and range of habitats and local
       conditions, but it only occurs in a few habitats in a localized area. Which of the following describes
       this species exploitation of its niche?
       a.   fundamental niche
       b.   general niche
       c.   required niche
       d.   specialized niche
    * e.   realized niche

26.   Specialist species
       a.   are very adaptable.
       b.   tolerate a wide range of environments.
    * c.   are more likely to become extinct.
       d.   eat a wide variety of food.
       e.   all of these answers.

27.   Which of the following is a specialist?
       a.   cockroach
       b.   fly
       c.   human
    * d.   giant panda
       e.   bear

28.   Which of the following statements is *false?*
       a.   Genetic diversity helps prevent a species from becoming extinct.
       b.   The phenomenon in which animals with favorable adaptation reproduce more rapidly is called
             differential reproduction.
       c.   Geographic isolation is a common mechanism contributing to speciation.
    * d.   By definition, the fittest animals are the largest and strongest animals.
       e.   A change in environmental conditions can lead to adaptation only for traits already present in the
             gene pool of a population.

29. Which of the following is *not* a common misconception about evolution?
    a.   Evolution is a grand plan of the perfecting of species.
    b.   In a Darwinian world, the strongest survive.
    c.   Humans evolved from apes.
*   d.   The key to survival in a Darwinian world is coexistence through occupying different niches.
    e.   Evolution is a plan in which species become increasingly more perfect.

5-4   SPECIATION, EXTINCTION, AND BIODIVERSITY

30. Geographic isolation may result from
    a.   a volcanic eruption.
    b.   an earthquake.
    c.   a mountain range.
*   d.   all of these answers.
    e.   a river.

31. Geographic isolation is *least* likely to give rise to
    a.   reproductive isolation.
    b.   speciation.
*   c.   convergent evolution.
    d.   divergent evolution.
    e.   none of these answers.

32. Patterns of speciation and extinction are least likely to be affected by
    a.   climatic changes.
    b.   continental drift.
    c.   meteorites crashing into the earth.
*   d.   changes in the weather.
    e.   human activity.

33. Biodiversity is believed to be the result of
    a.   divergent and convergent evolution.
*   b.   speciation and extinction.
    c.   speciation and coevolution.
    d.   extinction and coevolution.
    e.   divergent evolution and coevolution.

34. Biologists estimate that over _____% of the species that have ever lived are now extinct.
    a.   59
    b.   69
    c.   79
    d.   89
*   e.   99

35. Which of the following statements about extinctions is *false?*
    a.   Biologists estimate that 99% of all the species that have ever existed are now extinct.
    b.   Mass extinctions raise the extinction rate above the background extinction rate.
    c.   Most mass extinctions are believed to be due to global climatic changes.
*   d.   Earth has experienced over a dozen great mass extinctions.
    e.   none of these answers.

36. It takes on the order of _____ years for adaptive radiations to rebuild biological diversity after a mass extinction.
    a. 100
    b. 100 thousand
    c. 1 million
  * d. 10 million
    e. 100 million

CHAPTER 6
CLIMATE, TERRESTRIAL BIODIVERSITY, AND AQUATIC BIODIVERSITY

***

6-1   WEATHER AND CLIMATE: A BRIEF INTRODUCTION

1.   Weather occurs
    a.   in the troposphere.
    b.   at a particular place.
    c.   at a particular time.
*   d.   all of these answers.
    e.   none of these answers

2.   Climate
    a.   describes long-term weather patterns.
    b.   describes seasonal variations.
    c.   describes weather extremes.
*   d.   all of these answers.
    e.   none of these answers

3.   Climate is the general pattern of weather over a period of at least
    a.   10 years.
    b.   20 years.
*   c.   30 years.
    d.   50 years.
    e.   75 years

4.   The two most important factors in climate are
    a.   temperature and insulation.
    b.   precipitation and pressure.
    c.   humidity, clouds, and wind.
    d.   temperature and wind.
*   e.   temperature and precipitation.

5.   Climate is influenced by
    a.   the moon's gravity.
    b.   the size of the Earth.
*   c.   the distribution of land, ~~and~~ water and topography.
    d.   the distribution of thunderstorms.
    e.   the earth's gravity

6.   Which of the following statements is false?
    a.   The amount of solar energy reaching Earth's surface is dependent on latitude.
    b.   Hot air rises.
*   c.   Air at the lower latitudes tends to cool and fall or sink downward.
    d.   Cool air is denser than warm air.
    e.   Cool air falls.

7.   Which of the following statements of cause and effect is false?
    a.   The differential in solar energy striking the equator versus the poles sets up general global air circulation patterns.
*   b.   Earth's rotating faster under air at the poles causes the prevailing winds.
    c.   Earth's rotational tilt and revolution around the sun cause seasonal variations in temperature.
    d.   Greenhouse gases let in the sun's ultraviolet radiation and trap infrared waves radiated from Earth.
    e.   Heat from the sun evaporates ocean water and transfers hear from the oceans to the atmosphere.

8.   There are _____ separate belts of moving air or prevailing winds.
      a.   two
      b.   four
  *   c.   six
      d.   Eight
      e.   ten

9.   Which of the following wind patterns is found at the equator?
  *   a.   doldrums
      b.   trade winds
      c.   easterlies
      d.   southerlies
      e.   northerlies

10.   The term upwelling refers to the movement of
      a.   warm surface water.
  *   b.   cool nutrient-rich water from the bottom to the surface.
      c.   warm water replacing cool water.
      d.   cool water from the Arctic toward the equator.
      e.   warm nutrient-rich water from the bottom to the surface.

11.   Upwellings
      a.   cause the death of phytoplankton.
      b.   result in small populations of seabirds.
      c.   produce conditions that kill a large number of fish.
      d.   create El Niño -Southern Oscillation.
  *   e.   are highly productive areas.

12.   Where do upwellings characteristically occur?
      a.   in the open ocean.
      b.   on the east side of continents.
      c.   near coral reefs.
  *   d.   on steep western sides of continents.
      e.   they occur equally anywhere in the ocean.

13.   During an El Niño–Southern Oscillation (ENSO),
      a.   prevailing easterly winds weaken.
      b.   surface water along the South and North American coasts becomes cooler.
  *   c.   upwellings of cold, nutrient-rich water are suppressed.
      d.   upwellings of warm, nutrient-poor water are suppressed.
      e.   upwellings of cold, nutrient-rich water are increased.

14.   The term greenhouse effect
      a.   describes occupational diseases of florists.
  *   b.   describes the trapping of heat energy in the troposphere by certain gaseous molecules.
      c.   describes the trapping of heat energy in the stratosphere by nitrogen.
      d.   describes efforts by the White House to support environmental legislation.
      e.   describes the trapping of heat energy in the troposphere by nitrogen.

15.   All of the following are greenhouse gases except
      a.   carbon dioxide.
      b.   water vapor.
      c.   methane.
  *   d.   nitrogen.
      e.   chlorofluorocarbons (CFCs)

16. Ozone
    a. in the stratosphere is a pollutant.
    b. is formed in the stratosphere through the interaction of infrared radiation and molecular oxygen.
    c. filters out all harmful ultraviolet radiation.
    * d. in the stratosphere forms a thermal cap important in determining the average temperature of the troposphere.
    e. is O_3.

17. The rain shadow effect refers to
    a. more light on the windward side of mountain ranges.
    b. more light on the leeward side of mountain ranges.
    c. drier conditions on the windward side of mountain ranges.
    * d. drier conditions on the leeward side of mountain ranges.
    e. wetter conditions on the windward side of mountain ranges.

18. Microclimates are least likely to be produced by
    a. mountains.
    b. bodies of water.
    c. cities.
    * d. flat plains.
    e. sand dunes

19. A rain shadow is most likely to be produced by a
    a. forest.
    b. ocean.
    c. lake.
    d. sand dune.
    * e. mountain.

20. Which of the following microclimate effects is incorrectly described?
    a. The leeward sides of high mountains tend to show relatively dry conditions.
    b. Oceans and lakes modify temperature extremes.
    c. Forests have fewer temperature extremes and lower wind speeds than nearby open land.
    * d. Cities tend to have lower temperatures and higher wind speeds than the surrounding countryside.
    e. The windward sides of high mountains tend to show relatively wet conditions.

6-2   BIOMES: CLIMATE AND LIFE ON LAND

21. Large ecological regions with characteristic types of natural vegetation are called
    a. ecosystems.
    b. communities.
    c. populations.
    * d. biomes.
    e. niches

22. The distribution of the desert, grassland, and forest biomes is determined principally by
    a. temperature.
    * b. precipitation.
    c. latitude.
    d. sunlight.
    e. wind

23. The limiting factor that controls the vegetative character of a biome is
    a. light.
    * b. precipitation.
    c. nutrients.
    d. animal species.
    e. temperature

24. Climate and vegetation vary with
    a. latitude only.
    b. altitude only.
    * c. latitude and altitude.
    d. latitude and longitude.
    e. altitude and longitude

25. Trees of wet tropical rain forests tend to be
    a. succulent plants.
    * b. broadleaf evergreen plants.
    c. broadleaf deciduous plants.
    d. coniferous evergreen plants.
    e. coniferous deciduous plants.

26. Which of the following are examples of deciduous plants?
    * a. maples and oaks
    b. algae and seaweed
    c. bacteria
    d. pines and cedars
    e. fungi

27. Which of the following are examples of evergreen plants?
    a. maples and oaks
    b. algae and seaweed
    c. bacteria
    d. fungi
    * e pines and cedars

28. Succulent plants are *most* likely to be found in
    a. aquatic habitats.
    b. cold ecosystems.
    c. high altitudes.
    * d. deserts.
    e. coastal ecosystems

6-3 DESERT AND GRASSLAND BIOMES

29. Which of the following is not characteristic of desert plants?
    a. widespread, shallow root systems
    b. deep root systems
    * c. large leaves that droop in the bright sunlight
    d. succulent leaves or stems
    e. becoming dormant during dry periods.

30. All of the following are common adaptations made by animals to the desert *except*
    a. living underground during the heat of the day.
    b. having thick outer coverings to minimize water loss
    * c. drink and store large amounts of water
    d. become dormant during periods of extreme heat or drought
    e. excreting dry feces

31. The fragility of the desert ecosystem is indicated by
    a. the high growth rate of plants.
    b. moderate species diversity.
    c. abundant groundwater.
    * d. long regeneration time from vegetation destruction.
    e. having shallow roots.

32. Off-road vehicles are a major threat to
    a. grassland.
  * b. desert.
    c. tundra.
    d. taiga.
    e. tropical rainforest

33. Human impacts on deserts include
    a. encroachment by rapidly growing cities.
    b. disruption by extraction of mineral resources and building materials.
    c. lowering of the aquifers.
  * d. all of these answers.
    e. none of these answers.

34. A tropical grassland with scattered shrubs and stunted trees would be called a
    a. veld.
    b. steppes.
  * c. savanna.
    d. pampas.
    e. taiga

35. If you were a National Geographic reporter assigned to cover large herds of grazing, hoofed animals, where would you most likely journey?
    a. Arctic tundra
    b. tropical forest
    c. deciduous forest
    d. taiga
  * e. savanna

36. All of the following would be considered types of temperate grasslands except
    a. steppes.
    b. veldt.
  * c. taiga.
    d. pampas.
    e. tall-grass prairies

37. You read the data records of a field ecologist who reports the following varieties of species: beetles, spiders, grasshoppers, many insects and invertebrates, earthworms, prairie dogs, rabbits, squirrels, meadowlarks, coyotes, foxes, hawks. You conclude that the field ecologist is located in a
    a. desert.
    b. tropical grassland.
  * c. temperate grassland.
    d. arctic tundra.
    e. tropical rainforest

38. Many species of hoofed animals can live together in the African tropical savannas because they have _____ eating habits that _____ competition for resources.
    a. specialized . . . maximize
  * b. specialized . . . minimize
    c. generalized . . . maximize
    d. generalized . . . minimize
    e. none of the above.

39.   The _____ are located in Europe.
       a.   veldt
   *   b.   steppes
       c.   savanna
       d.   pampas
       e.   tall-grass prairies

40.   Recurring fires in summer and fall are most typical of
       a.   desert.
       b.   topical grassland.
   *   c.   temperate grassland.
       d.   polar grassland.
       e.   taiga

41.   You are going on a scientific expedition from the equator to the North Pole. As you leave the boreal
       forest behind, you anticipate next exploring
       a.   gases captured in the ice.
       b.   the fall leaves of New England.
       c.   patterns of cone design in coniferous trees.
       d.   germination patterns of tall-prairie grasses.
   *   e.   the role of lichens and mosses in boggy ecosystems.

42.   Permafrost and lichens are characteristic of the _____ biome.
       a.   tropical savanna
   *   b.   Arctic tundra
       c.   taiga
       d.   thorn woodland
       e.   deciduous forest

43.   Through your binoculars you observe a pack of wolves stalking a caribou separated from its herd.
       Geese take to the air, departing the boggy scene. You are most likely in
       a.   desert.
       b.   topical grassland.
       c.   temperate grassland.
   *   d.   polar grassland.
       e.   savanna

44.   Arctic tundra is perhaps Earth's most fragile biome because of
       a.   low rate of decomposition.
       b.   shallow soil.
       c.   slow growth rate of plants.
   *   d.   all of these answers.
       e.   bitter cold

45.   Humans have affected grasslands by
       a.   the introduction of livestock.
       b.   plowing and conversion to croplands.
       c.   oil exploration.
   *   d.   all of these answers.
       e.   none of these answers

46.   The primary limiting factor of the rain forest is
        a.   water.
   *   b.   nutrients.
        c.   temperature.
        d.   light.
        e.   wind

47.   A mature _____ has the greatest species diversity of all terrestrial biomes.
        a.   tundra
        b.   savanna
        c.   taiga
        d.   temperate deciduous forest
   *   e.   tropical rain forest

48.   Which of the following is not appropriate to use in describing a tropical rain forest?
        a.   humid
   *   b.   rich soil
        c.   stratified
        d.   diversity
        e.   rainfall

49.   Which of the following biomes would be considered least fragile?
   *   a.   temperate deciduous forest
        b.   desert
        c.   tropical rain forest
        d.   tundra
        e.   coral reef

50.   Which of the following is false? Deciduous forests
        a.   change significantly during four distinct seasons.
        b.   are dominated by a few species of broadleaf trees.
        c.   have trees that survive winter by dropping their leaves.
   *   d.   have nutrient-poor soil.
        e.   have a thick layer of slowly decaying leaf litter

51.   Which of the following does not belong with the others?
        a.   taiga
   *   b.   steppes
        c.   boreal forest
        d.   northern coniferous forest
        e.   none of these answers

52.   Cone-bearing trees are characteristic of the
   *   a.   taiga.
        b.   tropical rain forest.
        c.   temperate deciduous forest.
        d.   savanna.
        e.   desert

53.   Trees with needlelike leaves that are kept year round are especially abundant in which biome?
        a.   tundra
        b.   tropical rain forest
   *   c.   coniferous forest
        d.   temperate deciduous forest
        e.   desert

54. Which of the following is least descriptive of coniferous forest?
     a. carpet of needles on forest floor
     b. long, cold, dry winter
     c. short summer
   * d. high species diversity
     e. acidic soil

55. Clearing of forests often results in
     a. increased diversity.
     b. decreased rates of soil erosion.
   * c. loss of biodiversity.
     d. an increase in specialist species.
     e. none of these answers

56. The biome most likely to be found on the top of a very tall tropical mountain is the
     a. desert.
   * b. tundra.
     c. grassland.
     d. temperate deciduous forest.
     e. taiga

57. Mountain biomes
     a. have deep, rich soils.
     b. recover quickly from vegetation loss.
     c. do not affect climate
     d. have little biodiversity.
   * e. may act as sanctuaries for animal species driven from lowland areas.

58. Humans affect mountain biomes by
     a. expanding populations who may use the land in an unsustainable way.
     b. ecotourism and recreation.
     c. increase air pollution from urban areas.
   * d. all of these answers.
     e. none of these answers

6-5   AQUATIC ENVIRONMENTS: TYPES AND CHARACTERISTICS

59. In your explorations as a marine biologist, you find a new species of algae floating on the surface of a coastal zone. You would most likely classify this species as
   * a. phytoplankton.
     b. zooplankton.
     c. benthos.
     d. nekton.
     e. decomposer.

60. In a sample from a mud flat, you observe cyanobacteria under the microscope. You are most likely to classify this organism as
   * a. phytoplankton.
     b. zooplankton.
     c. benthos.
     d. nekton.
     e. decomposer.

61. Out on a fishing boat, a swordfish is caught. You would most likely classify this species as a member of the
    a. phytoplankton.
    b. zooplankton.
    c. benthos.
  * d. nekton.
    e. decomposer.

62. All of the following organisms would be considered part of the benthos *except*
  * a. cod.
    b. lobster.
    c. oysters.
    d. sand worms.
    e. crabs.

63. An aquatic environment
    a. concentrates toxic metabolic wastes.
    b. increases fluctuations in temperature.
    c. increases chances of overheating.
  * d. dissolves nutrients and makes them readily available.
    e. all of these answers.

64. Populations of organisms living in aquatic life zones may be limited by
    a. access to light.
    b. nutrient availability.
    c. dissolved oxygen.
  * d. all of these answers.
    e. none of these answers

65. Oxygen in the water varies widely because of
    a. number of consumers and producers.
    b. number of decomposers.
    c. temperature.
    d. number of consumers.
  * e. all of these answers.

6-6 SALTWATER LIFE ZONES

66. Oceans
    a. play a major role in controlling climate by distributing solar heat.
    b. function to dilute and disperse human wastes.
    c. participate in biogeochemical cycles.
  * d. all of these answers.
    e. none of these answers.

67. The ocean zone that covers the continental shelf is the
    a. estuary.
  * b. coastal zone.
    c. littoral zone.
    d. benthic zone.
    e. abyssal zone.

68. The coastal zone has ____% of the ocean's plant and animal life and ____% of its surface area.
    a. 95 . . . 5.
  * b. 90 . . . 10.
    c. 90 . . . 25.
    d. 80 . . . 25.
    e. 80 . . . 10.

69. The deepest part of the ocean is the
    * a. abyssal zone.
    b. euphotic zone.
    c. estuary zone.
    d. bathyal zone.
    e. riparian zone

70. Most photosynthesis in the open sea occurs in the
    * a. euphotic zone.
    b. abyssal zone.
    c. bathyal zone.
    d. coastal zone.
    e. benthic zone.

71. The twilight zone of the sea is the
    a. euphotic zone.
    b. abyssal zone.
    * c. bathyal zone.
    d. coastal zone.
    e. benthic zone.

72. The zone of the ocean with the highest net primary productivity is the
    a. euphotic zone.
    b. abyssal zone.
    c. bathyal zone.
    * d. coastal zone.
    e. benthic zone.

73. Which of the following trees is characteristic of tropical coastal wetlands?
    a. cypress
    b. coconut
    * c. mangrove
    d. palm
    e. live oak.

74. The relationship demonstrated by coral polyps and algae is
    a. predation.
    b. commensalism.
    c. parasitism.
    d. competition.
    * e. mutualism.

75. The least appropriate use of coastal wetlands is for
    a. spawning and nursery grounds.
    * b. condominiums and disposal of landfill waste.
    c. food production.
    d. recreational diving.
    e. education.

76. Estuaries and coastal wetlands are important for all of the following reasons except
    a. spawning and nursery grounds for marine fish and shellfish.
    b. filtering out waterborne pollutants from swimming and wildlife areas.
    c. breeding grounds for waterfowl.
    * d. providing coral for limestone production and the tourist trade.
    e. habitat for alligators.

77. Cities established on barrier islands are subject to
    a. beach erosion.
    b. hurricanes.
    c. flooding.
 * d. all of these answers.
    e. none of these answers

78. The relationship demonstrated by coral polyps and dinoflagellates is
    a. predation.
    b. commensalism.
    c. parasitism.
 * d. mutualism.
    e. partnerism

79. Coral reefs
    a. support a large variety of marine species.
    b. provide food, jobs, and building materials.
    c. protect coastlines from erosion.
 * d. all of these answers.
    e. none of these answers.

80. During the past 200 years, about _____ of the area of estuaries and coastal wetlands in the United
    States has been destroyed or damaged.
    a. one-quarter
    b. one-third
 * c. one-half
    d. two-thirds
    e. three-fourths

81. All of the following threaten the survival of coral reefs except
    a. runoff of toxic pesticides and industrial chemicals.
    b. eroded soil from deforestation and poor land management.
    c. depletion of stratospheric ozone.
 * d. predation by sharks.
    e. collection by tourists.

6-7   FRESHWATER LIFE ZONES

82. Lakes that have few minerals and low productivity are referred to as
    a. autotrophic.
    b. eutrophic.
 * c. oligotrophic.
    d. mesotrophic.
    e. neotrophic

83. Lakes with large nutrient supplies are called
    a. autotrophic.
 * b. eutrophic.
    c. oligotrophic.
    d. mesotrophic.
    e. neotrophic

84. In lakes, the nutrient-rich water near the shore is part of the
    a. limnetic zone.
    b. benthic zone.
 * c. littoral zone.
    d. profundal zone.
    e. abyssal zone.

85. In lakes, the open-water surface layer is called the
  * a. limnetic zone.
  b. benthic zone.
  c. littoral zone.
  d. profundal zone.
  e. abyssal zone.

86. Fish adapted to cool, dark water are most likely found in the zone of lakes called the
  a. limnetic zone.
  b. benthic zone.
  c. littoral zone.
  * d. profundal zone.
  e. abyssal zone.

87. The highest level of dissolved oxygen is most likely to be found in the _____ zone of a river system.
  * a. first
  b. second
  c. third
  d. fourth
  e. fifth.

88. A river is most likely to be wide and deep at its _____ zone.
  a. first
  b. second
  * c. third
  d. fourth
  e. fifth.

89. A mix of warm-water and cold-water fish are most likely to be found in the _____ zone of a river.
  a. first
  * b. second
  c. third
  d. fourth
  e. fifth.

90. Waterfalls are most likely to be found in the _____ zone of a river.
  * a. first
  b. second
  c. third
  d. fourth
  e. fifth.

91. Inland wetlands include all of the following except
  a. bogs.
  b. wet Arctic tundra.
  c. marshes.
  d. swamps.
  * e. estuaries.

92. Inland wetlands are valuable for providing
  a. wildlife habitat.
  b. improved water quality.
  c. regulated stream flow.
  * d. all of these answers.
  e. none of these answers.

93. Inland wetlands are often lost to
    a. croplands.
    b. mining.
    c. urban development.
*   d. all of these answers.
    e. none of these answers.

6-8 SUSTAINABILITY OF AQUATIC LIFE ZONES

94. Life in both saltwater and freshwater ecosystems can be limited by
    a. dissolved oxygen for respiration.
    b. temperature.
    c. access to sunlight for photosynthesis.
*   d. all of these answers.
    e. none of these answers.

95. Which of the following illustrations does not match the accompanying ecological concept.
    a. Coral reefs have high biodiversity.
    b. Estuaries have high productivity.
*   c. Dissolved oxygen is a primary limiting factor in the upper layer of a stratified lake.
    d. The open ocean is the least productive of aquatic life zones.
    e. Littoral zones have high biodiversity.

CHAPTER 7
COMMUNITY ECOLOGY: STRUCTURE, SPECIES INTERACTIONS, SUCCESSION, AND SUSTAINABILITY

1. The relationship between durian plants and flying foxes exemplifies
    a. mutualism and convergent evolution.
    * b. mutualism and coevolution.
    c. commensalism and convergent evolution.
    d. commensalism and coevolution.
    e. parasitism ad coevolution

2. Flying foxes are now listed as endangered because
    a. they congregate and are easy targets.
    b. they are hunted.
    c. of deforestation.
    * d. of all of these answers.
    e. none of these answers.

3. Flying foxes are recognized as a
    a. thriving species.
    b. alien species.
    c. native species.
    * d. keystone species.
    e. indicator species

4. Flying foxes contribute to the economy for the role they play in the production of
    a. tannins and dyes.
    b. animal fodder.
    c. fruits and medicines.
    * d. all of these answers.
    e. none of these answers.

7-1   COMMUNITY STRUCTURE AND SPECIES DIVERSITY

5. Of the following, ecosystem structure is *least* likely to include
    a. species abundance.
    b. species diversity.
    c. physical appearance.
    d. niche structure.
    * e. biochemical reactions in the intestines of detritus feeders.

6. What does *richness* refer to?
    a. the number of individuals of each species
    * b. the number of different species
    c. the number of edge effects
    d. the number of ecotones in an area
    e. the number of different communities

7. Where is most of the world's biodiversity?
    a. high-latitude forests
    b. middle-latitude grasslands
    * c. low-latitude forests
    d. polar grasslands
    e. none of these answers

8. Based on the theory of island biogeography, you would predict that large islands near the mainland would have relatively
    * a. high immigration and low extinction rates.
    b. high immigration and high extinction rates.
    c. low immigration and low extinction rates.
    d. low immigration and high extinction rates.
    e. not enough information to predict.

7-2   GENERAL TYPES OF SPECIES

9. Species that normally live and thrive in a particular ecosystem are known as
    a. nonnative species.
    * b. native species.
    c. keystone species.
    d. specialist species.
    e. indicator species

10. Species that serve as early warnings of environmental damage are called
    a. nonnative species.
    b. native species.
    c. specialist species.
    * d. indicator species.
    e. keystone species.

11. Species whose roles in an ecosystem are much more important than their abundance would suggest are called
    a. nonnative species.
    b. native species.
    * c. keystone species.
    d. specialist species.
    e. indicator species.

12. Species that migrate or are accidentally introduced into an ecosystem are called
    a. indicator species.
    b. native species.
    c. keystone species.
    d. specialist species.
    * e. nonnative species.

13. Which term means the opposite of the others?
    a. exotic species
    * b. native species
    c. alien species
    d. nonnative species
    e. introduced species

14. Which of the following statements about amphibians is *false?*
    a. The oldest of today's amphibians were living as long as 150 million years ago.
    b. Amphibians are important indicator species.
    c. Amphibians are experiencing sharp population declines in a variety of habitats.
    * d. Amphibians eat many insects, second in number only to birds.
    e. They are often considered indicator species.

15. Characteristics that make amphibians particularly sensitive to pollution include
    a. living part of their life cycle in water and part on land.
    b. soft, permeable skin.
    c. sensitivity to ultraviolet radiation.
* d. all of these answers.
    e. none of these answers.

16. Birds and trout make good
    a. nonnative species.
    b. native species.
    c. keystone species.
* d. indicator species.
    e. specialist species.

17. Wild African bees are best described as
* a. nonnative species.
    b. native species.
    c. keystone species.
    d. specialist species.
    e. indicator species.

18. Sea otters, dung beetles, and gopher tortoises are generally considered to be
    a. nonnative species.
    b. native species.
    c. indicator species.
    d. specialist species.
* e. keystone species.

7-3   SPECIES INTERACTIONS: COMPETITION AND PREDATION

19. Which of the following statements is *false?*
    a. When environmental conditions are changing rapidly, a generalist is usually better off than a specialist.
    b. The fundamental niche of a species is the full range of physical, chemical, and biological factors it could use if there were no competition.
    c. The competitive exclusion principle states that no two species with the same fundamental niche can indefinitely occupy the same habitat.
* d. Interspecific competition is competition between two members of the same species.
    e. Intraspecific competition is competition between two members of the same species.

20. Which of the following predators avoid competition by being active at different times?
    a. lions and tigers
    b. hummingbirds and bees
* c. hawks and owls
    d. zebras and antelopes
    e. lions and cheetahs

21. The relationship between fire ants and native ant populations is best described as
    a. mutualism.
    b. commensalism.
    c. intraspecific competition.
* d. interspecific competition.
    e. parasitism.

22. A new kitten is added to a home with an established older cat. The older cat is observed to gobble up its food as well as that of the younger cat. This behavior is best described as
    a. interference competition.
  * b. exploitation competition.
    c. mutualism.
    d. predation.
    e. sharing.

23. A new kitten is added to a home with an established older cat. You observe the older cat hiss and swat at the younger kitten in the kitchen where they are fed. This behavior is best described as
  * a. interference competition.
    b. exploitation competition.
    c. mutualism.
    d. predation.
    e. sharing.

24. Interspecific competition can be avoided by
    a. eating at different times.
    b. resource partitioning.
    c. character displacement.
  * d. all of these answers.
    e. none of these answers.

25. A shark is *least* likely to be killed
  * a. by a predator.
    b. for sport.
    c. out of fear.
    d. for food.
    e. for their jaws.

26. The obvious relationship demonstrated by a food chain is
    a. competition.
  * b. predation.
    c. parasitism.
    d. mutualism.
    e. commensalism

27. Prey are *least* likely to defend themselves against predators by
    a. camouflage.
    b. acute senses of sight and smell.
    c. protective shells.
    d. warning coloration.
  * e. pursuit and ambush.

28. You are an evolutionary entomologist. You have observed beetles that can raise their abdomens and give off a defensive chemical that generally repels predators. You discover a new species of beetle that raises its abdomen in a threatening way similar to the first species, but no defensive chemical is given off. You are most likely to characterize this defensive strategy as a form of
    a. camouflage.
    b. chemical warfare.
  * c. mimicry.
    d. flight mechanism.
    e. warning coloration

7-4   SPECIES INTERACTIONS: PARASITISM, MUTUALISM, AND COMMENSALISM

29. A relationship in which a member of one species obtains its nourishment by living on, in, or near a member of another species over an extended time is best labeled
    a.   competition.
    b.   predation.
    c.   mutualism.
  * d.   parasitism.
    e.   commensalism.

30. A relationship in which one species benefits while the other is neither helped nor harmed to any significant degree is best labeled
    a.   competition.
    b.   predation.
  * c.   commensalism.
    d.   parasitism.
    e.   mutualism.

31. A relationship in which both species benefit is best labeled
    a.   competition.
    b.   predation.
  * c.   mutualism.
    d.   parasitism.
    e.   commensalism.

32. Of the following relationships, the one most likely to be described as a positive feedback loop is
    a.   competition.
    b.   predation.
    c.   commensalism.
    d.   parasitism.
  * e.   mutualism.

33. The win-win relationship of animal behavior is
    a.   competition.
    b.   predation.
  * c.   mutualism.
    d.   parasitism.
    e.   commensalism.

34. Parasites
  * a.   rarely kill their hosts.
    b.   are usually larger than their hosts.
    c.   must be internal to their hosts.
    d.   may strengthen their hosts over a long period of time.
    e.   all of these answers.

35. All of the following are external parasites *except*
    a.   fleas and ticks.
    b.   mosquitoes.
    c.   mistletoe.
  * d.   tapeworms.
    e.   athlete's foot fungus.

36. Which of the following is *incorrect?*
    a. Parasites can promote biodiversity.
    b. Parasites can act to hold interacting species of an ecosystem together.
    * c. Parasites bring only bad news.
    d. Parasites can moderate population fluctuations of a species.
    e. none of these answers.

37. All of the following illustrate the relationship of mutualism *except*
    a. lichens.
    * b. epiphytes.
    c. ants and acacias.
    d. *Rhizobium* bacteria in root nodules of legumes.
    e. flowering plants and insects.

38. The relationship between clownfish and sea anemones is
    a. competition.
    b. predation.
    c. parasitism.
    * d. mutualism.
    e. commensalism.

7-5   ECOLOGICAL SUCCESSION: COMMUNITIES IN TRANSITION

39. How long does it take natural processes to produce fertile soil?
    a. weeks to months
    b. months to years
    c. decades to a few centuries
    * d. several centuries to several thousands of years
    e. several thousand years to millions of years.

40. Which of the following would exhibit primary succession?
    * a. rock exposed by a retreating glacier
    b. an abandoned farm
    c. a forest that had been clear-cut
    d. newly flooded land to create a reservoir
    e. a forest that has been burned.

41. Which of the following would undergo secondary succession?
    a. cooled volcanic lava
    b. an abandoned parking lot
    * c. a heavily polluted stream that has been cleaned up
    d. a bare rock outcrop
    e. a newly created shallow pond.

42. Soil formation in primary succession is encouraged by
    a. physical weathering.
    b. lichens and mosses trapping soil particles.
    c. secretion of acids by lichens.
    * d. all of these answers.
    e. none of these answers.

43. In immature ecosystems
    a. the species diversity is high.
    b. the decomposers are numerous.
    c. there are many specialized niches.
    d. there are few producers.
    * e. the food webs are simple.

44. In mature ecosystems
    a. most plants are annuals.
    b. species diversity is low.
  * c. the efficiency of energy use is high.
    d. the efficiency of nutrient recycling is low.
    e. there are few, mostly generalized, ecological niches.

45. Ecologists would consider all of the following to be natural disturbances *except*
    a. droughts.
    b. floods
  * c. deforestation.
    d. fires.
    e. landslides.

46. The immediate effects of a natural disturbance include
    a. maintaining the status quo and releasing resources.
  * b. changing conditions and releasing resources.
    c. maintaining the status quo and uptake of resources.
    d. changing conditions and uptake of resources.
    e. maintaining the status quo with no change in availability of resources.

47. Most terrestrial ecosystems are dynamic patchworks of vegetation providing
  * a. great biodiversity and sites for early successional species to gain a foothold.
    b. great biodiversity and sites that favor late successional species.
    c. moderate biodiversity and sites for all successional species.
    d. moderate biodiversity and sites for early successional species to gain a foothold.
    e. none of these answers.

48. According to the intermediate disturbance hypothesis, which of the following conditions is likely to result in communities with the greatest diversity of species?
    a. infrequent disturbances of any kind
    b. fairly frequent, large disturbances
  * c. fairly frequent, moderate disturbances
    d. very frequent, large disturbances
    e. very frequent, small disturbances.

49. Which of the following human-caused changes is *most* appropriately classified as a catastrophic change rather than a gradual change?
    a. salinization
  * b. plowing
    c. waterlogging
    d. compaction
    e. exotic species introduction

50. Which of the following natural changes would be considered gradual rather than catastrophic?
    a. drought
    b. landslide
    c. earthquake
    d. fire
  * e. climate change

51. Changes such as drought and earthquake are considered to be
  * a. natural and catastrophic.
    b. natural and gradual.
    c. human caused and catastrophic.
    d. human caused and gradual.
    e. human caused, natural and catastrophic.

52. Changes such as depletion of underground aquifers and waterlogging of irrigated soils are considered to be
   a. natural and catastrophic.
   b. natural and gradual.
   c. human caused and catastrophic.
 * d. human caused and gradual.
   e. human caused, natural and catastrophic.

53. Which of the following human activities most favor monocultures?
 * a. agriculture and plantation forestry
   b. agriculture and ecosystem restoration
   c. plantation forestry and ecosystem restoration
   d. agriculture and ecosystem rehabilitation
   e. ecosystem restoration and ecosystem rehabilitation.

7-6   ECOLOGICAL STABILITY AND SUSTAINABILITY

54. The ability of a population to maintain a certain size is known as
   a. stability.
   b. inertia.
 * c. constancy.
   d. resilience.
   e. persistence.

55. Which of the following characteristics of organisms includes the others?
 * a. stability
   b. inertia
   c. constancy
   d. resilience
   e. persistence

56. Which of the following refers to the ability of an ecosystem to return to its former condition after a period of stress?
   a. stability
   b. inertia
   c. constancy
 * d. resilience
   e. persistence

57. The tropical rain forest is characterized by all of the following *except*
   a. high persistence..
   b. high diversity.
   c. high inertia.
   d. high constancy.
 * e. high resilience

58. Compared to forests, grasslands have
   a. more diversity, more inertia.
   b. more diversity, more resilience.
   c. less diversity, more inertia.
 * d. less diversity, more resilience.
   e. more diversity, more constancy.

CHAPTER 8
POPULATION DYNAMICS, CARRYING CAPACITY, AND CONSERVATION BIOLOGY

8-1   POPULATION DYNAMICS AND CARRYING CAPACITY

1.   The changes in population size, density, dispersion, and age structure are known as
    a.   succession.
    b.   demography.
    c.   carrying capacity
    d.   biotic potential.
  *   e.   population dynamics.

2.   The most common pattern of population dispersion found in nature is
    a.   random.
    b.   uniform.
  *   c.   clumped.
    d.   dispersed.
    e.   none of these answers.

3.   You are an ecologist studying the population dynamics of an ecosystem. You observe that resources are not evenly distributed. You predict the population dispersion pattern is
    a.   uniform.
    b.   random.
  *   c.   clumped.
    d.   dispersed
    e.   none of these answers.

4.   You observe uniform dispersion in a species you are studying intensely. You predict that as you extend your work, you will find
  *   a.   intraspecific competition and evenly spread, scarce resources.
    b.   interspecific predation and evenly spread, scarce resources.
    c.   intraspecific competition and evenly spread, abundant resources.
    d.   commensalism and clumped resources.
    e.   interspecific competition and evenly spread, abundant resources.

5.   Which of the following is *not* one of the age structure categories?
    a.   prereproductive
    b.   reproductive
    c.   postreproductive
  *   d.   elderly
    e.   none of these answers.

6.   Emigration
    a.   is one-way movement of individuals into the area of an established population.
    b.   is one-way movement of individuals into an uninhabited area.
  *   c.   is one-way movement of individuals out of a particular population to another area.
    d.   is the repeated departure and return of individuals to and from a population area.
    e.   all of these answers.

7. The biotic potential of a population
  * a. is the maximum reproductive rate of a population.
    b. is the current rate of growth of a population.
    c. is an expression of how many offspring survive to reproduce.
    d. can be determined only by studying an age structure diagram.
    e. is the future rate of growth of a population.

8. Biotic potential is determined by
    a. reproductive age span.
    b. litter size.
    c. how many offspring survive to reproductive age.
  * d. all of these answers.
    e. none of these answers.

9. Environmental resistance is enhanced by
    a. the ability to compete for resources.
    b. the ability to resist disease and parasites.
  * c. a specialized niche.
    d. a high reproductive rate.
    e. all of these answers.

10. A population will increase if
    a. natality decreases.
    b. mortality increases.
  * c. the biotic potential increases.
    d. the environmental resistance increases.
    e. all of these answers.

11. Which of the following factors leads to an increase in biotic potential?
    a. too much or too little light
    b. low reproductive rate
    c. too many competitors
  * d. optimal level of critical nutrients
    e. specialized niche

12. Carrying capacity refers to
    a. reproductive rate.
    b. interaction of natality and mortality.
  * c. the maximum size of population the environment will support.
    d. the proportion of males to females.
    e. the intrinsic rate of increase.

13. A logistic growth curve depicting a population that is limited by a definite carrying capacity is shaped like the letter _____.
    a. J
    b. L
    c. M
  * d. S
    e. U

14. An exponential growth curve depicting an ever-growing population is shaped like the letter ____.
  * a. J
    b. L
    c. M
    d. S
    e. U

15. A population crash occurs when
    a. a population approaches its carrying capacity.
    b. environmental resistance comes into play gradually.
    c. resources are essentially unlimited.
  * d. a population overshoots carrying capacity and environmental pressures cause effects.
    e. the population growth rate slows.

16. A population grows, overshoots its carrying capacity, and crashes, most likely from
    a. a positive feedback loop.
    b. a negative feedback loop.
  * c. a time delay between a positive feedback loop and a negative feedback loop.
    d. an accumulation.
    e. none of these answers.

17. Humans have extended Earth's carrying capacity for the human species by
    a. controlling many diseases.
    b. using energy resources at a rapid rate.
    c. using material resources at a rapid rate.
  * d. all of these answers.
    e. increasing life span.

18. Carrying capacity is determined by
    a. climatic changes.
    b. predation.
    c. interspecific competition.
    d. resources.
  * e. all of these answers.

19. Density-dependent population controls include all of the following *except*
    a. disease.
  * b. human destruction of habitat.
    c. parasitism.
    d. competition for resources.
    e. predation.

20. Density-independent population controls include all of the following *except*
    a. drought.
    b. fire.
  * c. resource competition.
    d. unfavorable chemical changes in the environment.
    e. habitat destruction.

21. All of the following are general types of population change curves *except*
  * a. explosive.
    b. stable.
    c. cyclic.
    d. irruptive.
    e. irregular

22. Which of the following terms *best* describes the type of population change you would expect to find for a monkey in an undisturbed section of the Brazilian rain forest?
    a. explosive
  * b. stable
    c. cyclic
    d. irruptive
    e. irregular

23. Which of the following terms *best* describes the type of population change you would expect to find for a muskrat population in a state that has just outlawed trapping?
    a. explosive
    b. stable
    c. cyclic
  * d. irruptive
    e. irregular

24. Which of the following patterns would you expect to find for rabbits and coyotes in an undisturbed habitat?
    a. explosive
    b. stable
  * c. cyclic
    d. irruptive
    e. irregular

8-2 CONNEBTIONS: THE ROLE OF PREDATION IN CONTROLLING POPULATION SIZE

25. Wolves controlling deer populations are an example of
    a. bottom-up population control
  * b. top-down population control
    c. producer-level control
    d. predator control
    e. none of these answers.

8-3 REPRODUCTIVE PATTERNS AND SURVIVAL

26. An r-selected species generally
    a. has a low biotic potential.
    b. reproduce late in life.
    c. gives much parental care to its offspring.
    d. survives to reproduce.
  * e. is small and short-lived.

27. K-selected species
    a. have high genetic diversity.
    b. are more responsive to environmental changes than r-strategists.
    c. exhibit fast rates of evolution.
  * d. are generally less adaptable to change than r-strategists.
    e. reach reproductive age rapidly.

28. A K-selected species generally
  * a. has populations that follow an S-shaped growth curve.
    b. exhibits "boom-and-bust" cycles.
    c. has populations that rise quickly then crash.
    d. generally lives in a rapidly changing environment.
    e. have short generation times.

29. Which of the following is an r-selected species?
    a. human
    b. whale
    c. rhinoceros
    d. saguaro cactus
    * e. insect

30. Which of the following *best* describes the survivorship curve you would expect to find for a mountain gorilla?
    * a. late loss
    b. constant loss
    c. early loss
    d. no loss
    e. none of these answers.

31. Which of the following *best* describes the survivorship curve you would expect to find for a fish?
    a. late loss
    b. constant loss
    * c. early loss
    d. no loss
    e. none of these answers.

32. Which of the following connections among population cycle, survival strategies, and survivorship curves would you *most* expect to see?
    a. boom-and-bust; K-selected species; early-loss
    * b. boom-and-bust; r-selected species; early-loss
    c. stable; r-selected species; early-loss
    d. stable; K-selected species; early-loss
    e. stable; r-selected species; late loss

8-4 CONSERVATION BIOLOGY: SUSTAINING WILDLIFE POPULATIONS

33. Which of the following ethical principles does *not* apply to conservation biology?
    a. The best way to preserve Earth's genetic and species diversity and ecological integrity is to preserve its habitats, niches, and ecological interactions.
    b. Humans should not interfere with the ongoing processes of biological evolution.
    c. Biodiversity and ecological integrity are useful and necessary to all life on Earth and should not be reduced by human actions.
    * d. Humans should use genetic engineering to improve species as human resources.
    e. all of these apply to conservation biology.

34. Of the following strategies, the one emphasized *least* by conservation biologists is to
    a. sustain ecosystems.
    b. protect ecosystems.
    * c. protect individual species from human-initiated sharp declines.
    d. rehabilitate degraded ecosystems.
    e. none of these answers.

35. The ethical principle most important to conservation biology is:
    a. People should be held responsible for their own pollution.
    b. We should live lightly on the earth.
    * c. Do that which tends to maintain Earth's life-support systems for us and other species.
    d. No human culture should become extinct because of the actions of other humans.
    e. Human population growth must be reduced.

36. Which of the following questions is a conservation biologist least likely to ask?
    a. How can ecosystem integrity be maintained?
  * b. How does sulfur cycle in this ecosystem?
    c. What is the status of the natural populations in this ecosystem?
    d. What ecosystem services are we in danger of losing in this ecosystem?
    e. How can we sustain viable populations of wild species?

8-5 HUMAN IMPACTS ON ECOSYSTEMS: LEARNING FROM NATURE

37. Humans have interfered in the development of natural ecosystems by
    a. adding chemicals that alter natural cycles.
    b. overharvesting potentially renewable resources.
    c. eliminating predators and introducing new species.
    d. b and c only.
  * e. all of these answers.

38. The World Health Organization initiated spraying in North Borneo (Sabah) to
  * a. reduce the incidence of malaria.
    b. control sylvatic plague.
    c. eliminate small lizards.
    d. kill the caterpillars found in the thatched roofs.
    e. control the cat population.

39. The World Health Organization controlled sylvatic plague in North Borneo (Sabah) by
    a. spraying with pesticide.
  * b. parachuting healthy cats into the area.
    c. introducing lizards.
    d. burning all the huts that housed infected people.
    e. all of these answers.

40. Natural ecosystems
    a. require applications of pesticides.
    b. are subject to continuous invasion by pathogens and weeds.
  * c. are usually capable of self-maintenance and self-renewal.
    d. have most of their biomass in one species.
    e. require applications of nutrients.

41. All of the following are key features of living systems *except*
    a. interdependence.
    b. diversity.
  * c. predictability.
    d. limits.
    e. all of these are key features.

42. Which of the following is *not* one of the basic lessons from nature?
    a. Sunlight is the source of energy that sustains ecosystems.
    b. Soil, water, air, and organisms are renewed through natural processes.
  * c. All populations of organisms except humans are kept in check by natural means.
    d. Energy is required to maintain energy flow and recycle chemicals.
    e. There are always limits to population growth and resource consumption.

CHAPTER 9
ENVIRONMENTAL GEOLOGY: PROCESSES, MINERALS, AND SOILS

9-1 GEOLOGIC PROCESSES

1. Which of the following is *not* one of the Earth's interior concentric zones?
    a. the asthenosphere.
    * b. the crust.
    c. the mantle.
    d. the core.
    e. none of these answers.

2. The Earth zone with the most volume and mass is the
    a. lithosphere.
    b. core.
    c. crust.
    * d. mantle.
    e. oceanic crust.

3. Which of the following is *true?*
    * a. The most common element in the center of the earth's core is iron.
    b. The inner core is liquid, whereas the outer core is solid.
    c. Extreme pressure makes the interior of the earth liquid.
    d. The core of the earth occupies most of its volume.
    e. The thickest zone is the crust.

4. Which of the following statements about Earth's mantle is *false?*
    a. The mantle is Earth's largest zone.
    * b. The outermost part of the mantle is partially melted rock.
    c. The outermost part of the mantle is rigid.
    d. Iron is a major constituent of the mantle.
    e. The thinnest zone is the crust.

5. The asthenosphere is
    a. the outer atmosphere.
    b. the inner core of Earth.
    c. a plastic region in the crust.
    * d. a plastic region in the mantle.
    e. a solid region in the mantle.

9-2 INTERNAL AND EXTERNAL EARTH PROCESSES

6. The majority of earthquakes and volcanoes occur
    a. in the interior of continents.
    b. on oceanic islands.
    * c. along the edge of continents.
    d. in the open ocean.
    e. in the U.S.

7. The theory of plate tectonics explains
    a. the occurrence of earthquakes.
    b. the occurrence of volcanoes.
    c. movement of Earth's plates.
    * d. all of these answers.
    e. the occurrence of mountains.

8.   A ___ is *not* one of the three types of boundaries between lithospheric plates.
   a.   transform fault
* b.   mantle fault
   c.   convergent plate boundary
   d.   divergent plate boundary
   e.   lithosphere fault

9.   Which of the following is *false?* Tectonic plates
   a.   produce mountains.
* b.   are composed of crust and core.
   c.   move on the asthenosphere.
   d.   produce ocean trenches.
   e.   produce volcanoes.

10.   Tectonic plates move apart in opposite directions at a(n)
* a.   divergent plate boundary.
   b.   transform fault.
   c.   convergent plate boundary.
   d.   subduction zone.
   e.   mantle fault.

11.   Tectonic plates move in opposite but parallel directions along a fault at a(n)
   a.   divergent plate boundary.
   b.   mantle fault.
   c.   convergent plate boundary.
   d.   subduction zone.
* e.   transform fault.

12.   The movement of lithospheric plates is significant because it
   a.   explains the formation of waterfalls and river canyons.
* b.   predicts where certain natural hazards are likely to be found.
   c.   explains formation of ocean currents.
   d.   predicts where endangered species might be found.
   e.   explains the formation of weather.

13.   The energy sources primarily responsible for Earth's external geological processes are
   a.   energy from the sun and magnetism.
* b.   energy from the sun and gravity.
   c.   energy from the sun and heat from Earth's interior.
   d.   gravity and magnetism.
   e.   only gravity.

14.   The agent *most* responsible for erosion is
   a.   groundwater.
* b.   streams.
   c.   glaciers.
   d.   wind.
   e.   hurricanes.

15.   The *most* important agent of mechanical weathering is
   a.   gravity.
   b.   flowing water.
* c.   frost action.
   d.   wind.
   e.   groundwater.

16. Mechanical weathering accelerates chemical weathering because of an increase in
    a. temperature.
    b. pH.
    * c. surface area.
    d. solubility.
    e. moisture.

17. You are a scientist interested in chemical weathering. You are most likely to visit the
    * a. tropics.
    b. subtropics.
    c. temperate zone.
    d. subarctic.
    e. artic zone.

18. Chemical weathering is aided by
    a. mechanical weathering.
    b. higher temperatures.
    c. higher precipitation.
    d. a and c only.
    * e. all of these answers.

9-3   MINERALS, ROCKS, AND THE ROCK CYCLE

19. Which of the following is *not* a characteristic of a mineral?
    a. crystal structure
    * b. organic
    c. naturally occurring
    d. solid
    e. inorganic

20. All of the following are broad classes of rock *except*
    a. sedimentary.
    b. igneous.
    c. metamorphic.
    * d. crystal.
    e. plasticized

21. Lava is an example of _____ rock.
    a. metamorphic
    * b. igneous
    c. sedimentary
    d. plasticized
    e. crystal

22. The change of rocks from one type to another is known as
    a. metamorphism.
    * b. the rock cycle.
    c. petrography.
    d. consolidation.
    e. hydrogeology.

23. Igneous rocks
    * a. are an important source of many non-fuel mineral resources.
    b. include limestone and shale.
    c. are always formed on the surface.
    d. include schist and gneiss.
    e. can be derived from plant remains.

24. Which of the following does *not* belong with the others?
    a. basalt
    b. granite
    * c. sandstone
    d. volcanic rocks
    e. pumice

25. Which of the following rocks is most likely to be formed from compacted shells and skeletons?
    a. coal
    * b. limestone
    c. rock salt
    d. marble
    e. granite

26. Which of the following rocks is most likely to be formed from compacted plant remains?
    * a. coal
    b. limestone
    c. rock salt
    d. marble
    e. granite

27. Lignite and bituminous coal are _____ rocks.
    a. metamorphic
    b. igneous
    c. tectonic
    d. ore
    * e. sedimentary

28. The type of rock that covers most of Earth's land surface is
    a. metamorphic.
    b. igneous.
    * c. sedimentary.
    d. gemstones.
    e. plasticized.

29. Heat and pressure convert
    a. igneous rock into sedimentary rock.
    * b. sedimentary rock into metamorphic rock.
    c. metamorphic rock into igneous rock.
    d. sedimentary rock into igneous rock.
    e. metamorphic into sedimentary rock.

30. Slate, anthracite, and marble are _____ rocks.
    a. primary
    b. secondary
    * c. metamorphic
    d. igneous
    e. sedimentary

9-4   FINDING, REMOVING, AND PROCESSING NONRENEWABLE MINERAL RESOURCES

31. Mineral deposits are found by
    a. information about plate tectonics.
    b. aerial photos.
    c. studies of magnetic or gravitational fields.
    d. a and c only.
    * e. all of these answers.

32. All of the following are types of surface mining *except*
    a. mountaintop removal.
    b. dredging.
  * c. longwall mining.
    d. strip mining.
    e. none of these answers.

33. One example of subsurface mining is
    a. dredging.
    b. contour strip mining.
  * c. longwall mining.
    d. area strip mining.
    e. open-pit mining,

34. Compared to subsurface mining, surface mining
    a. is more dangerous.
    b. is more expensive.
  * c. disturbs more land.
    d. produces less waste material.
    e. all of these answers.

35. Extracting, processing, and using mineral resources
    a. requires enormous amounts of energy.
    b. causes land disturbance and erosion.
    c. produces solid and hazardous wastes.
    d. release of toxic chemicals into the atmosphere.
  * e. all of these answers.

36. Mining can cause
    a. collapse of land.
    b. acid mine drainage.
    c. spoils heaps and tailings.
    d. emission of toxic chemicals.
  * e. all of these answers.

37. Acid mine drainage
    a. occurs when anaerobic bacteria produce nitric acid from nitrogen oxides.
    b. enhances aquatic life.
    c. neutralizes the pH of surface waters.
  * d. may contaminate groundwater.
    e. reduces acidity of surface waters.

38. Runoff from underground mines may carry
  * a. sulfuric acid.
    b. soil nutrients.
    c. exotic species.
    d. carbon dioxide.
    e. all of these answers.

39. Waste soil and rock removed during surface mining is called
    a. hazardous waste.
  * b. spoil.
    c. gangue.
    d. tailings.
    e. smelt.

40. The fraction of the ore containing waste minerals is called the
     a. hazardous waste.
     b. spoil.
     c. smelt.
     d. tailings.
   * e. gangue.

41. When ore undergoes processing, a waste called _____ is produced.
     a. hazardous
     b. spoil
     c. gangue
   * d. tailings
     e. smelt.

42. Smelters of ore minerals may give off
     a. soot.
     b. lead.
     c. sulfur dioxide.
     d. a and c only.
   * e. all of these answers.

43. Environmental impact would be greatest mining for _____ ore.
     a. a high-grade
     b. a moderate-grade
   * c. a low-grade
     d. a plentiful
     e. a low to moderate-grade

9-5   SUPPLIES OF MINERAL RESOURCES

44. When a resource has been economically depleted, we can
     a. recycle or reuse what has already been extracted.
     b. cut down on unnecessary waste of the resource.
     c. find a substitute.
     d. do without.
   * e. all of these answers.

45. Depletion time is the time it takes to use up about _____% of the mineral reserves at a given rate.
     a. 50
     b. 60
     c. 70
   * d. 80
     e. 90

46. A depletion curve is typically used to
     a. project remaining undiscovered resources.
   * b. project the depletion time for a resource.
     c. predict when a resource will become a reserve.
     d. project when uneconomic resources will become economically feasible.
     e. none of these answers.

47. Which of the following statements is *false?*
    a. Depletion time is dependent on rate of use and the amount of known reserves.
    b. Usually, the first deposits of a mineral to be exploited are high-grade deposits.
    c. All of a resource will not be used because it is not economically feasible to continue to extract the resource.
  * d. Recycling, reusing, and reducing consumption cause a depletion curve to peak sooner and higher.
    e. none of these answers.

48. Depletion time can be extended by
    a. recycling and reuse.
    b. discoveries of new resources.
    c. reduced consumption.
  * d. all of these answers.
    e. better mining technology.

49. Scarcity of minerals does *not* raise the price of material goods much because
    a. investment capital is usually abundantly available.
    b. all resource supplies are theoretically infinite.
    c. the mining industry is fiercely competitive and poorly regulated.
  * d. raw materials typically account for only a small fraction of the price of consumer goods.
    e. all of these answers.

50. Which of the following statements is *false?*
  * a. Market prices clearly reflect dwindling mineral supplies.
    b. Consumers have few incentives to reduce demands before economic depletion occurs.
    c. Low mineral prices are caused by failure to include the external costs of mining.
    d. Low prices encourage waste and faster depletion.
    e. High prices encourage recycling and reuse.

51. Most of the world's easily accessible high-grade mineral deposits
    a. are not worth extracting at today's prices.
    b. cannot be located using known techniques.
    c. lie in unexplored areas of the developing countries.
  * d. have already been discovered.
    e. are still plentiful.

52. According to geological theory, if there were 10,000 sites where a deposit of a particular resource might be found, ____ could probably be (a) producing mine(s).
  * a. 1
    b. 10
    c. 100
    d. 1,000
    e. 10,000

53. The example of copper mining illustrates that
  * a. it can be profitable to mine low-grade ores.
    b. reserves of minerals decline each year.
    c. economic profits must be balanced with environmental costs.
    d. the reserves of some key metals are renewable.
    e. all of these answers.

54.   According to some analysts, mining of low-grade ores may be limited by
       a.   energy costs.
       b.   availability of fresh water.
       c.   land reclamation costs.
    * d.   all of these answers.
       e.   environmental impact of pollution.

55.   Advantages of using microorganisms for mining include all of the following *except* reduced
       a.   land disturbance.
       b.   air pollution.
       c.   water pollution.
    * d.   time to remove minerals.
       e.   none of these answers.

56.   High-temperature ceramic superconductors
    * a.   carry electricity without resistance.
       b.   may lead to better technology for car engines.
       c.   suffer from inefficient power transmission.
       d.   are not useful in electronics applications.
       e.   all of these answers.

57.   High-strength plastics and composite materials strengthened by carbon and glass fibers are advantageous because they are
       a.   stronger than metal.
       b.   less expensive because they use less energy.
       c.   easily molded into any shape.
    * d.   all of these answers.
       e.   don't need painting.

58.   Which of the following would be easiest to find a substitute for?
       a.   phosphates
       b.   helium
    * c.   steel
       d.   copper
       e.   manganese

9-6   NATURAL HAZARDS: EARTHQUAKES AND VOLCANIC ERUPTIONS

59.   An earthquake is most directly caused by
    * a.   the creation of a fault (fracture in rock) or shifting along an existing fault.
       b.   a change in ocean currents.
       c.   dumping of toxic wastes.
       d.   comets crashing into Earth.
       e.   mining.

60.   The strength of an earthquake is measured on the _____ scale.
    * a.   Richter
       b.   Miller
       c.   Mercalli
       d.   Geiger
       e.   Doppler.

61. An earthquake reported as magnitude 9 would be considered
    a. insignificant.
    b. minor.
    c. damaging.
    d. moderate.
* e. great.

62. Secondary effects from earthquakes include all of the following *except*
    a. urban fires.
* b. shaking and permanent vertical displacement of the ground.
    c. damaged coastal areas.
    d. mass wasting.
    e. tsunamis.

63. Of the following, the approach *least* likely to reduce earthquake hazards is
    a. better prediction of location and timing of earthquakes.
    b. location of active fault zones.
    c. establishment of building codes regulating placement and design of buildings in high-risk areas.
* d. filling of fault zones with rubberized cement.
    e. making maps of high-risk areas.

64. Ejecta is
* a. debris released from a volcano.
    b. substances injected into faults to relieve pressure.
    c. material released from rifts on the floor of the ocean.
    d. the depressed region inside the cone of an inactive volcano.
    e. lava flow.

65. What was the most important volcanic eruption in North America in recent times?
    a. Mt. Pinatubo, 1991
    b. Lassen Peak, 1953
* c. Mt. St. Helens, 1980
    d. Paracutin, 1941
    e. none of these answers.

66. Loss of human life from volcanic activity can be reduced by
    a. better land-use planning.
    b. development of effective evacuation plans.
    c. better prediction of volcanic eruptions.
    d. studying phenomena that precede eruptions.
* e. all of these answers.

9-7   SOIL RESOURCES: FORMATION AND TYPES

67. Soil is developed most directly through
    a. moving tectonic plates.
    b. earthquakes.
    c. volcanoes.
    d. mass wasting.
* e. weathering.

68. Soil is a complex mixture of
    a. mineral nutrients.
    b. eroded rock.
    c. air and water.
  * d. all of these answers
    e. decaying organic matter.

69. A cross-sectional view of the ___ in a soil is properly termed a soil ____.
  * a. horizons . . . profile
    b. horizons . . . sample
    c. profile . . . sample
    d. surface litter . . . profile
    e. profile … horizon.

70. The zones that compose a mature soil are known as
    a. strata.
    b. profiles.
  * c. horizons.
    d. laminae.
    e. samples.

71. The surface litter horizon is described by the letter
    a. A.
    b. B.
    c. C.
  * d. O.
    e. D

72. The ____-horizon of a soil contains no organic material and is composed of parent material.
    a. A
    b. B
  * c. C
    d. O
    e. D

73. The A-horizon of soil is commonly referred to as
  * a. topsoil.
    b. surface litter.
    c. subsoil.
    d. parent rock.
    e. humus.

74. The topsoil horizon is described by the letter
  * a. A.
    b. B.
    c. C.
    d. O.
    e. D.

75. Topsoil contains all of the following *except*
    a. plant roots.
    b. humus.
  * c. freshly fallen leaves.
    d. some inorganic minerals.
    e. bacteria.

76. As it is weathered, _____ gives rise to the C-horizon.
    a. parent material
    b. leaching
    c. subsoil
  * d. bed rock
    e. B-horizon.

77. The soil layer containing unique colors and often iron, aluminum, humus, and clay leached from higher layers is the
    a. parent material.
    b. zone of leaching.
    c. bed rock.
    d. topsoil.
  * e. subsoil.

78. Freshly fallen leaves, organic debris, and partially decomposed organic matter are indicative of the
  * a. surface litter.
    b. zone of leaching.
    c. parent material.
    d. subsoil.
    e. humus.

79. The dissolving of material from the upper layers of the soil and its movement to lower horizons is called
    a. percolation.
    b. weathering.
    c. accumulation.
  * d. leaching.
    e. humus.

80. Leaching occurs when
    a. humus is dissolved.
  * b. water removes soluble soil components.
    c. organic compounds slowly decay.
    d. rock is shattered by frost action.
    e. water stays in the soil.

81. Humus is
    a. indicative of poor soils.
    b. light colored or nearly white.
    c. poisonous to soil microorganisms.
  * d. partially decomposed organic matter.
    e. freshly, fallen leaves.

82. Topsoil that is _____ in color is the most highly fertile.
    a. gray
    b. red
    c. green.
    d. yellow
  * e. dark brown or black

83. Red and yellow colors in a soil horizon usually indicate a
    a. high percentage of sand.
    b. high percentage of lime and gypsum.
    c. lack of iron oxide.
  * d. low organic matter content.
    e. large number of soil organisms.

84. Leaf mold, a humus-mineral mixture, and silty loam are indicative of
    a. coniferous forest soil.
  * b. deciduous forest soil.
    c. tropical forest soil.
    d. grassland soil.
    e. desert soil.

85. A soil sample that is alkaline, dark, and rich in humus probably came from a
    a. coniferous forest.
    b. deciduous forest.
    c. tropical forest.
  * d. grassland.
    e. desert.

86. A soil sample of closely packed pebbles that is a mixture of minerals and low in humus probably came from a
    a. coniferous forest.
  * b. desert.
    c. deciduous forest.
    d. tropical forest.
    e. grassland.

87. Soil texture most directly determines
  * a. porosity.
    b. pH.
    c. color.
    d. nutrient content.
    e. mineral content.

88. Which of the following is *not* a particle size used to determine soil texture?
    a. silt
  * b. loam
    c. clay
    d. sand
    e. gravel

89. If you were a farmer, which type of soil would you choose for your crops?
    a. silt
  * b. loam
    c. clay
    d. sand
    e. gravel.

90. Which of the following types of soils has the *least* pore space?
    a. silt
    b. loam
    c. clay
  * d. sand
    e. they all have equal pore space.

91. Which of the following types of soils holds the *most* water?
    a. silt
    b. loam
    c. gravel
    d. sand
    * e. clay

92. Physical properties of clay include good
    * a. nutrient-holding capacity.
    b. water infiltration.
    c. air-holding capacity.
    d. aeration.
    e. workability

93. Clay has ____ permeability and ____ porosity.
    a. high . . . high
    b. high . . . low
    * c. low. . . high
    d. low. . . low
    e. none of these answers

94. Properties of sand do *not* include good
    * a. nutrient-holding capacity.
    b. water infiltration.
    c. percolation.
    d. aeration.
    e. workability

95. Sand has ____ permeability and ____ porosity.
    a. high . . . high
    * b. high . . . low
    c. low . . . high
    d. low . . . low
    e. none of these answers

96. Soil textures with moderate physical and chemical properties include
    a. clay and silt.
    b. sand and loam.
    c. clay and loam.
    d. sand and clay.
    * e. silt and loam.

97. Which of the soils would *most* likely become waterlogged?
    a. silt
    b. loam
    * c. clay
    d. sand
    e. gravel

98. Alkaline soil can be neutralized or made more acid by adding
    * a. sulfur.
    b. calcium.
    c. phosphates.
    d. sodium.
    e. water.

99.   An acidic soil is one with a pH of
       a.   10 or more.
       b.   exactly 10.
       c.   7 to 10.
  *   d.   less than 7.
       e.   exactly 6.5.

100. Acidic soil can be partially neutralized by adding
  *   a.   lime.
       b.   water-insoluble compounds.
       c.   phosphates.
       d.   sulfur.
       e.   calcium.

101. The addition of lime
       a.   makes soil more acidic.
  *   b.   causes decomposition of organic material.
       c.   increases porosity of the soil.
       d.   will change soil texture.
       e.   neutralizes alkalinity.

9-8   SOIL EROSION

102. Most soil erosion is caused by
  *   a.   moving water.
       b.   wind.
       c.   earthquakes.
       d.   volcanoes.
       e.   excess heat.

103. Of the following human activities, the one that probably contributes least to soil
      erosion is
       a.   urbanization.
       b.   off-road vehicles.
  *   c.   sustainable agriculture.
       d.   logging.
       e.   cutting forests.

104. Which term includes the others?
       a.   sheet erosion
       b.   rill erosion
  *   c.   soil erosion
       d.   gully erosion
       e.   none of these answers.

105. The greatest source of water pollution is
       a.   runoff of animal waste from farms.
       b.   runoff of agricultural chemicals.
       c.   drainage from urban areas.
       d.   industrial point sources.
  *   e.   sediment from erosion.

106. In tropical and temperate areas, 1 inch of topsoil takes an average of _____ years to form.
      a.   10–50
      b.   100–200
   * c.   200–1,000
      d.   1,000–2,000
      e.   2,000-5,000

107. Which of the following sites would be expected to have the *most* rapid erosion rates?
      a.   agricultural land
      b.   lumbering sites
      c.   rangeland
   * d.   construction sites
      e.   housing subdivisions

108. Currently, topsoil is eroding faster than it forms on about _____ of the world's croplands.
      a.   one-fourth
   * b.   one-third
      c.   one-half
      d.   two-thirds
      e.   three-fourths

109. In many developing countries, poor farmers plow up marginal land in order to survive. The resulting soil erosion and land degradation increases poverty. The relationship between poverty and soil erosion is best described as a
      a.   constructive positive feedback cycle.
      b.   constructive negative feedback cycle.
   * c.   destructive positive feedback cycle.
      d.   destructive negative feedback cycle.
      e.   none of these answers.

110. The United States has already lost about ___ of the original topsoil of the cropland in use today.
      a.   one-tenth
      b.   one-sixth
      c.   one-fifth
   * d.   one-third
      e.   one-half

111. The major erosion of U.S. cropland soil occurs in
      a.   the Northeast.
      b.   the Southeast.
      c.   areas whose crop output is not important.
      d.   areas with soil of low to very low fertility.
   * e.   the Great Plains.

112. The National Resources Conservation Service
      a.   was established in 1955.
      b.   is a regional service to the Great Plains.
   * c.   provides technical assistance to both farmers and ranchers.
      d.   solved the Great Plains' erosion problems.
      e.   studies weather patterns in the Great Plains.

113. Today, soil on agricultural land in the United States is
    a. forming 16 times faster than it is eroding.
    b. forming 6 times faster than it is eroding.
    c. is eroding 6 times faster than it is forming.
  * d. is eroding 16 times faster than it is forming.
    e. is eroding 2 times faster than it is forming.

114. Which of the following practices leads to desertification?
    a. irrigation
    b. overgrazing
    c. soil compaction
  * d. all of these answers
    e. surface mining

115. Salt buildup may
    a. increase crop growth.
    b. increase yields.
    c. eventually kill weeds.
  * d. eventually make the land unproductive.
    e. none of these answers.

116. Irrigation often results in
  * a. waterlogging.
    b. high pH.
    c. low pH.
    d. high nutrient levels.
    e. all of these answers.

9-9   SOLUTIONS: SOIL CONSERVATION

117. Plowing, breaking up, and smoothing soil in fall to plant in the spring is
  * a. conventional tillage.
    b. conservation tillage.
    c. contour farming.
    d. terracing.
    e. spring overturn

118. Conservation tillage
    a. increases labor costs.
    b. .increases erosion.
    c. increases energy consumption.
    d. accelerates water loss from the soil.
  * e. decreases erosion

119. Compared to conventional tillage, conservation tillage
  * a. reduces fuel and tillage costs.
    b. accelerates water loss from the soil.
    c. causes soil compaction.
    d. requires increased use of herbicides.
    e. all of these answers.

120. Which of the following statements is *false?* Conservation tillage
  a.   is used in 40% of U.S. cropland.
  b.   is not widely used outside the United States.
  c.   reduces soil compaction.
 * d.   reduces the number of crops that can be grown in an area in a year.
  e.   reduces decomposition of soil organic matter.

121. Which of the following practices both reduces erosion and increases soil fertility?
 * a.   strip cropping
  b.   terracing
  c.   contour farming
  d.   row cropping
  e.   line cropping

122. Contour farming involves
  a.   converting a steep slope into a series of terraces.
  b.   building a series of small dams.
 * c.   plowing at right angles to slopes.
  d.   plowing straight down slope or straight up slope.
  e.   none of these answers.

123. Planting crops in alternating rows of close-growing plants
  a.   creates windbreaks.
 * b.   is called strip cropping.
  c.   is called crop rotation.
  d.   increases erosion rates.
  e.   ally cropping

124. An agricultural style that prevents erosion on steep slopes is
  a.   conventional-tillage farming.
  b.   conservation-tillage farming.
  c.   alley cropping.
 * d.   terracing.
  e.   contour farming

125. In alley cropping,
 * a.   crops are planted between hedgerows of trees or shrubs that are used for fruits or fuelwood.
  b.   terraces are built to prevent swift water runoff.
  c.   plowing runs across slopes.
  d.   special tillers are used so the topsoil is not disturbed.
  e.   a row crops alternates in strips with another row crop.

126. Which of the following statements about gullies is *false?*
  a.   Gullies are created on slopes that are not covered by vegetation.
  b.   Small gullies can be seeded with quick-growing plants.
 * c.   Once gullies are formed, it is impossible to reclaim the land for agricultural purposes.
  d.   Deep gullies can be filled in by building small dams to collect silt.
  e.   none of these answers.

127. Which of the following is a *true* statement about shelterbelts (windbreaks) in the Great Plains?
  a.   Most are employed to channel water away from gullies.
  b.   They eliminate the need for other soil-conservation methods.
  c.   They are usually planted in an east-to-west direction.
  d.   They cause a loss of moisture in cropland.
 * e.   Many have been destroyed to make way for farming equipment.

128. Established by the 1985 Farm Act, a conservation reserve cannot be
    a. cut for hay.
    b. farmed.
    c. grazed.
  * d. all of these answers.
    e. farmers who violate their contracts must pay back all subsidies plus interest.

129. Which of the following is *not* one of the three major types of organic fertilizer?
    a. green manure
  * b. sewage sludge
    c. compost
    d. animal manure
    e. none of these answers.

130. Animal manure is normally not used as a crop fertilizer on large farms because it
    a. is low in fertility.
    b. lacks soil microorganisms.
    c. degrades soil structure.
  * d. is often unavailable or too costly to transport.
    e. smells bad.

131. Which of the following statements is *false?* Application of animal manure
    a. improves soil structure.
    b. stimulates the growth of soil bacteria and fungi.
  * c. has increased since farms have specialized in animal- or crop-farming operations.
    d. is expensive when manure must be transported from feedlots near urban areas to rural crop-growing areas.
    e. has declined since farms have specialized in animal- or crop-farming operations.

132. The process *least* likely to conserve soil nutrients is
    a. crop rotation.
    b. fertilizing with compost.
    c. fertilizing with green manure.
    d. fertilizing with animal manure.
  * e. irrigation.

133. Commercial inorganic fertilizers commonly contain all of the following *except*
  * a. organic nitrogen.
    b. phosphate.
    c. nitrate.
    d. potassium.
    e. none of these answers.

134. Commercially available inorganic fertilizers
  * a. lack trace elements.
    b. increase soil porosity.
    c. increase soil water-holding capacity.
    d. raise the oxygen content of soil.
    e. contain all trace elements.

CHAPTER 10
RISK, TOXICOLOGY, AND HUMAN HEALTH

1.   Of the following, the leading cause of death among adults in the United States is
*   a.   tobacco use.
     b.   alcohol use.
     c.   suicide.
     d.   accidents.
     e.   homicide.

2.   Of the following suggestions, the one *least* likely to reduce the health risks of smoking is to
*   a.   legalize the sale of tobacco products to all age groups.
     b.   ban cigarette vending machines.
     c.   eliminate federal subsidies to tobacco farmers and companies.
     d.   ban cigarette advertising.
     e.   use cigarette tax to finance anti-smoking advertising.

3.   Adding a $2–4federal tax to the price of a pack of cigarettes is a form of
     a.   life-cycle cost pricing.
     b.   externalizing internal costs.
     c.   operating cost pricing.
     d.   full-cost pricing.
*   e.   user-pays approach.

10-1   RISK, PROBABILITY, AND HAZARDS

4.   Risk is expressed as a probability of suffering from
     a.   disease.
     b.   economic loss.
     c.   environmental damage.
*   d.   all of these answers.
     e.   injury.

5.   The four main types of hazards include all of the following *except*
     a.   biological hazards.
     b.   physical hazards.
*   c.   global hazards.
     d.   chemical hazards.
     e.   none of these answers.

6.   All of the following are considered to be cultural hazards *except*
     a.   smoking.
*   b.   drought.
     c.   drugs.
     d.   diet.
     e.   unsafe sex.

7.   All of the following are considered to be biological hazards *except*
     a.   pollen.
     b.   parasites.
*   c.   diet.
     d.   bacteria.
     e.   bees

8.　All of the following are considered to be physical hazards *except*
　*　a.　driving.
　　b.　hurricanes.
　　c.　landslides.
　　d.　ionizing radiation.
　　e.　fires.

10-2　TOXICOLOGY

9.　Evaluating the potential harm to humans of a particular chemical requires determining
　　a.　the sources and amounts of exposure.
　　b.　the amounts absorbed and distributed throughout the body.
　　c.　the amount excreted.
　*　d.　all of these answers.
　　e.　whether a child or an adult is exposed.

10.　A person receiving background radiation from a low-level radioactive dumpsite for a lifetime has experienced
　*　a.　a chronic exposure.
　　b.　a subchronic exposure.
　　c.　an acute exposure.
　　d.　a subacute exposure.
　　e.　a superacute exposure.

11.　A person flying over the Chernobyl site two days after the explosion most probably experienced
　_____ to radioactive substances.
　　a.　a chronic exposure
　　b.　a subchronic exposure
　*　c.　an acute exposure
　　d.　a subacute exposure
　　e.　a superacute exposure

12.　A person experiencing dizziness after using a strong household cleaner is showing
　　a.　a chronic effect.
　　b.　a subchronic effect.
　*　c.　an acute effect.
　　d.　a subacute effect.
　　e.　a superacute effect.

13.　A person experiencing liver damage after a lifetime of alcohol abuse is showing
　*　a.　a chronic effect.
　　b.　a subchronic effect.
　　c.　an acute effect.
　　d.　a subacute effect.
　　e.　a superacute effect.

14.　A person with kidney damage after an acute exposure to a toxic chemical is showing
　　a.　a chronic effect.
　　b.　a subchronic effect.
　*　c.　an acute effect.
　　d.　a subacute effect.
　　e.　a superacute effect.

15. Dose and response may be affected by the chemical's
    a. solubility characteristics.
    b. biomagnification.
    c. antagonistic and synergistic interactions with other chemicals.
  * d. all of these answers.
    e. persistence.

16. Which statement is true?
    a. All chemicals are unsafe.
    b. Natural chemicals are safe, and synthetic chemicals are deadly.
    c. All chemicals are safe.
  * d. Some chemicals, whether synthetic or natural, are safe and others are deadly.
    e. All chemicals are safe expect those that cause cancer.

17. Suppose you accidentally drink a substance with an LD_{50} of 1mg/kg. You are *least* likely to
    a. call the poison hotline.
  * b. continue playing a board game.
    c. go to an emergency room.
    d. call your doctor.
    e. call 911.

18. The level of threat posed by a particular substance is determined by
    a. laboratory investigations.
    b. epidemiology.
    c. case reports.
  * d. all of these answers.
    e. none of these answers.

19. Case reports are most useful because
    a. the health status of the individuals studied is clearly known.
  * b. they provide clues about possible environmental hazards.
    c. acute dosages of harmful substances are documented.
    d. exposure of individuals to a variety of harmful substances is controlled.
    e. all of these answers.

20. Laboratory investigations involve all of the following *except*
    a. tests on live laboratory animals.
    b. controlled experiments.
    c. construction of dose-response curves.
  * d. extrapolation from fairly low dosages to high dosages.
    e. a control group.

21. Of the following, the *least* likely to be used in laboratory investigations of toxicity are
  * a. California condors.
    b. mice.
    c. bacteria.
    d. rats.
    e. rabbits.

22. Dose-response curves are generated from
    a. field studies.
    b. epidemiological studies.
  * c. laboratory studies comparing experimental to control groups of test animals.
    d. computer models.
    e. all of these answers.

23.	Dose-response curves
  *	a.	show the effects of various doses of toxic agents on a group of test organisms.
	b.	are extrapolated using mathematical models to project possible effects of high doses.
	c.	are extrapolated from humans to other primates.
	d.	all of these answers.
	e.	none of these answers.

24.	To assess acute effects, researchers often use high doses to
	a.	reduce the number of test animals needed.
	b.	cut the time needed to get results.
	c.	lower costs of testing.
	d.	a and c only.
  *	e.	all of these answers.

25.	Animal testing
	a.	extrapolates from low-dose levels to high-dose levels.
  *	b.	extrapolates from test animals to humans.
	c.	is noncontroversial.
	d.	usually involves low-dose levels.
	e.	c and d.

26.	The problem with using animal testing to determine dose levels for humans is
	a.	uncertainty about the accuracy of a threshold dose-response model.
	b.	uncertainty about the accuracy of a linear dose-response model.
	c.	that human metabolic processes differ from those of test animals.
	d.	we are going to run out of animals.
  *	e.	all of these answers.

27.	An epidemiological study showing a standard increase in physical effects for each rise in the dose of a toxic substance would imply
	a.	a threshold dose-response curve.
	b.	an exponential dose-response curve.
  *	c.	a linear dose-response curve.
	d.	no dose-response curve.
	e.	a nonlinear dose-response curve.

28.	A threshold dose-response model
  *	a.	implies there is a dose below which no detectable harmful effects occur.
	b.	errs on the side of safety.
	c.	implies that each dose of ionizing radiation or toxic chemical carries a risk of causing harm.
	d.	is useful for assessing chronic toxicity.
	e.	all of these answers.

29.	The model most often assumed because it errs on the side of safety is the
	a.	acute toxicity model.
	b.	chronic toxicity model.
	c.	threshold dose-response model.
  *	d.	linear dose-response model.
	e.	nonlinear dose-response model.

30. The study of the pattern of a disease in a population is called
    a. pathology.
    b. oncology.
*   c. epidemiology.
    d. ecology.
    e. bacteriology.

31. Epidemiological studies are limited by
    a. difficulty in selecting a sample because too many people have been exposed to high levels of hazardous substances.
*   b. difficulty in establishing cause and effect because people have been exposed to many different toxic agents.
    c. prohibitive costs.
    d. taking at least a decade to complete.
    e. all of these answers.

10-3 CHEMICAL HAZARDS

32. The principal types of chemical hazards include all of the following *except*
    a. toxic and hazardous substances.
    b. mutagens.
    c. teratogens.
*   d. zymogens.
    e. carcinogens.

33. Toxic substances
*   a. are fatal to over 50% of test animals at given concentrations.
    b. cause birth defects.
    c. are harmful because they are flammable, explosive, irritating to skin or lungs, or cause allergic reactions.
    d. cause mutations.
    e. are fatal to less than 50% of test animals at given conditions.

34. Hazardous chemicals include
    a. strong acids.
    b. asphyxiants.
    c. allergens.
    d. strong bases.
*   e. all of these answers.

35. Mutagens
    a. are fatal to humans in low doses.
    b. cause birth defects.
    c. are harmful because they are flammable, explosive, irritating to skin or lungs, or cause allergic reactions.
*   d. cause mutations.
    e. always cause cancer.

36. Mutagens directly change molecules of
    a. protein.
    b. carbohydrate.
*   c. DNA.
    d. fat.
    e. RNA

37. Teratogens
    a. are fatal to humans in low doses.
    * b. cause birth defects.
    c. are harmful because they are irritating to skin or lungs.
    d. cause mutations.
    e. cause allergic reactions.

38. Birth defects can be caused by
    a. radiation.
    b. viruses.
    c. chemicals.
    d. a and c only.
    * e. all of these answers.

39. Of the following chemicals, the least likely to cause birth defects is
    a. PCBs.
    b. thalidomide.
    * c. iodized sodium chloride.
    d. steroid hormones.
    e. heavy metals.

40. Carcinogens cause
    a. genetic defects.
    b. birth defects.
    * c. cancer.
    d. chronic health effects.
    e. allergic reactions.

41. Carcinogens may be
    a. viruses.
    b. radiation.
    c. chemicals.
    d. b and c only.
    * e. all of these answers.

42. According to the World Health Organization, which of the following plays the *most* important role in causing or promoting cancer?
    a. viruses
    b. genetic factors
    * c. cigarette smoke
    d. environmental pollutants
    e. bacteria

43. A delay of _____ years between initial exposure to a carcinogen and appearance of detectable symptoms is typical.
    a. 1–2
    b. 2–5
    c. 5–10
    * d. 10–40
    e. 40-60

44. The system responsible for defense against disease and harmful substances is the
   a. circulatory system.
   b. endocrine system.
 * c. immune system.
   d. excretory system.
   e. cardiovascular system.

45. Two lines of defense in the human body's immune system are
   a. antibodies and neurohumors.
 * b. antibodies and cellular defenses.
   c. hormones and antibodies.
   d. hormones and cellular defenses.
   e. antibodies and antibiotics.

46. The immune system can be made vulnerable to allergens, bacteria, and viruses through the action of
   a. some synthetic chemicals.
   b. ionizing radiation.
   c. viruses like HIV,
 * d. all of these answers.
   e. none of these answers.

47. All of the following are part of the nervous system *except*
   a. peripheral nerves.
   b. the brain.
   c. the spinal cord.
   d. spinal nerves.
 * e. the uterus.

48. Specialized cells, tissues, and organs which secrete hormones are part of the
   a. digestive system.
 * b. endocrine system.
   c. excretory system.
   d. circulatory system.
   e. immune system.

49. All of the following are synthetic neurotoxins that have been released into the environment *except*
 * a. estrogen.
   b. industrial solvents.
   c. chlorinated hydrocarbons.
   d. arsenic and mercury.
   e. lead.

50. The system responsible for growth, reproductive development, and much of our behavior is the
   a. circulatory system.
 * b. endocrine system.
   c. immune system.
   d. excretory system.
   e. digestive system.

51. All of the following are synthetic chemicals that can act as hormone mimics or blockers *except*
   a. dioxins.
 * b. adrenalin.
   c. PCBs.
   d. some pesticides.
   e. DDT.

52. The endocrine system is *least* likely to be disrupted by the intake of
    a. lead.
    b. PCBs.
    c. dioxins.
 * d. Vitamin E.
    e. DDT.

53. The intake of synthetic mimics can severely disrupt the
    a. digestive system.
    b. circulatory system.
    c. respiratory system.
    d. immune system.
 * e. endocrine system.

54. You would predict that a hormone disrupter would most effect a(n)
    a. producer.
    b. primary consumer.
    c. secondary consumer.
 * d. tertiary consumer.
    e. secondary producer.

55. You have been studying a large lake ecosystem. You learn that PCBs have been dumped into the water. You predict that the most affected population would be the
    a. algae.
    b. small fish.
 * c. predatory birds.
    d. zooplankton.
    e. phytoplankton.

10-4 BIOLOGICAL HAZARDS: DISEASE IN DEVELOPED AND DEVELOPING COUNTRIES

56. Vectors are
    a. dose levels.
    b. agents of infection.
 * c. agents of disease transmission.
    d. parasitic organisms.
    e. estrogen mimics.

57. A transmissible disease is *least* likely to be caused by a
    a. bacterium.
 * b. hazardous chemical.
    c. virus.
    d. parasite.
    e. protozoa.

58. All of the following are transmissible diseases *except*
 * a. diabetes.
    b. pneumonia.
    c. diarrhea.
    d. tuberculosis.
    e. AIDS.

59. All of the following are nontransmissible diseases *except*
    a. heart disease.
    b. cancer.
 * c. hepatitis-B.
    d. malnutrition.
    e. asthma.

60. In 1997, the world's leading cause of death was
    a. cancer.
    b. diabetes.
 * c. infectious diseases.
    d. heart disease.
    e. violence.

61. Which of the following infectious diseases is *not* among the four most deadly?
    a. acute respiratory infections
 * b. mumps
    c. malaria
    d. tuberculosis
    e. AIDS

62. In a developing country, you are most likely to fear health threats from
    a. ebola virus.
    b. hantavirus.
    c. diabetes.
 * d. unsanitary drinking water.
    e. HIV.

63. Outbreaks of infectious diseases often occur because of a change in the physical, social, or biological environment of
    a. hosts.
    b. carrier vectors.
    c. disease reservoirs.
 * d. any or all of these answers.
    e. none of these answers.

64. In which of the following situations would you predict an outbreak of an infectious disease is *least* likely to occur?
    a. Deforestation is rapid with large loss of biodiversity.
 * b. The system is stable with little change.
    c. It's an El Niño–Southern Oscillation year.
    d. Agriculture is spreading to more marginal land.
    e. both c and d.

65. Which of the following choices makes the statement *false?* Bacteria
    a. can develop resistance to antibiotics.
 * b. are K-selected species.
    c. have a high reproductive rate.
    d. are highly adaptable species.
    e. are r-selected species.

66. The factor which is probably *least* responsible for the rise in the incidence of bacterial diseases once controlled by antibiotics is
    a. the genetic adaptability of bacteria.
    b. the spread of bacteria around the globe.
 * c. the increased amount of ultraviolet light because of the thinning ozone layer.
    d. the use of antibiotics in the dairy industry.
    e. the overuse of antibiotics by doctors.

67. Tuberculosis is caused by
    a. mosquitoes.
    b. houseflies.
    c. viruses.
 * d. bacteria.
    e. protozoa.

68. The incidence of tuberculosis is increasing because
    a. strains of the TB bacterium have developed resistance to antibiotics.
    b. increased population size and the advanced age of the population.
    c. weakened immune systems from the spread of AIDS.
    d. poverty.
 * e. all of these answers.

69. All of the following are viral diseases *except*
 * a. Lyme disease.
    b. AIDS.
    c. ebola.
    d. influenza.
    e. rabies.

70. Each year, up to _____ Americans suffer a food-borne illness.
    a. 1 in 10
    b. 1 in 5
    c. 1 in 4
 * d. 1 in 3
    e. 1 in 20

71. About 80% of food-borne illness in the United States is caused by
    a. streptococcus and salmonella.
    b. streptococcus and cyanobacter.
 * c. cyanobacter and salmonella.
    d. cyanobacter and spirochete.
    e. streptococcus and spirochete.

72. Although most food in the United States is safe, there is an increasing risk of bacterial infections because of
    a. lax inspection.
    b. overuse of antibiotics by doctors and meat producers.
    c. changes in meat production.
    d. a and b only.
 * e. all of these answers.

73. Vaccines can help prevent all of the following diseases *except*
    a. polio.
    b. rabies.
  * c. AIDS.
    d. measles.
    e. mumps.

74. Malaria is caused by
    a. viruses.
    b. bacteria.
  * c. *Plasmodium* parasites.
    d. parasitic worms.
    e. mosquitoes.

75. Malaria is spread by
  * a. *Anopheles* mosquitoes.
    b. flies.
    c. worms.
    d. snails.
    e. bacteria.

76. All of the following are symptoms of malaria *except*
    a. general weakness and weakened immune system.
    b. chills and fever.
    c. enlarged spleen.
    d. anemia.
  * e. blindness.

77. During the mid-1900s, the spread of malaria decreased sharply from
    a. draining swamplands.
    b. draining marshes.
    c. spraying breeding areas with DDT and other pesticides.
    d. using drugs to kill the parasites in the bloodstream.
  * e. all of these answers.

78. Incidence of malaria has increased since 1970 because
    a. organisms causing malaria developed resistance to drugs.
    b. the vectors developed resistance to insecticides.
    c. reservoirs from hydropower have increased.
    d. none of these answers.
  * e. all of these answers.

79. The strategy *least* recommended for preventing incidence of malaria is
    a. increasing water flow in irrigation systems.
    b. using mosquito nets dipped in permethrin.
  * c. spraying heavier doses of DDT on swamps and estuaries.
    d. cultivating fish that feed on mosquito larvae.
    e. increasing public education.

10-5 RISK ANALYSIS

80. Which of the following includes the other four?
    a. risk assessment
    b. risk management
    * c. risk analysis
    d. risk communication
    e. none of these answers.

81. EPA science advisors consider all of the following to be high-risk ecological problems *except*
    a. global climate change.
    b. species extinction and loss of biodiversity.
    * c. groundwater pollution.
    d. stratospheric ozone depletion.
    e. wildlife habitat destruction.

82. Pesticides are considered by EPA science advisors to be
    a. high-risk ecological problems.
    * b. medium-risk ecological problems.
    c. low-risk ecological problems.
    d. medium-risk health problems.
    e. high-risk health problems.

83. EPA science advisors consider oil spills and thermal pollution to be
    a. high-risk ecological problems.
    b. medium-risk ecological problems.
    * c. low-risk ecological problems.
    d. high-risk health problems.
    e. medium-risk health problems.

84. EPA science advisors consider indoor and outdoor air pollution problems to be
    a. high-risk ecological problems.
    b. medium-risk ecological problems.
    c. low-risk ecological problems.
    d. medium-risk health problems.
    * e. high-risk health problems.

85. All of the following are part of the process of risk assessment *except*
    a. determining the types of hazards involved.
    b. estimating how many people are likely to be exposed.
    c. estimating the probability that each hazard will occur.
    * d. informing decision makers and the public about risks.
    e. none of these answers.

86. The major cause of a reduced human life span today is
    * a. poverty.
    b. smoking.
    c. cancer.
    d. high cholesterol.
    e. driving.

87. Susceptibility to environmental stresses is increased in people already affected by
    a. poverty.
    b. disease.
    c. malnutrition.
*   d. all of these answers.
    e. none of these answers.

88. The strategy which would contribute *least* to longer lifespan would be
    a. no smoking.
    b. regular exercise.
    c. safe driving.
*   d. regular sunbathing.
    e. good nutrition.

89. Technology reliability would be *least* improved by careful
    a. maintenance.
    b. monitoring.
*   c. job rotation.
    d. design.
    e. `none of these answers.

90. Human reliability is generally _____ technology reliability.
    a. much greater than
    b. slightly greater than
    c. slightly lower than
*   d. much lower than
    e. none of these answers.

91. Calculating the risk of a new technological system
*   a. requires assessment of technological reliability.
    b. requires careful economic analysis.
    c. requires assessment of human intelligence.
    d. is impossible.
    e. none of these answers.

92. The explosion of the space shuttle *Challenger* and the accidents at Three Mile Island and Chernobyl were caused
    a. by global climate change.
*   b. primarily by human error.
    c. by the northern lights interfering with normal electrical transmission.
    d. primarily by technological error.
    e. none of these answers.

93. Risk assessment and risk-benefit analyses are useful for all of the following *except* they
    a. focus on areas that need more research.
    b. help regulators decide how money for reducing risks should be allocated.
    c. organize available information.
*   d. eliminate uncertainties about planning the future.
    e. identify significant hazards.

94. Problems with risk assessment include:
    a. some technologies benefit one group and harm another group.
    b. people making risk assessments vary in their emphasis on long-term versus short-term risks
    c. there may be conflict of interest in those carrying out the risk assessment and review of
*   d. all of these answers.
    e. none of these answers.

95. Risk management involves trying to answer all of the following questions *except*
    a. Which of the risks have top priority?
    b. How reliable is the risk-benefit analysis or risk assessment?
    c. How much risk is acceptable?
  * d. Is it morally responsible to develop this risk?
    e. How much will it cost to reduce each risk to an acceptable level?

96. The general public perceives an innovation as a greater risk than the experts do when it
    a. is relatively familiar and simple.
  * b. is involuntarily thrust upon the public rather than being an individual choice.
    c. is viewed as beneficial and necessary rather than unnecessary.
    d. involves a large number of deaths spread out over a long period of time rather than deaths from a single catastrophic accident.
    e. the people affected are involved in the decision-making process.

CHAPTER 11
THE HUMAN POPULATION: GROWTH AND DISTRIBUTION

11-1 FACTORS AFFECTING HUMAN POPULATION SIZE

1. The population change in a particular year can be calculated by
    a. (deaths + emigration) - (births + immigration)
    *   b. (births + immigration) - (deaths + emigration)
    c. (deaths + immigration) - (births + emigration)
    d. (births + emigration) - (deaths + immigration)
    e. (births + deaths) – (immigration + emigration)

2. The crude birth rate is the number of live births per _____ persons in a given year.
    a. 50
    b. 100
    c. 500
    *   d. 1,000
    e. 10,000

3. The highest crude birth rate and crude death rate are in
    *   a. Africa.
    b. Latin America.
    c. Asia.
    d. Europe.
    e. Oceania.

4. Between 1963 and 2001, the rate of the world's annual population change
    *   a. dropped 39%.
    b. dropped 93%.
    c. remained stable.
    d. rose 39%.
    e. rose 93%.

5. Between 1963 and 2001, the human population size
    a. dropped 91%.
    b. dropped 39%.
    c. remained stable.
    d. rose 39%.
    *   e. rose 91%.

6. Which of the following statements about the world's population is *false?*
    a. Together, Chine and India make up 38% of the world's population.
    b. The most rapid population growth is taking place in the developing countries.
    c. Africa has the highest population growth rate.
    *   d. When the total fertility rate drops below the replacement-level fertility, the population is balanced and stops growing.
    e. Europe has a negative growth rate.

7. Which of the following countries would produce the greatest rise in population size from experiencing a growth rate of 1.2%?
    a. country A, with a population of 100,000
    b. country B, with a population of 1 million
    c. country C, with a population of 10 million
    *   d. country D, with a population of 1 billion
    e. country E, with a population of 100 million.

8.   Which of the following would contribute the greatest number to total population size in one year?
     a.   a country of 1.5 million people with a growth rate of 3%
     b.   a country of 5 million people with a growth rate of 2.5%
     c.   a country of 100 million people with a growth rate of 2%
*   d.   a country of 500 million people with a growth rate of 1.5%
     e.   a country of 10 million people with a growth rate of 2.5 %.

9.   The actual average replacement-level fertility for the whole world is slightly higher than
     a.   1 child per couple.
*   b.   2 children per couple.
     c.   3 children per couple.
     d.   4 children per couple.
     e.   6 children per couple.

10. The *most* useful measure of fertility for projecting future population change is the
     a.   replacement-level fertility.
     b.   one-year future fertility level.
*   c.   total fertility rate.
     d.   birth rate.
     e.   abortion rate.

11. The birth rate in the United States has been at or below replacement level for about
     a.   10 years.
     b.   20 years.
*   c.   30 years.
     d.   40 years.
     e.   50 years.

12. The total fertility rate in the United States reached a peak
     a.   when the United States was dominated by an agricultural economy during the late 1700s.
     b.   after the Civil War, in the 1870s.
     c.   after World War I, in the mid-1920s.
*   d.   after World War II, in the mid-1950s.
     e.   after the Viet man War, in the mid-1970's.

13. The industrialized country with the highest teenage pregnancy rate is
     a.   Japan.
     b.   Germany.
*   c.   the United States.
     d.   France.
     e.   Britain.

14. Social factors affecting birth and fertility rates include
     a.   attitudes toward large families and birth control.
     b.   average levels of education and affluence.
     c.   urbanization.
*   d.   all of these answers.
     e.   poverty.

15. Which of the following would decrease the likelihood of a couple having a child?
     a.   The child is part of the family labor pool.
     b.   Contraceptives are not available.
     c.   They have no public or private pension.
*   d.   Women have many opportunities to participate in the work force.
     e.   Infant mortality rates are high.

16. Of the following forms of birth control, the *most* effective is
    * a. total abstinence.
    b. condom (good brand).
    c. hormonal implant.
    d. diaphragm plus spermicide.
    e. Oral contraceptives.

17. Of the following forms of birth control, the *least* effective is
    a. IUD plus spermicide.
    b. oral contraceptive.
    c. hormonal implant.
    d. condom (good brand).
    * e. rhythm method.

18. An unreliable form of birth control is a
    a. cervical cap.
    * b. douche.
    c. condom.
    d. spermicide.
    e. IUD.

19. Which of the following statements is *false?*
    * a. The rise in the size of the human population is due primarily to a higher birth rate.
    b. Increased food supplies and medical care have increased life expectancy.
    c. Only a few countries annually accept a large number of immigrants or refugees.
    d. Migration within countries plays an important role in the population dynamics of cities, towns, and rural areas.
    e. Women with access to education and jobs usually have fewer children.

20. Two useful indicators of overall health in a country or region are
    a. birth rate and death rate.
    b. replacement-level fertility rate and total fertility rate.
    * c. life expectancy and infant mortality rate.
    d. life expectancy and death rate.
    e. population growth rate.

21. A high infant mortality rate is most often associated with
    a. a high standard of living.
    * b. undernutrition.
    c. balanced diets.
    d. a low incidence of infectious disease.
    e. affluence.

22. Infant mortality rate refers to the number of children out of 1,000 that die
    a. before birth.
    b. in their first month.
    c. in the first half-year of life.
    * d. by their first birthday.
    e. by their 5th birthday.

23. All of the following reasons help explain why the United States has one of the highest infant mortality rates of developed countries *except*
    a. lack of health care for children of the poor after birth.
  * b. the older age of pregnant women as a result of many women delaying having children.
    c. lack of adequate prenatal care.
    d. high birth rate for teenage women.
    e. none of these answers.

11-2 POPULATION AGE STRUCTURE

24. The age structure of a population is the number or percentage of
    a. females age 14 years or under.
    b. females age 15 to 44.
    c. males age 15 to 44.
  * d. persons of each sex at each age level.
    e. persons of each sex age 15 to 44.

25. Population age structure diagrams can be divided into all of the following categories *except*
  * a. infant.
    b. prereproductive.
    c. reproductive.
    d. postreproductive.
    e. a and b.

26. Age structure diagrams
    a. show only two age groups: reproductive and not reproductive.
    b. show the number of males and females in the infant category only.
    c. are strictly for present use and do not provide insight into future trends.
    d. are useful for studying developing countries but not developed countries.
  * e. are useful for comparing one population with another.

27. Countries that have achieved ZPG have an age structure that
    a. forms an inverted pyramid.
    b. has a broad-based pyramid.
  * c. shows little variation in population by age.
    d. has a large prereproductive population.
    e. has a large reproductive population.

28. Rapidly growing countries have an age structure that
    a. forms an inverted pyramid.
  * b. has a broad-based pyramid.
    c. shows little variation in population by age.
    d. has narrow pyramid.
    e. has a large postreproductive population.

29. Which of the following implies the greatest built-in momentum for population growth?
    a. a large population size
    b. a large number of people age 29 to 44
    c. a large number of people under age 34
  * d. a large number of people under age 15
    e. a large number of people over the age of 45.

30. A baby boomer is *least* likely to
    a. strongly influence demands for goods and services.
    b. influence politics.
 * c. take voluntary early retirement.
    d. place strains on Medicare as middle age approaches.
    e. place strains on social security as they retire.

31. Countries undergoing rapid population decline may experience a rise in the proportion of the population
    a. on social security.
    b. consuming a large fraction of medical services.
    c. who are older people.
 * d. who fit all of these answers.
    e. can face labor shortages.

11-3 SOLUTIONS: INFLUENCING POPULATION SIZE

32. All of the following countries accept large numbers of immigrants *except*
    a. the United States.
 * b. Mexico.
    c. Canada.
    d. Australia.
    e. b and d.

33. In 2001, legal and illegal immigration accounted for _____ of U.S. population growth.
    a. 13%
    b. 23%
    c. 33%
 * d. 43%
    e. 53%

34. Which of the following *least* characterizes U.S. immigration policy?
    a. The law prohibits hiring of illegal immigrants.
    b. Some environmentalists want to limit immigration to a small percentage of U.S. population growth.
    c. Some citizens feel that limiting immigration diminishes the U.S. role in providing a place of opportunity for poor and oppressed people.
 * d. Over the past decade, efforts to deport illegal immigrants have weakened.
    e. Some citizens are opposed to limiting immigration because immigrants pay taxes and take many menial, low-paying jobs.

35. Generally, proponents of population regulation say that
 * a. 1/6 of the human population does not get basic necessities.
    b. people are the world's most valuable resource.
    c. if a person produces more than he consumes, he is an asset.
    d. human ingenuity permits continued improvement in humanity's lot.
    e. all of these answers.

36. People who oppose population regulation are *least* likely to say that
    a. lack of a free and productive economic system in developing countries is the primary cause of poverty and despair.
    b. people are the world's most valuable resource for finding solutions to our problems.
    c. population regulation is a violation of religious beliefs and an intrusion into personal privacy and freedom.
 * d. increasing human population threatens the earth's life-support systems.
    e. many immigrants open businesses and create jobs.

37. People who support population regulation say that
* a. billions more people on the earth will intensify many environmental and social problems.
b. it is unethical for us to control birth rates.
c. the gap between the rich and poor has been narrowing since 1960.
d. we have the freedom to produce as many children as we want.
e. all of these answers.

38. The term *demographic transition* refers to
a. a requirement for a population to reach a specific size before it becomes stable.
b. the slowing down in the growth of a population as it approaches the carrying capacity.
* c. the decline in death rates followed by decline in birth rates when a country becomes industrialized.
d. the decline in death rates followed by a decline in birth rates that occurred when the germ theory of disease was discovered.
e. all of these answers.

39. The change that takes place in a demographic transition occurs when
a. one-third of the population is under 15 years of age.
b. the birth rate drops below the death rate.
* c. the economic development of a country changes the population growth pattern.
d. either immigration or emigration changes the population growth pattern.
e. a population reaches one million.

40. The demographic transition model helps to explain why
a. death rates rise in industrializing nations.
b. industrialization leads to population growth.
c. development requires large populations.
d. birth rates fall before death rates.
* e. death rates fall before birth rates.

41. During demographic transitions, birth rates of a population are high during the
a. preindustrial and industrial stages.
b. postindustrial and transitional stages.
c. industrial and postindustrial stages.
* d. preindustrial and transitional stages.
e. preindustrial and postindustrial stages.

42. In the demographic transition model, ZPG in a country is likely to occur during
a. the industrial stage.
* b. the postindustrial stage.
c. the transitional stage.
d. the preindustrial stage.
e. the time after the postindustrial stage.

43. In the demographic transition model, death rates fall while birth rates remain high during
a. the preindustrial stage.
b. the industrial stage.
c. the postindustrial stage.
* d. the transitional stage.
e. none of these answers.

44. In the demographic transition model, birth and death rates are high during
    * a. the preindustrial stage.
      b. the industrial stage.
      c. the postindustrial stage.
      d. the transitional stage.
      e. none of these answers.

45. Some experts fear that the developing countries lack sufficient ___ to allow the demographic transition to occur.
      a. people
    * b. capital
      c. cooperation
      d. commitment
      e. desire.

46. Basic family-planning policy in most countries includes all of the following *except*
    * a. limiting families to two children each.
      b. providing information about prenatal care.
      c. helping parents space births as desired.
      d. helping parents regulate family size.
      e. none of these answers.

47. Family-planning programs have been successful in reducing population growth in
      a. Haiti.
      b. India.
    * c. China.
      d. Nigeria.
      e. Guatemala

48. The success of a family planning program is enhanced when
      a. the leadership is apathetic.
      b. implementation is left to central planners.
    * c. contraceptives are widely available.
      d. the majority of the people live in the countryside.
      e. there is a high infant mortality rate.

49. Generally, women who are feeding their infant only with breast milk are ___ protected from pregnancy for six months after giving birth.
      a. 38%
      b. 58%
      c. 78%
    * d. 98%
      e. 18%

50. Government attempts to reduce population growth have included all of the following *except*
      a. paying couples who agree to use contraceptives.
      b. paying couples who agree to be sterilized.
      c. penalizing couples that have more than a certain number of children (usually one or two).
    * d. providing needed health care and food allotments to those who have more than a certain number of children.
      e. raising taxes for couples that have more than a certain number of children.

51. Economic rewards and penalties in population control strategies work *best* if they
    a. push rather than nudge people to have fewer children.
    b. are retroactive.
  * c. reinforce existing customs and trends.
    d. decrease a poor family's income or land.
    e. don't increase a poor families economic status.

52. Women tend to have fewer and healthier children when they
    a. live in societies in which their individual rights are protected.
    b. have access to paying jobs outside the home.
    c. have access to education.
    d. have access to birth control.
  * e. all of these answers.

53. Which of the following statements about women's employment/economic status is *false?*
    a. Women do more than half of the work gathering fuelwood.
    b. Women do more than half of the work involved in producing food.
  * c. Women have more than half of the world's assets.
    d. Women provide more of the world's health care than all of the world's organized health services put together.
    e. Women do almost all domestic work and child care.

54. Women possess _____% of the world's land.
  * a. less than 1
    b. 10
    c. 25
    d. 50
    e. 75

55. Women receive _____% of the world's income.
    a. 1
  * b. 10
    c. 25
    d. 50
    e. 75

11-4 CASE STUDIES: SLOWING POPULATION GROWTH IN INDIA AND CHINA

56. India _____ family-planning program.
  * a. had the world's first national
    b. has the world's most successful
    c. has the world's only national
    d. has the world's largest
    e. all of these answers.

57. India's family planning has yielded disappointing results for all of the following reasons *except*
    a. poor planning and bureaucratic inefficiency.
  * b. failure to employ sterilization.
    c. extreme poverty.
    d. low status of women.
    e. lack of administrative and financial support.

58. India's infant mortality rate is about _____ per 1,000 live births.
    a. 30
    b. 50
  * c. 70
    d. 90
    e. 100

59. Which of the following statements about India is (are) *true*?
    a. There is a strong preference for female children.
  * b. Many cultural norms favor large families.
    c. Indian women still have an average of 2.1 children.
    d. Government pensions have eliminated the need for large families.
    e. Women don't have access to birth control.

60. Which of the following statements about China is *false*?
  * a. In the last quarter century, China's crude birth rate dropped from 32 to 25 per 1,000 people.
    b. Total fertility dropped from 5.7 to 1.8 children per woman.
    c. Life expectancy is 12 years higher than India.
    d. Illiteracy is about one-third of India's rate.
    e. Married couples have access to free birth control.

61. China's population policy has included all of the following *except*
    a. encouraging later marriages.
    b. health, pension, and employment benefits for a one-child pledge.
    c. urging couples to have no more than one child.
    d. free access to birth control.
  * e. encouraging contraceptive use but banning abortion.

62. China's population control program does all of the following *except*
    a. employ freely available contraceptives.
    b. employ compulsory measures.
  * c. emphasize huge family-planning centers.
    d. offer economic incentives.
    e. preferential treatment in employment for a couples one child.

63. Perhaps the *most* important feature of China's population control program that could be transferred to other countries is
    a. focusing control efforts on males.
  * b. localizing the program rather than forcing people to travel to distant centers.
    c. requiring one of the parents to be sterilized when a couple has two children.
    d. encouraging couples to postpone marriage.
    e. none of these answers.

11-5 CUTTING GLOBAL POPULATION GROWTH: A NEW VISION

64. All of the following countries achieved replacement-level fertility within 15-30 years *except*
    a. Japan.
    b. Thailand.
  * c. India.
    d. Taiwan.
    e. South Korea.

65. Experience indicates that population growth can be slowed by .
    a. investing in family planning.
    b. elevating the status of women.
    c. reducing poverty.
  * d. a combination of all of these answers.
    e. improving the health care of infants, children, and pregnant women.

66. Which of the following strategies appear to play the *least* important role in slowing global population growth?
    a. reducing poverty
    b. investing in family planning
  * c. economic disincentives to have large families
    d. elevating the status of women
    e. improving the health care of infants, children and pregnant women.

67. Which of the following is *not* one of the goals of the 1994 UN Conference on Population and Development?
    a. Reduce and eliminate unsustainable patterns of production and consumption.
  * b. Increase access to education, especially for boys.
    c. Improve the health care of infants, children, and pregnant mothers.
    d. Improve employment opportunities for young women.
    e. Take steps to eradicate poverty.

68. Which of the following is *not* one of the goals of the 1994 UN Conference on Population and Development?
    a. Make population policies part of social and economic development policies.
  * b. Emphasize that child-rearing and family planning responsibilities belong to women.
    c. Take steps to eradicate poverty.
    d. Bring about more equitable relationship between the sexes.
    e. Increase access to education, especially for girls and women.

11-6 POPULATION DISTRIBUTION: URBANIZATION AND URBAN GROWTH

69. An urban area is any town, village, or city with a population of
    a. 750.
    b. 1,500.
  * c. 2,500.
    d. 5,000.
    e. 10,000.

70. Between 1850 and 2001, the global urban revolution resulted in urban population increasing from
  * a. 2% to 46%.
    b. 7% to 62%.
    c. 14% to 43%.
    d. 15% to 92%.
    e. 25% to 95%.

71. Today there are ____ megacities.
  * a. 19
    b. 29
    c. 39
    d. 49
    e. 59

72. The squatter settlement populations of most cities in developing countries
    a. have lower incomes than do the rural poor.
    b. are declining in number.
  * c. consist of poor people living in makeshift shelters.
    d. get the same services as other residents.
    e. have access to clean water.

73. Which of the following statements is *false?*
    a. Children in cities have a better chance for education.
    b. Politicians avoid giving services to the poor because this is costly and might attract more people to the cities.
    c. Jobs are difficult to find in cities.
  * d. Parents tend to have more children in urban than in rural environments.
    e. Parents tend to have fewer children in urban than in rural environments.

74. People migrate to cities
    a. because agriculture is becoming more mechanized.
    b. in search of a better life.
    c. for education, innovation, and culture.
    d. for jobs.
  * e. all of these answers.

75. The urban growth occurring in the developing countries is
  * a. caused by both migration and natural increase.
    b. generally well planned and orderly.
    c. generally offset by migration to rural areas.
    d. helping to eliminate urban poverty.
    e. all of these answers.

76. Those who migrate and find jobs in cities can expect all of the following *except*
    a. long hours and low wages.
    b. dangerous machinery.
  * c. health and retirement benefits.
    d. noise pollution.
    e. high crime rate.

77. Mexico City is characterized by
    a. severe air pollution.
    b. 2,000 rural immigrants every day.
    c. noise, congestion, and crime.
  * d. all of these answers
    e. high crime rate.

78. "Fecal snow" is characteristic of
    a. Sao Paulo.
  * b. Mexico City.
    c. Calcutta.
    d. Rio de Janeiro.
    e. Bombay.

79. Breathing the air of Mexico City is like smoking ____ pack(s) of cigarettes each day.
    a. 1
    b. 2
  * c. 3
    d. 4
    e. 5

80. Mexico City has severe air pollution because of
    a. motor vehicles.
    b. thermal inversions.
    c. high population.
*   d. all of these answers.
    e. factories.

81. Your text described all of the following actions to reduce Mexico City's air pollution *except*
    a. banning cars from a central zone.
*   b. tax incentives to improve energy efficiency.
    c. phasing out unleaded gasoline.
    d. trucks run only on LPG.
    e. planting 25 million trees.

82. The United States has about _____ metropolitan areas.
    a. 70
    b. 170
*   c. 270
    d. 370
    e. 470

83. To qualify as a metropolitan area, a city must have a population of _____ people.
    a. 25,000
*   b. 50,000
    c. 75,000
    d. 100,000
    e. 500,000

84. The U.S. population is
    a. shifting to the north and east.
    b. shifting to the north and west.
    c. shifting to the south and east.
*   d. shifting to the south and west.
    e. shifting to the north and south.

85. Since 1920, urban areas in the United States have seen improvements in
    a. housing conditions.
    b. medical care.
    c. air and water quality.
    d. sanitation.
*   e. all of these answers.

86. Which of the following shifts describes the most recent shift in U.S. internal human populations?
*   a. urban areas to rural areas
    b. agricultural areas to cities
    c. North and East to South and West
    d. large central cities to suburbs
    e. all of these answers.

87. Which of the following is not a factor that leads to urban sprawl?
*   a. high cost of gasoline
    b. state and local zoning laws
    c. availability of mortgages
    d. government loan guarantees to veterans
    e. ample land for expansion.

11-7 URBAN RESOURCES AND ENVIRONMENTAL PROBLEMS

88.   Today's cities are *not* self-sustaining because they import
      a.   minerals.
      b.   energy.
      c.   food.
      d.   manufactured goods.
   *   e.   all of these answers.

89.   With 46% of the world's population, urban dwellers occupy about _____ of the planet's land area, but to meet their demands has required using or disturbing about _____ of the earth's habitable land area.
      a.   20%. . . 73%
      b.   20%. . . 33%
      c.   44%. . . 88%
   *   d.   4%. . . 75%
      e.   50%...50%

90.   Which of the following is *not* an environmental benefit of urbanization?
      a.   Birth rates are lower.
      b.   Concentrating people preserves biodiversity.
   *   c.   Cities are self-sustaining.
      d.   Recycling is more economically feasible.
      e.   People have better access to environmental information.

91.   A sustainable city has _____ metabolism.
      a.   no
      b.   linear
      c.   exponential
   *   d.   circular
      e.   none of these answers.

92.   Vegetation improves the quality of life in urban areas by all of the following means *except*
      a.   muffling noise.
      b.   providing wildlife habitat.
      c.   absorbing air pollutants.
   *   d.   warming the air.
      e.   reduce soil erosion.

93.   The water problem *least* likely to be faced by an urban area is
      a.   water supply.
      b.   contaminated runoff.
      c.   flooding.
   *   d.   protection of wild streams and rivers.
      e.   none of these answers.

94.   Floodplains
      a.   are hard to develop.
      b.   are inaccessible.
   *   c.   are often sites of urbanization.
      d.   are considered poor land for development by developers.
      e.   all of these answers.

95. All of the following climate conditions are generally higher in urban areas than in suburbs and rural areas *except*
    a. cloud cover.
    * b. wind speeds.
    c. fog.
    d. precipitation.
    e. warmer.

96. Urban areas tend to alter climate by all of the following means *except*
    a. generating heat.
    b. absorbing heat.
    c. obstructing wind.
    * d. reducing tropospheric ozone.
    e. none of these answers.

97. A city may be identified by a(n)
    a. cool pocket.
    b. dust bowl.
    * c. heat island.
    d. increased wind speed.
    e. all of these answers.

98. Sound becomes painful at _____ decibels.
    a. 40
    b. 60
    c. 80
    d. 100
    * e. 120

99. The most widespread occupational hazard in the United States is
    a. pesticide poisoning.
    b. breathing smoke.
    * c. noise.
    d. landslides.
    e. physical injuries.

100. All of the following harmful effects have been linked to prolonged exposure to excessive noise *except*
    a. gastric ulcers.
    b. psychological disorders and irritability.
    c. high blood pressure and higher cholesterol levels.
    * d. skin cancer.
    e. hearing loss.

101. A sound registering 50 dbA compared to one registering 30 dbA means that the first sound is _____ times louder than the second sound.
    a. 12
    b. 30
    * c. 100
    d. 1,000
    e. 10,000

102. Definite hearing damage can be experienced by exposure to about _____ dbA.
*   a. 85
    b. 95
    c. 105
    d. 115
    e. 20

103. Which of the following produces the loudest sound?
    a. jackhammer
    b. chain saw
    c. rock music
    d. truck
*   e. military rifle

11-8 TRANSPORTATION AND URBAN DEVELOPMENT

104. Urban sprawl
    a. is a new video game.
    b. creates new natural habitat.
    c. defines a strong sense of community.
*   d. paves over some of the best farmland.
    e. none of these answers.

105. In the United States, _____% of all urban transportation is by car.
    a. 68
    b. 78
    c. 88
*   d. 98
    e. 48

106. With 4.7% of the people in the world, the United States has ___% of the cars.
    a. 5
    b. 15
    c. 25
*   d. 35
    e. 85

107. Advantages of automobiles include all of the following *except*
    a. freedom to go where you want when you want.
    b. adventure.
*   c. energy efficiency.
    d. provision of jobs.
    e. convenience of use.

108. Which of the following statements is *false*?
    a. About 18 million people have been killed by motor vehicles.
    b. Motor vehicles are the largest source of air pollution.
*   c. Constructing more roads reduces automobile travel and congestion.
    d. More Americans have been killed by automobiles than on battlefields in all U.S. wars.
    e. none of these answers.

109. In 1907, horse-drawn vehicles in Manhattan rode almost _____ as motorized vehicles today.
    a. 1/10 as fast
    b. 1/2 as fast
    c. the same speed
*   d. three times as fast
    e. 1/100 as fast

110. Which of the following statements is *false?*
    a. A bicycle requires less energy than walking.
    b. Bike-and-ride commuting is catching on in the United States.
    c. Annual sales of bicycles exceed sales of cars.
    d. Bicycles produce no pollution.
  * e. A bicycle is 8% less expensive to buy and operate than a car.

111. Electric bikes can do all of the following *except*
    a. allow cyclists to travel over hilly terrain.
    b. extend the range of bike trips.
    c. replace noisier, more highly polluting mopeds and motor scooters.
  * d. cost more than mopeds and motor scooters.
    e. help reduce air pollution.

112. The development of U.S. mass transit has been discouraged by
    a. the expansion of trolley systems.
    b. expensive gasoline prices.
    c. expensive cars.
  * d. federal gasoline taxes to build highways.
    e. all of these answers.

113. Mass transit is used most in
    a. West Germany.
    b. France.
  * c. Japan.
    d. the United States.
    e. Ethiopia.

114. Mass transit in the United States has been discouraged by
    a. 80% of the gasoline tax going for highways.
    b. employer-paid parking perks.
    c. the dismantling of the early trolley and streetcar systems.
  * d. all of these answers.
    e. none of these answers.

115. Compared to highway and air transport, rail systems
    a. are less energy efficient and produce more air pollution.
    b. cause more injuries and deaths.
  * c. are available to people who are too young, old, or disabled to drive or who can't afford to fly.
    d. take up more land.
    e. all of these answers.

116. Advantages of light rail include
    a. costing 1/10 as much to build as highways.
    b. low operating costs.
    c. sharing of rights-of way with other forms of transportation.
  * d. all of these answers.
    e. none of these answers.

117. All of the following cities have recently developed successful rapid-rail systems *except*
    a. Hong Kong.
    b. Mexico City.
  * c. Houston.
    d. Pittsburgh.
    e. none of these answers

118. In Western Europe and Japan, new high-speed regional trains have been found to be
    * a. ideal for trips of 120–620 miles.
    b. uncomfortable and dangerous.
    c. more polluting.
    d. least profitable along heavily used transportation routes.
    e. less energy efficient per person than cars.

119. Advantages of using buses for transportation include all of the following *except*
    a. flexibility of transportation routes.
    b. lower operating costs than heavy rail.
    * c. a comfortable, quiet ride.
    d. less capital investment than heavy rail.
    e. rarely getting caught in traffic.

120. Disadvantages of bus systems include all of the following *except*
    a. unreliability.
    b. noisy and uncomfortable rides.
    c. air pollution.
    d. getting caught in traffic.
    * e. high capital investment and operating costs.

121. If you visit Curitiba, Brazil, you would expect to find
    a. no recycling program.
    * b. a sophisticated bus system.
    c. urban blight.
    d. polluted air.
    e. no high rise apartments.

122. Which of the following statements is true?
    a. In the United States, more land is devoted to housing than cars.
    b. Three-fourths of the land in a U.S. city is devoted to cars and their services.
    c. Building more roads would solve traffic congestion.
    * d. With full-cost pricing of automobiles, demand for automobiles would go down.
    e. all of these answers.

123. When more roads are built, more cars are sold. Then more roads are built. This interaction exemplifies a(n)
    * a. positive feedback loop.
    b. negative feedback loop.
    c. synergistic interaction.
    d. antagonistic interaction.
    e. negative, synergistic interaction.

124. All of the following strategies could help developing countries avoid the "car trap" *except*
    a. investing in public transit systems.
    b. subsidizing ecocar development.
    * c. providing city-wide paths for bicycling and walking.
    d. instituting full-cost gasoline pricing.
    e. none of these answers.

11-9 MAKING URBAN AREAS MORE LIVABLE AND SUSTAINABLE

125. Ninety percent of the funds used to support government services (schools, roads, police and fire protection, welfare, and so on) come from
    a. income taxes.
    b. sales tax.
    c. fees and licenses.
    d. gifts.
  * e. property taxes.

126. Ecologically sound development can be discouraged by
    a. requiring environmental impact analysis for private and public projects.
    b. conservation easements.
    c. land trusts.
  * d. taxing land on the basis of the economically highest potential use.
    e. all of these answers.

127. Tools which can smooth uncontrolled growth and move toward more ecologically sound growth include
    a. requiring environmental impact analysis for all proposed developments.
    b. setting up land trusts to protect ecologically valuable land.
    c. offering conservation easements to landowners who use ecologically sound ways.
  * d. all of these answers.
    e. none of these answers.

128. Which of the following is *not* an appropriate method of land-use control?
    a. conservation easements
    b. land trusts
  * c. subsidy of farmers who use marginal land that is highly susceptible to erosion
    d. taxation of land on the basis of its current use
    e. none of these answers.

129. Local governments can control land use by
    a. not requiring building permits.
  * b. zoning.
    c. providing unlimited services.
    d. encouraging ecologically unsound development.
    e. all of these answers.

130. The world's *most* comprehensive land-use controls are found in
    a. Japan and North America.
    b. western Europe and Australia.
    c. western Europe and North America.
    d. North American and Australia.
  * e. Japan and western Europe.

131. Indications of problems in U.S. infrastructure include all of the following *except*
    a. substantial water losses in cities due to leaky pipes.
    b. roads needing repair.
  * c. statues being marred by acid deposition.
    d. maintenance required by public transportation.
    e. none of these answers.

132. In the current U.S. situation, it is unusual to pay infrastructure bills in a period of
    * a. record budget deficits.
      b. high inflation.
      c. strong citizen support for higher taxes.
      d. surpluses for federal building funds.
      e. all of these answers.

133. The reason for the extremely high cost of upgrading existing U.S. roads, bridges, transit systems, water-supply systems, and sewers is
      a. increased population.
      b. growth.
    * c. years of neglect.
      d. urbanization.
      e. all of these answers.

134. Which of the following is *not* one of the three types of new towns?
      a. satellite towns
      b. freestanding new towns
      c. in-town new towns
      d. urban towns.
    * e. suburban towns

135. A sustainable city does all of the following *except*
      a. use energy efficiently.
    * b. encourage fast flow-through of materials.
      c. encourage biodiversity.
      d. compost to improve soil quality.
      e. none of these answers.

136. All of the following strategies would make existing cities and suburbs more sustainable *except*
      a. developing a town center.
      b. cluster-housing.
    * c. zoning for larger lots with more lawns.
      d. offering alternative forms of transportation to the automobile.
      e. none of these answers.

CHAPTER 12
AIR AND AIR POLLUTION

1.   A lichen is a mutualistic relationship between
  *   a.   an alga and a fungus.
      b.   a dinoflagellate and a coral.
      c.   a coral and a fungus.
      d.   a coral and an alga.
      e.   a sea anemone and a clown fish.

2.   Lichens are particularly useful for indicating
      a.   water pollution.
  *   b.   air pollution.
      c.   toxic-waste sites.
      d.   pesticides.
      e.   old growth forests.

3.   Lichens can track air pollution to its source because they
      a.   live a long time.
      b.   stay in one place.
      c.   are widespread.
  *   d.   all of these answers
      e.   none of these answers,

12-1   THE ATMOSPHERE

4.   The correct sequence of layers of the atmosphere from innermost to outermost is
      a.   mesosphere—stratosphere—thermosphere—troposphere.
  *   b.   troposphere—stratosphere—mesosphere—thermosphere.
      c.   stratosphere—thermosphere—troposphere—mesosphere.
      d.   thermosphere—stratosphere—mesosphere—troposphere.
      e.   thermosphere-mesosphere-stratosphere-troposphere.

5.   The atmosphere is divided into spherical layers based upon the
      a.   density of each layer.
      b.   concentration of ozone in each layer.
  *   c.   temperature changes from variations in absorption of solar energy.
      d.   concentration of oxygen in each layer.
      e.   precipitation in each layer.

6.   The atmospheric layer containing 75% of the mass of Earth's air is the
      a.   thermosphere.
      b.   mesosphere.
      c.   stratosphere.
  *   d.   troposphere.
      e.   none of these answers.

7.   If the Earth were an apple, the lower layer of the atmosphere would be the thickness of
      a.   the core.
      b.   the part of the apple we eat.
  *   c.   the skin.
      d.   the whole apple.
      e.   a seed.

8.   Most of Earth's weather occurs in the
   * a.   troposphere.
      b.   thermosphere.
      c.   mesosphere.
      d.   stratosphere.
      e.   all of these answers.

9.   You send up a weather balloon that monitors temperature changes in the atmosphere. Initially, the temperature drops as the balloon rises. Suddenly, there is a reversal and the temperature starts to rise. This boundary would be the
   * a.   the tropopause.
      b.   the stratopause.
      c.   the minipause.
      d.   the mesopause.
      e.   the menopause.

10.   The troposphere differs from the stratosphere in that it has
      a.   1,000 times less oxygen by volume.
      b.   1,000 times more ozone by volume.
   * c.   1,000 times less ozone by volume.
      d.   1,000 times more nitrogen.
      e.   1,000 times less moisture by volume.

11.   Stratospheric ozone
      a.   screens out ultraviolet radiation.
      b.   allowed the evolution of life on land.
      c.   prevents ozone formation in the troposphere.
   * d.   all of these answers.
      e.   helps protect humans from sunburn and cataracts.

12.   There is evidence that humans are _____ ozone in the troposphere and _____ ozone in the stratosphere.
      a.   increasing. . . increasing
   * b.   increasing. . . decreasing
      c.   decreasing. . . decreasing
      d.   decreasing. . . increasing
      e.   none of these answers.

12-2 OUTDOOR AIR POLLUTION

13.   Ozone which contributes to the formation of smog is found in the
   * a.   troposphere.
      b.   thermosphere.
      c.   mesosphere.
      d.   stratosphere.
      e.   mesopause.

14.   Each of the following is one of the major classes of outdoor pollutants *except*
      a.   carbon oxides.
   * b.   smog.
      c.   nitrogen oxides.
      d.   sulfur oxides.
      e.   photochemical oxidants.

15. According to the World Health Organization, one in every _____ persons live in urban areas with air that is unhealthy to breathe.
    a. two
  * b. six
    c. ten
    d. twenty
    e. fifty

16. All of the following are volatile organic compounds (VOCs) *except*
    a. methane.
    b. chlorofluorocarbon.
  * c. carbon monoxide.
    d. benzene.
    e. none of these answers.

17. All of the following are photochemical oxidants *except*
  * a. dioxin.
    b. hydrogen peroxide.
    c. peroxyacyl nitrates (PANs).
    d. aldehydes, such as formaldehyde.
    e. none of these answers.

18. All of the following are suspended particles *except*
    a. dust and soot.
    b. pesticides.
    c. sulfuric acid.
    d. PCBs.
  * e. chlorofluorocarbons.

12-3 PHOTOCHEMICAL AND INDUSTRIAL SMOG

19. Photochemical smog generally requires the presence of
    a. nitrogen oxides.
    b. sunlight.
    c. volatile organic compounds.
    d. b and c only.
  * e. all of these answers.

20. Photochemical smog is formed when primary pollutants interact with
  * a. sunlight.
    b. water vapor.
    c. sulfur dioxide.
    d. oxygen.
    e. carbon.

21. You are enjoying a sunny day in Los Angeles. In late afternoon, your respiratory tract becomes irritated. Of the following substances, the one *least* likely to be causing your problem is
    a. PANS
    b. aldehydes.
    c. ozone.
  * d. carbon dioxide.
    e. carbon monoxide.

22. Photochemical smog is characteristic of urban areas with many vehicles and a climate that is
    a. cool, wet, and cloudy.
    b. cool, dry, and sunny.
  * c. warm, dry, and sunny.
    d. warm, wet, and cloudy.
    e. warm, wet and sunny.

23. Primary pollutants from burning coal include all of the following *except*
    a. carbon monoxide.
    b. sulfur dioxide.
    c. soot.
    * d. ozone.
    e. none of these answers.

24. Gray-air smog comes from suspended particles of
    a. carbon dioxide.
    b. ammonium salts.
    * c. soot.
    d. carbonic acid.
    e. ozone.

25. The frequency and severity of smog in an area depends *least* upon the
    a. local climate and topography.
    b. fuels used in industry, heating, and transportation.
    * c. size of the ozone hole over the Arctic.
    d. density of the population.
    e. open fires.

26. Which of the following statements is *true?*
    a. Thermal inversion occurs when a layer of cold air prevents warm air from rising.
    * b. Thermal inversions exacerbate pollution problems.
    c. Thermal inversions last only a few minutes to a few hours.
    d. Normally, cool air near Earth's surface expands and rises, carrying pollutants higher into the troposphere.
    e. Thermal inversions help prevent air pollution.

27. A thermal inversion is the result of
    a. precipitation.
    b. cold air drainage.
    * c. a lid of warm air on top of cooler, stagnant air.
    d. a cold blanket of air that prevents warm air from rising.
    e. mixing of cool and warm air.

28. Which of the following areas would be *least* likely to have a temperature inversion?
    a. an area near the coast
    * b. an area in the central plains
    c. a valley surrounded by mountains
    d. the leeward side of a mountain range
    e. none of these answers.

29. The US city with the toughest pollution control program and the greatest air pollution problem is
    a. New York City.
    b. Birmingham, Alabama.
    * c. Los Angeles.
    d. Boston.
    e. Atlanta.

12-4 REGIONAL OUTDOOR AIR POLLUTION FROM ACID DEPOSITION

30. Tall chimneys
    a. are expensive ways to disperse pollution.
    b. cannot carry the pollutants above any local inversion layer.
    * c. are an output approach to pollution.
    d. increase pollution in upwind areas.
    e. all of these answers.

31. Acid deposition is properly defined as the _____ deposition of _____ pollutants onto Earth's surface.
    a. wet . . . secondary
    b. dry . . . secondary
    c. wet and dry . . . primary
  * d. wet and dry . . . secondary
    e. dry . . . primary

32. Typical rain in the eastern United States has a pH of
    a. 3.6.
    b. 4.6.
  * c. 5.6.
    d. 6.6.
    e. 7.6.

33. Acid deposition is best classified as a
    a. local problem.
    b. state problem.
  * c. regional problem.
    d. national problem.
    e. international problem.

34. All of the following describe soils that are vulnerable to acid deposition *except*
    a. thin.
    b. low in buffering ions.
  * c. high in hydroxyl (OH-) ions.
    d. acidic.
    e. soils that have been depleted by decades of acid deposition.

35. Experts rate acid rain as a
    a. high-risk ecological and human health problem.
  * b. medium-risk ecological problem and high-risk human health problem.
    c. high-risk ecological and low-risk human health problem.
    d. medium-risk ecological and human health problem.
    e. high-risk ecological problem and no-risk human health problem.

36. In general, acid deposition has harmful effects for terrestrial ecosystems when it falls below a pH level of
    a. 3.6.
    b. 4.6.
  * c. 5.6.
    d. 6.6.
    e. 7.6.

37. Acid deposition has been linked to
    a. contamination of fish with highly toxic methylmercury.
    b. excessive soil nitrogen levels.
    c. reduced nutrient uptake by tree roots.
  * d. all of these answers.
    e. weakening trees so they become more susceptible to other types of damage.

38. Of the following strategies to reduce acid deposition, the *least* effective is probably
    a. removing sulfur from coal before it is burned.
    b. reducing energy use.
    c. switching to natural gas.
  * d. adding lime to neutralize the acids.
    e. improving energy efficiency.

39. Acid shock that damages aquatic life in the Northern Hemisphere is the result of the sudden runoff of acid water with dissolved
    a. lead.
    b. chromium.
    c. fluorine.
 * d. aluminum.
    e. all of these answers.

40. Most of the 9,000 lakes threatened by excess acidity in the United States are in the
    a. Southeast and lower Midwest.
    b. Northwest and upper Midwest.
    c. Southwest and lower Midwest.
    d. Southwest and upper Midwest.
 * e. Northeast and upper Midwest.

41. Acid deposition
    a. increases the mobility of toxic metals.
    b. kills many species of fish.
    c. damages statues, buildings, and car finishes.
 * d. all of these answers.
    e. decreases atmospheric visibility.

12-5 INDOOR AIR POLLUTION

42. Experts rate indoor air pollution as a
 * a. high-risk health problem for humans.
    b. medium-risk health problem for humans.
    c. low-risk health problem for humans.
    d. high-risk ecological problem.no-risk health problem for humans.
    e. none of these answers.

43. Of the following, the *least* vulnerable to air pollution are
    a. sick people.
    b. pregnant women.
    c. infants and children.
 * d. white-collar workers.
    e. smokers.

44. *Sick Building Syndrome* is linked to all of the following *except*
    a. headaches.
    b. coughing and sneezing.
 * c. lung cancer.
    d. chronic fatigue.
    e. burning eyes.

45. According to the EPA, at least _____ of all U.S. commercial buildings are considered "sick" from indoor air pollutants.
    a. 7%
 * b. 17%
    c. 27%
    d. 37%
    e. 47%

46. All of the following are on EPA's "four most dangerous indoor air pollutants list" *except*
    a. asbestos
    b. radon-222
    c. cigarette smoke
    d. formaldehyde
 * e. sulfur dioxide

47. Furniture stuffing, paneling, particleboard, and foam insulation may be sources of
    a. chloroform.
    * b. formaldehyde.
    c. carbon monoxide.
    d. asbestos.
    e. sulfur dioxide.

48. Formaldehyde is used in
    a. particle board.
    b. paneling.
    c. plywood.
    d. foam insulation.
    * e. all of these answers.

49. Exposure to indoor formaldehyde pollution is *least* likely to cause
    * a. ulcers.
    b. headaches.
    c. chronic breathing problems.
    d. dizziness.
    e. sore throat.

50. Pipe insulation and vinyl ceiling and floor tiles may be sources of
    a. chloroform.
    b. formaldehyde.
    c. carbon monoxide.
    * d. asbestos.
    e. sulfur dioxide.

51. Asbestos has been used for all of the following *except*
    a. fireproofing.
    * b. insulation of refrigerators.
    c. insulation of heaters and pipes.
    d. wall and ceiling decoration.
    e. none of these answers.

52. Radioactive _____ is a product of uranium decay and an indoor air pollutant.
    * a. radon
    b. radium
    c. plutonium
    d. lead
    e. hydrogen.

53. Radon-222 is
    a. a nauseating gas.
    b. a product of organic decay.
    c. particularly concentrated in underground deposits of limestone and sandstone.
    * d. basically a problem in confined spaces, such as basements, and underground wells over radon-containing deposits.
    e. not dangerous because it is easily seen and smelled.

54. In 1988, the EPA and the U.S. Surgeon General recommended that everyone living in a detached house or the first three floors of an apartment building test for radon. By 2001, ___% of all households had tested for radon.
    * a. 6
    b. 12
    c. 24
    d. 48
    e. 68

55. You have been looking for your first house for months. You find one in just the right neighborhood at just the right price for you. In the course of negotiations, you have a radon test done and find that the level is 1 picocurie/liter. A reasonable course of action would be to
    a. get out of the housing market.
    b. back out of the deal quickly and look for another house.
    c. make a purchase offer, but recognize you will need to make some changes over the course of a few years.
    d. call the police and report the homeowner.
 * e. make a purchase and move in happily ever after.

56. You have been looking for your first house for months. You find one in just the right neighborhood at just the right price for you. In the course of negotiations, you have a radon test done and find that the level is 250 picocuries/liter. A reasonable course of action would be to
    a. get out of the housing market.
 * b. back out of the deal quickly and look for another house.
    c. make a purchase offer, but recognize you will need to make some changes over the course of a few years.
    d. make a purchase and move in happily ever after.
    e. call the police and report the homeowner.

12-6 EFFECTS OF AIR POLLUTION ON LIVING ORGANISMS AND MATERIALS

57. Humans are protected from air pollution by
    a. sneezing and coughing.
    b. mucus capturing small particles.
    c. nasal hairs filtering out large particles.
    d. tiny mucus-coated hairlike structures called cilia.
 * e. all of these answers.

58. Years of smoking and exposure to air pollutants can contribute to the incidence of
    a. emphysema.
    b. chronic bronchitis.
    c. lung cancer.
    d. asthma.
 * e. all of these answers.

59. The people *least* vulnerable to air pollution are
    a. infants.
    b. elderly people.
 * c. adult males.
    d. people with heart and respiratory disease.
    e. pregnant women.

60. Sources of carbon monoxide include all of the following *except*
    a. cigarette smoking.
 * b. anaerobic respiration.
    c. motor vehicles.
    d. faulty heating systems.
    e. airplanes.

61. Carbon monoxide
    a. causes the blood to carry too much oxygen.
    b. speeds up reflexes.
 * c. causes headaches and dizziness.
    d. sharpens thinking and perceptions.
    e. prevents sleep.

62. Pollutants that can penetrate the lungs' natural defenses include
    a. large suspended particles.
    * b. fine and ultrafine suspended particles.
    c. ozone.
    d. acid rain.
    e. none of these answers.

63. Fine and ultrafine particles are emitted by
    a. radial tires.
    b. wind erosion.
    c. power and industrial plants.
    d. wood-burning fireplaces.
    * e. all of these answers.

64. Fine and ultrafine particles lodged in the lungs may
    a. cause lung cancer.
    b. trigger asthma attacks.
    c. interfere with gas exchange between the blood and the lungs.
    * d. all of these answers.
    e. aggravate other lung diseases.

65. All of the following are chronic diseases adversely affected by ozone in photochemical smog *except*
    * a. diabetes.
    b. asthma.
    c. bronchitis.
    d. emphysema.
    e. heart disease.

66. According to the EPA and the American Lung Association, air pollution in the US costs at least
    _____ annually.
    a. $1 billion
    b. $10 billion
    c. $15 billion
    d. $100 billion
    * e. $150 billion

67. According to a 1999 study by Australia's Commonwealth Science Council, at least _____ people die prematurely each year from the effects of indoor and outdoor air pollution.
    * a. 1 million
    b. 3 million
    c. 5 million
    d. 10 million
    e. 25 million

68. Chronic exposure of tree leaves and needles to air pollutants can
    a. cause a waxy coating to build up.
    b. increase uptake of nutrients.
    c. cause leaves or needles to turn bright red and drop off.
    d. reduces susceptibility to pests.
    * e. increase the chance of damage from diseases, pests, drought, and frost.

69. Waldsterben in Europe
    a. kills small rodents.
    b. increases plant resistance to drought and disease.
    * c. kills large forests.
    d. spreads bubonic plague.
    e. prevents air pollution.

70. Air pollution in the United States has *most* seriously affected trees
    a. along the shores of lakes.
    b. lining major interstate highways.
 * c. on high-elevation slopes facing moving air masses.
    d. in the low-lying swamps in the Southeast.
    e. in the central United States.

71. U.S. air pollution has *most* seriously affected trees in the
 * a. Appalachian Mountains.
    b. Rocky Mountains.
    c. Olympic Mountains.
    d. Sierra Nevada Mountains.
    e. all of these answers.

72. Air pollution, mostly ozone, has reduced crop production by 5% to 10% especially in
    a. corn.
    b. wheat.
    c. soybeans.
 * d. alfalfa.
    e. peanuts.

73. Which of the following would you expect to show the *least* damage from air pollution?
    a. clothing
 * b. plastic swimming pool
    c. marble statue
    d. exterior paint on a car
    e. roofing material

12-7 SOLUTIONS: PREVENTING AND REDUCING AIR POLLUTION

74. National ambient air quality standards
    a. have been established for almost 100 air pollutants.
    b. must be met by 50 major U.S. metropolitan areas that are responsible for implementation plans.
    c. are established by Congress.
 * d. specify the maximum allowable level, averaged over a specific time period, for a certain outdoor air pollutant.
    e. specify the minimum allowable level, averaged over a specific time period, for a certain outdoor air pollutant.

75. Which of the following policies prevents industries from moving into those areas with air cleaner than national requirements?
    a. the Clean Air Act of 1970
    b. the National Ambient Air Quality Standards (NAAQS)
    c. national emission standards
 * d. Prevention of Significant Deterioration (PSD) standards
    e. all of these answers.

76. The effectiveness of the pollution prevention approach is *best* illustrated by the sharp drop in atmospheric
    a. ozone.
    b. sulfur dioxide.
 * c. lead.
    d. carbon monoxide.
    e. nitrogen oxide.

77. Environmentalists criticize the Clean Air Act of 1990 for all of the following *except*
    * a. failing to establish primary ambient air quality standards.
      b. failing to increase the fuel-efficiency standards for cars and light trucks.
      c. doing too little to reduce emissions of greenhouse gases.
      d. relying primarily on pollution cleanup rather than pollution prevention.
      e. not adequately regulating emissions from inefficient, two-cycle gasoline engines.

78. An emissions trading policy tried on _____ cut U.S. emissions by 30%.
      a. carbon oxides.
    * b. sulfur dioxide.
      c. asbestos.
      d. lead.
      e. carbon dioxide.

79. In 1997, the EPA proposed a voluntary emission trading program involving smog-forming _____ for 22 eastern states.
      a. ozone
      b. particulates
    * c. nitrogen oxides
      d. carbon monoxide
      e. carbon dioxide.

80. Of the following strategies to reduce emissions of pollutants from stationary sources, the one which is *least* likely to help over the *long run* is
      a. burning low-sulfur coal.
      b. removing sulfur from coal.
    * c. dispersing pollutants above the thermal inversion layer.
      d. shifting to less polluting fuels.
      e. convert coal to a liquid or gaseous fuel.

81. Particulates can be removed from stack exhaust gases by all of the following methods *except*
      a. baghouse filters.
      b. wet scrubbers.
    * c. mini-incinerators.
      d. cyclone separators.
      e. electrostatic precipitator.

82. Which of the following would function as a pollution cleanup method for motor vehicles?
      a. Improve motor efficiency.
      b. Rely on mass transit and bicycles.
    * c. Use emission-control devices.
      d. Add a charge to new cars based on the amount of pollution they produce.
      e. all of these answers.

83. Methods to *prevent* pollution from motor vehicle emissions include all of the following *except*
      a. improving fuel efficiency and modifying the internal combustion engine to reduce emissions.
      b. raising annual registration fees on older, more polluting cars.
    * c. using pollution control devices.
      d. giving subsidies to car makers for each low-polluting, energy-efficient car they sell.
      e. restrict driving in polluted areas.

84. Of the following motor vehicle fuels, the greatest polluter is
    * a. gasoline.
      b. hydrogen gas.
      c. alcohol.
      d. natural gas.
      e. battery.

85. Recently, a University of Colorado professor developed a one-second highway test for automobile emissions of
   a. nitrogen oxides.
   b. carbon monoxide.
   c. hydrocarbons.
   * d. all of these answers.
   e. none of these answers.

86. Indoor air pollution could be sharply reduced by
   a. modifying building codes to prevent radon infiltration.
   b. requiring exhaust hoods or vent pipes for stoves, refrigerators, or other appliances burning natural gas or other fossil fuels.
   c. setting emission standards for building materials.
   d. use office machine in well-ventilated areas.
   * e. all of these answers.

87. One way to help protect the atmosphere would be to
   a. quickly burn all remaining fossil fuels to encourage faster change to alternative fuels.
   b. compartmentalize air pollution, water pollution, and energy policies so that each department has its own focus.
   c. emphasize local control and responsibility for air pollution.
   * d. control population growth.
   e. decrease use of renewable energy.

88. Which of the following strategies would help protect the atmosphere?
   a. Use a city-by-city rather than regional approach to air quality control.
   b. Shift from renewable to more efficient nonrenewable energy resources.
   * c. Integrate air pollution, water pollution, energy, land-use, and population regulation policies.
   d. Exclude social costs of air pollution from pricing strategies.
   e. Decrease use of renewable energy.

CHAPTER 13
CLIMATE CHANGE AND OZONE LOSS

13-1 PAST CLIMATE CHANGE AND THE NATURAL GREENHOUSE EFFECT

1. Which of the following best describes the Earth's average surface temperature for the past 900,000 years?
    a. a steady warming trend
    b. fairly steady temperatures until recently
    *   c. many fluctuations of several °C
    d. fairly steady with occasional cool spells
    e. fairly steady with a recent cooling trend.

2. Over the last million years, glacial periods lasting about _____ years have alternated with interglacial periods lasting about _____.
    *   a. 10,000 . . . 100,000
    b. 1,000 . . . 10,000
    c. 10,000 . . . 10,000
    d. 5,000 . . . 10,000
    e. 50,000 . . . 500,000

3. The *greenhouse effect* is best described as
    *   a. consensus science.
    b. pioneer science.
    c. fantasy.
    d. a convention of florists.
    e. junk science.

4. The major greenhouse gases include all of the following *except*
    a. chlorofluorocarbons (CFCs).
    b. carbon dioxide and water vapor.
    *   c. sulfur dioxide.
    d. ozone and nitrous oxide.
    e. ozone

5. The two predominant greenhouse gases in the troposphere are
    a. carbon dioxide and ozone.
    *   b. carbon dioxide and water vapor.
    c. nitrogen and water vapor.
    d. nitrous oxide and sulfur dioxide.
    e. ozone and nitrogen.

6. Which of the following statements about the greenhouse effect is *false?*
    a. The amount of heat trapped in the troposphere depends on concentrations of greenhouse gases.
    *   b. The greenhouse effect is a new theory that explains the warming of the atmosphere.
    c. Heat trapped by greenhouse gases keeps the planet warm enough for life.
    d. The two predominant greenhouse gases are water vapor and carbon dioxide.
    e. It has been confirmed by numerous lab experiments and measurements of atmospheric temperatures at different altitudes.

7. Estimated variations in Earth's mean surface temperature over the past 135 years correlate closely with
   a. ozone.
   b. water vapor.
   c. CFCs.
   d. nitrous oxide.
   * e. carbon dioxide.

13-2 CLIMATE CHANGE AND HUMAN ACTIVITIES

8. Since 1860, mean global temperature has risen _____ degree(s) Centigrade.
   a. 0.1–0.3
   * b. 0.6-0.7
   c. 0.8-1.1
   d. 1.0–1.5
   e. 2.0-2.5

9. All of the following greenhouse gases have increased in recent decades *except*
   a. carbon dioxide.
   b. methane.
   * c. water vapor.
   d. nitrous oxide.
   e. CFCs

10. Increased greenhouse gases originate from
    a. burning fossil fuels.
    b. use of CFCs.
    c. deforestation.
    d. none of these answers.
    * e. all of these answers.

13-3 PROJECTING FUTURE CHANGES IN THE EARTH'S CLIMATE

11. Major climate models project all of the following *except*
    a. a 1.0- to 3.5-degree centigrade rise in Earth's mean surface temperature by 2100.
    b. an Earth warmer than at any time in the last 10,000 years.
    * c. the falling of global sea levels.
    d. more warming in the Northern Hemisphere than in the Southern Hemisphere.
    e. none of these answers.

12. All of the following have been reported and are possible signs of global warming *except*
    a. spread of some tropical diseases away from the equator.
    b. bleaching of coral reefs in tropical areas with warmer water.
    * c. homestead farming in Antarctica.
    d. increased retreat of some glaciers on the tops of mountains in the Northern Cascades.
    e. northward migration of some warm-climate fish.

13. We have the most certainty about
    a. variations in solar output.
    b. the role the oceans will play in global warming.
    * c. patterns of glacial and interglacial periods in Earth's history.
    d. the role of polar ice in global warming.
    e. how changes in the Earth's reflectivity will affect atmospheric temperature.

13-4   FACTORS AFFECTING CHANGES IN THE EARTH'S AVERAGE TEMPERATURE

14.   We are uncertain about how
  a.   carbon dioxide will affect the rate of photosynthesis.
  b.   increased temperatures will affect insect populations.
  c.   gas trapped in the permafrost will affect global warming.
  d.   how air pollution might affect climate.
  * e.   all of these answers.

15.   Solar output varies in 13-year and 22-year cycles by about
  a.   0.001%.
  b.   0.01%.
  * c.   0.1%.
  d.   1.0%.
  e.   10.0%

16.   About 29% of the carbon dioxide released into the atmosphere by human activities
  a.   remains in the atmosphere.
  * b.   is absorbed by the oceans.
  c.   is absorbed by the growth of plants.
  d.   is absorbed by the soil.
  e.   none of these answers

17.   Pollutants might affect climate change by
  a.   cooling effects of particles from volcanic eruptions.
  b.   warming and cooling effects from sulfur dioxide emissions.
  c.   cooling effects from particles in smoke from large-scale burning.
  * d.   all of these answers.
  e.   none of these answers.

18.   As global warming progresses, methane
  a.   might be absorbed as permafrost melts in the arctic tundra.
  b.   might be absorbed from natural wetlands with rising carbon dioxide.
  * c.   may be released from oceanic muds as ocean waters warm.
  d.   may be reduced by bacteria in tundra soils.
  e.   all of these answers.

19.   Projections from global climate models might be off by a factor of
  a.   10.
  b.   5.
  * c.   2.
  d.   50%.
  e.   25%

13-5   SOME POSSIBLE EFFECTS OF A WARMER WORLD

20.   Evidence indicates that climate belts would shift toward the poles _____ miles for every 1°C increase.
  a.   10–30
  b.   30–60
  * c.   60–90
  d.   90–120
  e.   120-150

21. Regarding food production, global climate models have projected a
   * a. 10% to 50% loss in current cropland area.
     b. 10% to 50% gain in current cropland area.
     c. no change in the amount of land available to grow food.
     d. 10% to 70% gain in yields of food crops.
     e. 20% to 75% loss in current cropland area.

22. In the event of global warming, food production might be negatively affected by all of the following *except*
     a. poorer soil in new crop-growing regions.
     b. increased insect populations.
     c. lack of irrigation water in some areas.
   * d. decreased UV radiation resulting from increased ozone.
     e. changes in crop yields.

23. The consequences of rapid climate change over decades might include
     a. premature deaths from lack of food.
     b. reduction in earth's biodiversity.
     c. social and economic chaos.
     d. increased death from heat and disease.
   * e. all of these answers.

24. Tree species typically move _____ mile(s) per decade.
     a. 1
   * b. 5
     c. 10
     d. 20
     e. 50

25. If climate belts move faster than trees migrate, there could be
     a. a large increase of forest area.
   * b. mass extinctions of species that couldn't migrate.
     c. an increase in forest diversity.
     d. tropical forests in New England.
     e. all of these answers.

26. A warmer world is *least* likely to result in
     a. decreased food production.
     b. reductions in biodiversity.
     c. a rise in sea level.
   * d. more moderate weather.
     e. spread of tropical diseases.

27. A rise in sea level is *least* likely to
     a. flood areas where one-third of the world's human population lives.
   * b. save the coral reefs.
     c. accelerate coastal erosion.
     d. contaminate coastal aquifers.
     e. disrupt coastal fisheries.

28. In a warmer world, we would expect more
     a. droughts.
     b. hurricanes.
     c. prolonged heat waves.
     d. desert expansion.
   * e. all of these answers.

29. Which of the following niches is likely to be *most* effected by global warming?
    a. generalist
  * b. specialist
    c. keystone
    d. indicator
    e. spectator.

30. Which of the following statements about the potential effects of global warming on human health is *false?*
    a. Food and freshwater supplies are likely to be disrupted.
    b. People are likely to be displaced.
  * c. Insect-borne diseases are likely to decrease in today's temperate zones.
    d. Sanitation systems in coastal cities may be flooded.
    e. Increased respiratory disease.

31. In a warmer world, increasing numbers of environmental refugees would likely cause
  * a. political instability.
    b. more good will among people.
    c. the quicker emergence of the fourth world order.
    d. quicker evolutionary adaptation among humans.
    e. a lower death rate.

13-6 SOLUTIONS: DEALING WITH THE THREAT OF CLIMATE CHANGE

32. Scientists who claim the global climate system is so complex we will never have the level of certainty wanted by decision makers urge
    a. take no action now because global warming is all hype.
  * b. take action now based on the precautionary principle.
    c. take no action until we get more data.
    d. continuing monitoring of the data.
    e. take no action until we see a greater effect.

33. The quickest, cheapest, and most effective way to reduce the buildup of carbon dioxide in the atmosphere is to
    a. switch from fossil fuels to nuclear fuels.
  * b. increase the efficiency of energy use.
    c. plant trees to trap more carbon dioxide.
    d. stop deforestation.
    e. slow population growth

34. The threat of global warming can be addressed by
    a. using energy more efficiently.
    b. halting deforestation.
    c. slowing population growth.
  * d. all of these answers.
    e. shifting to renewable resources.

35. All of the following are prevention approaches to global warming *except*
    a. taxing gasoline and carbon dioxide emissions.
    b. shifting to perpetual and renewable energy sources.
    c. improving energy efficiency; transfer energy-efficiency and pollution prevention technologies to developing countries.
    d. slowing population growth.
  * e. dispersing methane from landfills to prevent explosions.

36. Prevention approaches to global warming include all of the following *except*
  * a. increase beef production to strengthen public health.
    b. reduce deforestation.
    c. switch to sustainable agriculture.
    d. slow population growth.
    e. improve energy efficiency.

37. It has been suggested that the threat of global warming can be addressed by all of the following "technofixes" except
    a. adding iron to the oceans.
    b. using foil-surfaced sun shields in space.
    c. injecting sulfate particulates into the stratosphere.
  * d. covering the oceans with Styrofoam chips.
    e. releasing billions of helium-filled reflective balloons into the atmosphere.

38. At the 1992 Earth Summit in Rio de Janeiro, _____ nations committed themselves to reducing greenhouse gas emissions to 1990 levels by the year 2000.
    a. 25
    b. 50
    c. 75
  * d. over 100
    e. over 200

13-7 WHAT IS BEING DONE TO REDUCE GREENHOUSE GAS EMISSIONS?

39. The 1997 Kyoto treaty to reduce global warming would
    a. not require developing countries to make any cuts in their greenhouse gas emission unless they choose to do so.
    b. allow emissions trading.
    d. allow forested countries to get a break in their quotas.
    d. none of these answers.
  * e. all of these answers.

13-8 OZONE DEPLETION IN THE STRATOSPHERE?

40. Which of the following statements is *false?*
    a. The formation of the ozone layer enabled life on land to evolve.
    b. CFCs are odorless and stable.
    c. CFCs are nonflammable, nontoxic, and noncorrosive.
  * d. Fluorine atoms are most responsible for the breakdown of ozone to molecular oxygen.
    e. CFCs are cheap to produce.

41. Chlorofluorocarbons are
  * a. nontoxic.
    b. corrosive.
    c. odorous.
    d. flammable.
    e. expensive.

42. Chlorofluorocarbons are used in all of the following *except*
    a. air conditioners.
    b. aerosol spray cans.
    c. sterilants for hospital equipment.
  * d. fire extinguishers.
    e. cleaners for computer chips.

43. The story of the discovery of the effects of CFCs and the political response to that knowledge best illustrates which of the following components of complex systems?
    a. negative feedback loop
    b. positive feedback loop
    c. synergistic interaction
    * d. lag time
    e. all of these answers.

44. Which of the following statements is *false?*
    a. Over 44 years passed from the first production of CFCs until the first awareness that they could cause environmental damage.
    b. CFCs are stable, odorless, nonflammable, nontoxic, and noncorrosive chemicals.
    c. CFCs are found in bubbles in Styrofoam and insulation.
    * d. CFCs are important because they help screen out ultraviolet radiation from reaching Earth's surface.
    e. CFCs remain in the troposphere because they are insoluble in water and chemically unreactive.

45. Which of the following statements is *false?*
    a. CFCs are relatively unreactive compounds.
    * b. CFCs are heavy molecules that will sink in the atmosphere.
    c. Ultraviolet radiation will cause CFCs to break down and release chlorine.
    d. One chlorine molecule may convert 100,000 molecules of ozone to molecular oxygen.
    e. all the statements are true

46. Between the first warnings about CFCs from the scientific community and a response to reduce CFCs from the political community there was a ____-year lag.
    a. one
    b. five
    c. ten
    * d. fifteen
    e. twenty-five

47. All of the following chemicals are ozone-eaters *except*
    a. methyl bromide.
    * b. PCBs.
    c. halons.
    d. methyl chloroform.
    e. CFCs

48. CFCs take _____ years to reach the stratosphere.
    a. 1–2
    b. 5–10
    * c. 10–20
    d. 20–30
    e. 30-50

49. CFCs are used for all of the following *except*
    a. coolants in refrigerators and air conditioners.
    b. propellants in aerosol spray cans.
    c. sterilants in hospitals.
    * d. fuels in camp stoves.
    e. cleaners for electronic parts.

50. CFCs are released into the atmosphere by all of the following *except*
    a. spray cans.
    b. discarded refrigerators.
 * c. burning of artificial logs in fireplaces.
    d. leaking of air conditioners.
    e. cleaning computer chips.

51. A single chlorine atom can convert as many as _____ ozone molecules to molecular oxygen molecules.
    a. 100
    b. 1,000
    c. 10,000
 * d. 100,000
    e. 1,000,000

52. The single greatest contributor to CFC emissions in the United States is
    a. spray cans.
    b. discarded refrigerators.
    c. burning of artificial logs in fireplaces.
    d. cleaning computer chips.
 * e. leaking air conditioners.

53. Chemicals capable of destroying ozone include all of the following *except*
    a. chlorofluorocarbons.
 * b. formaldehyde used as a preservative.
    c. halons in fire extinguishers and crop fumigants.
    d. carbon tetrachloride used as a solvent.
    e. methyl bromide used as a fumigant.

54. In the 1980s, researchers discovered a _____% loss of ozone in the upper stratosphere over the Antarctic during the Antarctic springtime.
    a. 5—10
    b. 20—25
 * c. 40—50
    d. 70—80
    e. 80—90

55. Which of the following statements is *false?*
 * a. The ozone hole is larger in the Northern Hemisphere than in the Southern Hemisphere.
    b. Up to 50% of the ozone over Antarctica is destroyed each year.
    c. The large annual decrease in ozone over the South Pole is caused by spinning vortices with clouds of ice crystals with absorbed CFCs on their surfaces.
    d. 10—38% ozone loss has been reported in the Arctic springtime.
    e. none of these answers.

56. Increases in ultraviolet radiation will cause an increase in all but which one of the following?
    a. skin cancers
 * b. yields of food crops
    c. eye cataracts
    d. suppression of the human immune system
    e. increased breakdown of materials such as paints and plastics.

57. Human health problems closely associated with ozone depletion include all of the following *except*
    a. skin cancer.
    b. eye cataracts.
    * c. increased incidence of heart disease.
    d. suppression of the immune response.
    e. none of these answers.

58. The fact that increased skin cancer rates may not show up for 15–40 years following ozone depletion illustrates the concept of
    a. positive feedback.
    b. negative feedback.
    * c. lag time.
    d. suppression of the immune system.
    e. synergistic interaction.

59. Damage to the ecological structure and function of lakes because of deeper penetration of UV light is cause by
    a. ozone depletion only.
    b. acid deposition only.
    c. global warming only.
    * d. a synergistic interaction among ozone depletion, acid deposition, and global warming.
    e. a and b only.

13-9 SOLUTIONS: PROTECTING THE OZONE LAYER

60. We can slow the rate of ozone hole creation by
    a. stopping production of ozone-depleting chemicals.
    b. recovering and reusing ozone-depleting chemicals.
    c. finding substitutes for CFCs.
    * d. all of these answers.
    e. none of these answers.

61. In 1987, 36 nations meeting in Montreal, Canada, developed the Montreal Protocol to reduce production of
    a. carbon dioxide.
    b. nitrous oxide.
    * c. CFCs.
    d. toxic wastes.
    e. halons.

62. To help protect the ozone layer, individuals should do all of the following *except*
    a. avoid purchasing products that contain CFCs.
    * b. buy halon fire extinguishers.
    c. pressure legislators to ban all uses of CFCs, halons, and methyl bromide by 1995.
    d. buy new refrigerators that use vacuum insulation and helium as a coolant.
    e. encourage all countries to ban all ODCs.

CHAPTER 14
WATER RESOURCES AND WATER POLLUTION

1. All of the following are downstream countries that could suffer from an upstream country withdrawing more water from a shared river *except*
    a. Egypt.
    b. Jordan.
    c. Israel.
    d. Iraq.
    * e. Turkey.

2. There is potential for conflict over water resources among all of the following pairs of countries *except*
    a. Sudan and Egypt.
    b. Syria and Jordan.
    c. Syria and Israel.
    * d. Turkey and Egypt.
    e. Syria and Iraq.

14-1 WATER'S IMPORTANCE AND UNIQUE PROPERTIES

3. Water covers about _____% of the earth's surface.
    a. 51
    b. 61
    * c. 71
    d. 81
    e. 91

4. Water
    a. provides habitats for many organisms.
    b. maintains Earth's climate.
    c. makes up most of living organisms.
    d. dissolves a variety of substances.
    * e. all of these answers.

5. Which of the following statements is *false?*
    a. Water has a very high heat capacity and changes temperatures very slowly.
    b. Water helps distribute heat throughout the earth.
    * c. Water has a low heat of vaporization; that is, it evaporates very easily.
    d. Water functions well as a coolant.
    e. Water dissolves a variety of substances.

6. Which of the following statements is *false?*
    a. Water is easily polluted because it is a good solvent.
    * b. Water has a low surface tension; it is not attracted and does not adhere to other molecules.
    c. Water exhibits capillarity, the ability to rise through small pores.
    d. Water expands when it freezes.
    e. Water helps distribute heat throughout the earth.

7. Water
    a. contracts when it freezes and expands when it melts.
    b. reaches its maximum density when it freezes.
    * c. breaks rocks during weathering.
    d. is used as a lubricant in engines.
    e. all of these answers.

8. Which of the following statements is *false?*
   * a. Water is one of the better-managed resources.
   b. We do not charge enough for water.
   c. We waste and pollute water.
   d. More than 50% of organisms' weight is water.
   e. Water expands when it freezes.

14-2 SUPPLY, RENEWAL, AND USE OF WATER RESOURCES

9. Approximately _____% of the earth's water is fresh rather than salt water.
   * a. 3
   b. 9
   c. 27
   d. 60
   e. 85

10. Only about _____% of the world's total water supply exists as uncontaminated fresh water on or close to the surface and readily available for human use.
   a. 0.0003
   * b. 0.003
   c. 0.03
   d. 0.3
   e. 3.0

11. The hydrologic cycle will naturally purify and recycle fresh water as long as humans don't
   a. pollute the water faster than it is replenished.
   b. withdraw it from groundwater supplies faster than it is replenished.
   c. overload it with slowly degradable and nondegradable wastes.
   d. a and b only.
   * e. all of these answers.

12. During which of the following does water move in a direction different from the others?
   a. percolation
   * b. transpiration
   c. infiltration
   d. precipitation
   e. runoff

13. Porous water-saturated layers of underground rock are known as
   * a. aquifers.
   b. recharge areas.
   c. watersheds.
   d. runoff areas.
   e. water tables.

14. Which of the following statements is *false?*
   a. Recharging of water is a slow process.
   b. Fossil aquifers are nonrenewable resources on a human time scale.
   c. Aquifers could be called slow moving underground lakes.
   * d. Groundwater is stationary and does not move.
   e. The water table is located at the top of the zone of saturation.

15. Throughout the world, the most water is used for
    * a. irrigation.
    b. industrial processes.
    c. needs of animals and humans.
    d. transportation.
    e. cooling towers of power plants.

16. Averaged globally, about two-thirds of the water withdrawn each year is used for
    a. industrial processes.
    b. cooling towers of power plants.
    * c. irrigation of croplands.
    d. domestic use.
    e. transportation.

17. Worldwide, energy production accounts for _____% of withdrawn water.
    a. 5
    b. 15
    * c. 25
    d. 35
    e. 45

18. Which of the following uses tends to consume the smallest amount of water?
    a. irrigation
    * b. public use
    c. industry
    d. power plant cooling
    e. transportation

19. In the western United States as compared to the eastern United States, the major water problem(s) is (are)
    a. flooding.
    b. insufficient water for some urban areas.
    * c. chronic drought and insufficient runoff.
    d. pollution of rivers, lakes, and groundwater.
    e. insufficient water for industry.

20. Of the following uses for water, the one, which is least significant in the eastern United States, is
    * a. irrigation.
    b. energy production.
    c. cooling.
    d. manufacturing.
    e. transportation.

21. In the western United States, the largest use for water is
    * a. irrigation.
    b. energy production.
    c. cooling.
    d. manufacturing.
    e. transportation.

22. The least important water concern in the East is
    a. occasional urban shortages.
    b. water pollution.
    * c. shortage of runoff caused by low precipitation.
    d. flooding.
    e. lack of water for industry.

23. The most serious water problem in the West is
    a. occasional urban shortages.
    b. water pollution.
 * c. shortage of runoff caused by low precipitation.
    d. flooding.
    e. lack of water for industry.

14-3 TOO LITTLE WATER: PROBLEMS AND SOLUTIONS

24. Water can be scarce because of
    a. water stress.
    b. aridity.
    c. desiccation.
    d. drought.
 * e. all of these answers.

25. Water scarcity from long-term shortage of water due to a dry climate is called
    a. water stress.
 * b. aridity.
    c. drought.
    d. desiccation.
    e. acute shortage.

26. Water scarcity from drying up of the soil because of deforestation or overgrazing is called
    a. water stress.
    b. aridity.
    c. drought.
    d. acute shortage.
 * e. desiccation.

27. Water scarcity from increasing numbers of people relying on fixed levels of runoff is called
 * a. water stress.
    b. aridity.
    c. drought.
    d. desiccation.
    e. acute shortage.

28. Water scarcity during a period when precipitation is lower than normal and evaporation is higher than normal is called
    a. water stress.
    b. aridity.
 * c. drought.
    d. desiccation.
    e. acute shortage.

29. About _____ of the world's 214 major river systems are shared by two or more countries.
    a. 20
    b. 50
    c. 100
 * d. 150
    e. 200

30   Conflicts over water supplies are most serious in
*   a.   the Middle East.
       b.   the southwestern United States.
       c.   California.
       d.   Southeast Asia.
       e.   China.

31.   Water supply can be increased by
       a.   water diversion projects.
       b.   construction of dams and reservoirs.
       c.   improving efficiency of water use.
       d.   withdraw groundwater.
*   e.   all of these answers.

32.   Large dams and reservoirs
       a.   reduce danger of flooding upstream.
       b.   are inexpensive to build.
       c.   cannot be used for outdoor recreation.
*   d.   can be used to provide electric power.
       e.   all of these answers.

33.   Which of the following statements about disadvantages of large dams is *false?*
       a.   Reservoir formation displaces people and destroys wildlife habitat.
       b.   They can contribute to the incidence of earthquakes.
       c.   Eventually siltation requires their abandonment.
*   d.   They often cause flooding downstream.
       e.   They cause water loss through evaporation.

34.   Water transfer projects best illustrate the ecological principle that
*   a.   you can never do just one thing.
       b.   external costs should be internalized.
       c.   matter is conserved.
       d.   energy is conserved.
       e.   all of these answers.

35.   All of the following are large water distribution projects *except*
       a.   the Aral Sea Project.
       b.   the James Bay Project in Canada.
*   c.   the Boston Harbor Project.
       d.   the California Water Project.
       e.   none of these answers.

36.   California's basic water problem stems from the fact that _____% of the population lives south of Sacramento, but _____% of the rain falls north of it.
       a.   50 . . . 50
*   b.   75 . . . 75
       c.   50 . . . 75
       d.   75 . . . 50
       e.   50 . . . 25

37. Someone from northern California is likely to express concern over which of the following uses of water?
   a. urban use
 * b. dilution of pollution
   c. irrigation for agriculture
   d. power plant cooling
   e. all of these answers.

38. The volume of the world's fourth largest freshwater lake in Uzbekistan and Kazakhstan has been decreased by two thirds to provide water for
 * a. agriculture.
   b. drinking.
   c. industry.
   d. energy production.
   e. transportation.

39. Which of the following statements about the Aral Sea is *false?*
 * a. Water has been diverted from the Aral Sea and the two rivers that replenish its water for use in manufacturing.
   b. The volume of the Aral Sea has dropped by 75%.
   c. The salinity levels have risen dramatically.
   d. Most native fish species have disappeared.
   e. The surface area has decreased by 54%.

40. Strategies that could improve the situation at the Aral Sea include all of the following *except*
   a. charging farmers more for irrigation water to reduce waste.
 * b. removing trees that block the diversion project.
   c. introducing water-saving technologies.
   d. using groundwater to supplement irrigation water.
   e. construct wetlands and artificial lakes.

41. The term *subsidence* refers to
   a. failure of the groundwater supply.
   b. accumulation of silt behind a dam.
 * c. sinking of ground when water has been withdrawn.
   d. intrusion of salt water into a freshwater aquifer.
   e. loss of water due to evaporation.

42. Currently in the United States, groundwater is being withdrawn _____ times faster than it is being replaced.
   a. 2
 * b. 4
   c. 8
   d. 10
   e. 20

43. The Ogallala Aquifer
   a. is a fossil aquifer and has a slow recharge rate.
   b. will be depleted by one-fourth by 2020 if current withdrawal rates continue.
   c. is the largest known aquifer in the world.
 * d. all of these answers.
   e. is located in the United States.

44. Which of the following will occur first?
    a. The Ogallala Aquifer will dry up.
    b. We will reach the year 2020.
    c. The Ogallala Aquifer will reverse direction.
    * d. The high cost of pumping water from the dropping water tables will force a change in agriculture.
    e. The Ogallala Aquifer will be fully recharged.

45. Desalination may be accomplished by
    a. desiccation.
    * b. reverse osmosis.
    c. salt-eating bacteria.
    d. halide adsorption.
    e. all of these answers.

46. Which of the following statements about desalination is *true?*
    a. The common methods of desalination are reverse osmosis and evaporation.
    * b. Desalination is expensive.
    c. The removed salt can simply be dumped back into the ocean.
    d. Desalination is the best approach to solving irrigation problems.
    e. Desalination is the best method of acquiring clear water for drinking.

47. Desalination
    a. is expensive.
    b. uses vast amounts of energy.
    c. produces large amounts of salt and other minerals.
    d. is more common in arid regions of the world.
    * e. all of these answers.

48. Which choice completes the sentence *incorrectly?* Cloud seeding
    * a. is most useful in very dry areas.
    b. could change regional rainfall patterns.
    c. could introduce large amounts of cloud-seeding chemicals into natural ecosystems.
    d. is impeded by legal disputes.
    e. none of these answers.

49. It is most economically and environmentally sound to focus water resource management on
    a. increasing the water supply.
    b. controlling the "mining" of groundwater.
    * c. increasing the efficiency of the way we use water.
    d. developing desalination plants.
    e. cloud seeding and towing icebergs to arid regions.

14-4 REDUCING WATER WASTE

50. According to the World Resources Institute, what percentage of the water that people use throughout the world is unnecessarily wasted?
    a. 25-30%
    b. 35–40%
    c. 45–50%
    d. 55–60%
    * e. 65–70%

51. The world's largest water user is
    a. India.
    b. China.
  * c. the United States.
    d. Russia.
    e. Australia.

52. Which of the following statements is *false?*
    a. Lasers could be used to aid in contouring agricultural fields to increase even distribution of water.
    b. Seepage from irrigation canals can be reduced by use of plastic and tile liners.
  * c. Clearing land will increase its water retention.
    d. Small check dams of earth and stone can be used in developing countries to retain more water.
    e. Drip irrigation systems waste less water than center-pivot sprinkler systems.

53. The trickle and drip irrigation systems were developed in
    a. Egypt.
  * b. Israel.
    c. China.
    d. Japan.
    e. United States.

54. Which of the following offers the greatest conservation of water?
    a. center-pivot sprinkler systems
    b. low-energy precision-application (LEPA) sprinkler systems
  * c. trickle or drip irrigation
    d. gravity-flow canal systems
    e. diagonal-pivot systems

55. Irrigation efficiency can be improved by
    a. using traditional farming techniques.
  * b. using computer-controlled systems that deliver water to crops as needed.
    c. planting salt-sensitive crops.
    d. planting only genetically engineered crops.
    e. all of these answers.

56. All of the following are available to improve water efficiency *except*
    a. xeriscaping.
    b. policies allowing use of gray water.
    c. systems to purify and completely recycle wastewater from houses, apartments, or office buildings.
  * d. condensing water vapor from indoor air.
    e. using water meters to monitor and charge for municipal water use.

14-5 TOO MUCH WATER: PROBLEMS AND SOLUTIONS

57. Benefits of floods include all of the following *except*
    a. provision of productive farmland downstream.
    b. refilling of wetlands.
    c. provision of important breeding and feeding grounds for wildlife.
  * d. filling up of soil air spaces to prevent oxidation of nutrients.
    e. none of these answers.

58. People like to settle on floodplains for all of the following reasons *except*
    a. good transportation.
    b. flat sites for buildings.
  * c. security.
    d. fertile soil.
    e. availability of nearby rivers.

59. Floods and droughts are
    a. strictly natural disasters.
  * b. influenced by human activities.
    c. decreased by increases in human population.
    d. independent of human activity.
    e. all of these answers.

60. Humans increase the likelihood of flooding by
    a. building on floodplains.
    b. urbanization.
    c. removing water-absorbing vegetation.
    d. draining wetlands.
  * e. all of these answers.

61. Which of the following conditions in the Himalayan watershed contribute(s) to flooding in Bangladesh?
    a. rapid population growth
    b. deforestation
    c. unsustainable farming practices
  * d. all of these answers
    e. none of these answers.

62. To reduce flooding risks, an environmentalist is most likely to choose
  * a. floodplain management.
    b. a flood control dam.
    c. channelization of streams.
    d. artificial levees.
    e. none of these answers.

63. Floodplain management includes
    a. prohibiting building in high-risk zones.
    b. constructing floodways to minimize damage when flooding occurs.
    c. elevating buildings in flood-zones.
    d. a and b only.
  * e. all of these answers.

14-6   TYPES, EFFECTS, AND SOURCES OF WATER POLLUTION

64. Of the following organisms, the group that is *least* likely to cause disease is
    a. bacteria.
    b. protozoa.
  * c. algae.
    d. parasitic worms.
    e. viruses.

65. A good indicator of water quality for drinking or swimming is the number of colonies of
   * a. coliform bacteria.
   b. algae.
   c. dinoflagellates.
   d. manatees.
   e. protozoa.

66. For drinking water, the World Health Organization recommends a level of _____ coliform bacteria colonies per 100 milliliters of water sample.
   * a. 0
   b. 5
   c. 10
   d. 100
   e. 200

67. A body of water can be depleted of its oxygen by
   a. viruses and parasitic worms.
   * b. organic wastes.
   c. sediments and suspended matter.
   d. organic compounds such as oil, plastics, solvents, and detergents.
   e. all of these answers.

68. Which of the following statements is *false?*
   a. Heat can lower dissolved oxygen and make fish vulnerable to disease.
   b. Organic wastes that can be decomposed by aerobic bacteria reduce the amount of oxygen in the water supply.
   c. Radioactive wastes and toxins can be concentrated by biological amplification.
   * d. Inorganic nutrients such as fertilizers have no adverse effects on aquatic ecosystems.
   e. Sediment can cloud water and reduce photosynthesis.

69. Nitrates and phosphates are examples of
   a. disease-causing agents.
   b. oxygen-demanding wastes.
   c. organic plant nutrients.
   * d. inorganic plant nutrients.
   e. sediment.

70. Acids, salts, and metals are examples of
   a. oxygen-demanding wastes.
   b. organic plant nutrients.
   c. inorganic plant nutrients.
   * d. water-soluble inorganic chemicals.
   e. sediment.

71. Heat, organic wastes, and inorganic plant nutrients may all deplete dissolved _____ from water.
   a. nitrogen
   * b. oxygen
   c. particulate matter
   d. minerals
   e. hydrogen.

72. One class of pollutants that can cause a population explosion of aerobic bacteria is
    a. disease-causing agents.
  * b. oxygen-demanding wastes.
    c. inorganic chemicals.
    d. organic chemicals.
    e. sediment.

73. One class of pollutants that can cause excessive growth of algae is
    a. radioactive substances.
    b. oxygen-demanding wastes.
  * c. inorganic plant nutrients.
    d. organic chemicals.
    e. sediment.

74. The greatest source of water pollution in terms of total weight is
    a. fertilizers.
  * b. sediments.
    c. oxygen-demanding wastes.
    d. water-soluble inorganic chemicals.
    e. organic chemicals.

75. Which of the following decrease(s) photosynthesis in bodies of water?
    a. disease-causing organisms
    b. inorganic plant nutrients
  * c. sediment or suspended matter
    d. heat
    e. organic chemicals.

76. Introduction of alien species through waterways is a type of _____ pollution.
    a. inorganic
    b. sediment
  * c. genetic
    d. thermal
    e. organic.

77. All of the following are nonpoint sources of water pollution *except*
  * a. offshore oil wells.
    b. livestock feedlots.
    c. urban lands.
    d. croplands.
    e. parking lots.

78. Which of the following is a point source of pollution?
    a. acid deposition
    b. urban streets
  * c. oil tanker
    d. suburban lawns
    e. parking lots.

79. Which of the following is a nonpoint source of water pollution?
    a. sewage treatment plant
    b. electric power plant
    c. active and inactive coal mines
  * d. logged forest
    e. factories.

14-7 POLLUTION OF FRESHWATER STREAMS, LAKES, AND GROUNDWATER

80. Which of the following statements is *false?*
   a. Because of their flow, dilution, and bacterial decay, most streams recover rapidly from pollution by heat and biodegradable waste.
   b. In rapidly flowing rivers, dissolved oxygen is replaced quickly.
   c. The amount of oxygen in rivers declines in dry seasons.
 * d. The amount of oxygen in rivers increases as the water's temperature rises.
   e. The amount of oxygen in rivers increases as the water's temperature falls.

81. Oxygen sag curves
   a. usually occur during a rainy spring.
 * b. may occur when oxygen-demanding wastes are added to the water.
   c. may develop in fast-moving rivers.
   d. may occur upstream from a sewage treatment plant.
   e. all of these answers.

82. Which of the following statements is *false?*
   a. Requiring cities to withdraw water downstream of the city would reduce pollution.
 * b. Slow-flowing rivers are less susceptible to pollutants than fast-flowing streams.
   c. The width and depth of the oxygen sag curve depend on water volume and flow rate.
   d. Streams can recover from degradable pollutants as long as they are not overloaded.
   e. Oxygen sag curves show the time and distance needed for a stream to recover.

83. The water pollution and control laws enacted in the 1970s have done all but which one of the following?
   a. reduced or eliminated point source pollution on rivers
   b. increased the number and quality of wastewater treatment plants
   c. held the line against disease-causing agents and oxygen-demanding wastes
 * d. forced municipalities to take their water supply from the downstream side of the city
   e. none of these answers.

84. Which of the following statements about lake stratification is *true?*
   a. Stratified layers of lakes are characterized by vertical mixing.
   b. Stratification increases levels of dissolved oxygen, especially in the bottom layer.
 * c. Lakes are more vulnerable than streams to contamination by plant nutrients, oil, pesticides, and toxic substances that can destroy bottom life.
   d. Lakes have more flushing than streams.
   e. all of these answers.

85. Of the following chemicals, which is *least* likely to be biologically magnified as it moves through food webs?
   a. radioactive isotopes
   b. mercury compounds
 * c. nitrates
   d. PCBs
   e. DDT

86. Which of the following statements is *false?*
 * a. Rivers are more vulnerable than lakes to contamination by plant nutrients, oil, toxins, and pesticides.
   b. Acid deposition and fallout represent a more serious hazard to lakes than rivers.
   c. Eutrophication is a natural process and can occur without the influence of humans.
   d. Human activities can induce cultural eutrophication
   e. Eutrophication is caused by inputs of nutrients and silt from the surrounding land basin.

87. Cultural eutrophication is caused by
    a. infestations of zebra mussels.
    b. water supply intakes.
  * c. fertilizer runoff.
    d. decomposing algae.
    e. natural runoff.

88. Which of the following developments of cultural eutrophication would occur last?
    a. fish kills
    b. blooms of algae
    c. increase in aerobic bacteria
    d. increase of plants such as duckweed.
  * e. increase in anaerobic bacteria

89. In cultural eutrophication, game fish die from
    a. acid deposition.
  * b. suffocation from lack of oxygen.
    c. toxic substances in the water.
    d. salt.
    e. loss of space.

90. About _____ of the 100,000 medium to large lakes in the US suffer from cultural eutrophication.
    a. one-fifth
    b. one-fourth
  * c. one-third
    d. one-half
    e. one-tenth

91. All of the following strategies would help prevent cultural eutrophication *except*
    a. banning the use of phosphate detergents.
    b. preventing the runoff of fertilizer from agricultural fields.
    c. advance treatment of municipal sewage.
  * d. stopping release of toxic heavy metal pollution.
    e. land-use control to reduce nutrient runoff.

92. Which of the following would *not* reduce cultural eutrophication?
    a. Dredge lake bottoms.
    b. Pump oxygen into lakes.
    c. Land-use control to prevent nutrient runoff.
  * d. Ban cloud seeding.
    e. removing excess weeds.

93. The Great Lakes possess _____% of all the surface fresh water in the United States.
    a. 55
    b. 65
    c. 75
  * d. 95
    e. 45

94. Which of the following most closely approximates the percentage of water entering the Great Lakes that flows out the St. Lawrence River each year?
  * a. 1%
    b. 10%
    c. 20%
    d. 30%
    e. 40%

95. Since 1972, the massive pollution control program for the Great Lakes has reduced
   * a. the coliform level.
     b. the dissolved oxygen level.
     c. the amount of fishing (sport and commercial).
     d. swimming.
     e. all of these answers.

96. Currently, the greatest problem facing the Great Lakes is
     a. point-source emission of toxins.
     b. phosphates in detergents.
   * c. toxins found in runoff water as well as atmospheric deposition.
     d. oil spills from tankers using the St. Lawrence Seaway.
     e. none of these answers.

97. The Great Lakes have suffered invasions by all of the following *except* the
     a. quagga mussel.
     b. zebra mussel.
     c. sea lamprey.
     d. round goby.
   * e. American muskrat.

98. Zebra mussels are least known for their ability to
     a. clog irrigation pipes.
     b. grow in masses on boat hulls.
   * c. filter pollutants from the bottoms of lakes.
     d. deplete the food supply for other lake species.
     e. displace other mussel species.

99. Groundwater
     a. has turbulent flows that dilute pollutants.
     b. has large populations of decomposing bacteria that break down degradable wastes.
   * c. is cold, which slows down decomposition rates.
     d. may take 5 to 10 years to cleanse itself of wastes.
     e. is quickly renewable.

100. Which of the following statements about underground contaminants is *false?*
     a. Degradable organic wastes do not decompose as rapidly underground as they do on the surface.
     b. There is little dissolved oxygen to aid in degradation of wastes.
   * c. Waste products are diluted and dispersed quickly in underground aquifers.
     d. It can take hundreds to thousands of years for contaminated groundwater to cleanse itself of degradable wastes.
     e. In some coastal areas, groundwater has been contaminated by saltwater intrusion.

101. Groundwater would be least protected by
     a. storing hazardous liquids above ground in tanks with leak-detecting systems.
   * b. putting double hulls on tankers.
     c. monitoring aquifers near landfills.
     d. requiring liability insurance for underground tanks storing hazardous liquids.
     e. requiring leak detecting systems for underground tanks used to store hazardous waste.

102.   Which of the following aquatic ecosystems is most capable of diluting, dispersing, and degrading large amounts of sewage, sludge, and oil?
     a.   estuary
     b.   swiftly flowing stream
*   c.   deep-water ocean
     d.   coastal parts of the ocean
     e.   slow-moving river.

103.   Which of the following marine ecosystems is least polluted from ocean dumping and coastal development?
     a.   mangrove swamps
*   b.   deep-ocean trenches
     c.   coral reefs
     d.   wetlands
     e.   estuaries

104.   The largest estuary in the United States is
     a.   Mobile Bay.
*   b.   Chesapeake Bay.
     c.   San Francisco Bay.
     d.   Puget Sound.
     e.   Gulf of Mexico.

105.   In Chesapeake Bay, 60% by weight of phosphates come from _____ and 60% by weight of nitrates come from _____.
*   a.   point sources, nonpoint sources
     b.   point sources, nitrate rocks
     c.   nonpoint sources, point sources
     d.   phosphate rocks, nonpoint sources
     e.   phosphate rocks, point sources

106.   Of the following sources of oil in the environment, the one that contributes least is
*   a.   tanker accidents and blowouts at offshore drilling rigs.
     b.   washing tankers and releasing the oily water.
     c.   normal operation of offshore wells.
     d.   pipeline leaks.
     e.   none of these answers.

107.   The majority of the oil pollution of the ocean comes from
     a.   blowouts (rupture of a borehole of an oil rig in the ocean).
     b.   tanker accidents.
     c.   environmental terrorism.
*   d.   runoff from land.
     e.   normal operation of offshore wells.

108.   The effects of an oil spill depend on the
     a.   time of year.
     b.   type of oil (crude or refined).
     c.   weather conditions.
     d.   amount released.
*   e.   all of these answers.

109. The *most* common problem encountered by seabirds coated with oil is
   a. immediate death.
   b. vulnerability to predators.
 * c. loss of buoyancy and insulation, causing deaths from exposure.
   d. poisoning by taking in the oil internally.
   e. starvation.

110. Of the following organisms, the ones *least* likely to be killed by heavy oil components are
   a. oysters.
 * b. marine birds.
   c. crabs.
   d. clams.
   e. mussels.

111. The oil company responsible for the oil spill of the *Valdez* was
   a. Alyeska.
   b. Gulf.
 * c. Exxon.
   d. Sunoco.
   e. Texaco.

112. Which of the following is *false?*
   a. Oil evaporates and undergoes decomposition.
 * b. The environment recovers more slowly from crude oil spills than from refined oil spills.
   c. Recovery from oil spills is faster in warm water than in cold water.
   d. Estuaries and salt marshes suffer the most damage from oil pollution.
   e. Oil spills can have a negative economic impact on coastal residents.

14-9 SOLUTIONS: PREVENTING AND REDUCING SURFACE WATER POLLUTION

113. The leading nonpoint source of water pollution is
   a. municipal landfills.
   b. runoff from city streets and storm sewers.
 * c. agriculture.
   d. industrial wastes.
   e. leaks from offshore oil wells.

114. Farmers can reduce pesticide runoff by
   a. applying pesticides only when needed.
   b. using biological methods of pest control.
   c. using integrated pest management.
   d. control runoff.
 * e. all of these answers.

115. Livestock growers can control runoff of animal wastes from feedlots and barnyards by
   a. increasing animal density.
 * b. diverting runoff of animal wastes into detention basins.
   c. removing buffers between stockyards and surface water.
   d. locating feedlots on gently sloping land so rainwater will naturally clean off the stockyards.
   e. all of these answers.

116. Reforestation
  * a. reduces soil erosion and pollution from sediment.
    b. increases the severity of flooding.
    c. helps accelerate projected global warming.
    d. decreases biodiversity.
    e. all of these answers.

117. Which of the following would *not* reduce nonpoint source pollution?
    a. Require buffer zones of permanent vegetation between cultivated fields and surface water.
    b. Divert runoff of animal wastes into detention basins to be used as fertilizer.
  * c. Establish wastewater lagoons.
    d. Use biotic control or integrated pest management.
    e. Reduce the need for fertilizers.

118. The Clean Water Act and Water Quality Act attempt to maintain the _____ integrity of U.S. waters.
    a. biological
    b. chemical
    c. physical
    d. a and c only.
  * e. all of these answers

119. In 1995, using the strategy of controlling the air pollutant sulfur dioxide as a model, the EPA proposed to reduce water pollution through
    a. more regulations.
    b. educating the public to prevent water pollution.
    c. changing American lifestyles.
  * d. a discharges trading policy.
    e. more water testing.

120. The Clean Water Act could be strengthened by all of the following strategies *except*
    a. prevention and control of toxic water pollution.
    b. more funding for watershed planning.
    c. allowing citizens to bring lawsuits to ensure that water pollution laws are enforced.
  * d. establishing national effluent standards.
    e. requiring states to do a better job of monitoring and enforcing water pollution laws.

121. Which of the following types of sewage treatment are properly matched?
    a. primary—biological process
    b. secondary—mechanical process
  * c. advanced—physical and chemical processes
    d. secondary—chemical process
    e. primary- chemical process

122. Which of the following types of sewage treatment are properly matched?
    a. primary—removal of pollutants particular to a given area
  * b. secondary— removal of oxygen-demanding wastes
    c. advanced— removal of suspended solids
    d. all of these answers
    e. none of these answers

123. Which of the following substances are removed to the greatest extent by combined primary and secondary wastewater treatment?
    a. organic pesticides
    * b. organic oxygen-demanding wastes
    c. toxic metals and synthetic organic chemicals
    d. radioactive isotopes
    e. all of these answers

124. Of the following, the *most* ecologically reasonable way to dispose of sewage sludge is
    a. incineration.
    b. dumping into the deep trenches of the ocean.
    c. conventional landfills.
    * d. treating with heat and using as fertilizer.
    e. none of these answers.

125. All of the following are used to disinfect or to purify water *except*
    a. ozone
    b. chlorine
    * c. iodine
    d. ultraviolet radiation
    e. a and b

126. Sustainable use of the earth's water resources involves
    * a. an integrated approach to managing water resources and water pollution throughout each watershed.
    b. continued subsidizing of the market price of water so that there is fair distribution of water.
    c. emphasis on waste management over waste prevention.
    d. emphasis on individual and community responsibility rather than cooperation among political entities.
    e. all of these answers.

127. A change in the U.S. Safe Drinking Water Act that is *least* likely to be recommended by an environmentalist is
    a. banning all lead in new plumbing pipes, faucets, and fixtures.
    * b. increased reliance on voluntary compliance to drinking water standards.
    c. strengthening public notification requirements of drinking water violations.
    d. reducing testing and administrative costs and improving treatment by combining smaller water systems into larger ones.
    e. combining small water treatment facilities with larger ones nearby.

14-10 SOLUTIONS: ACHIEVING A MORE SUSTAINABLE WATER FUTURE

128. To further sustainable use of water supplies, environmentalists are *least* likely to call for
    a. reduction of pollution sources.
    b. reuse of wastewater.
    * c. decentralization of control of water supply and quality.
    d. moving from pollution treatment to pollution prevention.
    e. elimination of national drinking water tests.

CHAPTER 15
SOLID AND HAZARDOUS WASTE

1.   Love Canal is located in
     a.   Ohio.
 *   b.   New York.
     c.   California.
     d.   Panama.
     e.   Georgia.

2.   The company responsible for the dumping of toxic and cancer-causing wastes into an old canal
     excavation called the Love Canal was
     a.   DuPont.
     b.   Monsanto.
 *   c.   Hooker Chemical and Plastics Corporation.
     d.   the 3M Company.
     e.   Intel.

3.   After Love Canal was abandoned, it was sold and used for
 *   a.   an elementary school and housing project.
     b.   a shopping mall.
     c.   an amusement park.
     d.   an industrial park.
     e.   an office building.

4.   The Love Canal incident demonstrates that
 *   a.   preventing pollution is safer and cheaper than cleaning it up.
     b.   political officials are alert and sympathetic to their constituents.
     c.   pollutants can be stored safely underground for a long time.
     d.   polluting companies can escape from the costs and responsibility of their actions.
     e.   all of these answers.

15-1 WASTING RESOURCES

5.   With 4.7% of the world's population, the United States produces _____ of the world's solid waste.
     a.   4.6%
     b.   13%
     c.   23%
 *   d.   33%
     e.   43%

6.   Garbage produced directly by households and businesses accounts for _____% of the solid waste
     produced in the United States.
 *   a.   less than 2
     b.   5
     c.   10
     d.   15
     e.   20

7. The single largest category of U.S. solid waste is
   * a. mining wastes.
   b. agricultural wastes.
   c. industrial wastes.
   d. municipal wastes.
   e. agricultural wastes.

8. The amount of solid waste currently produced in the United States would fill a convoy of garbage trucks stretching around the world almost
   a. 2 times.
   b. 4 times.
   c. 6 times.
   * d. 8 times.
   e. 10 times.

9. The recycling/composting rate of municipal solid waste produced in the United States is about
   a. 5%.
   b. 15%.
   * c. 30%.
   d. 45%.
   e. 60%.

10. U.S. consumers throw away enough aluminum to rebuild the country's commercial airline fleet every
    a. 3 weeks.
    * b. 3 months.
    c. 6 months.
    d. 1 year.
    e. 2 years.

11. A waste is considered hazardous if it possesses one of four properties. Which of the following is *not* one of those properties?
    a. flammable
    b. unstable
    * c. soluble
    d. corrosive
    e. carcinogenic, mutagenic or teratogenic.

12. If a small business produces less than ___ pounds of a waste per month, the EPA does not consider the material hazardous.
    a. 22
    * b. 220
    c. 2200
    d. 2220
    e. 22220

13. The EPA estimates that approximately _____ metric tons of hazardous wastes are produced for each person in the United States per year.
    a. 2
    b. 10
    * c. 20
    d. 30
    e. 40

14. _____% of the U.S. hazardous waste is not regulated by hazardous-waste laws.
    a. 35
    b. 55
    c. 75
  * d. 95
    e. 25

15. Legally designated and controlled forms of hazardous waste make up about _____ of the total hazardous waste produced.
  * a. 5%
    b. 15%
    c. 25%
    d. 35%
    e. 45%

15-2 PRODUCING LESS WASTE AND POLLUTION

16. In a low-waste approach, which of the following strategies should be given *top* priority?
    a. incinerate
    b. reuse
  * c. reduce
    d. bury
    e. recycle.

17. In a low-waste approach, which of the following strategies should be given *lowest* priority?
    a. incinerate
    b. reuse
    c. reduce
  * d. bury
    e. recycle.

18. Company plans to reduce waste and pollution
    a. can increase energy and resource use.
  * b. are usually less costly on a life-cycle basis than waste management strategies.
    c. worsen worker health and safety.
    d. increase environmental impacts of extracting, processing, and using resources.
    e. all of these answers.

19. A low-waste approach
  * a. eliminates unnecessary packaging.
    b. makes a product require frequent replacement.
    c. uses more material.
    d. encourages built-in obsolescence.
    e. all of these answers.

20. Which is the *most* advanced approach?
    a. recycling materials
    b. using biodegradable material
    c. creating more durable products
  * d. reducing the amount of materials used
    e. reusing materials

21. Of the following methods of reducing hazardous wastes, the *most* desirable is
    a. incineration.
    * b. conversion to less hazardous materials.
    c. perpetual storage.
    d. deposit in ocean trenches.
    e. bury waste in landfills.

22. Lois Marie Gibbs feels we should analyze tough issues by
    a. cost-benefit analysis.
    b. asking if the economy will grow.
    c. asking if more jobs will be created.
    * d. asking who will benefit and who will pay the cost.
    e. all of these answers.

15-3 SOLUTIONS: CLEANER PRODUCTION AND SELLING SERVICES INSTEAD OF THINGS

23. Industrial ecology tries to
    a. maximizing the input of energy per unit of output.
    b. maximizing the input of matter resources per unit of output.
    c. make resource use an open system.
    * d. adjust inputs and outputs to the carrying capacity of the environment.
    e. all of these answers.

24. Minnesota Mining and Manufacturing Company (3M) is famous for its
    a. clean-burning incinerator.
    b. waste treatment program.
    * c. Pollution Prevention Pays program.
    d. recycling model.
    e. waste reduction program.

25. Xerox Corporation now leases most of its copy machines, providing maintenance and upgrades for the length of the least. This is an example of the shift towards
    a. a material flow economy
    * b. a service flow economy
    c. a resource intensive economy
    d. a no-sell economy
    e. a high-sell economy.

15-4 REUSE

26. Studies by two soft-drink companies indicate that 16-oz bottles of soft drinks cost _____ in refillable bottles.
    a. three times more
    b. two times more
    c. one-half less
    * d. one-third less
    e. four times more

27. _____ has a beverage-container deposit fee that is 50% of the cost of the drink, to encourage use of refillable bottles.
    a. Italy
    * b. Ecuador
    c. Germany
    d. Canada
    e. United States

28. At the checkout counter, an environmentalist is most likely to
    a. say "plastic please."
    b. say "paper please."
  * c. say "I brought my own bag."
    d. walk out of the store.
    e. say "either plastic or paper."

15-5 RECYCLING

29. The most desirable type of recycling is
  * a. primary, or closed-loop recycling.
    b. secondary, or open-loop recycling.
    c. tertiary, or figure-eight recycling.
    d. materials-recovery facility recycling.
    e. secondary or closed-loop recycling.

30. Which of the following statements is *false?*
    a. It is more economical to have consumers separate trash before pickup than to use materials-recovery facilities.
    b. Glass, iron, and aluminum can be recovered from solid wastes.
    c. Source separation involves consumers separating trash into categories like glass, paper, and metal.
  * d. Materials-recovery facilities provides many more jobs than source separation recycling.
    e. Materials-recovery facilities need a large input of garbage to be financially successful.

31. Source separation differs from materials-recovery facilities in all but which of the following?
    a. It is cheaper.
    b. It provides greater income for unskilled labor and volunteer organizations.
    c. It produces less air and water pollution.
  * d. It is the most common type of recycling strategy.
    e. It saves more energy and provides more jobs per unit of material recycled.

32. Critics of recycling are *most* likely to claim
    a. it isn't worth the effort.
    b. there is no solid-waste problem.
    c. incineration is the safest and most efficient way to dispose of solid wastes.
  * d. it doesn't make sense to recycle if it costs more than sending wastes to a landfill or an incinerator.
    e. there is abundant landfill space in all areas.

33. Obstacles to recycling in the United States include
    a. lack of inclusion of environmental costs in market prices.
    b. tax breaks for mining virgin materials.
    c. lack of large, steady markets for recycled materials.
  * d. all of these answers.
    e. none of these answers.

34. Obstacles to recycling can be overcome by all of the following *except*
    a. requiring households and businesses to pay directly for garbage collection based on how much they throw away.
    b. encouraging government purchases of recycled products.
    c. requiring ecolabels that evaluate life-cycle environmental costs.
  * d. enacting a national aluminum-can bill.
    e. providing subsidies for reuse and postconsumer waste recycling.

35. As Germany's reduced-packaging initiative progressed, higher fees were charged for
    a. cardboard.
    b. glass.
    c. metal.
  * d. plastic and composite materials.
    e. paper.

36. Which of the following is *false?* Recycling aluminum
    a. produces 95% less air pollution than using virgin ore.
    b. produces 97% less water pollution than using virgin ore.
  * c. requires 50% less energy than using virgin ore.
    d. is done at a 74% rate in the United States.
    e. uses 95% less energy than using virgin ore.

37. Environmentalists would *most* like to see aluminum cans
    a. buried in landfills.
    b. burned in incinerators.
    c. recycled.
  * d. replaced by refillable bottles.
    e. outlawed.

38. In 2000, the United States recycled about _____ of all its wastepaper.
    a. 19%
    b. 29%
  * c. 49%
    d. 69%
    e. 89%

39. Recycling paper
  * a. saves energy.
    b. increases water and air pollution.
    c. eliminates jobs.
    d. increases production costs.
    e. all of these answers.

40. Consumers of recycled products are most effective when they maximize the amount of
    _____ waste in the products.
    a. pre-producer
    b. post-producer
    c. pre-consumer
  * d. post-consumer
    e. producer

41. Plastic materials are a problem because
    a. they do not decompose readily in landfills.
    b. toxic lead and cadmium can leach out of plastics.
    c. they can harm animals that swallow them or become entangled in them.
  * d. all of these answers.
    e. they are unnecessarily and excessively used as single-use and throw-away packaging.

42. Of the following materials, the most difficult to recycle is
    a. glass.
  * b. plastic.
    c. paper.
    d. aluminum.
    e. cardboard.

43. Plastic is desirable because of its
    a. reusability.
    b. light weight.
    c. durability.
    * d. all of these answers.
    e. unbreakability.

44. Environmentalists would most object to plastics used in
    a. lunch boxes.
    b. shampoo bottles.
    * c. single-use packaging.
    d. refrigerator storage containers.
    e. cars.

15-6 DETOXIFYING, BURNING, BURYING, AND EXPORTING WASTES

45. The *most* comprehensive and effective hazardous-waste detoxification program is in
    a. France.
    * b. Denmark.
    c. Norway.
    d. Yugoslavia.
    e. United States.

46. Bioremediation
    a. involves training bacteria to eat new foods.
    b. results in the production of low-level hazardous wastes.
    * c. may be used at considerably less expense than landfills and incineration if toxin-degrading bacteria can be found.
    d. is widely accepted as the best way to cut hazardous wastes.
    e. does not exist.

47. Evaluations of bioremediation indicate that it is most effective for
    a. toxic metals.
    b. concentrated chemical wastes.
    c. complex mixtures of toxic chemicals.
    * d. a few specific organic wastes.
    e. none of these answers.

48. Hazardous waste experts point out that all incinerators burning waste
    * a. release toxic air pollutants.
    b. can eliminate air pollution by using electrostatic precipitators.
    c. can eliminate air pollution by using baghouse filters.
    d. can eliminate air pollution by using scrubbers.
    e. all of these answers.

49. Because of health and financial costs to their citizens, incineration was banned in
    a. Michigan and Ohio.
    b. Virginia and West Virginia.
    * c. Rhode Island and West Virginia.
    d. Rhode Island and Massachusetts.
    e. Michigan and Massachusetts.

50. Components of a modern state-of-the-art landfill include
   a. wells to monitor potential contamination of groundwater.
   b. plastic liners on the bottom of the landfill.
   c. collection, storage, and treatment of leachate.
 * d. all of these answers.
   e. methane gas recovery well.

51. Sanitary landfills typically have problems with
   a. rodents and insects.
   b. odor.
   c. open, uncovered garbage.
 * d. traffic, noise, and dust.
   e. spread of disease.

52. Underground anaerobic decomposition in a landfill produces
   a. volatile organic compounds.
   b. methane.
   c. hydrogen sulfide.
 * d. all of these answers.
   e. none of these answers.

53. Which of the following statements about landfill leaching is *false?*
   a. Rain filtering through landfills leaches toxic materials.
   b. Contaminated leachate can seep from the bottom of landfills.
 * c. Contaminated groundwater is not a problem at landfills.
   d. Older, unlined landfills may have particularly bad water pollution problems.
   e. none of these answers.

54. According to Fred Lee, a landfill consultant,
   a. most landfills should be abandoned.
 * b. applying water and collecting and treating leachate will hasten breakdown of landfill wastes and prevent groundwater pollution.
   c. bioremediation can hasten breakdown of landfill wastes, which can then be used for compost.
   d. all landfill liners will leak sometime.
   e. we should not disturb old landfills.

55. Deep-well disposal of liquid hazardous wastes is
   a. a complex process.
 * b. less visible than other waste-disposal methods.
   c. more carefully regulated than other waste-disposal methods.
   d. the most expensive waste-disposal method.
   e. all of these answers.

56. Hazardous waste deposited in ponds or lagoons
   a. may evaporate into the atmosphere.
   b. may enter groundwater when there are no liners or when liners leak.
   c. may contaminate surface water.
 * d. may do all of these answers.
   e. may do none of these answers.

57. The real cost of dumping hazardous wastes is borne by the
   a. producer of the waste.
   b. disposer of the waste.
   c. haulers of the waste.
 * d. taxpayers who pay to clean up disposal messes.
   e. recyclers of the waste.

58. Which of the following statements about disposal of hazardous wastes is *false?*
    a. Waste-disposal firms in the United States and other industrialized nations have shipped hazardous wastes to other countries.
  * b. Most legal U.S. exports of hazardous waste go to Mexico and Panama.
    c. Hazardous wastes have been labeled "exports for recycling" even though they are often dumped in importing countries.
    d. In 1994, the United States was the only one of a 64-country meeting not to sign a ban on exporting hazardous wastes from developed countries to developing countries.
    e. Waste disposal firms can charge high prices for picking up hazardous wastes.

15-7 CASE STUDIES: LEAD, MERCURY, CHLORINE, AND DIOXINS

59. In the United States, lead comes from
    a. paint used in new homes.
  * b. drinking water that runs through pipes held together with lead solder.
    c. today's ceramics industry.
    d. burning pine logs in fireplaces.
    e. recycling paper.

60. Of the following sources of lead in the United States, the one that probably causes the *least* problems is
  * a. chewing on pencils.
    b. atmospheric lead that settles on the ground.
    c. paints used in older buildings.
    d. lead solder from seamed food cans.
    e. lead glazing in ceramicware used to serve food.

61. Which of the following would *least* protect children from lead poisoning?
    a. eliminating leaded paint and contaminated dust in housing
  * b. switching from wooden to mechanical pencils
    c. testing all community sources of drinking water for lead contamination
    d. testing for lead glazing in ceramics
    e. removing lead from piping.

62. Most atmospheric emissions of dioxins in the United States are released by
    a. landfills.
    b. paper mills.
  * c. medical and municipal solid-waste incinerators.
    d. refrigerator manufacturers.
    e. coal-fired power plants.

63. Dioxin can
    a. cause immunological effects.
    b. affect the immune system.
    c. promote cancers.
  * d. all of these answers.
    e. disrupt the reproductive system.

64. Chlorine is used to
    a. purify water.
    b. produce hundreds of organic compounds.
    c. bleach paper and wood pulp.
  * d. do all of these answers processes.
    e. produce PVC plastics.

65. Which of the following is *not* one of the top three uses of chlorine?
   * a. laundry bleach
   b. plastics
   c. paper and pulp bleaching
   d. solvents
   e. none of these answers.

66. All of the following *except* _____ can help replace many chlorinated organic solvents.
   a. citrus-based solvents
   b. soap and water
   c. steam cleaning
   * d. ozone
   e. physical cleaning.

67. Chlorine bleaching of wood pulp and paper can be replaced by using
   a. oxygen.
   b. hydrogen peroxide.
   c. ozone.
   * d. all of these answers.
   e. none of these answers.

68. Which country achieved completely chlorine-free paper production in the early 1990s?
   a. the United States
   b. Japan
   * c. Germany
   d. Sweden
   e. England

15-8 HAZARDOUS WASTE REGULATION IN THE UNITED STATES

69. The Resource Conservation and Recovery Act of 1976
   a. requires the EPA to identify hazardous wastes.
   b. requires the EPA to set standards for hazardous-waste management.
   c. requires all firms that handle more than 100 kilograms of hazardous waste per month to have a permit stating how such wastes are to be managed.
   * d. all of these answers.
   e. none of these answers.

70. The Superfund program pays
   * a. to clean up inactive or abandoned hazardous-waste dump sites.
   b. to monitor hazardous wastes.
   c. for testing for lead in paint, water, and air samples.
   d. the doctors' bills and lawyers' fees for pollution events.
   e. all of these answers.

71. Which of the following statements about hazardous-waste cleanup is *false?*
   a. Cleaning up toxic military dumps is estimated to cost $100–200 billion over 30 years.
   * b. The Department of the Interior will need to spend more than any other agency for cleanup.
   c. Pollution prevention is cheaper than cleanup strategies.
   d. Cleaning up contaminated Department of Energy sites used to make nuclear weapons will run between $200 billion and $400 billion over 30 to 50 years.
   e. all of these answers.

72. Enforcement of Superfund has failed because
   a. polluters deny responsibility.
   b. polluting businesses campaign that toxic dumps are not that threatening.
   c. big polluters sue local governments and small businesses to make them responsible for cleanup.
 * d. of all the above reasons.
   e. of none of the above reasons.

73. It is generally accepted that enforcement of Superfund could be improved by
   a. creating a form of triage in which hazardous-waste sites are classified by severity and the worst ones get treated first.
   b. involving people and local governments where sites are located in the decision-making process.
   c. setting up an Environmental Insurance Resolution Fund.
 * d. all of these answers.
   e. none of these answers.

15-9 SOLUTIONS: ACHIEVING A LOW-WASTE SOCIETY

74. The environmental justice movement attempts to dismantle
   a. exclusionary zoning ordinances.
   b. differential enforcement of environmental regulations.
   c. dumping of toxic waste on the poor and people of color in the United States and in developing countries.
   d. discriminatory land-use practices.
 * e. all of these answers.

75. All of the following are called for by the grass-roots movement for environmental justice *except*
 * a. NIMBY (Not in My Backyard).
   b. holding polluters and elected officials who support them personally accountable.
   c. opposing hazardous-waste landfills, deep-disposal wells, and incinerators.
   d. demanding wider distribution of unwanted industries and waste facilities.
   e. none of these answers.

76. Which of the following principles contributes *least* to the transition to a low-waste society?
   a. There is no "away."
   b. The best priorities for dealing with waste are to reduce, reuse, and recycle.
   c. Everything is connected.
 * d. Economic growth and free markets are the keys to waste reduction.
   e. Dilution is not always the solution to pollution.

CHAPTER 16
FOOD RESOURCES

16-1 HOW IS FOOD PRODUCED?

1.   Approximately _____ plant and animal species supply 90% of human food.
     a.   13
  * b.   23
     c.   33
     d.   43
     e.   53

2.   All of the following are among the world's major food crops *except*
     a.   wheat.
  * b.   soybean.
     c.   potato.
     d.   rice.
     e.   grits.

3.   Which of the following types of agriculture is most characteristic of developing countries?
     a.   plantation agriculture
  * b.   traditional agriculture
     c.   industrialized agriculture
     d.   minimum-tillage agriculture
     e.   high-input agriculture

4.   Which of the following types of agriculture is most characteristic of developed countries?
     a.   plantation agriculture
     b.   traditional agriculture
  * c.   industrialized agriculture
     d.   minimum-tillage agriculture
     e.   maximum-tillage agriculture

5.   All of the following crops are commonly grown in plantation agriculture *except*
  * a.   corn.
     b.   bananas.
     c.   cacao.
     d.   coffee.
     e.   sugarcane.

6.   A single type of crop is generally grown in
     a.   plantation agriculture.
     b.   traditional intensive agriculture.
     c.   traditional subsistence agriculture.
  * d.   industrialized agriculture.
     e.   minimum-tillage agriculture.

7.   Which of the following is a type of subsistence agriculture?
  * a.   shifting cultivation on small plots in tropical forests
     b.   intensive crop cultivation plots
     c.   cultivation of large cornfields
     d.   coffee plantations
     e.   monoculture plantations.

8. Industrialized agriculture requires large inputs of
   a. fossil fuels.
   b. water.
   c. inorganic fertilizers.
   * d. all of these answers.
   e. pesticides.

16-2 PRODUCING FOOD BY GREEN REVOLUTION AND TRADITIONAL TECHNIQUES

9. Since 1950, the majority of the increase in food production is a result of the _____ revolution.
   a. red
   b. blue
   * c. green
   d. yellow
   e. purple.

10. Genetic research of the second green revolution produced _____ specially bred for tropical and subtropical climates.
    a. sugarcane and pineapples.
    * b. rice and wheat.
    c. corn and potatoes.
    d. bananas and coconuts.
    e. corn and sugarcane.

11. The plants of the second green revolution are
    a. dwarf varieties.
    b. fast growing, allowing multiple cropping.
    c. high-yield varieties.
    * d. all of these answers.
    e. producing more food on less land.

12. All of the following factors contributed to a doubling of U.S. food productivity since 1940 *except*
    a. increased use of fossil fuels.
    * b. increased amount of cultivated land.
    c. increased use of pesticides.
    d. increased use of inorganic fertilizers.
    e. increased use of irrigation.

13. Increased yields from green revolution crops may become limited by
    a. soil erosion and loss of soil fertility.
    b. waterlogged soil and salinization.
    c. pests that have developed genetic immunity to widely used pesticides.
    * d. all of these answers.
    e. none of these answers.

14. Which of the following industries has the largest total annual sales in the United States?
    a. automotive
    b. housing
    * c. agricultural
    d. steel
    e. transportation.

15. Agriculture contributes ____% to the GNP of the United States.
    a. 5
    b. 8
* c. 18
    d. 28
    e. 38

16. In the *whole* U.S. food system, it takes about _____ units of fossil-fuel energy to put 1 unit of food energy on the table.
    a. 1
* b. 10
    c. 15
    d. 20
    e. 25

17. Which of the following requires the greatest input of energy?
* a. feedlot beef
    b. soybeans
    c. intensive wheat or rice
    d. milk produced by grass-fed cows
    e. corn

18. Intercropping involves growing
    a. several varieties of one crop on a plot of land.
* b. two or more different crops on a plot of land at the same time.
    c. trees and crops together.
    d. crops in alternate rows.
    e. rotating crops from year to year.

19. All of the following are types of interplanting *except*
    a. agroforestry.
    b. polyvarietal cultivation.
* c. monoculture.
    d. intercropping.
    e. polyculture.

16-3   FOOD PRODUCTION, NUTRITION, AND ENVIRONMENTAL EFFECTS

20. Between 1950 and 1990, which of the following statements is *false?*
    a. Grain production almost tripled.
    b. Per capita food production increased.
    c. Food prices, even adjusted for inflation, dropped.
* d. Most of the world's countries are self-sustaining in food.
    e. The amount of food traded in the world market quadrupled.

21. The term *undernutrition* refers to people who
* a. eat less than the basic minimum number of daily calories.
    b. eat balanced meals.
    c. eat too much.
    d. suffer from poor food quality.
    e. eat too much protein.

22. The term *malnutrition* refers to people who
    a. eat less than the basic minimum number of daily calories.
    b. eat balanced meals.
    c. eat too much.
  * d. suffer from lack of protein and other key nutrients.
    e. eat too much protein.

23. Marasmus is a
    a. weather pattern that has replaced the monsoon in Africa.
  * b. result of lack of calories and protein.
    c. vitamin deficiency.
    d. parasitic infection.
    e. is a result of lack of protein.

24. Kwashiorkor
    a. occurs in newborn children.
  * b. is a result of lack of protein.
    c. is a lack of sufficient calories.
    d. is a severe form of diarrhea.
    e. is a vitamin deficiency.

25. Administration of _____ will prevent the majority of blindness in developing countries in the world.
    a. iodine
    b. immunizing shots
    c. sugar and salt in a glass of water
  * d. vitamin A capsules
    e. protein.

26. Anemia can be the result of a deficiency in
    a. cobalt.
    b. iodine.
  * c. iron.
    d. calcium.
    e. oxygen.

27. Goiter can result from a deficiency in
    a. cobalt.
  * b. iodine.
    c. iron.
    d. calcium.
    e. oxygen.

28. Which of the following statements is *false*?
    a. The estimated number of malnourished people fell from 940 million in 1970 to 828 million in 1996.
    b. Almost 90% of the malnourished people in the world live in Asia and Africa.
    c. The proportion of people suffering from chronic undernutrition fell from 36% to 14% in the last quarter century.
  * d. One of every ten people in developing countries is undernourished or malnourished.
    e. People who are underfed and underweight, like those overweight and overfed, have a lower life expectancy.

29. The UNICEF program to sharply reduce childhood deaths from improper nutrition would include all of the following *except*
   * a. discouraging breastfeeding.
   b. preventing dehydration by giving infants sugar and salt in water.
   c. giving vitamin A supplements.
   d. providing family planning services.
   e. giving iron supplements.

30. The term *overnutrition* refers to people who
   a. eat less than the basic minimum number of daily calories.
   b. eat balanced meals.
   * c. eat more than the basic minimum number of daily calories.
   d. suffer from poor food quality.
   e. eat too much protein.

31. Overnutrition is characterized by diets
   * a. high in fat.
   b. high in fruit and fiber.
   c. high in fresh vegetables.
   d. low in meats.
   e. all of these answers.

32. If everyone at the typical diet of a person living in a developed country, the current agricultural system could support only about _____ billion people.
   a. 1.0
   * b. 2.5
   c. 4.0
   d. 5.5
   e. 6.0

33. Which of the following activities causes more pollution and environmental degradation than any other human activity?
   a. transportation
   * b. agriculture
   c. industry
   d. recreation
   e. building houses

34. In most modern agriculture, which of the following effects is agriculture *least* likely to have on soil resources?
   * a. replenishment of soil fertility
   b. salinization
   c. waterlogging
   d. desertification
   e. water deficits and droughts.

35. Which of the following effects is agriculture as it is currently practiced *least* likely to have on water resources?
   a. cultural eutrophication
   b. sediment pollution from erosion
   * c. recharging of aquifers
   d. flooding from land cleared to grow crops
   e. increased runoff and flooding from cleared land.

36. Agriculture as it is currently practiced can cause
    a. human illness from drinking groundwater polluted by nitrates.
    b. loss of genetic diversity through habitat degradation.
    c. contamination of recreational waters with livestock wastes.
    d. soil erosion.
  * e. all of these answers.

16-4 INCREASING WORLD CROP PRODUCTION

37. Agricultural experts hope to increase food production with plants that do all of the following *except*
    a. grow in salty soil.
    b. make their own nitrogen fertilizer.
  * c. do not require light to produce their food.
    d. are resistant to drought.
    e. more resistant to pests.

38. Which of the following statements *best* describes how we hope to improve agricultural yields in the future?
    a. If the soil is deficient in minerals, we add fertilizer.
    b. If the land is dry, we add irrigation.
  * c. If the plants don't fit the environment, we use genetic engineering.
    d. If the insects produce problems, we add pesticides.
    e. If biodiversity decreases, we don't worry about it.

39. Which of the following is the most controversial agricultural practice?
    a. cultivating more land.
  * b. genetically modifying food.
    c. increasing irrigation.
    d. gene banking.
    e. pesticide use.

40. Which of the following statements is *true?*
    a. Green-revolution plants are less expensive than regular varieties.
  * b. Loss of biodiversity limits green-revolution approaches.
    c. Green-revolution plants require less water and fertilizer.
    d. Monocultures of newly developed plants lead to greater plant diversity.
    e. all of these answers.

41. Storing the world's varieties of seeds in seed banks, agricultural centers, and botanical gardens is *least* likely to be constrained by
    a. power failures and fires.
    b. space and money.
  * c. lack of knowledge about how to store seeds.
    d. varieties that do not store well.
    e. death of stored seeds unless they are periodically planted and then stored again.

42. Which of the following plants has been called "supermarket on a stalk"?
    a. peanut
    b. soybean
  * c. winged bean
    d. rice
    e. corn.

43.   Use of perennial crops would reduce
      a.   the amount of water used.
      b.   sediment water pollution.
      c.   soil erosion.
   * d.   all of these answers.
      e.   none of these answers.

16-5   PRODUCING MORE MEAT

44.   What is *metabolic reserve*?
      a.   the caloric content of beef
   * b.   growing leaf bases of grasses
      c.   the nutrient content of the soil
      d.   nutrients contained in livestock manure
      e.   the fat content of beef

45.   Which of the following is a major environmental impact of livestock production?
      a.   bad smells
   * b.   water pollution
      c.   dispersion of livestock operations throughout the country
      d.   animal rights groups releasing domestic livestock
      e.   diets high in beef contain too much fat

46.   Which of the following is the most energy efficient to produce?
      a.   pigs
      b.   chicken
   * c.   catfish
      d.   cattle
      e.   goats

47.   Most overgrazing is caused by
      a.   drought.
      b.   climate changes.
      c.   large populations of wild herbivores.
   * d.   too many grazing animals for too long a time.
      e.   all of these answers.

48.   The major goal of range management is
      a.   soil conservation.
   * b.   maximizing livestock productivity without overgrazing.
      c.   recreation.
      d.   mining of fossil fuel.
      e.   water management.

49.   Riparian vegetation
      a.   is a kind of algae in watering holes for cattle.
      b.   is poisonous to cold-water fish.
      c.   can destroy a grassland ecosystem.
   * d.   can be destroyed by trampling and overgrazing.
      e.   is not accessed by cattle.

50. Sustainable management of rangelands would include
    a. elimination of riparian areas.
    b. increasing livestock grazing in underutilized areas.
  * c. allowing no or limited grazing on riparian areas.
    d. reducing grazing fees.
    e. all of these answers.

16-6 CATCHING AND RAISING MORE FISH AND SHELLFISH

51. Most of the commercial fish catch comes from
    a. freshwater rivers.
  * b. coastal waters.
    c. the open sea.
    d. the abyssal zone.
    e. estuaries.

52. The world's marine catch is projected to
  * a. decline.
    b. stay the same.
    c. increase.
    d. oscillate.
    e. decline for a few years and then rebound.

53. The tonnage of annual commercial fish catch from all sources
    a. has increased nearly ten times since 1950.
  * b. has increased nearly five times since 1950.
    c. has stayed constant over the last forty-five years.
    d. peaked in 1950 and has been declining ever since.
    e. has been declining since 1990.

54. Sustainable yield is difficult to estimate because
    a. counting aquatic populations isn't easy.
    b. pollution levels change.
    c. harvesting one species' surplus may affect another species' food supply.
  * d. all of these answers.
    e. none of these answers.

55. Overfishing can lead to which of the following?
    a. increased stocks
    b. larger catches
  * c. commercial extinction
    d. larger individual fish
    e. reduced bycatch levels

56. The world's marine catch is not expected to increase significantly. The factor *least* responsible for this trend is
    a. increased population growth.
  * b. global warming.
    c. overfishing.
    d. water pollution.
    e. none of these answers.

57. Aquaculture supplies ____% of the world's commercial fish harvest.
   a. 5
   b. 10
   c. 15
 * d. 20
   e. 35

58. _____ is the world leader in aquaculture.
   a. North Korea
   b. Japan
 * c. China
   d. Brazil
   e. United States

59. Fish ranching is useful for
   a. carp.
 * b. salmon.
   c. tilapia.
   d. lake trout.
   e. tuna.

60. Fish species cultivated in aquaculture include all of the following *except*
 * a. trout.
   b. carp.
   c. clams.
   d. tilapia.
   e. oysters.

61. In developed and some rapidly developing countries, aquaculture primarily benefits
   a. lower-income people.
 * b. sports fishermen.
   c. bears.
   d. developing countries.
   e. all of these answers.

16-7 GOVERNMENT AGRICULTURAL POLICY

62. Governments often provide assistance to farmers because farmers have little control over
   a. weather.
   b. crop prices.
   c. crop pests.
 * d. all of these answers.
   e. interest rates.

63. Governments can influence the food supply by
   a. keeping food prices artificially high.
 * b. giving farmers subsidies.
   c. establishing price controls.
   d. encouraging irrigation.
   e. all of these answers.

64. Governments in many developing countries keep food prices low
   a. to prevent surplus.
 * b. to prevent political unrest in the cities.
   c. to exert political control over the farmers.
   d. to feed their armies.
   e. all of these answers.

65. Government subsidies may
    a. produce local shortages.
    b. cause a rise in global food prices.
  * c. reduce the incentives for farmers to grow crops.
    d. cause the government to export food.
    e. all of these answers.

66. Large amounts of food aid can
    a. inflate local food prices.
  * b. discourage receiving governments from investing in rural agricultural development to grow
       sustainable crops.
    c. stimulate mass migration from cities to rural areas.
    d. increase food production.
    e. all of these answers.

67. Food made available to a country may not reach the poor and hungry because of
    a. transportation problems.
    b. robbery, graft, and bribes.
    c. pests and storage problems.
    d. a and b only.
  * e. all of these answers.

16-8 PROTECTING FOOD RESOURCES: USING CONVENTIONAL CHEMICAL PESTICIDES TO CONTROL PESTS

68. Which of the following categories includes all of the others?
    a. insecticides
    b. herbicides
  * c. pesticides
    d. fungicides
    e. nematocides.

69. Which of the following would be used to kill rats and mice?
    a. herbicides
  * b. rodenticides
    c. fungicides
    d. insecticides
    e. nematocides

70. Which of the following would be used to kill weeds?
  * a. herbicides
    b. rodenticides
    c. fungicides
    d. insecticides
    e. nematocides

71. Rachel Carson
    a. was a scientist for the EPA.
    b. reviewed the literature on the environmental effects of fertilizers.
  * c. defended her work against a well-funded campaign to discredit her findings.
    d. wrote *A Black Day in Bhopal.*
    e. wrote the first textbook on ecology.

72. According to pesticide proponents, pesticides
    a. work faster than alternate controls.
    b. increase profit for farmers.
    c. save lives and money.
    d. they increase food supplies and lower costs.
 * e. all of these answers.

73. Some beneficial changes in pesticides and their use include all of the following *except*
    a. pesticides which are less damaging to the environment.
    b. pesticides which are safer to the users.
    c. genetic engineering which may lead to pest-resistant crop strains.
 * d. pesticides which kill only the target pest and do no harm to any other species.
    e. very low rates per unit area are needed.

74. The ideal pesticide would
 * a. kill only the target pest.
    b. be persistent.
    c. allow the development of genetic resistance.
    d. be of equal value to the damage the pest would have caused.
    e. kill every plant it came into contact with.

75. The ideal pesticide would
    a. be persistent.
    b. attract target organisms to the poison.
 * c. not allow the development of resistance in the pest.
    d. kill organisms related to the target.
    e. kill every plant it came into contact with.

76. The most serious drawback to using chemicals to control pests is
 * a. the development of genetic resistance.
    b. the killing of other forms of life.
    c. magnification in the food chain.
    d. their persistence in nature.
    e. their expense.

77. Since 1945, approximately ____ species of insects have developed resistance to one or more insecticides.
    a. 20
    b. 50
 * c. 500
    d. 2,000
    e. 5,000

78. Broad-spectrum pesticides may increase the number of a pest species through
    a. development of genetic resistance.
    b. killing of predators of the pest species.
    c. killing of parasites that may have kept the population of the pest low.
    d. b and c only.
 * e. all of these answers.

79. According to the U.S. Department of Agriculture (USDA), no more than _____% of the insecticides applied to crops by aerial spraying reach the target pests.
   * a. 2
   b. 10
   c. 25
   d. 50
   e. 75

80. Which of the following approaches would be the *least* beneficial in trying to reduce insect damage?
   a. rotating crops and delayed planting
   b. photodegradable plastic
   * c. planting monocultures
   d. planting barrier hedges around agricultural fields
   e. planting polycultures

81. Limits to building in resistance to pests include
   a. long development time.
   b. expense.
   c. evolution operating to overcome the resistance.
   * d. all of these answers.
   e. none of these answers.

16-9 PROTECTING FOOD RESOURCES: ALTERNATIVES TO CONVENTIONAL CHEMICAL PESTICIDES

82. Biological control
   a. costs more money than pesticides to use.
   b. is not target specific.
   c. is easily produced and quickly applied.
   * d. is often self-perpetuating once established.
   e. is faster acting than conventional pesticides.

83. Which of the following statements is *false?*
   * a. Biological control is a good, quick fix.
   b. U.S. farmers save $25 for each $1 invested in biological controls.
   c. Biological control is slower acting than pesticides.
   d. Biological control is harder to apply than pesticides.
   e. Biological control focuses on selected species.

84. Insect control by sterilization involves irradiating
   a. eggs.
   * b. males.
   c. females.
   d. larvae.
   e. pupae.

85. A pheromone is
   a. a new form of chemical insecticide waiting approval by FIFRA.
   b. a strong herbicide.
   * c. a species-specific chemical sex attractant.
   d. a bloodstream chemical that controls an organism's growth and development.
   e. a safe, natural pesticide.

86. Which of the following statements is a weakness of using pheromones?
  * a. They are costly and time-consuming to produce in the laboratory.
    b. They are more effective in the juvenile stage than the adult stage.
    c. Insects develop resistance to pheromones.
    d. They are biologically magnified in nontarget species.
    e. They only work in large amounts.

87. Pheromones
    a. are non-species-specific.
    b. cause genetic resistance.
    c. are only effective in large amounts.
  * d. are not harmful to nontarget species.
    e. all of these answers.

88. A hormone is
    a. a new form of chemical insecticide waiting approval by FIFRA.
    b. a strong herbicide.
    c. a species-specific chemical sex attractant.
  * d. a chemical that controls an organism's growth and development.
    e. a strong pesticide.

89. Which of the following statements is *false?*
  * a. Insect development and metamorphosis are controlled by pheromones.
    b. Each step in the life cycle of a typical insect is controlled by hormones.
    c. Insect hormones can be synthesized in the laboratory.
    d. When applied at certain times during the life cycle, insect hormones cause developmental abnormalities.
    e. Hormones are inexpensive to produce.

90. Integrated pest management _____ than pesticides.
  * a. requires more expert knowledge about individual pest-crop situations
    b. is faster acting
    c. requires more fertilizer and irrigation
    d. is more expensive
    e. none of these answers.

91. Which of the following statements is *false?*
  * a. The goal of integrated pest control is the complete eradication of the pest.
    b. Integrated pest management is a multidimensional control program.
    c. Integrated pest management involves much sampling to keep up with the pest population.
    d. In integrated pest management, small amounts of pesticides are used at critical times to control pest populations.
    e. In integrated pest management, controlling pests may include vacuuming up harmful bugs.

92. An integrated pest management program can
    a. increase inputs of fertilizer and irrigation water.
  * b. reduce pre-harvest pest-induced crop losses by 50%.
    c. increase pesticide use.
    d. decrease yields and increase costs.
    e. increase the development of disease resistant pests.

93. Switching to integrated pest management
    a. will be easy to do because it is very simple.
    * b. is strongly opposed by politically and economically powerful agricultural chemical companies.
    c. is difficult because it only works for a few pests.
    d. is strongly opposed by environmentalists.
    e. all of these answers.

94. Integrated pesticide management (IPM) could be promoted by all of the following strategies *except*
    a. setting up federally supported IPM demonstration projects in each county.
    b. adding a sales tax on pesticides to fund IPM research and education.
    c. training USDA field personnel and county farm agents so they can help farmers with this strategy.
    * d. gradually phasing in subsidies for farmers who depend primarily on pesticides.
    e. providing federal or state subsidies for farmers who use IPM.

95. To help protect the food supply and fight pests responsibly, individuals can
    a. use larger amounts of pesticides when necessary.
    b. dispose of unused pesticide where it will continue to kill pests.
    * c. allow native plants to cover most of their property.
    d. use powerful synthetic to pesticides.
    e. help eradicate all pests everywhere.

96. Which of the following would *not* reduce the threat of pesticide in the food you eat?
    * a. Use imported food whenever possible.
    b. Scrub all food in soapy water.
    c. Grow your own fruits and vegetables using organic gardening methods.
    d. Purchase organically grown foods.
    e. none of these answers.

16-10 SOLUTIONS: MORE SUSTAINABLE AGRICULTURE

97. Sustainable agriculture is characterized by all of the following *except*
    * a. promoting monoculture.
    b. lack of requirements of massive amounts of fossil fuels.
    c. conserving and building topsoil.
    d. lack of use of many artificial chemicals.
    e. promoting polyculture.

98. All of the following are characteristic of sustainable agriculture *except*
    a. perennial plants.
    b. nontraditional crops.
    c. diversity of fruits and vegetables.
    * d. large-scale monoculture.
    e. reduced erosion.

99. Sustainable agriculture
    a. uses pesticides.
    * b. minimizes erosion.
    c. requires high inputs of fossil fuel.
    d. employs massive fertilization programs.
    e. wastes water.

100. In order to switch to sustainable agriculture, which of the following practices would *not* be favorable?
   a. Give subsidies and tax breaks to those that use the method.
   b. Shift to full-cost pricing.
   c. Increase government support of research on sustainable agriculture.
 * d. Expand the use of the crops of the green revolution.
   e. Discourage monocultures.

101. An individual can support the concept of sustainable-Earth agriculture by
   a. eating higher on the food chain.
 * b. developing a home garden using appropriate principles.
   c. using genetically altered vegetables.
   d. using chemical pest control.
   e. using more fertilizer.

CHAPTER 17
SUSTAINING BIODIVERSITY: THE ECOSYSTEM APPROACH

17-1   HUMAN IMPACTS ON BIODIVERSITY

1.   How much of the Earth's land surface have been disturbed or degraded by human activities?
      a.   10-20%
      b.   20-30%
      c.   30-40%
*   d.   40-50%
      e.   60-70%

2.   It is estimated that global extinction rates may be _____ what they would be without human-induced changes.
      a.   1-2 times
      b.   2-10 times
      c.   10-20 times
*   d.   100-1,000 times
      e.   1000-10,000 times

17-2   LAND USE IN THE WORLD AND THE UNITED STATES

3.   The country that has set aside the largest portion of its land area for the public's use and enjoyment is
      a.   Brazil.
*   b.   the United States.
      c.   Great Britain.
      d.   Germany.
      e.   Australia.

4.   In the United States, about _____% of the land is public land.
      a.   17
      b.   25
      c.   33
*   d.   42
      e.   67

5.   About three-quarters of federally managed public lands are in
      a.   New York State.
      b.   Colorado.
*   c.   Alaska.
      d.   Arizona.
      e.   Hawaii.

6.   The national forests are managed on
*   a.   a sustainable-yield multiple-use basis.
      b.   a restricted-use basis.
      c.   a maximum timber production schedule.
      d.   the basis of political expediency.
      e.   all of these answers.

7.   Which of the following is managed on a multiple-use basis?
      a.   national wildlife refuges
      b.   national wilderness areas
      c.   national parks
*   d.   national resource lands
      e.   national forests

8.   Which of the following is managed on a restricted-use basis?
  * a. national parks
    b. national forests
    c. national resource lands
    d. national wildlife refuges
    e. national wilderness areas

9.   Which of the following is managed as moderately restricted-use land?
    a. national parks
    b. national forests
    c. national resource lands
  * d. national wildlife refuges
    e. national wilderness areas

10.   Which of the following principles would most environmentalists *not* want to see being a
      guide to governance of public lands?
    a. All users of public lands should be responsible for correcting any environmental damage they
        cause.
    b. Protection of biodiversity and ecological integrity should be the most important goal.
  * c. Public lands should be used to enrich individual citizens to make a strong U.S. economy.
    d. No one should be given subsidies or tax breaks for extracting resources on public lands.
    e. The American people deserve fair compensation for the use of their property.

11.   The takings/property rights movement
    a. gives local zoning, land-use, and environmental plans precedence over federal laws.
    b. requires the federal government to compensate landowners for property values diminished
        because of regulations.
    c. greatly weakens federal environmental legislation.
  * d. is described by all of these answers.
    e. is described by none of these answers.

12.   Federally administered public lands contain a large portion of the country's
    a. energy resources.
    b. commercial timber.
    c. minerals.
  * d. all of these answers.
    e. none of these answers.

13.   Restricted use lands are generally governed by
    a. a wise use philosophy.
  * b. a preservationist philosophy.
    c. the whim of the current director of the Bureau of Land Management.
    d. a philosophy of utilitarian conservation.
    e. a horoscope.

14.   Management of multiple-use public lands could include
    a. logging.
    b. mining.
    c. grazing.
    d. farming.
  * e. all of these answers.

17-3 MANAGING AND SUSTAINING FORESTS

15.   Forests cover about ____ of the land surface of the earth.
  *   a.   one-fourth
        b.   one-third
        c.   one-half
        d.   two-thirds
        e.   three-fourths

16.   Most temperate forests are _____ forests; most tropical forests are _____ forests.
        a.   old-growth . . . old-growth
        b.   old-growth . . . second-growth
        c.   second-growth . . . second-growth
  *   d.   second-growth . . . old-growth
        e.   third-growth . . . second-growth

17.   Old growth forests
        a.   result from primary succession.
        b.   developed after the abandonment of agricultural lands.
        c.   are the predominant forest form in the United States.
  *   d.   are the predominant forest form in the tropics.
        e.   are the predominant forest form in Europe.

18.   Secondary forests
        a.   result from primary succession.
        b.   develop on volcanic lava flows.
  *   c.   are the predominant forest form in the United States.
        d.   are the predominant forest form in the tropics.
        e.   are the only type that exists on earth today.

19.   Utilitarian functions of forests include
        a.   lumber for housing.
        b.   fuelwood.
        d.   medicines.
  *   d.   all of these answers.
        e.   none of these answers.

20.   Forests
  *   a.   control erosion and reduce sedimentation.
        b.   increase surface runoff.
        c.   aid depletion of aquifers.
        d.   increase severity of flooding.
        e.   all of these answers.

21.   Which of the following statements is *false?*
        a.   Forests affect humidity, which affects the climate of an area.
  *   b.   Forests play a minor role in biodiversity.
        c.   Through photosynthesis, forests play an important role in the carbon cycle and global warming.
        d.   Forests absorb some air pollutants.
        e.   Forests reduce erosion and drying.

22. The goal of even-aged management of a forest is
   a. maintenance of maximum biological diversity.
   b. production of high-quality timber.
   c. a long-term ecologically oriented approach.
 * d. grow and harvest monoculture forests.
   e. multiple use of the forest for timber, watershed protection, and recreation.

23. A tree grower using uneven-aged management most likely has the goal of
   a. decreasing biological diversity.
 * b. maintaining long-term production of high-quality timber.
   c. producing quick economic return.
   d. producing fiber for paper mills.
   e. increasing erosion.

24. Logging roads
   a. cause erosion and increased sedimentation of waterways.
   b. can expose forests to invasion of pests.
   c. open up land for development.
   d. increase habitat fragmentation and biodiversity loss.
 * e. all of these answers.

25. Selective cutting
   a. encourages crowding of trees.
   b. encourages growth of more mature trees.
 * c. maintains an uneven-aged stand of trees of different species, ages, and sizes.
   d. requires a special seed-distribution plan.
   e. requires crop rotation.

26. In the lumber industry, the term *high-grading* means
 * a. harvesting only the best-quality trees.
   b. cutting selectively.
   c. removing all trees.
   d. harvesting the timber in an area as quickly as possible.
   e. harvesting timber in higher elevations only.

27. Which of the following types of cutting involves at least three cuttings?
   a. selective cutting
   b. seed-tree cutting
   c. clear-cutting
 * d. shelterwood cutting
   e. strip-cutting

28. Which of the following cutting methods leaves only a few mature seed-producing, wind-resistant trees for regeneration of the forest?
   a. selective cutting
 * b. seed-tree cutting
   c. clear-cutting
   d. shelterwood cutting
   e. strip cutting

29. The removal of all trees from a given area in a single cutting to establish a new even-aged stand is called
   a. selective cutting.
   b. seed-tree cutting.
 * c. clear-cutting.
   d. shelterwood cutting.
   e. strip cutting

30. Which of the following statements is *false?*
    a. Clear-cutting increases the amount of timber produced per acre.
    b. Lumber companies prefer clear-cutting because it takes less skill and planning than other methods.
    c. Clear-cutting shortens rotation time.
  * d. Clear-cutting requires more roads.
    e. permits reforestation with genetically improved stocks of fast-growing trees.

31. Clear-cutting on a large scale leads to
    a. erosion.
    b. flooding.
    c. sediment water pollution.
    d. loss of biodiversity.
  * e. all of these answers.

32. Clear-cutting, if done properly, can be useful for some
    a. shade-tolerant species.
  * b. shade-intolerant species.
    c. species that prefer acid soils.
    d. species that prefer alkaline soils.
    e. species that prefer alkaline soils and shade.

33. A form of clear-cutting that can allow a sustainable timber yield without widespread destruction is called
    a. selective cutting.
    b. seed-tree cutting.
  * c. strip cutting.
    d. shelterwood cutting.
    e. straight cutting.

34. Which of the following statements is the best and cheapest way to protect trees from insects and disease?
  * a. Maintain the biological diversity of the forest.
    b. Use antibiotics on only the infected trees.
    c. Clear-cut and burn all infected areas.
    d. Develop disease-resistant tree species.
    e. Use pesticides.

35. Which of the following is the most dangerous type of fire?
    a. surface
    b. prescribed
  * c. crown
    d. ground
    e. cool.

36. Which of the following statements is *false?*
    a. Wildlife and mature trees are relatively unharmed by surface fires.
  * b. Frequent surface fires increase the chance of a severe crown fire.
    c. Surface fires release minerals that are locked up in vegetation.
    d. Surface fires may actually benefit some plant species and some game animals.
    e. Surface fires burn away flammable ground material and help prevent more destructive fires.

37. Which of the following statements is *false?*
   a. Prescribed burning is a controlled surface fire.
   b. Prescribed burning is done at specific times to reduce the amount of air pollution.
 * c. Surface fires kill much wildlife, and such burning should be prevented.
   d. Some wildlife species depend on surface fires to maintain their habitats.
   e. Surface fires release valuable nutrients tied up in slowly decomposing litter and undergrowth.

38. Which of the following statements is *false?*
   a. Fire may help to release minerals locked up inside organisms.
 * b. Fire is universally a dangerous and destructive force that reduces productivity.
   c. Fire may occur periodically without the interference of humans.
   d. Surface fires may be prescribed to reduce the chance of serious fires.
   e. Crown fires kill more trees than surface fires.

39. Which of the following animals do *not* require periodic fires to maintain their habitats?
   a. quail
   b. deer
   c. muskrats
 * d. squirrels
   e. moose

40. Which of the following statements is *false?*
   a. Conifers are more susceptible to air pollution than hardwoods.
   b. Pollution makes trees more vulnerable to disease and insects.
 * c. Forests at low elevations are exposed to more pollutants.
   d. The only solution to pollution is to reduce it drastically.
   e. Forests downwind from urban and industrial centers are harmed more than those upwind.

41. In the next few decades, a threat to temperate and boreal forests that is expected to become more significant is
   a. clear-cutting to create croplands.
   b. insects.
 * c. climate change.
   d. air pollution.
   e. water pollution.

17-4 FOREST RESOURCES AND MANAGEMENT IN THE UNITED STATES

42. U.S. forests
   a. are a setting for outdoor recreation.
   b. sustain the country's biodiversity by providing wildlife habitat.
   c. provide wood and wood products.
   d. provide hunting habitats.
 * e. all of these answers.

43. The national forests are managed on
 * a. a sustainable-yield multiple-use basis.
   b. a restricted-use basis.
   c. a maximum timber production schedule.
   d. the basis of political expediency.
   e. all of these answers.

44. _____ has built as much road as the entire U.S. interstate highway system.
    a. A team of Alaskan pipeline workers.
    b. The U.S. interstate system.
*   c. The U.S. Forest Service.
    d. Australia.
    e. Europe.

45. The Forest Service keeps most of the money it makes on timber sales. The Forest Service has allowed timber harvesting to become the dominant use of most national forests. The Forest Service makes more money. Money increases size, power, and influence. This situation best illustrates which of the following components of a complex system?
*   a. a positive feedback loop
    b. a negative feedback loop
    c. a delay
    d. an accumulation
    e. none of these answers

46. Sustainable use of U.S. forests would be encouraged by all of the following *except*
    a. making biodiversity and ecological integrity the top priority of national forest management policy.
*   b. building more roads to encourage recreational use of national forests.
    c. moving toward full-cost pricing of U.S. timber.
    d. disallowing the Forest Service to keep money from timber sales.
    e. certification of timber grown by sustainable methods.

47. Sustainable use of U.S. forests would be encouraged by all of the following *except*
    a. disallowing returns of gross receipts from national forests to county governments.
*   b. emphasizing even-aged management in old-growth forests.
    c. using more recreational user fees to fund the Forest Service.
    d. taxing exports of raw logs.
    e. minimize fragmentation of remaining larger blocks of forest.

48. A lumber company viewing a forest is *least* likely to see
    a. the economic value of giant living trees.
    b. jobs.
    c. improved economy.
*   d. recreational opportunity.
    e. pulp to make paper.

49. An environmentalist viewing a forest is *least* likely to see
    a. ecological value.
    b. aesthetic value.
*   c. economic value.
    d. scientific value.
    e. wildlife habitat.

17-5 TROPICAL DEFORESTATION

50. About _____% of the earth's land area is tropical forest.
    a. 1
*   b. 6
    c. 12
    d. 16
    e. 20

51.   About _____ of the world's tropical forests have already been cleared or damaged.
       a.   1/4
       b.   1/3
   *   c.   1/2
       d.   2/3
       e.   3/4

52.   Tropical forests supply
       a.   hardwood.
       b.   coffee and spices.
       c.   tropical fruits and nuts.
       d.   nuts.
   *   e.   all of these answers.

53.   Over 50 years, harvesting of nonwood products from tropical forests would generate _____ revenue
       as clearing for timber.
       a.   three times as much
   *   b.   twice as much
       c.   the same
       d.   one-half as much
       e.   one-tenth as much

54.   Key active ingredients in one-fourth of the world's drugs come from
   *   a.   tropical rain forests.
       b.   coniferous forests.
       c.   deciduous forests.
       d.   cacti.
       e.   grasslands.

55.   Which of the following important food crops did *not* have original strains predominantly from the
       tropical forests?
       a.   rice
       b.   corn
   *   c.   potatoes
       d.   wheat
       e.   none of these answers

56.   As a best approximation, less than _____% of the flowering plant species in the tropical forests have
       been examined closely for their possible use as human resources.
   *   a.   1
       b.   5
       c.   10
       d.   15
       e.   20

57.   The Neem tree
       a.   can reforest bare land quickly.
       b.   has been called a "village pharmacy."
       c.   seeds contain a strong spermicide.
       d.   provide fuelwood and lumber.
   *   e.   all of these answers.

58. Tropical forest are being destroyed and degraded by
    a. economic growth and development.
    b. international policies.
    c. population growth.
    d. cattle ranching.
  * e. all of these answers.

59. Shifting ranching
    a. is against government policy in developing countries.
  * b. is very destructive to nutrient-poor soils in the tropics.
    c. is a way to use tropical grasslands.
    d. is a form of nomadic herding.
    e. all of these answers.

60. Currently, the greatest user of tropical lumber is
    a. Indonesia.
  * b. Japan.
    c. Canada.
    d. the United States.
    e. Europe.

61. Economic steps that can help reduce the destruction and degradation of tropical forests include all of the following *except*
    a. phase in full-cost pricing.
  * b. providing economic incentives to convert fuelwood plantations to croplands.
    c. phasing out funding for dams and other projects that are not sustainable.
    d. creating enforceable debt-for-nature swaps.
    e. phasing out government subsidies that encourage unsustainable agriculture and forestry.

62. Political steps that can help reduce the destruction and degradation of tropical forests include all of the following *except*
    a. slowing population growth.
    b. establishing programs to teach settlers sustainable agriculture and forestry strategies.
    c. reforming timber-cutting regulations.
  * d. encouraging migration to undisturbed tropical forests.
    e. reducing poverty.

63. Fuelwood scarcity is associated with
    a. deforestation.
    b. accelerated soil erosion.
    c. reduced cropland productivity.
  * d. all of these answers.
    e. none of these answers.

64. Eucalyptus are
    a. small mammals.
  * b. fast-growing fuelwood trees.
    c. small farms in tropical rain forests.
    d. an endangered species.
    e. small reptiles.

17-6 MANAGING AND SUSTAINING NATIONAL PARKS

65   Today there are over _____ parks in the world.
    a. 50
    b. 100
    c. 500
  * d. 1,100
    e. 2,500

66.   The first national park system was created in
    a. Kenya.
    b. Antarctica.
    c. Costa Rica.
  * d. the United States.
    e. Europe.

67.   Currently, the national parks are threatened by
    a. popularity.
    b. uncontrolled populations of prey because of the decline in predators.
    c. lack of funding.
    d. invasion of nonnative species.
  * e. all of these answers.

68.   Wolves
    a. culled herds of herbivores.
    b. protected species dependent upon vegetation.
    c. strengthened the gene pool of their prey.
    d. are ancestors to dogs.
  * e. all of these answers.

69.   In developed countries, many national parks are threatened by
    a. air and water pollution.
    b. invasion of alien species.
    c. roads and noise.
    d. lack of funding.
  * e. all of these answers.

70.   Of the following, the biggest problem for U.S. national and state parks *today* is
  * a. increased number of park visitors.
    b. too many concessions.
    c. invasion of alien species.
    d. rock collectors.
    e. soil erosion.

71.   Currently, the greatest danger to the national parks is
  * a. human activities in nearby areas.
    b. uncontrolled populations of prey because of the decline in predators.
    c. pollution.
    d. lack of funding.
    e. soil erosion.

72. The Wilderness Society and the National Parks and Conservation Association suggested all of the following proposals *except*
    a. establishing the National Park Service as an independent agency.
    b. significantly increasing the pay and number of park rangers.
    c. blocking mining and timbering at park boundaries.
  * d. locating most commercial park facilities only along the main road through the park.
    e. none of these answers

17-7 ESTABLISHING, DESIGNING, AND MANAGING NATURE RESERVES

73. Of Earth's remaining wilderness areas, about _____% are strictly or partially protected by law from exploitation.
  * a. 8
    b. 16
    c. 26
    d. 36
    e. 46

74. Currently, there are about _____ established biosphere reserves.
    a. 15
    b. 150
    c. 250
  * d. 350
    e. 500

75. A well-designed biosphere reserve has all of the following zones *except*
    a. buffer zone.
    b. transition zone.
    c. core.
  * d. mantle.
    e. none of these answers.

76. The zone of a biosphere reserve where there would be little, if any, disturbance from human activities would be the
    a. buffer zone.
    b. transition zone.
  * c. core.
    d. mantle.
    e. biozone.

77. The Wilderness Society estimates that a wilderness area should contain at least _____ square miles.
    a. 1.5
    b. 15
    c. 150
  * d. 1,500
    e. 5,000

78. About _____ of Earth's land area is undeveloped wilderness.
    a. 1/10
    b. 1/5
    c. 1/4
  * d. 1/3
    e. 2/3

79. Wilderness areas are needed for
    a. aesthetic reasons.
    b. recreation.
    c. preserving biological diversity.
    d. people to improve their mental and physical health.
 * e. all of these answers.

80. Wilderness recovery areas can be created by all of the following *except*
    a. reintroducing species that have been driven away.
    b. closing nonessential roads in large areas of public lands.
    c. allowing natural fires to burn.
 * d. removing buffer zones between core wilderness areas and developed areas.
    e. restoring wildlife habitat.

81. Good wilderness management would do all of the following *except*
    a. extensively patrol the accessible, popular areas.
    b. offer permits to selected areas for those who have demonstrated wilderness skills.
    c. leave some areas undisturbed by humans.
 * d. allow citizens to camp anywhere at their own risk.
    e. limit number of people using sites at any one time.

82. Activities allowed in the national Wild and Scenic Rivers System include all of the following *except*
    a. camping.
    b. canoeing.
 * c. motor boating.
    d. fishing.
    e. kayaking.

17-8 PROTECTING AND SUSTAINING AQUATIC SYSTEMS

83. Which of the following occurs in protected marine reserves?
    a. fish populations remain steady
    b. fish reproduction decreases
    c. fish size declines
 * d. there is increased fish diversity
    e. species diversity decreases

84. What does integrated coastal management accomplish?
    a. enlarges the exclusive economic zone
    b. reduces the number of marine protected areas
    c. supercedes the "Law of the Sea"
 * d. provides a variety of protection and use levels
    e. allows for unlimited development.

85. What has helped to reduce annual wetland loss by up to 75% in the last 30 years?
    a. a federal law prohibiting wetland development
 * b. a federal permit system for dredging or filling wetlands larger than 3 acres
    c. grassroots environmental groups that blockade wetlands development projects
    d. federal endangered species laws
    e. a federal law allowing unlimited wetland development.

17-9 ECOLOGICAL RESTORATION

86. All of the following are approaches to restore ecosystems *except*
    a. rehabilitation
*   b. secondary succession
    c. replacement
    d. creating artificial ecosystems
    e. restoration.

CHAPTER 18
SUSTAINING BIODIVERSITY: THE SPECIES

1. Alexander Wilson, an ornithologist in the early 1800s, described a flock of _____ that he estimated was 240 miles long and 1 mile wide and consisted of over 2 million birds.
   a. Carolina parakeets
   b. starlings
   c. sparrows
   * d. passenger pigeons
   e. California condors

2. The passenger pigeon became extinct in
   a. 1874.
   b. 1894.
   * c. 1914.
   d. 1934.
   e. 1954

3. Passenger pigeons
   a. were used as fertilizer.
   b. were good to eat.
   c. were suffocated by burning grass or sulfur below their roosts.
   d. feathers were used to stuff pillows.
   * e. all of these answers.

18-1 SPECIES EXTINCTION

4. In 1996, conservation biologists estimate that the rate of extinction was _____ than the estimated natural background extinction rate.
   a. ten times lower
   b. ten times higher
   c. hundreds times higher
   * d. thousands times higher
   e. two times higher

5. The current extinction crisis differs from previous mass extinctions in that
   a. ecosystems that store genes for future radiations are being protected.
   * b. the current crisis is caused by the human species.
   c. it is taking place at a slower rate.
   d. recovery is likely to be faster because of genetic engineering.
   e. it is making the planet healthier.

6. Habitat loss may result in extinction over several generations. Which feature of a model is illustrated by this example?
   a. a positive feedback loop
   b. a negative feedback loop
   * c. a delay
   d. an accumulation
   e. a synergistic interaction

7. Mathematical models indicate that organisms most vulnerable to habitat loss may be the
   a. producers.
   b. herbivores.
   c. decomposers.
   * d. top competitors.
   e. bacteria.

8. Wilson estimates that a 1.8% per year loss of tropical forest results in roughly a _____ loss of species.
   * a. 0.5%
     b. 1.0%
     c. 1.5%
     d. 1.8%
     e. 5%

9. In a 1998 survey, 70% of the biologists polled believe
     a. their estimates of species loss are precise and cannot be ignored.
     b. if 300 biosphere reserves are not established immediately, the resultant species loss will be irreplaceable.
   * c. we are in the midst of a mass extinction and that this loss of species will pose a major threat to human existence in the next century.
     d. there is a clear correlation between the rates of habitat loss and species loss.
     e. all of these answers.

10. A biologist is most likely to say that the passenger pigeon is
     a. endangered.
     b. locally extinct.
     c. ecologically extinct.
   * d. biologically extinct.
     e. threatened.

11. You are an ecologist studying alligators in the outback. You find that the population of alligators is so depleted that organisms that depend on alligator holes for their survival are also hurting. You would most likely label the alligators
     a. threatened.
     b. endangered.
     c. locally extinct.
   * d. ecologically extinct.
     e. biologically extinct.

12. An endangered species is any species that can
     a. undergo alteration of its genetic traits.
     b. become rare within the next century.
   * c. soon become extinct in all or part of its range.
     d. eventually become threatened or rare.
     e. be considered economically important but is rare.

13. The California condor and whooping crane are
   * a. endangered species.
     b. threatened species.
     c. imported species.
     d. overpopulated species.
     e. biologically extinct.

14. The grizzly bear and American alligator are
     a. endangered species.
   * b. threatened species.
     c. imported species.
     d. overpopulated species.
     e. biologically extinct.

15. The whooping crane is vulnerable to extinction because of
    a. its small size.
    b. its call.
*   c. its low reproduction rate.
    d. its variable migration patterns.
    e. competition.

16. The blue whale is extinction prone for all of the following reasons *except*
    a. low reproduction rate.
*   b. feeding at the top trophic level.
    c. specialized feeding habits.
    d. fixed migratory patterns.
    e. none of these answers.

17. The timber wolf is extinction prone because of its
    a. large size.
    b. specialized breeding areas.
    c. fixed migratory patterns.
*   d. preying on livestock.
    e. none of these answers.

18. All of the following characteristics would make a species more prone to extinction *except*
    a. low population density.
*   b. small body size.
    c. specialized niche.
    d. low reproductive rate.
    e. fixed migratory patterns.

19. Small populations of species
    a. may be below the critical population density.
    b. are vulnerable to catastrophic events.
    c. may have a reduced evolutionary potential for survival.
*   d. all of these answers.
    e. none of these answers.

20. The type of species that offers the best opportunity to apply the prevention principle is the
    a. keystone species.
    b. alien species.
*   c. indicator species.
    d. endemic species found in only one part of the world.
    e. endangered species.

21. If you eat cashews, avocados, or bananas, you can thank a
*   a. bat.
    b. manatee.
    c. bee.
    d. hummingbird.
    e. butterfly.

22. Bats are endangered for all of the following reasons *except* that
    a. they live in habitats vulnerable to destruction.
    b. they have a slow reproduction rate.
    c. people are fearful of them.
*   d. people appreciate their ecological role.
    e. people are fearful of them.

23. Fruit-eating bats on many tropical islands are
  * a. keystone species.
    b. alien species.
    c. indicator species.
    d. generalists.
    e. endangered.

18-2 WHY SHOULD WE CARE ABOUT SPECIES EXTINCTION?

24. Biologists claim that species have
    a. ecological value.
    b. economic value.
    c. medical and scientific value.
  * d. all of these answers.
    e. intrinsic value.

25. About _____ of today's food crops were domesticated from wild tropical plants.
    a. 20%
    b. 30%
    c. 50%
    d. 70%
  * e. 90%

26. Wild plant species have economic value as
    a. fiber.
    b. dyes.
    c. oils.
    d. medicines.
  * e. all of these answers.

27. Economic services performed by wild species include
    a. nitrogen-fixation.
    b. production of medicines.
    c. pollination of crops.
    d. fuelwood and lumber.
  * e. all of these answers.

28. The ecosystem service *least* likely to be provided by wild species is
    a. recycling nutrients and decomposition of organic wastes.
    b. diversifying the gene pool.
  * c. balancing all the impacts of human activities.
    d. moderating Earth's climate.
    e. natural pest and disease control.

29. People regard wildflowers as beautiful, and this is evidence that wildflowers have _____ importance.
    a. economic
  * b. aesthetic
    c. medical
    d. ecological
    e. recreational

30. An environmentalist is *least* likely to go on an ecotour which
    a. takes precautions to reduce the tour's impact on the local ecosystem.
    b. contributes a high percentage of the tour company's profits to local environmental projects.
    c. hires naturalists and local people.
  * d. provides lodging in internationally owned lodging.
    e. collects specimens.

31. People who believe that wild species have an inherent right to exist generally believe that species have
    a. economic value.
    b. extrinsic value.
*   c. intrinsic value.
    d. utilitarian value.
    e. recreational value.

18-3 EXTINCTION THREATS FROM HABITAT LOSS AND DEGRADATION

32. Underlying causes of extinction and reduction of wildlife populations include all of the following *except*
    a. affluence.
    b. human population growth.
*   c. sustainable development.
    d. governmental policies that undervalue ecological services.
    e. rising resource use.

33. The cause of endangerment and extinction of wild species with the longest delay is
    a. habitat fragmentation.
*   b. human population growth.
    c. poaching and commercial hunting.
    d. pollution.
    e. climate change.

34. The greatest threat to most species is
*   a. reduction of habitats.
    b. water pollution.
    c. parasites.
    d. sport hunting.
    e. climate change.

35. The greatest species terminator is habitat destruction of
    a. coral reefs.
    b. grasslands.
*   c. tropical forests.
    d. deserts.
    e. temperate forests.

36. Since Europeans first settled North America, _____% of the tall-grass prairies in the United States have been destroyed.
    a. 28
    b. 38
    c. 58
    d. 78
*   e. 98

37. National parks can be viewed as habitat islands surrounded by
    a. logging.
    b. industrial activity.
    c. energy extraction.
    d. agriculture.
*   e. all of these answers.

38. Which of the following is *false?* Habitat islands
   * a. are wildlife preserves set aside to sustain endangered species.
   b. can create small populations vulnerable to inbreeding.
   c. are often too small to support the minimum number of individuals required to sustain a population.
   d. may be national parks, protected areas, or freshwater lakes.
   e. are more vulnerable to competition from nonnative and pest species.

39. Fragmentation of tropical forests would be harmful to
   a. skunks.
   b. cowbirds.
   * c. migrating songbirds.
   d. raccoons.
   e. opossums.

40. Habitat fragmentation
   a. can create barriers that limit the ability of species to find food and mates.
   b. increases edge areas that make some species more vulnerable to predators.
   c. may create habitats too small to support the minimum breeding population of some species.
   d. may limit the ability of some species to disperse and colonized new areas.
   * e. all of these answers.

18-4   EXTINCTION THREATS FROM NONNATIVE SPECIES

41. The introduction of nonnative species often results in unforeseen consequences. This experience indicates that when introducing nonnative species, we would be well-advised to apply the
   a. first law of thermodynamics.
   b. law of common property.
   * c. precautionary principle.
   d. law of supply and demand.
   e. second law of thermodynamics.

42. About _____ of the species on the U.S./ official list of endangered and threatened species are there in part because of population declines caused by nonnative species.
   a. 1/5
   b. 1/4
   c. 1/3
   * d. 1/2
   e. 3/4

43. Japanese kudzu vine offers all of the following *except*
   a. starch used in Asian beverages and herbal remedies.
   b. control of soil erosion.
   * c. toxic berries that deplete bird populations.
   d. a source of tree-free paper.
   e. herbal remedies for diseases.

44. The rapid doubling of a water hyacinth population in nutrient-rich waters with no predators is an example of
   * a. a positive feedback loop.
   b. a negative feedback loop.
   c. an accumulation.
   d. a synergistic interaction.
   e. a delay.

45. Which of the following is *false?* The water hyacinth
    a. is native to Central and South America.
    b. entered Florida via transplanting from an exhibit.
    c. has rapidly displaced native species.
 * d. is successfully controlled by mechanical harvesting and herbicides.
    e. clogs waterways.

46. Water hyacinths have been *most* effectively controlled by
 * a. manatees, which are a threatened species.
    b. mechanical harvesting.
    c. plastic or canvas covers that deprive them of light.
    d. herbicides.
    e. sea turtles.

47. Water hyacinths can
    a. absorb toxic chemicals in sewage treatment lagoons.
    b. be fermented to form biogas fuel.
    c. be used as a mineral and protein supplement in cattle feed.
 * d. all of these answers.
    e. none of these answers.

48. All of the following are organisms imported into the United States that cause damage *except* the
 * a. prairie dog.
    b. sea lamprey.
    c. Japanese beetle.
    d. house sparrow.
    e. kudzu.

18-5 EXTINCTION THREATS FROM HUNTING AND POACHING

49. Illegal hunting for profit is called
    a. subsistence hunting.
    b. sport hunting.
 * c. poaching.
    d. commercial hunting.
    e. all of these answers.

50. A threatened species causes demand for the species to increase. The species becomes endangered. Which of the following characteristics of complex systems is best applied to this sequence?
    a. negative feedback loop
 * b. positive feedback loop
    c. delay
    d. antagonistic interaction
    e. a synergistic interaction

51. Which of the following is *least* responsible for the strong decline in elephant populations?
 * a. global climate change
    b. legal ivory trade
    c. habitat loss
    d. poaching
    e. low reproductive rate

52. As a result of the ban on elephant ivory sales, killing of bull walruses and hippos has increased. Which of the following principles best describes this event?
    a. We lose quality of energy every time an energy transformation takes place.
    b. Public resources will be overused by a few.
* c. We can never do just one thing.
    d. Habitat loss most severely affects the top predators.
    e. none of these answers.

53. The Carolina parakeet was exterminated because it
* a. fed on fruit crops.
    b. was an alien species.
    c. carried a viral disease that killed domesticated parakeets.
    d. spread histoplasmosis, a fungal disease.
    e. over collected for the pet trade.

54. All of the following species *except* _____ are threatened or endangered because they are a nuisance to some humans.
    a. coyotes
* b. parrots
    c. prairie dogs
    d. elephants
    e. wolves

18-6 OTHER EXTINCTION THREATS

55. Prairie dogs have almost been driven to extinction by
    a. imported black-footed ferrets.
* b. poison.
    c. coyotes.
    d. shotguns and rifles.
    e. wolves.

56. Which of the following is almost extinct because its prime source of food has been killed by poison?
    a. wolverines
* b. black-footed ferrets
    c. manatees
    d. alligators
    e. coyotes

57. Importing exotic birds for households may
    a. be hazardous to the owners' health.
    b. result in the decline of tourist income from exporting countries.
    c. result in a 90% animal death rate.
* d. result in all of these answers.
    e. endangered or threaten bird species.

58. The pet trade has depleted populations of
    a. birds.
    b. mammals.
    c. tropical fish.
* d. all of these answers.
    e. reptiles.

59. Some exotic plant species that may bring $5,000 to $15,000 to collectors are *most* likely
    a. mushrooms.
    * b. orchids or cacti.
    c. bromeliads or ferns.
    d. bonsai or dwarf trees.
    e. lilies.

60. Even with the best management, wildlife reserves may be depleted in a few decades because of
    a. depletion of fossil fuels.
    * b. climatic change brought about by projected global warming.
    c. demands for sport trophies.
    d. biological magnification of pesticides.
    e. the pet trade.

61. DDT can harm wildlife by
    a. making them more vulnerable to diseases.
    b. making them more vulnerable to parasites and predators.
    c. killing them directly.
    * d. all of these answers.
    e. decreasing reproductive rates.

62. Which of the following bird species would *least* likely show the harmful effects of biological magnification?
    a. falcon
    * b. cardinal
    c. pelican
    d. sparrow hawk
    e. owl

18-7 PROTECTING WILD SPECIES FROM DEPLETION AND EXTINCTION: THE RESEARCH AND LEGAL APPROACH

63. Which of the following is *not* one of the three major approaches to protecting wildlife?
    a. the species approach
    b. the ecosystem approach
    c. the wildlife management approach
    * d. the kinder, gentler human approach
    e. the sanctuary approach.

64. Bioinformatics includes
    a. providing means for communicating biological information, such as the Internet.
    b. building computer databases to organize and store useful biological information.
    c. providing computer tools to find, visualize, and analyze biological information.
    * d. all of these answers.
    e. none of these answers.

65. CITES is
    * a. a treaty controlling the international trade in endangered species.
    b. a set of regulations controlling the introduction of exotic species.
    c. a pact that supports critical ecosystems that support wildlife.
    d. an international organization dedicated to the preservation of endangered species.
    e. all of these answers.

66. CITES is limited by
    a. violators receiving only small fines.
    b. spotty enforcement.
    c. member countries exempting themselves from protecting some species.
    d. much of the illegal trade in wildlife goes on in countries that have not signed the treaty.
  * e. all of these answers.

67. Transporting of live or dead wild animals across U.S. state borders without a federal permit is prohibited by
    a. CITES.
  * b. the Lacey Act.
    c. the Endangered Species Act.
    d. the Delaney Act.
    e. the Amber Act.

68. The Endangered Species Act of 1973
    a. is one of the world's toughest environmental laws.
    b. allows the use of endangered species for approved scientific purposes or if the use enhances the survival of the species.
    c. authorizes identification of endangered species solely on a biological basis.
    d. requires all commercial shipments of wildlife enter or leave the U.S. through one of nine designated ports.
  * e. all of these answers.

69. Animals listed as endangered or threatened cannot be _____ in the United States.
    a. injured
    b. hunted
    c. collected
    d. killed
  * e. any of the above

70. Identification and listing of endangered species is done by the
  * a. Fish and Wildlife Service.
    b. Environmental Protection Agency.
    c. National Park Service.
    d. Department of the Interior.
    e. Nature Conservancy.

71. Over the last quarter century, the number of species found exclusively on the U.S. list
  * a. increased about ten times.
    b. increased about five times.
    c. stayed the same.
    d. decreased by about 50%.
    e. decreased by about 20%.

72. All of the following are candidates for delisting from the endangered and threatened species list *except* the
  * a. California condor.
    b. gray wolf.
    c. bald eagle.
    d. peregrine falcon.
    e. American alligator.

73. All of the following would strengthen the Endangered Species Act *except*
    a. giving private landowners tax breaks for helping protect endangered ecosystems.
    b. surveying the species and ecosystems we have.
  * c. making the protection of endangered species on private land voluntary.
    d. locating and protecting the most endangered species.
    e. give private landowners financial incentives and technical help for helping protect endangered species.

74. When wildlife experts must judge which species to save, they are *least* likely to choose a species because
    a. it has the best chance for survival.
  * b. it is furry and charismatic.
    c. it has the most ecological value to the ecosystem.
    d. it is potentially useful for agriculture or medicine.
    e. none of these answers.

18-8   PROTECTING WILD SPECIES FROM DEPLETION AND EXTINCTION: THE SANCTUARY APPROACH

75. The group of animals *most* protected by wildlife refuges are
    a. small mammals.
  * b. migratory waterfowl.
    c. large mammals.
    d. songbirds.
    e. reptiles.

76. The vast majority of area included in the national wildlife refuge system is found in
    a. Hawaii.
    b. Texas.
    c. the Northwest.
  * d. Alaska.
    e. California.

77. Over four decades, a large system of private natural areas and wildlife sanctuaries has been created by
    a. the National Wildlife Federation.
    b. Ducks Unlimited.
    c. the National Audubon Society.
  * d. the Nature Conservancy.
    e. World Wildlife Fund.

78. Prudhoe Bay is a
    a. gem of biodiversity that shelters several habitat islands.
  * b. site of oil drilling in Alaska.
    c. wildlife refuge in Alaska.
    d. site of a disastrous oil spill in the 1970s.
    e. bay in the Great Lakes.

79. Wildlife refuges have been instrumental in helping all of the following species recover *except*
  * a. the snail darter.
    b. key deer.
    c. trumpeter swan.
    d. brown pelican.
    e. American alligator.

80. Seed gene banks are
   * a. refrigerated environments with low humidity.
   b. refrigerated environments with high humidity.
   c. warm environments with low humidity.
   d. warm environments with high humidity.
   e. frozen environments with low humidity.

81. A drawback of gene banks, arboreta, and botanical gardens is that
   a. there is not enough funding to provide storage of all endangered species.
   b. there is too little storage capacity.
   c. seeds in storage do not evolve and therefore become less fit for reintroduction into a changed environment.
   d. some plant seeds do not store well.
   * e. all of these answers.

82. Egg pulling refers to
   a. techniques used to extend the breeding span of captured birds.
   * b. collecting eggs from the wild and hatching them in zoos or research centers.
   c. using fertility drugs to increase productivity.
   d. production of hybrids in captive breeding programs.
   e. collecting unfertilized eggs from ovaries of wild animals.

83. Captive breeding programs in zoos
   a. eliminate the need to preserve critical habitats.
   b. can be used for most species except mammals.
   c. increase the genetic variability of species.
   * d. require the captive population to number between 100 and 500.
   e. is very unsuccessful.

84. Recent genetic research indicates that _____ or more individuals are needed for an endangered species to maintain its capacity for biological evolution.
   a. 10
   b. 100
   c. 1,000
   * d. 10,000
   e. 100,000

18-9 WILDLIFE MANAGEMENT

85. Most wildlife management in the United States is keyed to
   a. protection of endangered species.
   b. control of population sizes and habitats to maintain diversity.
   * c. management of population sizes and habitats to favor game species.
   d. maximizing of bird diversity.
   e. protection of threatened species.

86. Wildlife managers have to make plans based on all of the following principles *except*
   a. ecological succession.
   b. food and habitat requirements for each species.
   * c. laws of thermodynamics.
   d. number of potential hunters.
   e. wildlife population dynamics.

87.   Weedy pioneer species are found primarily in
 *   a.   early-successional stages.
       b.   mid-successional stages.
       c.   late-successional stages.
       d.   wilderness.
       e.   pre-early-successional stages.

88.   Wilderness species would be expected to flourish *best* in
       a.   early-successional stages.
       b.   mid-successional stages.
       c.   late-successional stages.
 *   d.   mature, relatively undisturbed habitats.
       e.   pre-early-successional stages.

89.   Moderate-size, old-growth forest refuges are required by
       a.   early-successional species.
       b.   mid-successional species.
 *   c.   late-successional species.
       d.   wilderness.
       e.   pre-early-successional stages.

90.   Partially open areas with plenty of edge habitat are required by
       a.   early-successional species.
 *   b.   mid-successional species.
       c.   late-successional species.
       d.   wilderness.
       e.   pre-early-successional stages.

91.   Flyways are
       a.   insect infestation routes.
 *   b.   migration routes.
       c.   routes connecting islands.
       d.   areas that require insecticide treatment.
       e.   airplane flight plans.

92.   Waterfowl management includes
       a.   developing ponds.
       b.   protecting existing habitats.
       c.   building artificial nesting sites.
       d.   regulating hunting.
 *   e.   all of these answers.

CHAPTER 19
NONRENEWABLE ENERGY RESOURCES

1. Chernobyl resulted in all of the following *except*
   a. evacuation of many families from land they had farmed for centuries.
   b. separation of families from their pets.
   * c. nuclear winter.
   d. cancers, thyroid tumors and eye cataracts..
   e. about 62,000 acres of contaminated land.

19-1 EVALUATING ENERGY RESOURCES

2. All of the following are *indirect* forms of solar energy *except*
   a. waterfalls.
   b. biomass.
   * c. sunlight.
   d. wind.
   e. none of these answers.

3. The most important supplement to solar energy in most developing countries is
   a. oil.
   b. hydropower.
   * c. biomass.
   d. coal.
   e. wind.

4. The most important supplement to solar energy in the United States is
   * a. oil.
   b. hydropower.
   c. fuelwood.
   d. coal.
   e. wind.

5. With 4.7% of the world's population, the U.S. uses about ___% of the world's commercial energy.
   a. 10
   b. 15
   c. 20
   * d. 25
   e. 50

6. Affordable oil supplies will probably be depleted in
   a. 10–20 years.
   b. 20–30 years.
   c. 30–50 years.
   * d. 40–80 years.
   e. 80-100 years.

7. Which is our *best* immediate energy option?
   a. Find and burn more forms of oil, natural gas, and coal.
   * b. Cut out unnecessary energy waste by improving energy efficiency.
   c. Build more and better conventional nuclear power plants.
   d. Increase efforts to develop breeder nuclear fission and nuclear fusion.
   e. Dramatically decrease transportation.

8.   It takes at least _____ years to phase in new energy alternatives.
     a.   5
     b.   10
     c.   30
  * d.   50
     e.   100

9.   To make decisions about energy alternatives, we need to ask:
     a.   How much will be available in the short term, intermediate term, and long term?
     b.   How much will it cost to develop, phase in, and use?
     c.   What are potential environmental impacts?
     d.   What is this source's net energy yield?
  * e.   All of these answers.

10. The concept of net energy most closely reinforces the
     a.   first law of energy.
  * b.   second law of energy.
     c.   law of conservation of matter and energy.
     d.   principle that everything is connected to everything else.
     e.   precautionary principle.

11. Net energy is
     a.   the usable amount of low-quality energy from a given quantity of energy resource.
     b.   the total useful energy available from an energy resource.
     c.   analogous to total income.
  * d.   the total useful energy from an energy resource minus the amount of energy used and wasted in producing it.
     e.   the amount of energy used and wasted to produce useful energy.

12. The net energy ratio is
     a.   the ratio of the energy it took to produce it to the new useful energy produced.
  * b.   the ratio of the useful energy produced to the useful energy used to produce it.
     c.   high when the net energy yield is high.
     d.   high when the net energy yield is low.
     e.   none of these answers.

13. The energy source with the highest net energy ratio for space heating is
     a.   oil.
     b.   active solar.
  * c.   passive solar.
     d.   electric resistance heating.
     e.   wind.

14. The energy source with the highest net energy ratio for high-temperature industrial heat is
     a.   coal gasification.
  * b.   coal.
     c.   oil.
     d.   direct solar.
     e.   wind.

15. The energy source with the highest net energy ratio for transportation is
     a.   gasoline.
     b.   coal liquefaction.
  * c.   natural gas.
     d.   oil shale.
     e.   wind.

16. Oil currently has a _____ net energy ratio that is expected to _____ in the future.
    a. low . . . stay low
    b. low . . . increase
    c. high . . . stay high
    * d. high . . . decline
    e. high . . . increase

19-2 OIL

17. Petroleum is a gooey liquid consisting primarily of
    * a. hydrocarbon compounds.
    b. nitrogen.
    c. sulfur.
    d. oxygen.
    e. phosphorus.

18. Crude oil components are separated by
    a. gravity.
    * b. heat.
    c. pressure.
    d. filtration.
    e. combustion.

19. Petrochemicals are
    * a. used as raw materials in industrial chemicals.
    b. removed from oil before it is refined.
    c. impurities that must be burned or buried.
    d. additives to bring up the octane level of gasoline.
    e. all of these answers.

20. You can thank petrochemicals if you use
    a. aluminum cans.
    b. glass bottles.
    * c. plastics and synthetic fibers.
    d. organic fertilizers.
    e. all of these answers.

21. World oil supplies and prices are expected to be controlled over the long term by
    a. Russia.
    b. the United States.
    c. Mexico.
    * d. OPEC.
    e. Saudi Arabia

22. The greatest use of oil in the United States is for
    * a. transportation.
    b. generation of electricity.
    c. commercial and residential heating and cooling.
    d. industrial uses.
    e. agriculture.

23. At present consumption rates, projected world crude oil reserves will be depleted in _____ years.
    a. 4-8
    b. 10-40
    * c. 42-93
    d. 80-140
    e. 150-200

24. Oil is widely used because it
    a. is easily transported.
    b. has a high net useful energy yield.
    c. is very versatile.
    d. has an artificially low cost.
  * e. all of these answers.

25. A strategic disadvantage of oil is that it
    a. produces more carbon dioxide than any other fuel.
    b. produces destruction of nature through oil spills.
    c. can contaminate groundwater supplies.
  * d. will be commercially depleted within 42 to 93 years.
    e. all of these answers.

26. Oil has all of the following disadvantages *except*
  * a. difficulty in transport between countries.
    b. release of heat-trapping carbon dioxide.
    c. release of air pollutants that harm people and other species.
    d. contamination of groundwater with brine.
    e. artificially low price encourages waste.

27. Kerogen is
    a. the active ingredient in kerosene.
    b. a waste product from production of oil from oil shale.
    c. a fuel supplement added to diesel oil.
    d. sludge from sewage plants.
  * e. a waxy mixture of hydrocarbons in oil shale.

28. Shale oil and tar sands
    a. are principal sources of conventional crude oil.
  * b. contain large supplies of heavy oils.
    c. constitute a small but cheap supply of crude oil.
    d. are usable only for aviation fuel.
    e. all of these answers.

29. Shale oil is
    a. pure in its naturally occurring form.
    b. a light oil found in ancient sand deposits.
  * c. extracted from the kerogen in oil shale.
    d. commercially produced in about 25 nations.
    e. all of these answers.

30. All of the following states have potentially recoverable deposits of shale oil except
    a. Colorado.
  * b. Iowa.
    c. Utah.
    d. Wyoming.
    e. none of these answers.

31. Shale oil processing requires large amounts of
  * a. water.
    b. electricity.
    c. zinc.
    d. time.
    e. all of these answers..

32. Disadvantages of shale oil as an energy source include all of the following *except*
    a. massive land disruption.
    b. air and water pollution.
    c. considerable energy input for the energy output obtained.
    d. low grade energy.
  * e. potentially recoverable U.S. deposits are only enough to meet the country's crude oil demand for five years.

33. Shale oil and tar sands _____ than conventional oil deposits.
    a. are easier to extract
  * b. have lower net useful energy yield
    c. have less environmental impact
    d. are the source of more useful products
    e. are less expensive to produce.

34. Bitumen is
    a. a type of coal.
    b. a deep shale oil deposit.
  * c. high-sulfur heavy oil.
    d. an octane-raising gasoline additive.
    e. a type of natural gas.

35. Tar sand normally contains all but which of the following?
  * a. coal
    b. bitumen
    c. sand
    d. water
    e. clay

36. Which of the following countries has the greatest tar sand deposits?
    a. Saudi Arabia
  * b. Canada
    c. Venezuela
    d. Kuwait
    e. United States

19-3 NATURAL GAS

37. Natural gas from wells consists of 50% to 90% _____.
  * a. methane
    b. ethane
    c. propane
    d. butane
    e. ethanol

38. Liquefied petroleum gas consists of
    a. methane.
  * b. butane and propane.
    c. ammonia.
    d. nitrogen oxides.
    e. ethanol.

3

39. The countries with the largest reserves of natural gas are
   a. Canada and the United States.
 * b. Russia and Kazakhstan.
   c. Nigeria and Algeria.
   d. India and Pakistan.
   e. United States and Pakistan.

40. The world's supplies of conventional natural gas are projected to last
   a. at least 300 years at 1984 usage rates.
   b. about 200 years if annual usage increases at 2% a year.
 * c. at least 125 years at present consumption rates.
   d. until unconventional natural gas technologies are fully developed.
   e. at least 1000 years at present consumption rates.

41. Natural gas has a _____ net useful energy yield and is a _____ fuel compared to coal.
   a. high . . . dirty
 * b. high . . . clean-burning
   c. low . . . dirty
   d. low . . . clean-burning
   e. none of these answers.

42. Which of the following statements about liquefied natural gas (LNG) is *false?*
   a. Natural gas has to be liquefied before it can be transported by ship.
 * b. Shipment of LNG is safe and inexpensive.
   c. LNG requires refrigeration and pressure.
   d. Conversion of natural gas to LNG reduces net energy yield by one-fourth.
   e. This liquid is highly flammable.

43. A key option during the switch from oil to other new energy sources is
   a. coal.
   b. nuclear.
   c. biomass.
 * d. natural gas.
   e. ethanol.

19-4 COAL

44. Which of the choices below lists stages of coal in order from highest to lowest heat content?
 * a. anthracite—bituminous—lignite—peat
   b. peat—anthracite—bituminous—lignite
   c. anthracite—lignite—bituminous—peat
   d. peat—bituminous—lignite—anthracite
   e. bituminous-peat-anthracite-lignite

45. Because of high heat content and low sulfur content, the most desirable type of coal is
   a. bituminous.
   b. lignite.
 * c. anthracite.
   d. peat.
   e. black.

46. Currently coal provides about _____ % of the world's commercial energy.
   a. 11
 * b. 21
   c. 31
   d. 41
   e. 51

47. Coal supplies _____ of the electricity generated in the United States.
    a. 223%
    b. 32%
    c. 42%
    * d. 52%
    e. 82

48. About two-thirds of the world's proven coal reserves are found in
    a. the Middle East.
    * b. China, the United States, and the former Soviet Union.
    c. Canada.
    d. Mexico.
    e. Russia.

49. The world's *most* abundant conventional fossil fuel is
    a. crude oil.
    b. natural gas.
    c. biomass.
    d. tar sand.
    * e. coal.

50. _____ is the dirtiest fossil fuel to burn.
    a. Oil
    b. Natural gas
    * c. Coal
    d. Wood
    e. Biomass

51. The world's identified coal reserves should last about _____ years at current usage rates.
    a. 10
    b. 50
    c. 100
    * d. 220
    e. 550

52. Two major reasons that burning solid coal is a popular means of producing electricity and high-temperature heat are
    a. high heat content and low carbon dioxide output.
    * b. great abundance and high net useful energy yield.
    c. low net useful energy yield and high versatility.
    d. ease of pollution control and relative abundance.
    e. a and c only.

53. Land subsidence can result from
    a. surface mining.
    b. higher ocean levels.
    * c. underground coal mining.
    d. natural gas extraction.
    e. strip mining.

54. Using coal
    a. causes severe land disturbance.
    b. releases large amounts of sulfur dioxide, nitrogen oxides, and particulate matter.
    c. produces more carbon dioxide per unit of energy than other fossil fuels.
    d. high land use.
    * e. all of these answers.

55. Fluidized-bed combustion is a method of burning coal
  * a. more cleanly and efficiently.
    b. to produce extremely hot ionized gases.
    c. in underground deposits too deep to mine.
    d. without having to crush or powder it.
    e. which is cheap but pollutes more than conventional methods.

56. Coal can be converted to
    a. hydrogen gas.
    b. synthetic gasoline.
    c. synthetic natural gas.
    d. methanol.
  * e. all of these answers.

57. Which of the following statements about synfuels is *false?*
    a. Synfuels can be transported by pipeline.
    b. Synfuels are more expensive than coal.
  * c. Synfuel combustion, by itself, produces more air pollution than coal.
    d. Synfuels are more versatile than coal.
    e. Synfuels have large potential supply availability.

19-5 NUCLEAR ENERGY

58. Which of the following reasons for developing nuclear power in the United States is *incorrect?*
    a. The Atomic Energy Commission promised that nuclear power would produce electricity at a much lower cost than coal and other alternatives.
  * b. There was a surplus of tax money, and nuclear power looked like a good investment opportunity.
    c. Congress passed the Price-Anderson Act to protect the nuclear industry from significant liability to the general public in case of accidents.
    d. The U.S. government paid about a quarter of the construction costs for the first group of reactors.
    e. none of these answers.

59. The Atomic Energy Commission convinced utilities to use nuclear power to generate electricity because
    a. government picked up one-fourth the cost with no cost overruns allowed.
    b. it was predicted that nuclear energy would produce electricity at extremely low costs.
    c. the utilities were protected from liability to the general public.
  * d. all of these answers.
    e. none of these answers.

60. Since 1978, _____ new nuclear power plants have been ordered in the United States.
  * a. no
    b. 4
    c. 8
    d. 12
    e. 15

61. In 2000, the 103 licensed nuclear power plants in the United States generated about _____ % of the country's electricity.
    a. 1
    b. 10
  * c. 20
    d. 30
    e. 50

62. The nuclear power industry in the United States has declined because of
    a. high construction costs.
    b. accidents at Chernobyl and Three Mile Island.
    c. concerns about radioactive waste disposal.
    d. public opposition.
  * e. all of these answers.

63. Light-water reactors generate about _____% of the nuclear-generated electricity.
    a. 95
  * b. 85
    c. 75
    d. 65
    e. 55

64. The fissionable fraction of the fuel in a nuclear reactor is _____.
  * a. uranium-235
    b. uranium-238
    c. uranium-239
    d. plutonium-239
    e. iodine-125

65. Control rods in a reactor
    a. contain uranium.
  * b. absorb neutrons.
    c. contain plutonium.
    d. reduce heat.
    e. eject electrons.

66. The moderator in a nuclear reactor
    a. releases neutrons.
    b. absorbs neutrons.
    c. reflects neutrons.
  * d. slows down neutrons.
    e. speeds up neutrons.

67. The *most* common moderator used in nuclear reactors is
    a. graphite.
    b. boron.
    c. argon.
    d. air.
  * e. water.

68. Each year, about _____ of the fuel assemblies in a nuclear reactor must be replaced because of their spent condition.
    a. one-tenth
    b. one-fifth
    c. one-fourth
  * d. one-third
    e. one-half

69. All of the following countries have nuclear fuel reprocessing plants *except*
  * a. Russia.
    b. France.
    c. Japan.
    d. West Germany.
    e. Canada.

70. The nuclear fuel cycle includes all of the following *except*
   a. the uranium mine.
   b. fuel fabrication.
 * c. the cyclotron.
   d. interim underwater storage.
   e. spent fuel reprocessing.

71. If the fuel pellets in spent fuel rods are processed to remove plutonium and other very long-lived radioactive isotopes, the remaining radioactive waste should be safely stored on the order of _____ years.
   a. 100
   b. 1,000
 * c. 10,000
   d. 100,000
   e. 1,000,000

72. A meltdown of the reactor core would occur if
   a. control rods were inserted into the core.
 * b. too much coolant was lost.
   c. the proportion of uranium-238 was too high.
   d. the containment building developed an air leak.
   e. all of these answers.

73. Three Mile Island is located in
   a. New Jersey.
 * b. Pennsylvania.
   c. Massachusetts.
   d. Connecticut.
   e. California.

74. The accident at the Three Mile Island nuclear power plant in 1979 involved all of the following *except*
   a. a series of mechanical failures.
   b. operator errors unforeseen in safety studies.
   c. loss of unknown amounts of ionizing radiation.
 * d. a complete reactor core meltdown.
   e. none of these answers.

75. Which one of the following statements about U.S. low-level radioactive waste disposal is *false?*
   a. From the 1940s to 1970, low-level waste was dumped into the ocean in steel drums.
   b. Since 1970, low-level waste has been buried at government-run landfills.
 * c. Prior to 1970, low-level waste was sealed in glass in stable salt deposits.
   d. In 1995, Westinghouse Electric proposed burial in old mine shafts in Russia.
   e. The United Kingdom and Pakistan dispose of low-level radioactive waste in steel drums dumped into the ocean.

76. Suggestions to bury radioactive wastes underground include converting the radioactive waste to a solid form and fusing it with
   a. salt.
   b. lead.
   c. limestone.
 * d. glass.
   e. gas.

77. Suggestions to handle radioactive waste include
 a. sending it into outer space.
 b. burying it in Antarctic ice sheets.
 c. dumping it into downward-descending, deep-ocean sediments.
 d. shooting it to the sun.
 * e. all of these answers.

78. Which of the following proposals for disposing of high-level radioactive wastes is at present a technological impossibility because we don't know how it could be done?
 a. Shoot it into the sun.
 * b. Convert it into harmless isotopes.
 c. Bury it under ice sheets in Antarctica.
 d. Dump it into downward descending bottom sediments.
 e. Bury it in thick deposits of mud on the deep ocean floor.

79. The useful operating life of today's nuclear power plants is supposed to be _____ years.
 a. 20
 b. 30
 * c. 40
 d. 50
 e. 100

80. Nuclear power plants wear out when
 a. the reactor's pressure vessels become brittle through neutron bombardment.
 b. pipes and valves corrode.
 c. pressure and temperature changes weaken tubes.
 * d. all of these answers.
 e. none of these answers.

81. All of the following are methods of decommissioning nuclear power plants *except*
 a. immediate dismantling.
 b. entombment.
 * c. decomposition.
 d. mothballing.
 e. physical barrier.

82. Today at least _____ countries sell nuclear technology in the international marketplace.
 a. 5
 * b. 15
 c. 25
 d. 35
 e. 45

83. There are enough nuclear weapons on Earth to kill every person on Earth _____ times.
 a. 2
 b. 5
 c. 25
 * d. 30
 e. 50

84. Breeder nuclear fission reactors convert
 a. fast-moving neutrons into slow-moving ones.
 b. high-level wastes into harmless isotopes.
 * c. uranium-238 into plutonium-239.
 d. uranium-235 into uranium-238.
 e. uranium-235 into iodine-125.

85. Which of the following statements is *false?*
    a. Breeder reactors would generate more fuel than they consume.
    b. If the breeder reactor's safety system failed, the reactor could lose some of its liquid sodium coolant.
    c. Many experimental breeder reactors built so far have caught fire.
  * d. Breeder reactors would not extend the supplies of uranium in the world.
    e. Breeder reactors produce plutonium extremely slowly.

86. Plans to build full-size commercial breeder reactors have been abandoned in
    a. the United Kingdom.
    b. Germany.
    c. Japan.
  * d. all of these answers.
    e. none of these answers.

87. A construction project completed in 1986 brought the world's first full-sized commercial breeder reactor into operation in
    a. the United States.
    b. the Commonwealth of Independent States.
    c. Germany.
  * d. France.
    e. the United Kingdom.

88. The coolant employed in a breeder reactor is liquid
  * a. sodium.
    b. plutonium.
    c. nitrogen.
    d. lithium.
    e. water.

89. In nuclear fusion research, deuterium and tritium atoms have been forced together with
    a. bombardment by high-speed particles.
    b. high-powered laser beams.
    c. electromagnetic reactors.
  * d. all of these answers.
    e. none of these answers.

CHAPTER 20
ENERGY EFFICIENCY AND RENEWABLE ENERGY

20-1   THE IMPORTANCE OF IMPROVING ENERGY EFFICIENCY

1.   What percentage of the commercial energy used in the United States is wasted?
     a.   14%
     b.   24%
     c.   44%
     d.   64%
 *   e.   84%

2.   What percentage of the commercial energy used in the United States is wasted *unnecessarily?*
     a.   13%
     b.   23%
     c.   33%
 *   d.   43%
     e.   53%

3.   According to energy expert Amory Lovins, the easiest, fastest, and cheapest way to get more energy with the least environmental impact is to
     a.   improve photovoltaics.
     b.   develop wind power.
     c.   initiate the second wave of nuclear power plants in the United States.
 *   d.   reduce energy consumption.
     e.   switch to natural gas transportation.

4.   Energy consumption can be reduced by all of the following except
     a.   using mass transit instead of individual automobiles.
 *   b.   turning the thermostat up in wintertime.
     c.   turning off unused lights.
     d.   purchasing only needed products.
     e.   reducing packaging.

5.   When purchasing appliances, consumers can make more economically and environmentally conscious decisions by considering
     a.   initial cost.
     b.   operating cost.
     c.   external cost.
 *   d.   life-cycle cost.
     e.   consumer cost.

6.   We can conserve energy by
 *   a.   increasing the efficiency of our equipment.
     b.   recycling the energy we use.
     c.   using nonrenewable resources.
     d.   using high-quality energy whenever possible.
     e.   all of these answers.

7.   The *least* efficient method of space heating is
     a.   passive solar heat.
 *   b.   electricity produced by nuclear power plants.
     c.   natural gas furnaces.
     d.   oil furnaces.
     e.   none of these answers.

8. The most expensive way to provide space heat is by using
    a. propane.
*   b. electricity.
    c. kerosene.
    d. oil
    e. no heat.

9. If the United States wanted to make the most difference in tightening up energy efficiency of widespread energy-using devices, which one of the following is likely to attract the *least* attention?
    a. internal combustion engines
    b. nuclear power plants
*   c. refrigerators
    d. incandescent light bulbs
    e. heating and air conditioning systems

10. Improving energy efficiency is *least* likely to
    a. reduce environmental damage.
    b. lessen the need for military intervention in the Middle East.
*   c. decrease competitiveness in the international marketplace.
    d. give us more time to phase in renewable energy resources.
    e. none of these answers.

20-2 WAYS TO IMPROVE ENERGY EFFICIENCY

11. Cogeneration
    a. involves instruments like heat pumps that can generate heating and cooling.
    b. combines passive solar and active solar technologies.
    c. involves both electricity and natural gas.
*   d. uses waste heat to produce electricity.
    e. uses heat from the earth to produce electricity.

12. Utilities make money by selling electricity. To make more money, they have often encouraged customers to use even more electricity. This lack of incentive to improve energy efficiency creates a
    a. harmful negative feedback loop.
*   b. harmful positive feedback loop.
    c. helpful negative feedback loop.
    d. helpful positive feedback loop.
    e. synergistic effect.

13. At this time, the most important way to save energy and money in transportation is to
    a. switch to hydrogen-powered cars.
    b. switch to electric engines.
*   c. increase the fuel efficiency of motor vehicles.
    d. ban cars in cities.
    e. require mandatory mass transportation.

14. Since 1985, at least 10 automobile companies have made fuel-efficient cars that
    a. carry four or five passengers.
    b. meet or exceed 1990 safety standards.
    c. meet or exceed 1990 pollution control standards.
    d. are manufactured with light and strong materials.
*   e. all of these answers.

15. Ecocars
    a. are made from composite materials that won't rust and can be recycled.
    b. manufacturing would create jobs.
    c. could operate emission-free in urban areas.
    d. a and c only.
  * e. all of these answers.

16. Demand for ecocars would be increased by all of the following strategies *except*
    a. a rebate system which gives people money for buying fuel-efficient cars and charges people more for buying gas-guzzling vehicles.
    b. establishing higher average fuel-efficiency standards for all new cars.
    c. raising gasoline taxes with tax relief for the poor and lower middle class.
  * d. maintaining the status quo.
    e. b and c.

17. Requiring higher average fuel-efficiency standards would do all of the following *except*
    a. save huge amounts of energy.
    b. reduce air pollution.
  * c. cost jobs.
    d. reduce emissions of heat-trapping carbon dioxide.
    e. b and d.

18. The weakness of electric cars is their
    a. noise level.
    b. maintenance cost.
  * c. energy-storage system.
    d. slow acceleration.
    e. all of these answers.

19. The textbook cites the _____ as a very energy-efficient structure.
    a. Empire State Building in New York
    b. Sears Tower in Chicago
  * c. Georgia Power Company building in Atlanta
    d. Transamerica building in San Francisco
    e. Whitehouse

20. The energy efficiency of buildings can be improved by all of the following strategies *except*
    a. microprocessors to monitor indoor temperatures and sunlight angles.
    b. "smart windows."
    c. plugging leaks.
  * d. building big windows into the northern side of new housing.
    e. energy-efficient lighting.

21. The cheapest and *most* energy-efficient way to heat a house is superinsulation coupled with
    a. active solar heating and a natural gas furnace.
    b. active solar heating and electric resistance heating produced by a nuclear power plant.
  * c. passive solar heating and a natural gas furnace.
    d. passive solar and electric resistance heating produced by a nuclear power plant.
    e. heat pump

22. The *most* effective water heater
    a. is an electric water tank.
    b. is a gas water heater.
    c. is an oil water heater.
  * d. is a tankless instant water heater fired by natural gas or LP gas.
    e. is a propane water heater.

20-3 USING SOLAR ENERGY TO PROVIDE HEAT AND ELECTRICITY

23. Renewable energy resources include all of the following *except*
    a. the sun.
    b. the wind.
    c. biomass.
  * d. natural gas.
    e. water.

24. The solar envelope house is heated and cooled
    a. actively by solar energy and thermal exchange with timbers and Earth.
    b. actively by solar energy and tree plantings.
  * c. passively by solar energy and thermal exchange with timbers and Earth.
    d. passively by solar energy with a natural gas backup system.
    e. none of these answers.

25. Which of the following is *true* of passive but *not* of active solar systems, compared to other heating systems?
    a. The technology is well developed and can be installed quickly.
  * b. The system adds 5–10% to the initial cost but reduces lifetime costs by 30–40%.
    c. They require more materials and more maintenance.
    d. The systems deteriorate more readily and need to be replaced more often.
    e. all of these answers.

26. Advantages of solar space heating include all of the following *except*
    a. a free energy source.
  * b. low to moderate net useful energy.
    c. well-developed active and passive technologies.
    d. no carbon dioxide additions to the atmosphere.
    e. c and d.

27. Disadvantages of solar heating systems include all of the following *except*
    a. high initial costs.
    b. solar collectors are not aesthetically pleasing to some people.
  * c. long payback times.
    d. owners need laws to prevent blockage of access to light.
    e. a and b.

28. All of the following can be used for cooling a house in warm weather *except*
    a. cooling vents in the roof.
    b. earth tubes and tanks buried 20 feet underground.
    c. deciduous trees.
  * d. foil sheets under the floor.
    e. b and c.

29. The solar technology that most strongly focuses the sun's rays is the
    a. active solar heating system.
  * b. solar power tower.
    c. nonimaging optical solar concentrator.
    d. solar cooker.
    e. solar wind tunnel.

30. A type of distributed receiver system that has captured a fraction of the commercial market is the
    a. active solar heating system.
    b. solar power tower.
    c. nonimaging optical solar concentrator.
    d. solar wind tunnel.
  * e. solar thermal plant.

31. A promising solar technology noted for its high efficiency is
    a. active solar heating system.
    b. solar power tower.
  * c. nonimaging optical solar concentrator.
    d. solar cooker.
    e. solar wind tunnel.

32. Solar power plants
    a. pollute air and water.
    b. take three to five years to construct.
    c. require more land than coal-burning plants plus coal deposit lands.
  * d. require less land than most hydropower projects.
    e. are most as cost effective as nuclear power plants.

33. Solar cookers reduce all of the following *except*
    a. deforestation.
  * b. the time it takes to cook food.
    c. indoor air pollution.
    d. the time and labor it takes to collect fuelwood.
    e. oil reserves.

34. Cells that convert solar energy directly into electricity are called
    a. electrosolar chips.
  * b. photovoltaic cells.
    c. helioelectric units.
    d. photoelectric cells.
    e. solarelectric cells.

35. All of the following are characteristic of solar cells *except*
    a. durability up to 30 years.
    b. quick installation.
    c. easy expansion of the system as needed.
  * d. primarily metal composition.
    e. no carbon dioxide emissions.

36. Which of the following statements is *false?*
    a. Solar cells are reliable and quiet and have no moving parts.
    b. Solar cells require minimal maintenance.
  * c. The U.S. government is the current global leader in photovoltaic research.
    d. Solar cells could provide at least one-third of the electricity needed by the United States by 2050.
    e. a and d.

37. Photovoltaic cells
    a. should last 30 years or more if encased in glass or plastic.
    b. can be installed quickly and easily.
    c. produce minimal air and water pollution during operation.
    d. can provide electricity.
  * e. all of these answers.

20-4 PRODUCING ELECTRICITY FROM MOVING WATER AND FROM HEAT STORED IN WATER

38. Hydroelectric power may be
    a. large scale.
    b. small scale.
    c. pumped storage.
    d. a and b only.
  * e. all of these answers.

39. Pumped-storage hydropower systems
  * a. are used to produce power during peak periods.
    b. involve the use of large dams.
    c. depend on stream flow to control power generation.
    d. may vary in output during different seasons.
    e. all of these answers.

40. Within a few years, the world's largest producer of electricity from hydropower is likely to be
    a. Australia.
    b. the United States.
  * c. China.
    d. Austria.
    e. Russia.

41. Which of the following countries produces the greatest proportion of its electricity by hydroelectric plants?
    a. Austria
    b. Switzerland
  * c. Norway
    d. Italy
    e. United States

42. Hydroelectric plants
    a. need to be shut down frequently for maintenance checks.
    b. offer low net useful energy yield.
    c. have relatively high operating and maintenance costs.
  * d. help control flooding and supply a regulated flow of irrigation water to areas below the dam.
    e. all of these answers.

43. Which of the following is a disadvantage of hydroelectric plants?
    a. high pollution
  * b. high construction costs
    c. high operation and maintenance costs
    d. low functional life span
    e. all of these answers

44. Which of the following statements about disadvantages of large dams is *false?*
  * a. They are useful only for flood control.
    b. Reservoir formation displaces people and destroys wildlife habitat.
    c. They can contribute to the incidence of earthquakes.
    d. They last only 40 to 200 years before siltation requires their abandonment.
    e. All of these statements are false.

45. Tidal power
    a. is generated from watering flowing in and out of bays three times per day.
  * b. uses tides to spin turbines to produce electricity.
    c. is widely used in France and Canada.
    d. has a high net energy yield.
    e. will be an important power source in the future.

46. Which of the following statements about wave power is *false?*
    a. Wave power is created primarily by wind.
  * b. Wave power is expected to be a key contributor to global electric production by 2110.
    c. Net useful energy is moderate.
    d. Equipment may be damaged by storms.
    e. all of these answers.

47. Freshwater solar ponds
  * a. can be used for hot water and space heating.
    b. are located in isolated mountain areas.
    c. are found in salt flats and deserts.
    d. provide both cooling and heating.
    e. all of these answers.

48. All of the following are characteristic of freshwater ponds *except*
    a. moderate construction and operating costs.
    b. moderate net energy yield.
    c. no energy storage and backup systems.
  * d. moderate air and water pollution.
    e. a and c.

20-5 PRODUCING ELECTRICITY FROM WIND

49. Wind power
    a. offers quick construction time.
    b. has a moderate to high net useful energy yield.
    c. emits no air pollution during operation.
  * d. all of these answers.
    e. no CO^2 emissions.

50. What is a major disadvantage of wind power?
    a. low net energy
  * b. high noise levels
    c. time consuming to construct
    d. low efficiency
    e. low land use

20-6 PRODUCING ENERGY FROM BIOMASS

51. A major disadvantage of using biomass for energy is
  * a. large land, water, and fertilizer requirements.
    b. higher nitrous oxide and sulfur dioxide emissions than other sources of energy.
    c. lack of versatility in its use and application.
    d. that it is not renewable.
    e. very expensive.

52. Gaseous and liquid biofuels include
    a. biogas.
    b. wood alcohol.
    c. liquid ethanol.
    d. ethanol.
  * e. all of these answers.

53. Biogas digesters are
  * a. very efficient, slow, and unpredictable.
    b. very efficient, fast, and predictable.
    c. very inefficient, slow, and unpredictable.
    d. very inefficient, fast, and predictable.
    e. very inefficient, fast and unpredictable.

54. Gasohol is gasoline mixed with
  * a. ethanol.
    b. methane.
    c. methanol.
    d. butane.
    e. propane.

55. About _____% of the people living in developing countries heat their dwellings and cook their food by burning wood or charcoal from wood.
    a. 10
    b. 30
    c. 50
  * d. 70
    e. 100

56. Which country leads the world in using wood as an energy source?
    a. Canada
  * b. Sweden
    c. China
    d. Brazil
    e. Russia

57. A-55 fuel
    a. consists of about half water and half naptha plus additives.
    b. can be used in almost any combustion engine.
    c. is cleaner, safer, and cheaper than conventional gasoline and diesel fuel.
    d. a and c only.
  * e. all of these answers.

20-7 THE SOLAR-HYDROGEN REVOLUTION

58. Which of the following statements is *false?*
    a. When burned, hydrogen produces virtually no air pollutants.
    b. Some metals can store and release hydrogen.
  * c. Fuel tanks of metal-hydrogen compounds would tend to explode in an accident.
    d. Experimental cars have been running on hydrogen fuel.
    e. None of these statements is false.

59. Which of the following statements is *false?*
    a. The costs of using solar energy to produce electricity are coming down.
    b. Hydrogen gas could be stored at high pressures and distributed by pipeline.
  * c. Burning hydrogen releases low amounts of carbon dioxide.
    d. Hydrogen gas is easier to store than electricity.
    e. a and c.

60. Large-scale funding of hydrogen research would generally be *least* opposed by
    a. electric utilities.
  * b. sustainable developers.
    c. fossil-fuel companies.
    d. automobile manufacturers.
    e. heating and air conditioning manufacturers.

61. The Solar-Hydrogen Revolution could be encouraged by
    a. convincing private investors to risk capital in investing in hydrogen.
    b. convincing the government to put up some money for hydrogen development as it did for fossil fuels and nuclear energy in the past.
    c. phasing in full-cost pricing of fossil fuels.
  * d. all of these answers.
    e. none of these answers.

20-8 GEOTHERMAL ENERGY

62. Geothermal energy is stored in the form of
    a. dry steam.
    b. wet steam.
    c. hot water.
    d. b and c only.
  * e. all of these answers.

63. Geothermal energy can be used for all of the following *except*
    a. heating space.
    b. producing electricity.
  * c. transportation fuel.
    d. producing high-temperature heat for industry.
    e. a and d.

64. Magma is
    a. a deep source of fossil fuel.
  * b. molten rock.
    c. an air pollutant given off by geothermal energy.
    d. cooled lava flow.
    e. volcanic ash.

65. Which of the following statements about geothermal power is *false?*
    a. Use of geothermal energy is limited by scarcity of sites and economics.
    b. It releases air pollution.
  * c. It releases more carbon dioxide than fossil fuels.
    d. It results in moderate to high water pollution.
    e. It has very high efficiency.

66.   An advantage associated with the development and use of geothermal energy systems is that
 *   a.   little or no carbon dioxide is produced.
       b.   geothermal power plants do not require cooling water.
       c.   all geothermal energy sources are renewable.
       d.   there is no risk of harmful environmental impact.
       e.   it requires high land use.

20-9   ENTERING THE AGE OF DECENTRALIZED MICROPOWER

67.   What are micropower systems?
       a.   miniaturized photovoltaic cells
 *   b.   small power stations distributed throughout a region
       c.   a way of transmitting electricity via microwaves
       d.   installing electrical generators in individual homes and buildings
       e.   regional computer stations

20-10 SOLUTIONS: A SUSTAINABLE-EARTH ENERGY STRATEGY

68.   Which of the following statements is *false?*
       a.   There is not enough financial capital to develop all energy alternatives.
       b.   We should not depend on only one source of energy but should develop a mix of perpetual and
             renewable energy resources.
 *   c.   Energy production should be centralized as much as possible to increase efficiency.
       d.   Improving energy efficiency is the best option available to produce more energy.
       e.   a and b only.

69.   Which of the following approaches emphasizes today's prices for short-term economic gain and
       inhibits long-term development of new energy resources?
 *   a.   free-market competition
       b.   energy prices kept artificially high
       c.   energy prices kept artificially low
       d.   intense regulation
       e.   b and d only.

70.   Governments use _____ to manipulate the energy playing field.
       a.   tax breaks
       b.   regulations
       c.   subsidies
       d.   b and c only.
 *   e.   all of these answers

71.   Keeping energy prices artificially low
       a.   encourages waste and rapid depletion of energy resources getting favorable treatment.
       b.   protects consumers from sharp price increases.
       c.   discourages the development of energy alternatives not getting favorable treatment.
       d.   a and b only.
 *   e.   all of these answers.

72.   Keeping energy prices artificially high does all of the following *except*
       a.   encourage improvements in energy efficiency.
       b.   reduce dependence on imported energy.
       c.   dampen economic growth.
 *   d.   cause high unemployment.
       e.   none of these answers.

73. A sustainable energy future is *least* likely to encourage
    a. greatly increased use of perpetual and renewable resources.
    b. phasing out of government subsidies for nonrenewable resources.
    c. taxing of fossil fuels with energy assistance to the poor.
*   d. no government influence on personal decisions about purchases of energy-consuming goods.
    e. cutting coal use.

74. A sustainable energy future is *least* likely to encourage
*   a. requiring that all energy systems supported by government funds be based on cost-benefit analysis.
    b. requiring that electrical production be on a least-cost basis.
    c. reducing use of nonrenewable resources.
    d. permitting utilities to earn money by reducing electricity demand.
    e. tax credits for buying efficient cars.

APPENDIX A

CONCEPT MAPS

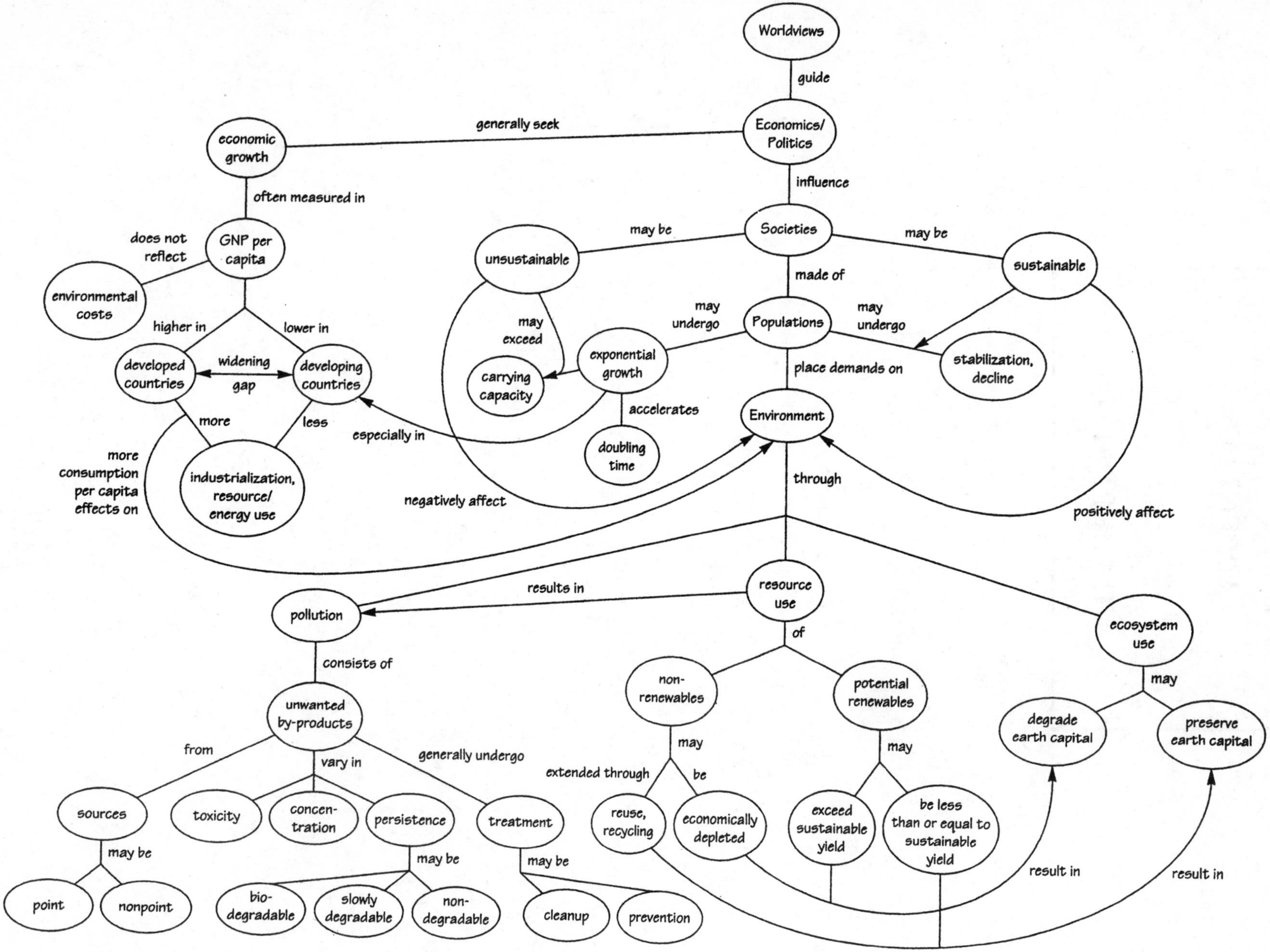

Worldviews —guide→ Economics/ Politics —influence→ Societies —made of→ Populations —place demands on→ Environment —through→ resource use —of→

Economics/Politics —generally seek→ economic growth —often measured in→ GNP per capita

GNP per capita —does not reflect→ environmental costs

GNP per capita —lower in→ developing countries

GNP per capita —higher in→ developed countries

developing countries ←widening gap→ developed countries

developed countries —more→ industrialization, resource/ energy use

developing countries —less→ especially in

more consumption per capita effects on

Societies —may be→ sustainable

Societies —may be→ unsustainable

sustainable —positively affect→ Environment

unsustainable —negatively affect→ Environment

Populations —may undergo→ stabilization, decline

Populations —may undergo→ exponential growth —accelerates→ doubling time

exponential growth —may exceed→ carrying capacity

resource use —results in→ pollution

ecosystem use —may→ preserve earth capital

ecosystem use —may→ degrade earth capital

resource use —of→ potential renewables —may→ be less than or equal to sustainable yield

potential renewables —may→ exceed sustainable yield

resource use —of→ non-renewables —may→ be economically depleted

non-renewables —may→ be reuse, recycling

be less than or equal to sustainable yield —result in→ preserve earth capital

exceed sustainable yield —result in→ degrade earth capital

non-renewables —extended through→ reuse, recycling

pollution —consists of→ unwanted by-products

unwanted by-products —generally undergo→ treatment —may be→ cleanup

treatment —may be→ prevention

unwanted by-products —vary in→ persistence —may be→ non-degradable

persistence —may be→ slowly degradable

persistence —may be→ biodegradable

unwanted by-products —vary in→ concentration

unwanted by-products —vary in→ toxicity

unwanted by-products —from→ sources —may be→ point

sources —may be→ nonpoint

Map 1A. Overview

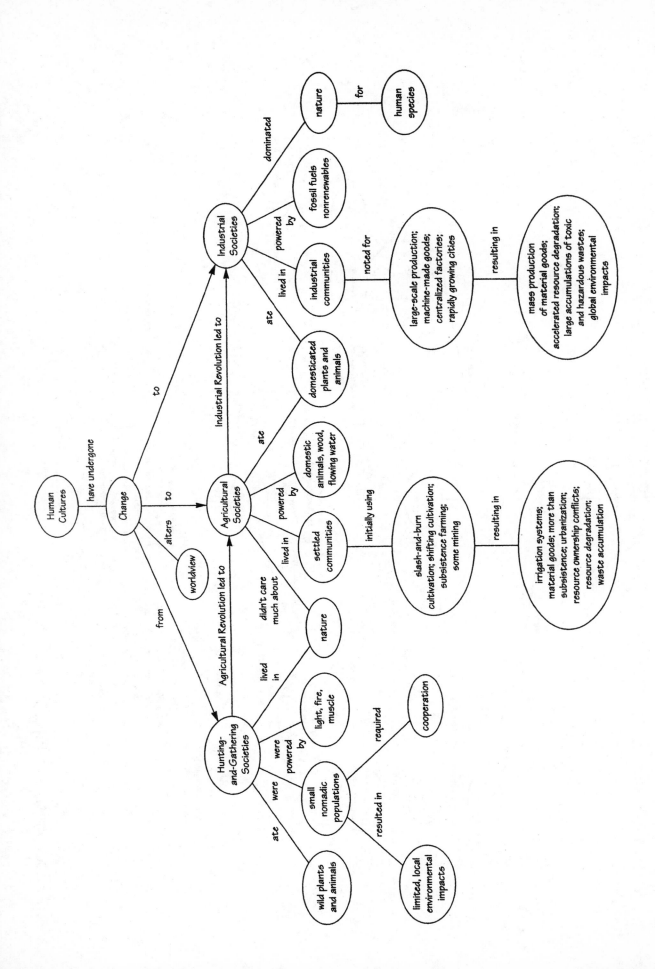

Map 1B. Cultural Changes

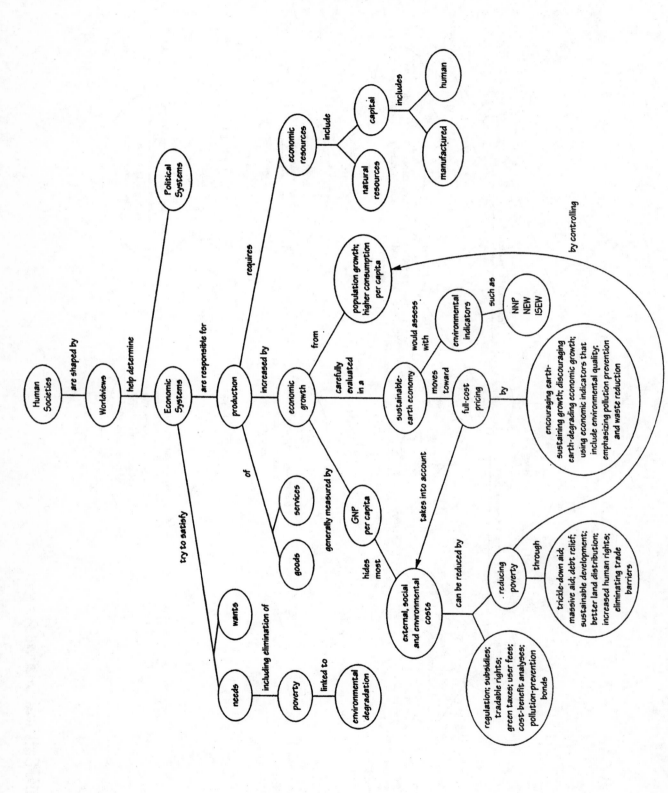

Map 2. Economics and Environment

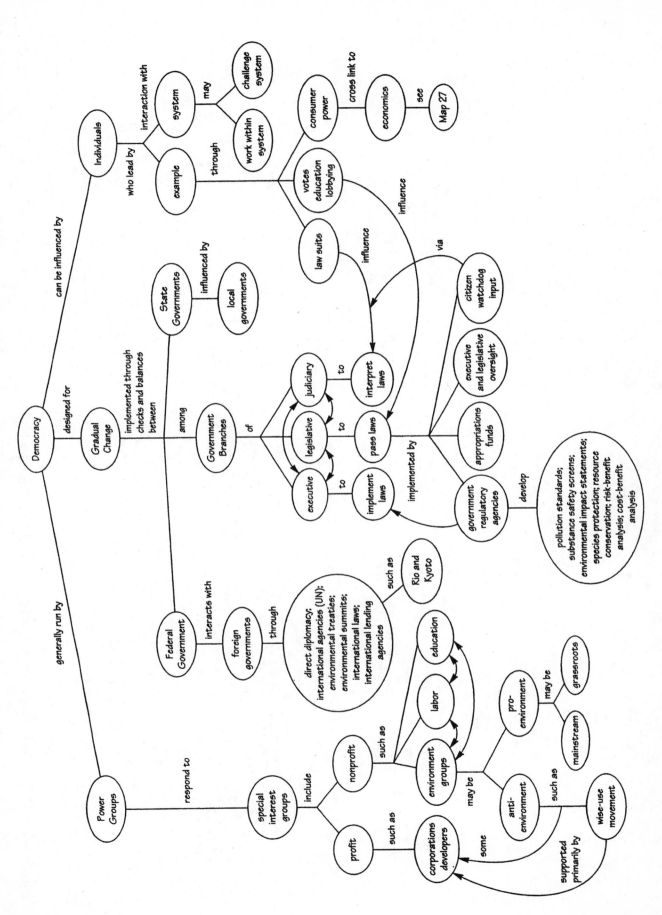

Map 3. Politics and Environment

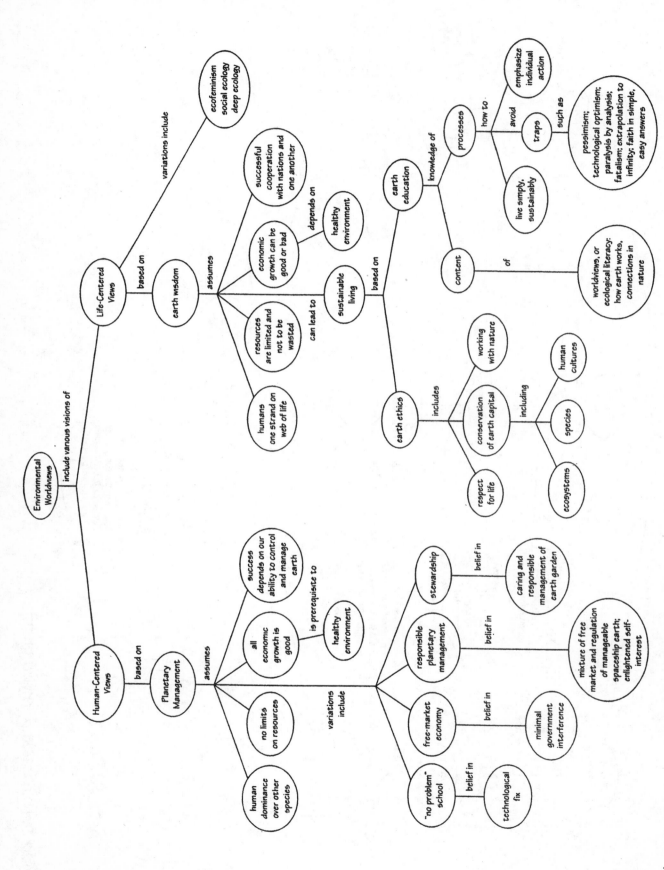

Map 4. Environmental Worldviews, Ethics, and Sustainability

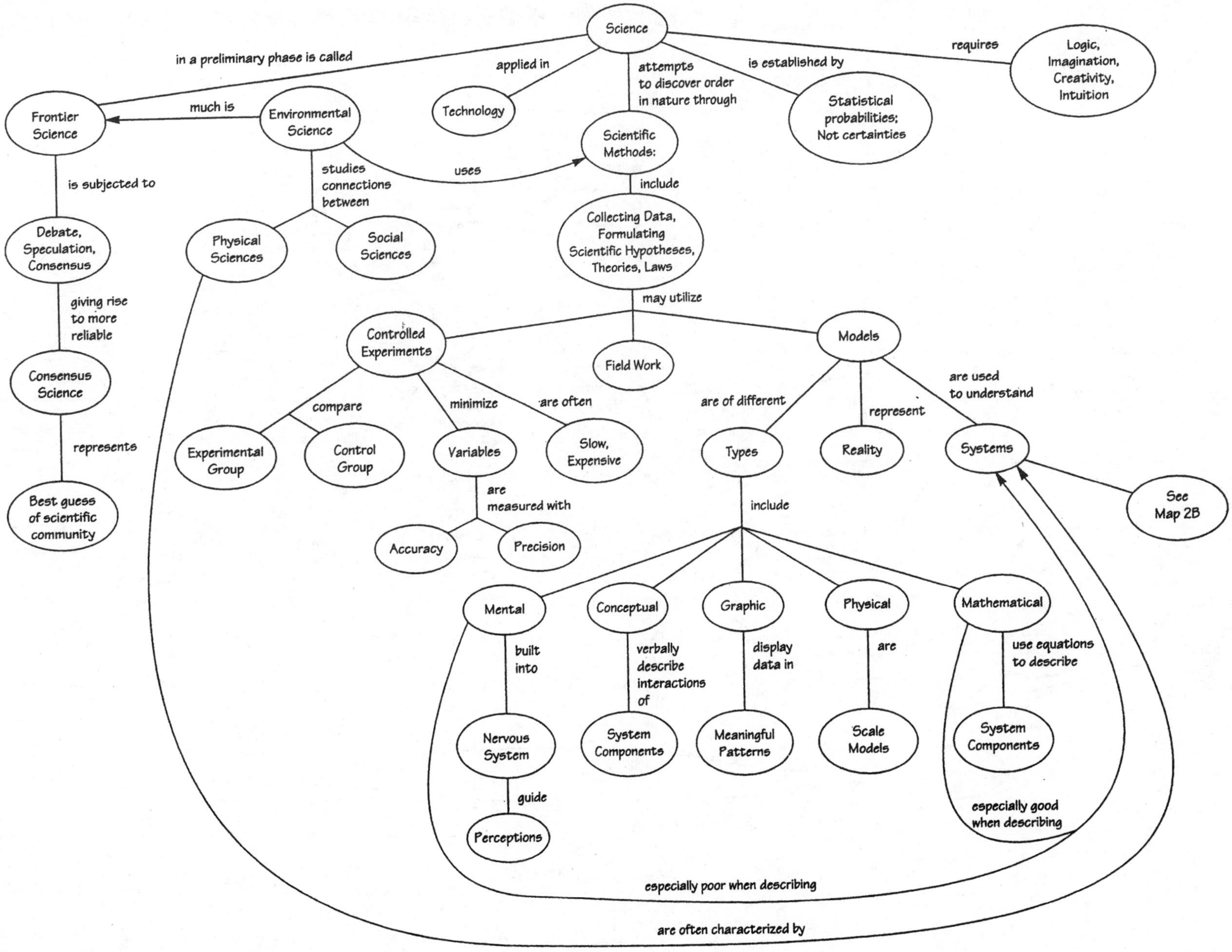

Map 5A. Science and Models

Science
- requires → Logic, Imagination, Creativity, Intuition
- is established by → Statistical probabilities; Not certainties
- attempts to discover order in nature through → Scientific Methods:
- applied in → Technology
- in a preliminary phase is called → Frontier Science

Scientific Methods:
- include → Collecting Data, Formulating Scientific Hypotheses, Theories, Laws
- may utilize → Field Work
- uses → Environmental Science

Environmental Science
- studies connections between → Social Sciences / Physical Sciences
- much is → Frontier Science

Frontier Science
- is subjected to → Debate, Speculation, Consensus
- giving rise to more reliable → Consensus Science

Consensus Science
- represents → Best guess of scientific community

Controlled Experiments
- are often → Slow, Expensive
- minimize → Variables
- compare → Control Group / Experimental Group

Variables
- are measured with → Precision / Accuracy

Models
- are used to understand → Systems
- represent → Reality
- are of different → Types

Systems
- See Map 2B

Types include:
- Mathematical → use equations to describe → System Components → especially good when describing
- Physical → are → Scale Models
- Graphic → display data in → Meaningful Patterns
- Conceptual → verbally describe interactions of → System Components
- Mental → built into → Nervous System → guide → Perceptions

especially poor when describing

are often characterized by

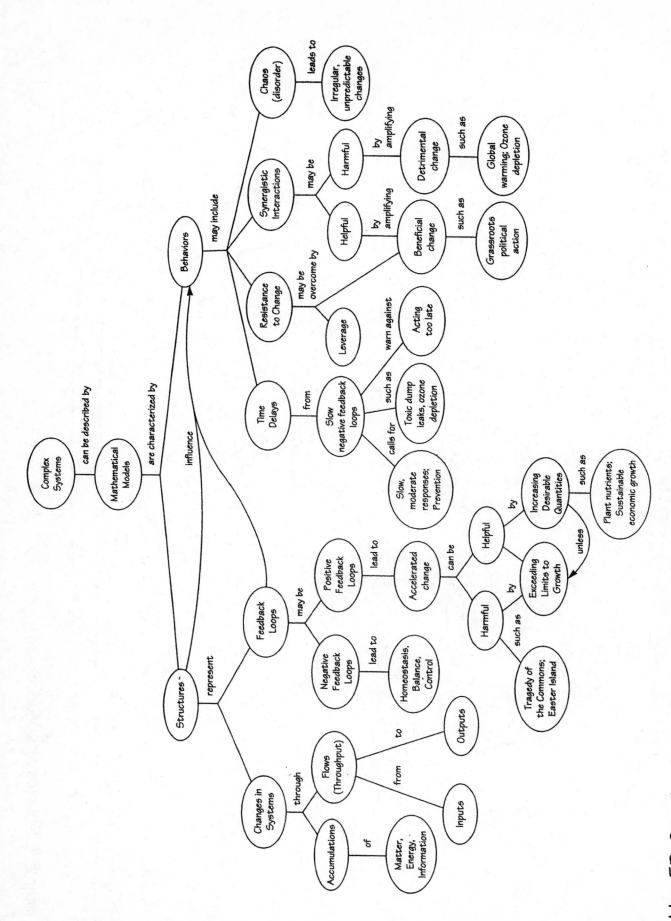

Map 5B. Complex Systems: Structures and Behaviors

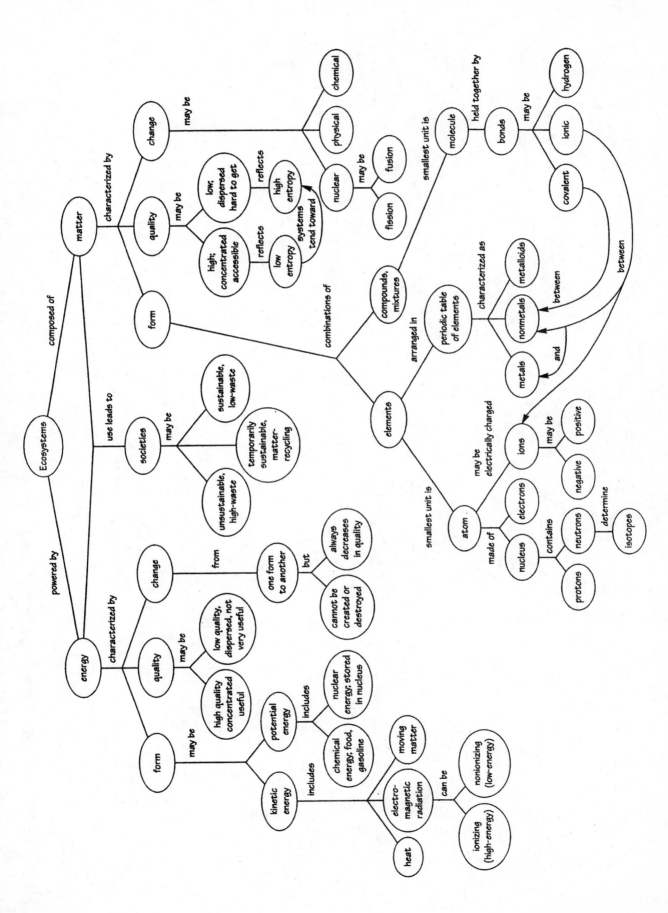

Map 6. Matter and Energy Resources

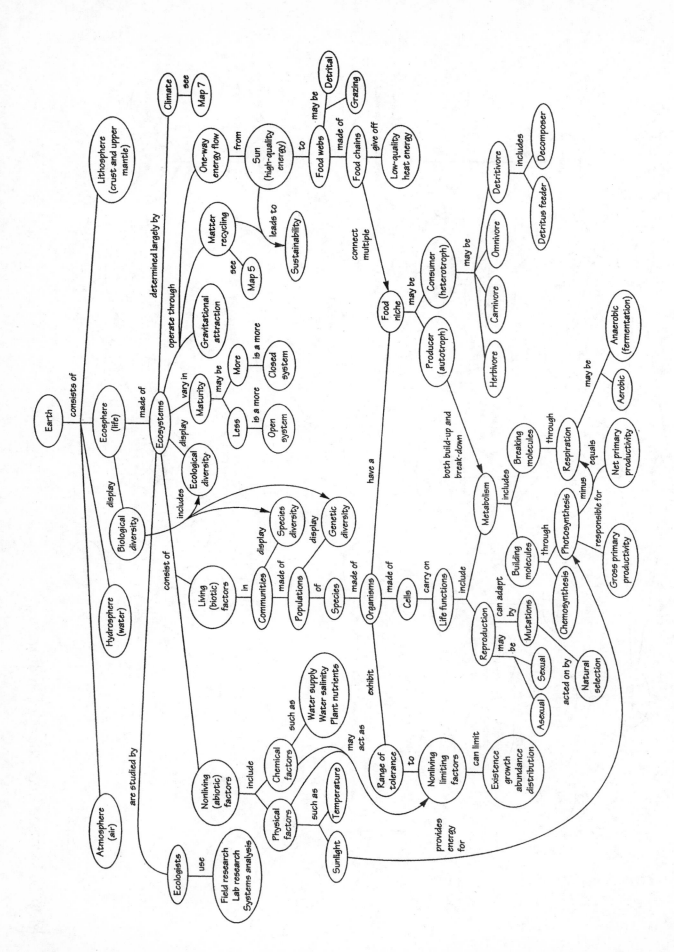

Map 7. Ecology, Ecosystems, and Food Webs

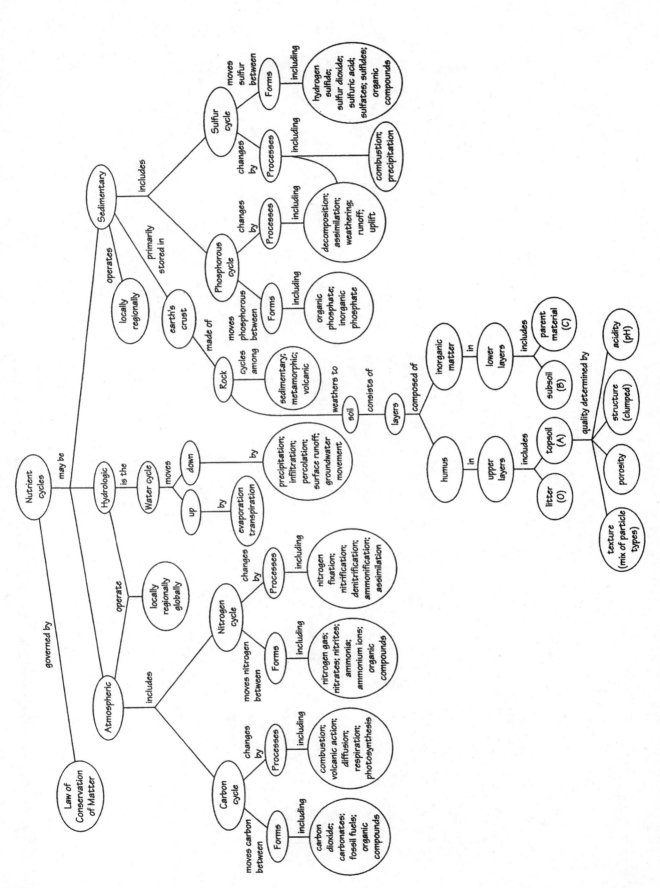

Map 8. Nutrient Cycles and Soils

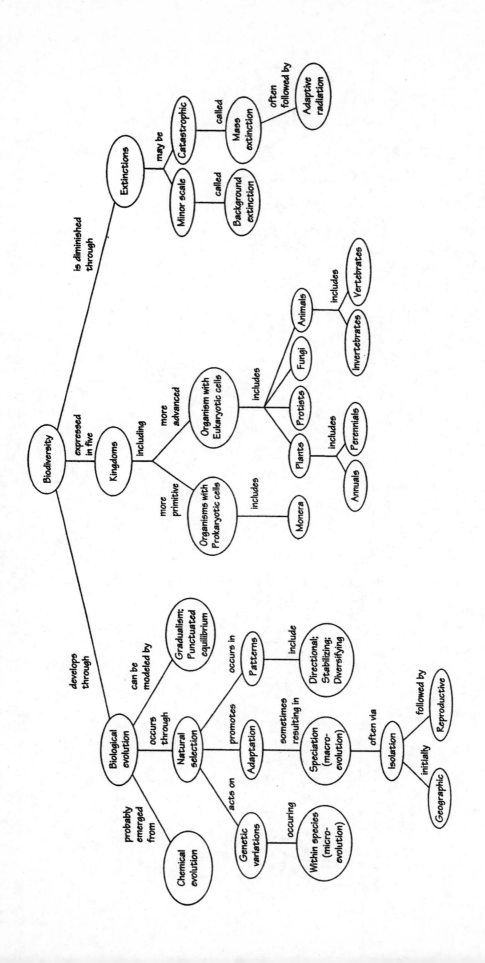

Map 9. Evolution and Biodiversity: Origins, Niches, and Biodiversity

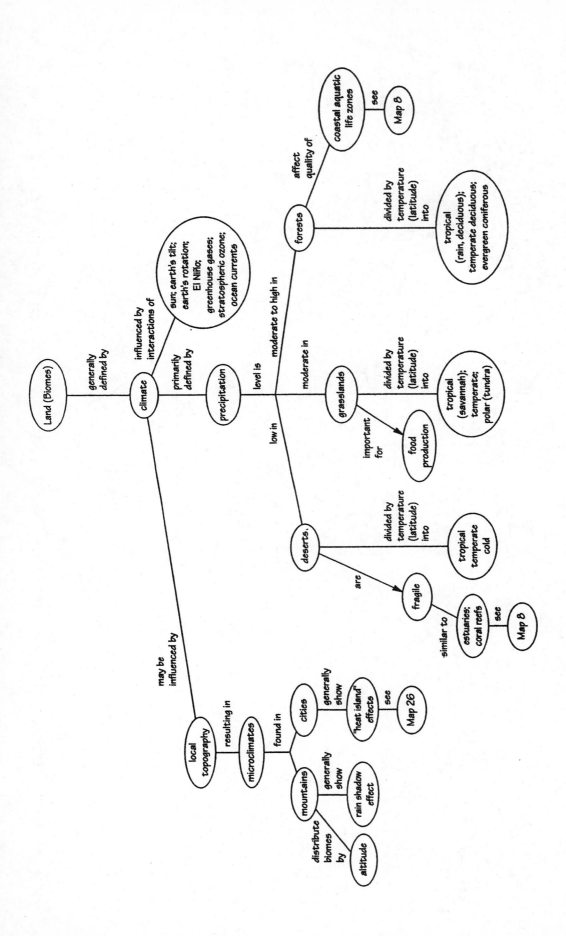

Map 10. *Geographical Ecology: Climate and Biomes*

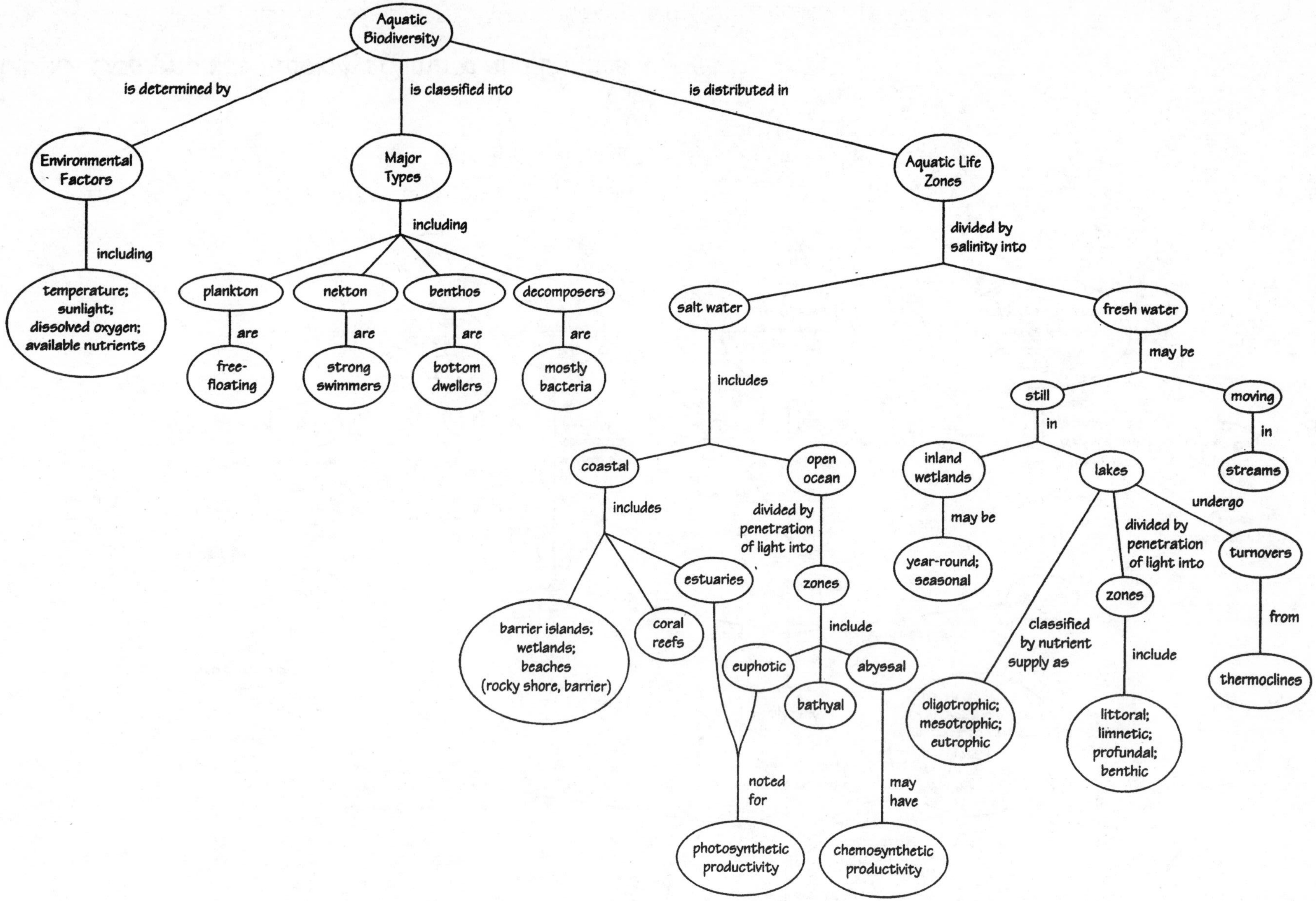

Map 11. Aquatic Ecology

Aquatic Biodiversity
— is determined by → **Environmental Factors**
— including → temperature; sunlight; dissolved oxygen; available nutrients

Aquatic Biodiversity
— is classified into → **Major Types**
— including →
- **plankton** — are → free-floating
- **nekton** — are → strong swimmers
- **benthos** — are → bottom dwellers
- **decomposers** — are → mostly bacteria

Aquatic Biodiversity
— is distributed in → **Aquatic Life Zones**
— divided by salinity into → **fresh water** and **salt water**

fresh water — may be →
- **moving** — in → **streams**
- **still** — in →
  - **lakes**
    - divided by penetration of light into → **zones** — include → littoral; limnetic; profundal; benthic
    - undergo → **turnovers** — from → **thermoclines**
    - classified by nutrient supply as → oligotrophic; mesotrophic; eutrophic
  - **inland wetlands** — may be → year-round; seasonal

salt water — includes →
- **open ocean**
  - divided by penetration of light into → **zones** — include →
    - **euphotic** — noted for → **photosynthetic productivity**
    - **bathyal**
    - **abyssal** — may have → **chemosynthetic productivity**
- **coastal** — includes →
  - **estuaries**
  - **coral reefs**
  - barrier islands; wetlands; beaches (rocky shore, barrier)

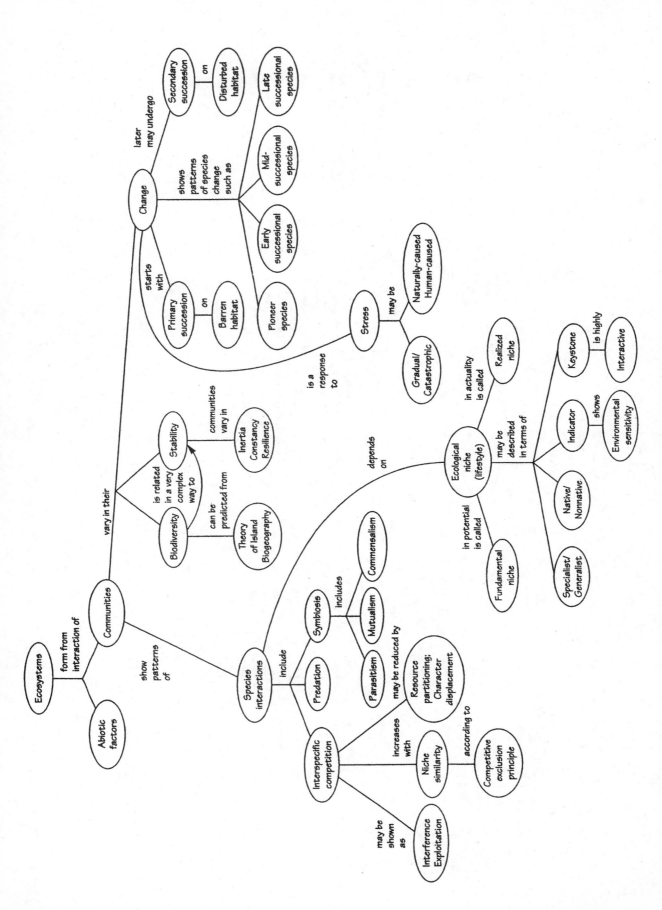

Map 12. Community Processes: Species Interactions and Succession

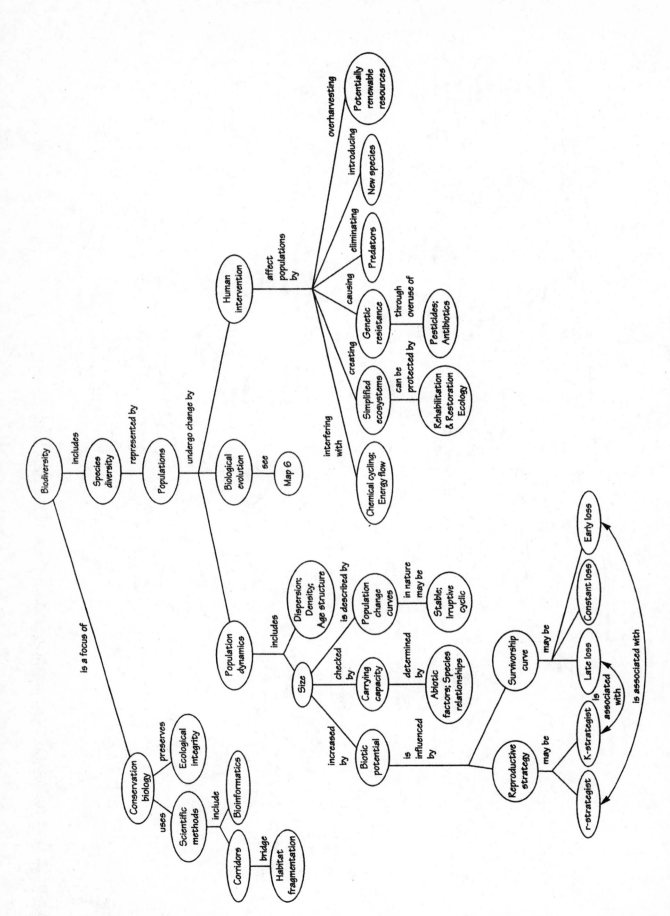

Map 13. Population Dynamics, Carrying Capacity, and Conservation Biology

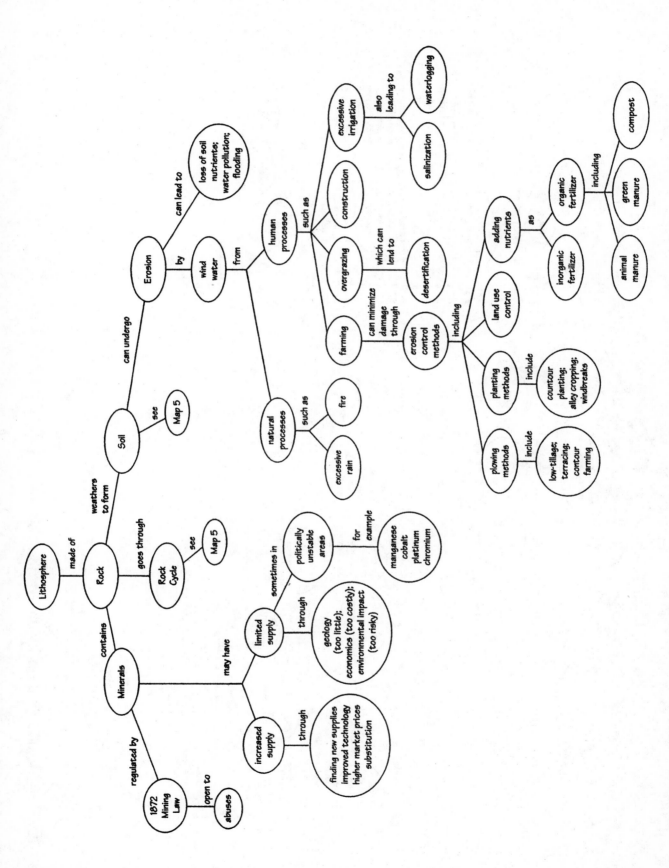

Map 14. Mineral and Soil Resources

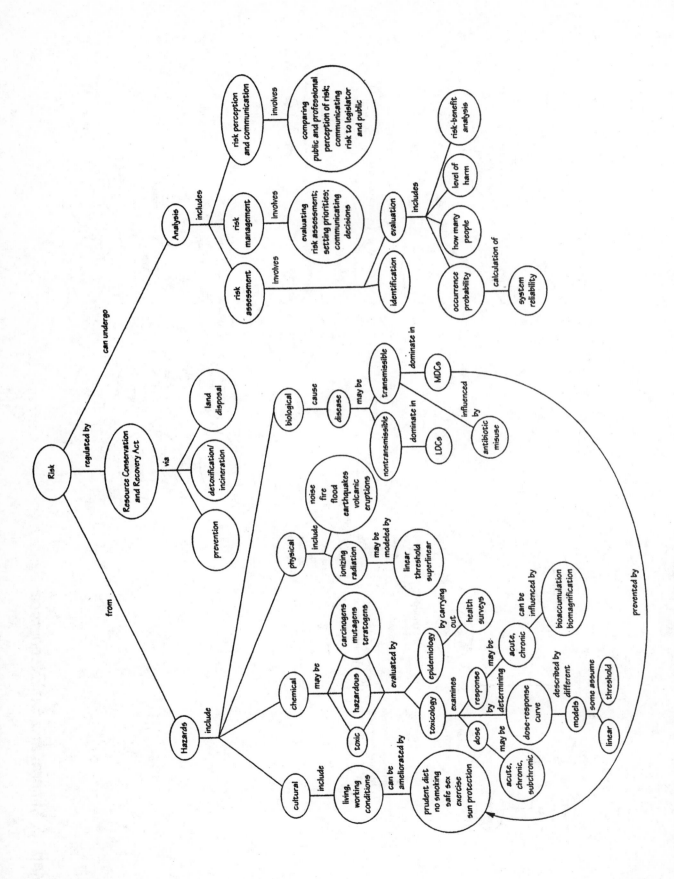

Map 15. Risk, Toxicology, and Human Health

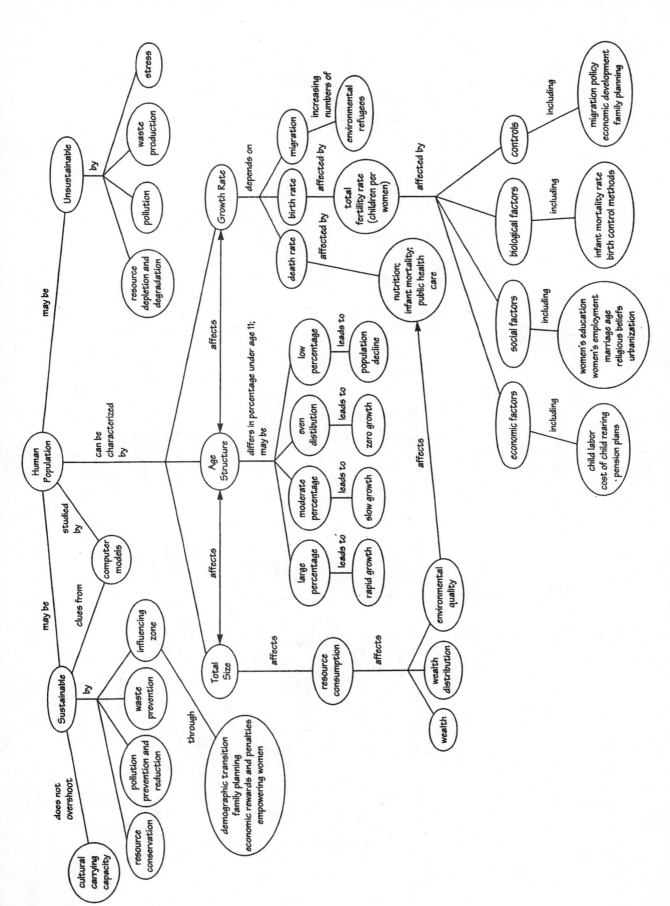

Map 16. Human Population: Growth, Demography, and Carrying Capacity

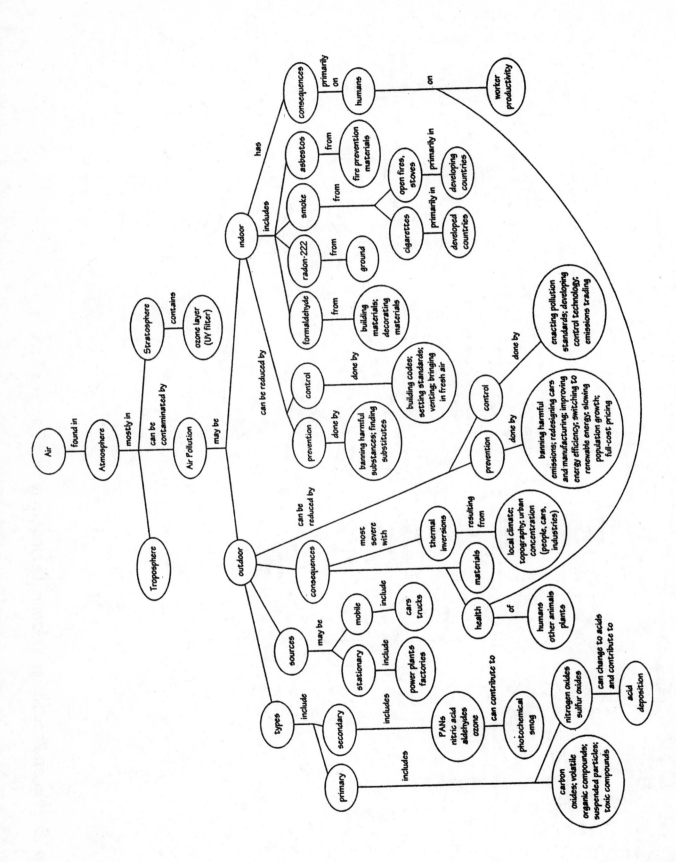

Map 17. Air Pollution

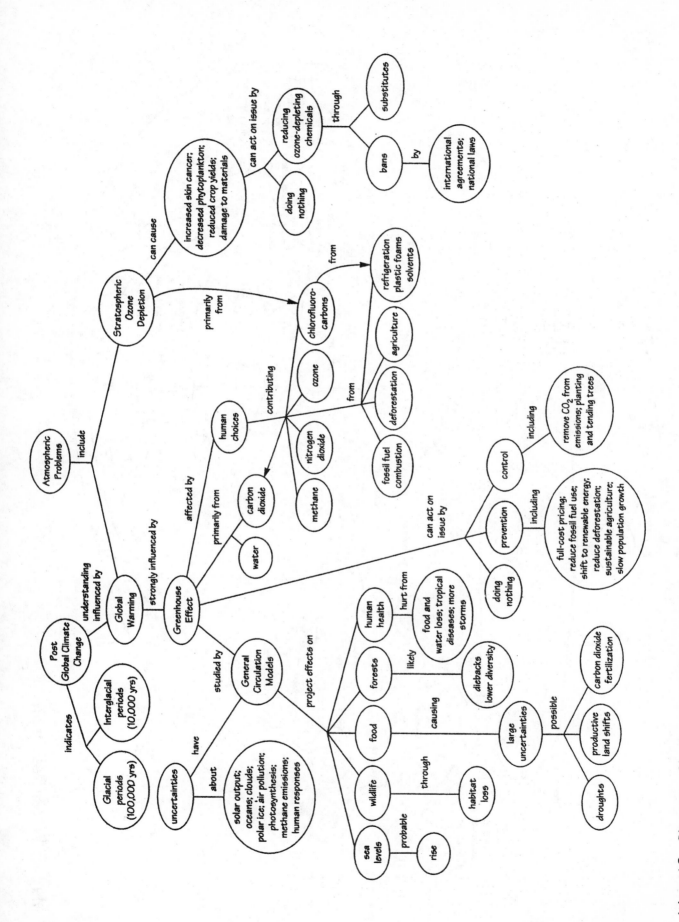

Map 18. Climate Change and Ozone Loss

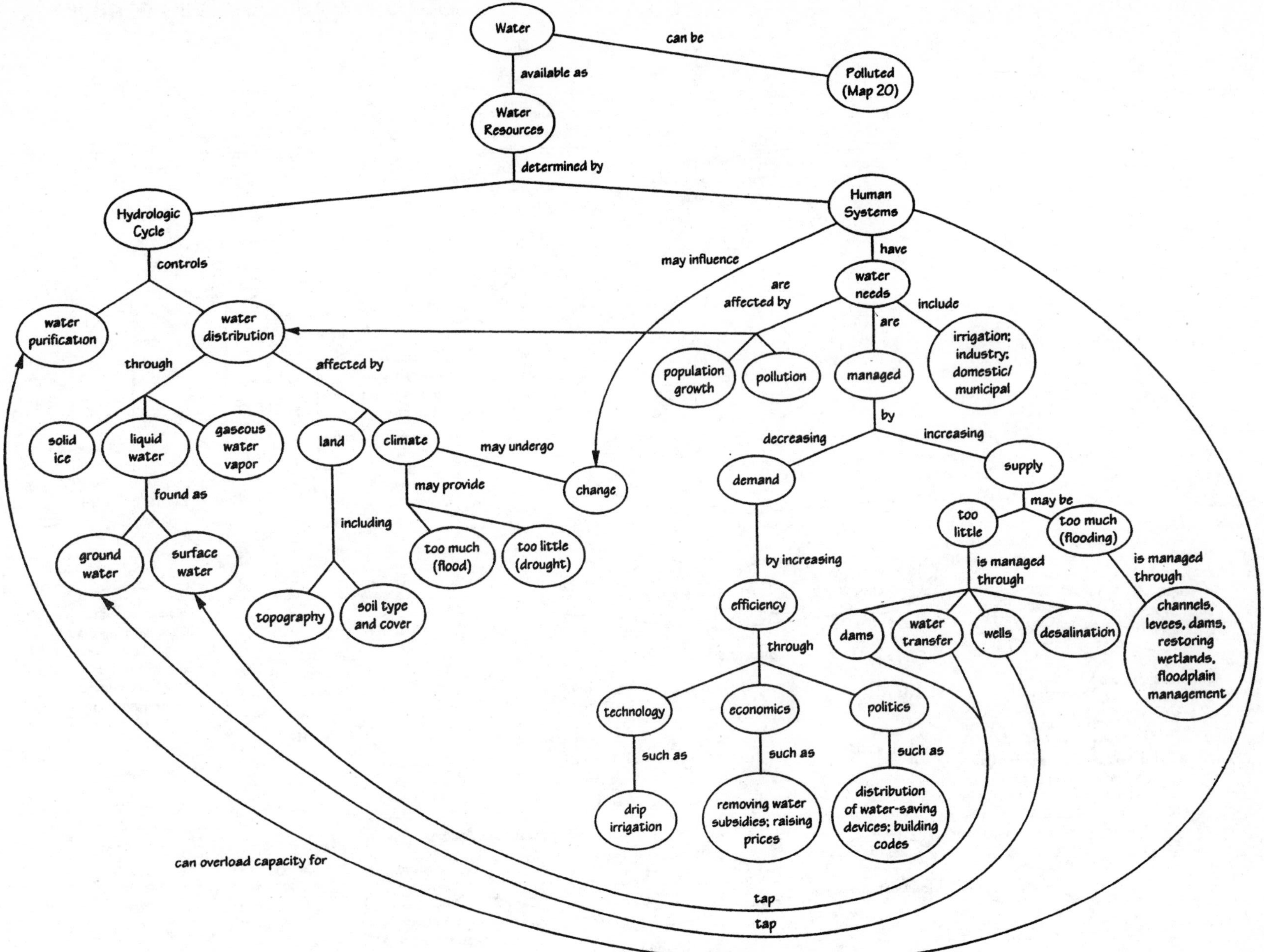

Map 19. Water Resources

Water — available as → Water Resources — determined by → Hydrologic Cycle

Water — can be → Polluted (Map 20)

Hydrologic Cycle — controls → water distribution

water distribution — through → water purification

water distribution — found as:
- solid ice
- liquid water
- gaseous water vapor

liquid water — found as:
- surface water
- ground water

Hydrologic Cycle — may influence → Human Systems

water distribution — affected by → climate

climate — may undergo → change

climate — may provide:
- too much (flood)
- too little (drought)

climate — including → land

land — including:
- topography
- soil type and cover

Human Systems — have → water needs

Human Systems — are affected by:
- population growth
- pollution

water needs — include → irrigation; industry; domestic/municipal

water needs — are → managed

managed — by:
- increasing → supply
- decreasing → demand

supply — may be:
- too much (flooding) — is managed through → channels, levees, dams, restoring wetlands, floodplain management
- too little — is managed through:
  - desalination
  - wells
  - water transfer
  - dams

demand — by increasing → efficiency

efficiency — through:
- politics — such as → distribution of water-saving devices; building codes
- economics — such as → removing water subsidies; raising prices
- technology — such as → drip irrigation

surface water / ground water — tap

can overload capacity for → water purification

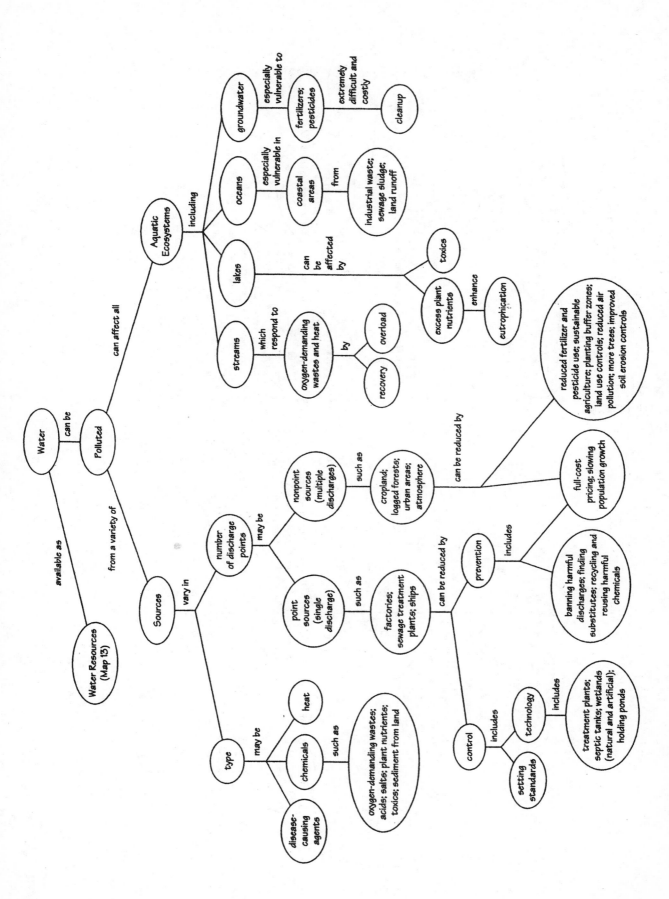

Map 20. Water Pollution

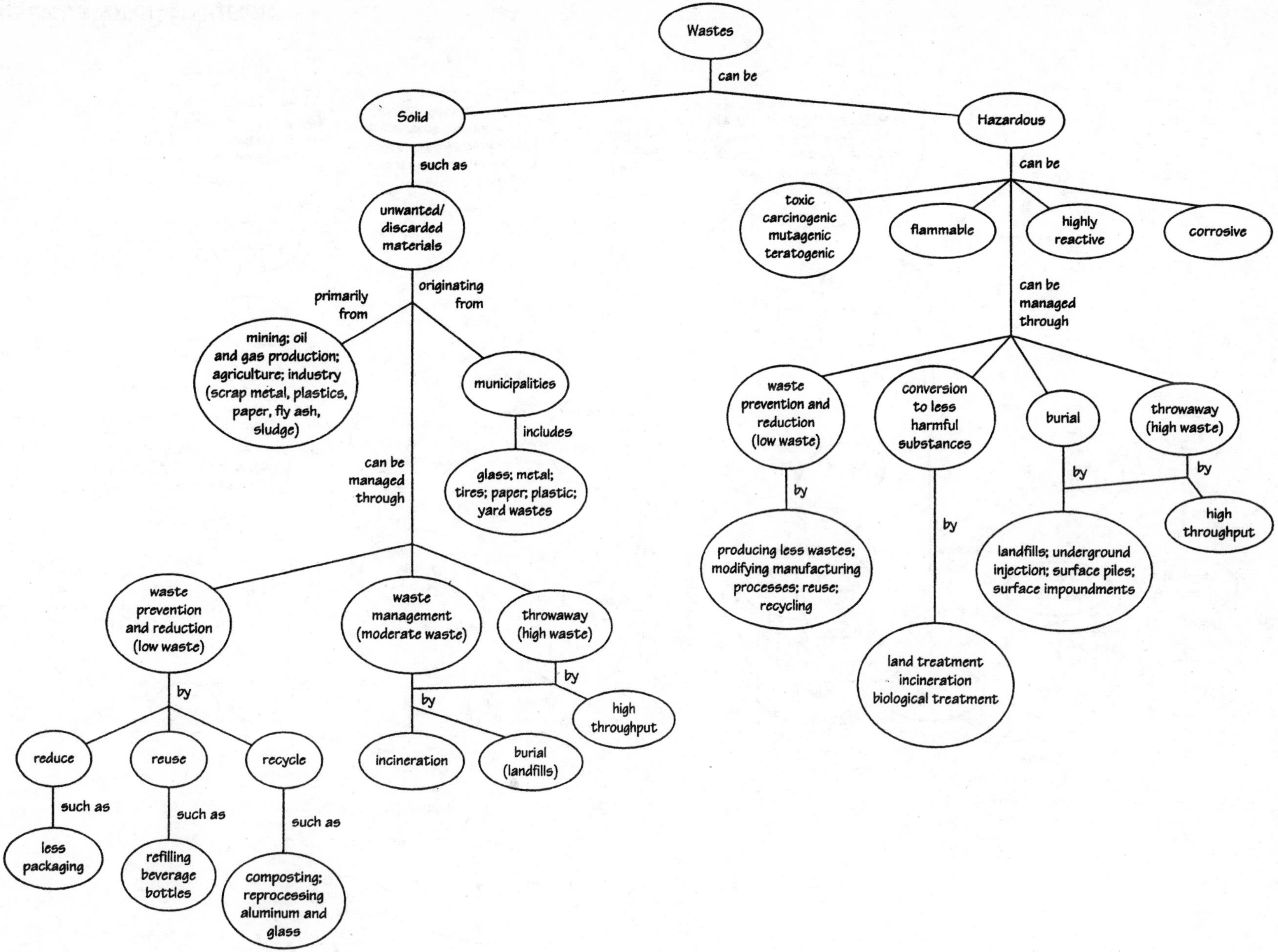

Map 21. Wastes

Wastes
— can be —

Hazardous
— can be —
- toxic, carcinogenic, mutagenic, teratogenic
- flammable
- highly reactive
- corrosive

— can be managed through —

- **waste prevention and reduction (low waste)**
  — by —
  producing less wastes; modifying manufacturing processes; reuse; recycling

- **conversion to less harmful substances**
  — by —
  land treatment incineration biological treatment

- **burial**
  — by —
  landfills; underground injection; surface piles; surface impoundments

- **throwaway (high waste)**
  — by —
  high throughput

Solid
— such as —
unwanted/discarded materials

— primarily from —
mining; oil and gas production; agriculture; industry (scrap metal, plastics, paper, fly ash, sludge)

— originating from —
municipalities
— includes —
glass; metal; tires; paper; plastic; yard wastes

— can be managed through —

- **waste prevention and reduction (low waste)**
  — by —
  - reduce
    — such as —
    less packaging
  - reuse
    — such as —
    refilling beverage bottles
  - recycle
    — such as —
    composting; reprocessing aluminum and glass

- **waste management (moderate waste)**
  — by —
  - incineration
  - burial (landfills)

- **throwaway (high waste)**
  — by —
  high throughput

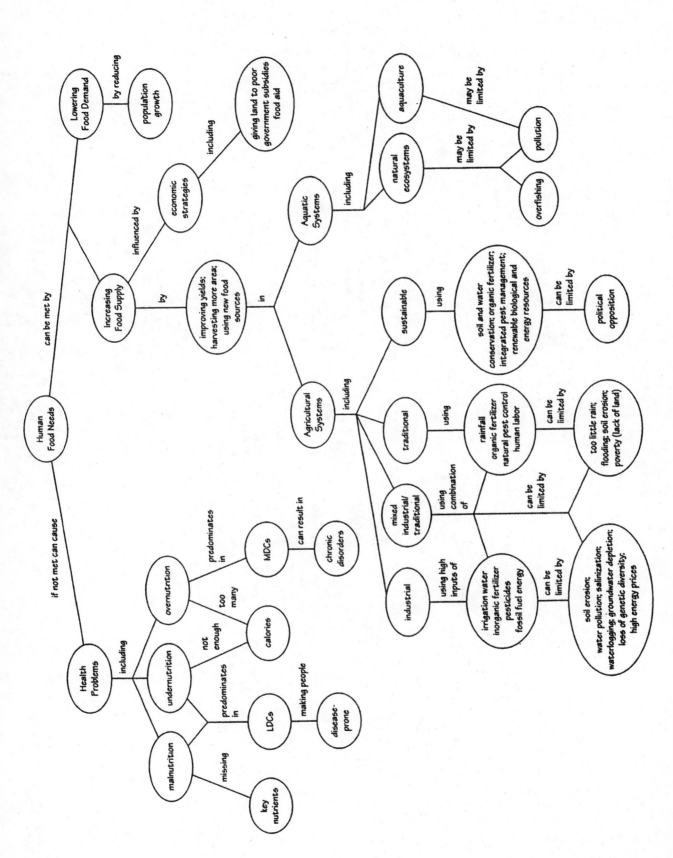

Map 22. Food Resources

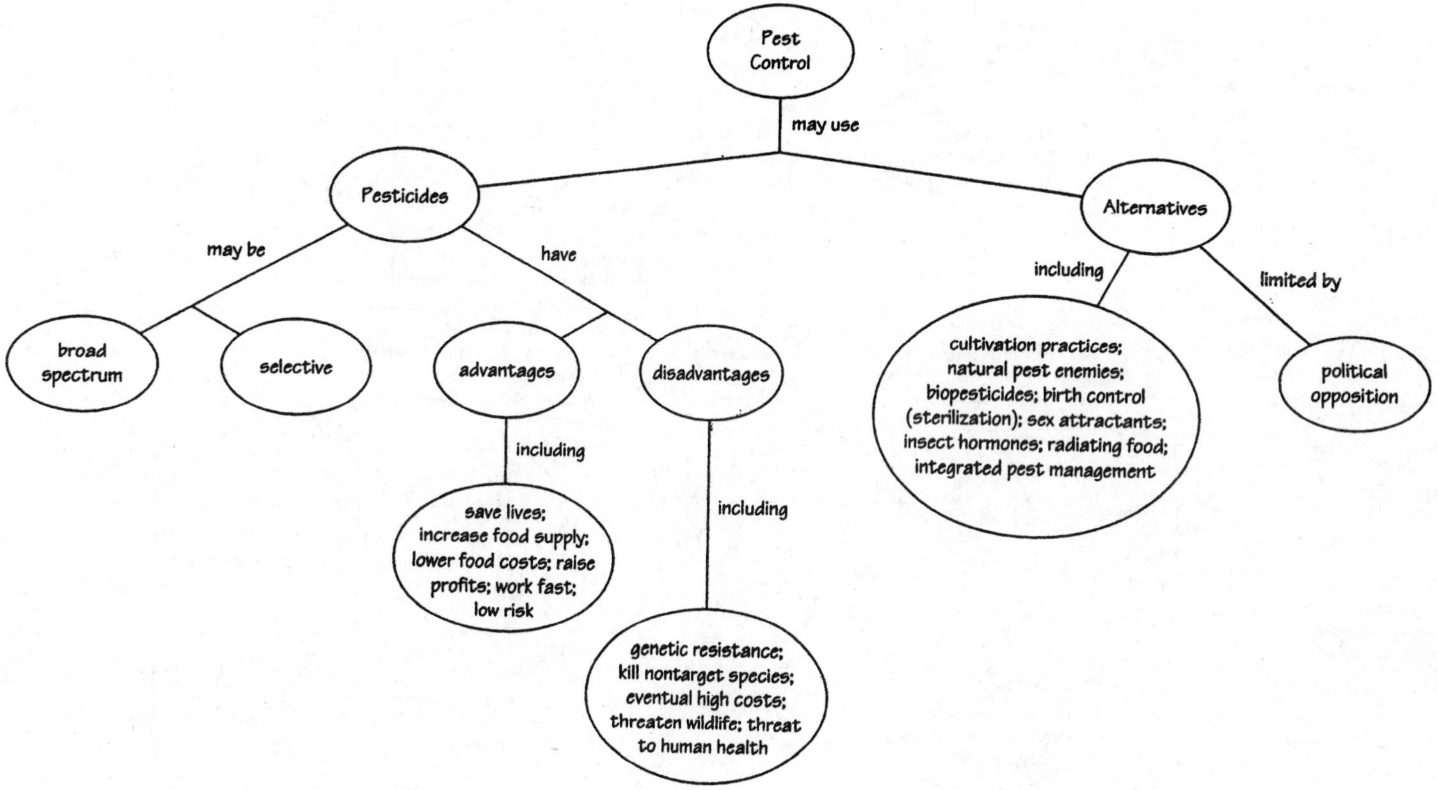

Pest Control

Pest Control —may use—> Alternatives

Alternatives —limited by—> political opposition

Alternatives —including—> cultivation practices; natural pest enemies; biopesticides; birth control (sterilization); sex attractants; insect hormones; radiating food; integrated pest management

Pest Control —may use—> Pesticides

Pesticides —may be—> selective, broad spectrum

Pesticides —have—> advantages, disadvantages

advantages —including—> save lives; increase food supply; lower food costs; raise profits; work fast; low risk

disadvantages —including—> genetic resistance; kill nontarget species; eventual high costs; threaten wildlife; threat to human health

Map 23. Pest Control

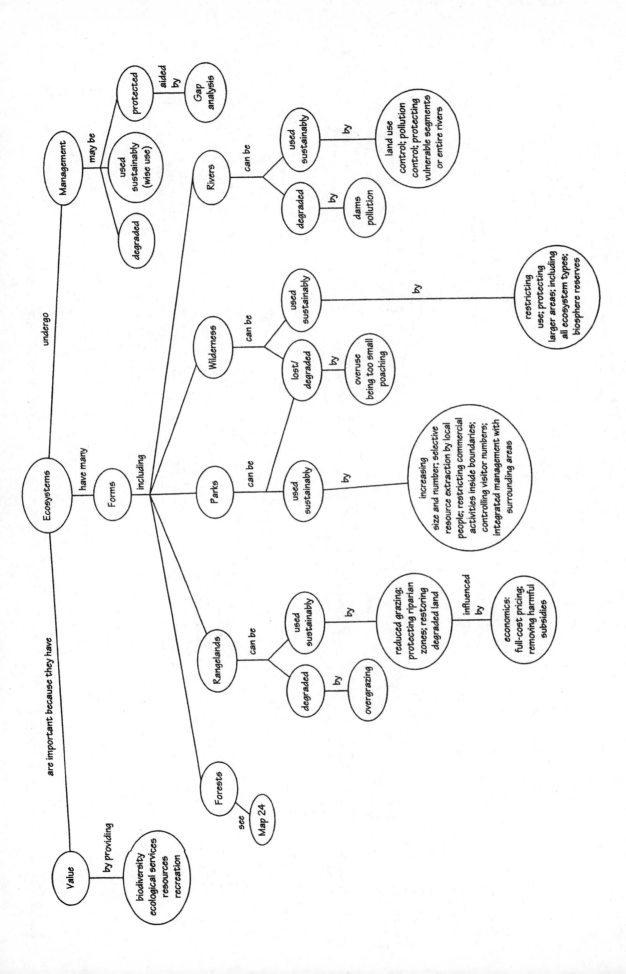

Map 24. Sustaining Ecosystems: Land Use, Conservation, and Management

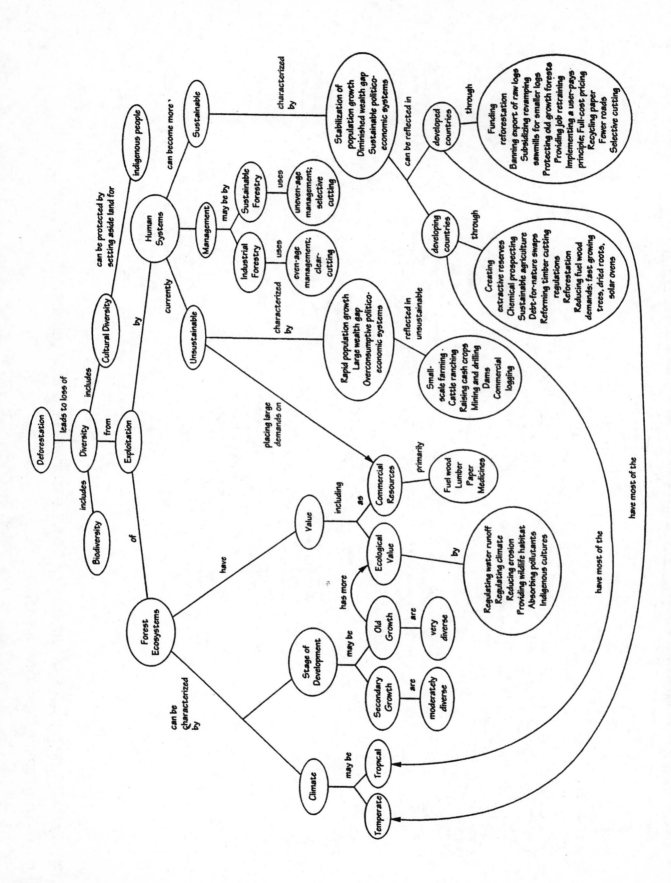

Map 25. Sustaining Ecosystems: Deforestation, Biodiversity, Forest Management

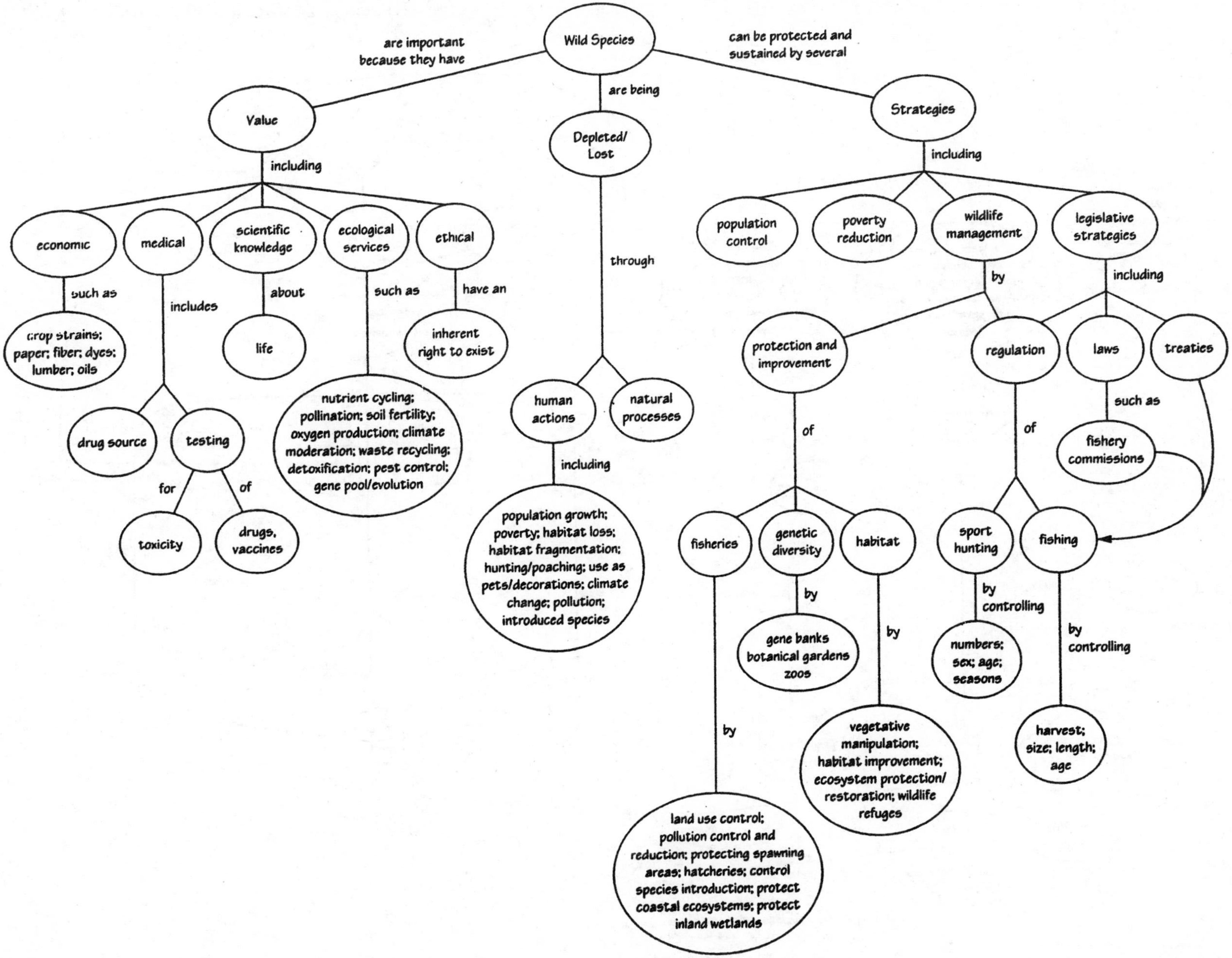

Map 26. Sustaining Wild Species

Wild Species

- **are important because they have** → **Value**
  - **including**
    - **economic** — *such as* — crop strains; paper; fiber; dyes; lumber; oils
    - **medical** — *includes* — **testing**
      - *of* — drugs, vaccines
      - *for* — toxicity
      - **drug source**
    - **scientific knowledge** — *about* — life
    - **ecological services** — *such as* — nutrient cycling; pollination; soil fertility; oxygen production; climate moderation; waste recycling; detoxification; pest control; gene pool/evolution
    - **ethical** — *have an* — inherent right to exist

- **are being** → **Depleted/Lost**
  - **through**
    - **natural processes**
    - **human actions** — *including* — population growth; poverty; habitat loss; habitat fragmentation; hunting/poaching; use as pets/decorations; climate change; pollution; introduced species

- **can be protected and sustained by several** → **Strategies**
  - **including**
    - **population control**
    - **poverty reduction**
    - **wildlife management** — *by*
      - **regulation** — *of*
        - **fishing** — *by controlling* — harvest; size; length; age
        - **sport hunting** — *by controlling* — numbers; sex; age; seasons
      - **protection and improvement** — *of*
        - **habitat** — *by* — vegetative manipulation; habitat improvement; ecosystem protection/ restoration; wildlife refuges
        - **genetic diversity** — *by* — gene banks; botanical gardens; zoos
        - **fisheries** — *by* — land use control; pollution control and reduction; protecting spawning areas; hatcheries; control species introduction; protect coastal ecosystems; protect inland wetlands
    - **legislative strategies** — *including*
      - **treaties**
      - **laws** — *such as* — fishery commissions

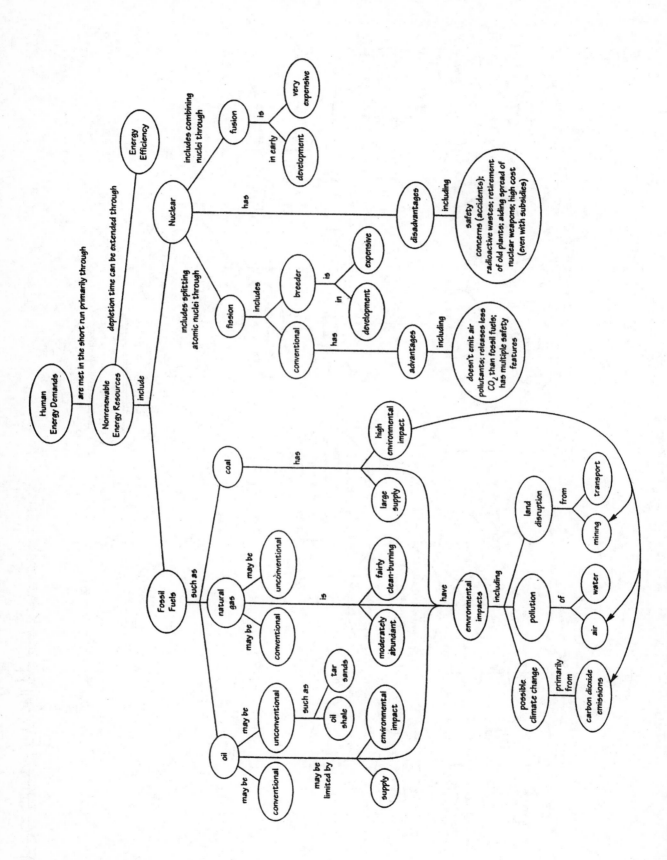

Map 27. Nonrenewable Energy Resources

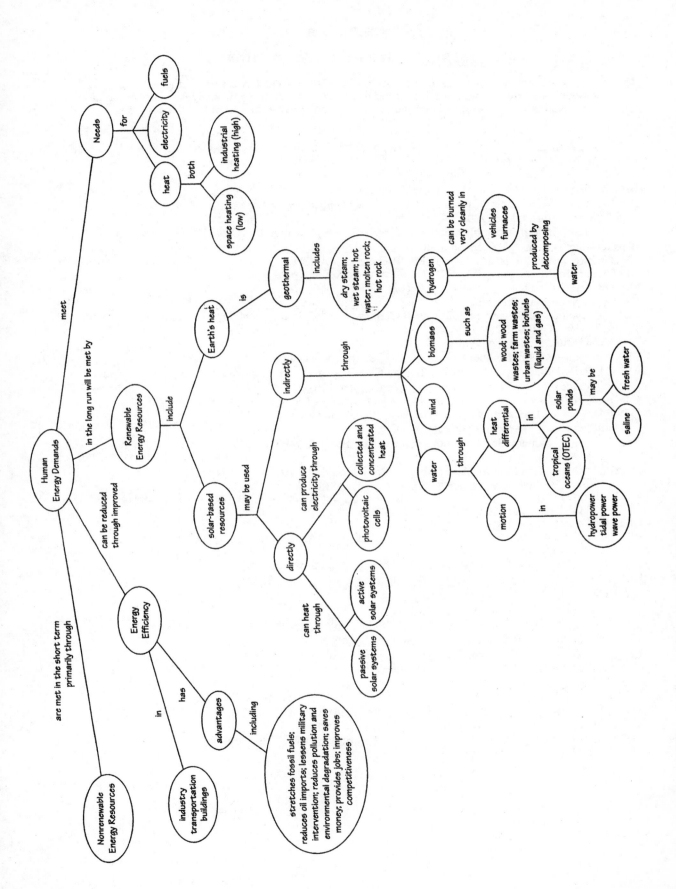

Map 28. Energy Efficiency and Renewable Energy

APPENDIX B

MEDIA SOURCES AND DISTRIBUTORS

The following abbreviations were used in the AUDIOVISUAL AIDS subsections of the Goals and Activities material in this manual. Addresses and/or phone numbers of media sources are given. Some general suggestions about obtaining environmental films are given at the end of the abbreviations.

ACPB The Annenberg/CPB Project, 901 E Street, N.W., Washington, D.C. 20004-2006 (800–LEARNER) www.learner.org

ATA All Things Arctic www.allthingsarctic.com

BBC British Broadcasting Company www.bbcshop.com

BBC-A British Broadcasting Company, America www.bbcamericashop.com

BFF Bullfrog Films, Oley, PA 19547 (800-543-3764) www.bullfrogfilms.com

CBS Carolina Biological Supply Company, 2700 York Rd., Burlington, NC 27215CBS Canadian Broadcasting System www.cbcboutique.ca

CF Commonwealth Films, 1500 Brook Rd., Richmond, VA 23220

CPr Cinnamon Productions (203-221-0163) www.nativevideos@AOL.com

DIS Discovery Channel. www.discovery.com

EA Ecology Action (California) 707 459-0150 http://essenes.crosswinds.net

EBEC Encyclopedia Britannica Educational Corporation, 310 South Michigan Ave., Chicago, IL 60604 (312-347-7000)

ENC ENC Online. www.ency.org

EPA United States Environmental Protection Agency www.epa.gov

EREC Energy Efficiency & Renewable Energy Clearinghouse. www.eere.energy.gov EV Encounter Video 800 677-4607 www.info@encountervideo.com

F-H Finley-Holiday Film Corporation 800 345-6707 www.finley-holiday.com

FHS Films for the Humanities & Sciences, Box 2053, Princeton, NJ 08543

GF Gulliver Films www.gullivermedia.com.au

NA+ National Audubon Society (with Turner Broadcasting & WETA) 212 979-3000 www.audubon.org

NCAP Northwest Coalition for Alternatives to Pesticides, P.O. Box 1393, Eugene OR 97440 (503-344-5044) www.pesticide.org/inertspage.html

NG National Geographic Society Educational Services, Department 88, Washington, D.C. 20036 (800-368-2728) www.nationalgeographic.com

OCE Oceanwatch oceanwatch@AOL.com

PBS Public Broadcasting Service Video, 1320 Braddich Pl., Alexandria, VA 22314 (800-424-7963) 7963 www.shop.pbs.org

RCO Recycling Council of Ontario Library www.rco@rco.on.ca

RMI RMI Media Productions. www.rmimedia.com

RV Richter Video www.richterviedos.com

SA Scientific American www.shoppbs.com

TA Thinking Allowed. 800 999-4415 www.thinking-allowed.com

TVE Television Trust for the Environment. www.tve.org

USD U. S. Dept. of Agriculture. Forest Service. 800 683-8366 www.fs.fed.us

VP The Video Project, 5332 College Ave., Suite 101, Oakland, CA 94618 (510-655-9050) www.videoproject.net

VT Video 301 881-0270 vidtrans@erols.com online video: http://refuges.fws.gov

WBG World Bank Group. 800 645-7247 www.web.worldbank.org

WS Wilderness Society (of Australia). www.wilderness.org.au

WS Wilderness Society (of U. S.) www.wilderness.org/library [PDF files online]

ZF Zipporah Films. www.zipporah.com

GENERAL SOURCES FOR ENVIRONMENTAL FILMS/VIDEOS

From the sources listed above, catalogues are strongly recommend from the Video Project (http://www.videoproject.net/), Bullfrog Films (http://www.bullfrogfilms.com/), Carolina Biological Supply (http://www.carolina.com/), the Race to Save the Planet Series, and National Geographic (http://www.nationalgeographic.com/education/teacher_store/edmedia/index.html).

North American Association of Environmental Education, P.O. Box 400, Troy, Ohio 45373. (513-698-6493) (http://naaee.org/) This professional organization offers a number of environmental education publications including a Festival of Film and Video Series and Curriculum and Resource Fair Catalogs.

Global Tomorrow Coalition.(http://habitat.igc.org/projects/gtc.htm) *The Global Ecology Handbook: What You Can Do About the Environmental Crisis*, edited by Walter H. Corson. Beacon Press, Boston, 1990. This book is an excellent source of teacher support materials as well as films and videos.

SAFE PLANET: The Guide to Environmental Film and Video offers a source of high-quality documentaries. It is available to individuals for $7.50 plus $3 postage and handling. Make checks payable to Media Network, 39 W. 14th St., Suite 403, New York, NY 10011 (212-929-2663) http://www.evc.org/screening/cat_env.html

APPENDIX C

COMPUTER SOFTWARE

In this section, you will find some computer simulations and models listed by chapter. Each entry includes title of the program, purpose of the program, and source where the program may be obtained. We are expanding this section and would appreciate receiving suggestions of appropriate software and sources from you.

Complete descriptions of most of the programs listed here, as well as many more, are found in *Managing a Nation: The Microcomputer Software Catalog, second edition*, 1991, edited by Gerald O. Barney, W. Brian Kreutzer, and Martha J. Garrett, published in cooperation with the Institute for 21st Century Studies, Westview Press, Boulder, San Francisco, and Oxford. Each entry includes title, purpose, description, theory and assumptions, an evaluation of the program, hardware and software requirements, and source. The book also includes a list of data sources.

Some of the courseware below (*) is listed in *Computer-Aided Environmental Education*, edited by W. J. Rohwedder, Ph.D.; North American Association for Environmental Education, P.O. Box 400, Troy, Ohio 45373. (513-339-6835) This publication is a collection of articles classified into environmental hypermedia, computer simulation/modeling, interactive software, and telecommunications.

An excellent resource for computer modeling of ecological systems (including population dynamics, competition, predator/prey, succession, and ozone depletion) is *Critical Thinking Software Tools and Workbook* (1992) for Starr and Taggart's *Biology: The Unity and Diversity of Life*, sixth edition, Wadsworth Publishing Company, Belmont, California.

Chapter 1: Environmental Problems, Their Causes, and Sustainability

Tragedy of the Commons
-Illustrates Garrett Hardin's principle of the Tragedy of the Commons—that increased exploitation of a common resource is desirable in the short term for each individual in a community, but disastrous in the long term to the whole community.
-National Collegiate Software, Duke University Press, 6697 College Station, Durham, NC 27708

International Futures Simulation (IFS)
-Provides a framework for evaluating the widely different public statements made about the workings of the global development system and about probable global futures.
-CONDUIT, The University of Iowa, Oakdale Campus, Iowa City, Iowa 52242

World Economic Model (WEM)
-Offers a consistent quantitative framework for carrying out prospective analysis and policy design exercises in the area of international economic relations.
-Dr. A.R. Gigengack, World Model Project, State University of Groningen, P.O. Box 800, 9700 AV Groningen, The Netherlands

*SimEarth
-To modify, manage, and nurture a planet from creation, through the formation of life, to the development of technology; based on the Gaia theory.
-Maxis, 2 Theatre Square, #230, Orinda, CA 94563 (510-254-9700)

*Balance of the Planet
-Role play the "High Commissioner of the Environment" by levying taxes and granting subsidies to solve a variety of global environmental problems.
-Accolade, 550 W. Winchester Blvd., Suite 200, San Jose, CA 95128 (800-245-7744)

Chapter 2: Environmental Economics, Politics, and Worldviews

Dynamic Synthesis of Basic Macroeconomic Theory (DSBMT)
-Provides, in a single model, a synthesis of the major theoretical macroeconomic models used by economists to provide advice on the management of the economies of nations and thereby reduce disagreement among economists on economic policy.
-System Dynamics Group, Sloan School of Management, Massachusetts Institute of Technology, 50 Memorial Dr., Cambridge, MA 02139

Environmental Assessment System (EASY)
-Provides a flexible decision support system for political decisions involving multiple decision makers and complex issues, such as the environment.
-R. Janssen and W. Hafkamp, Institute for Environment and Energy, Free University, P.O. Box 7161, 1007 Amsterdam, The Netherlands

Chapter 10: Risk, Toxicology, and Human Health

Waterborne Toxic Risk Assessment Model (WTRISK)
-Estimates the risks of adverse human health effects from substances emitted into the air, surface water, soil, and groundwater from sources such as coal-fired power plants.
-Manager, Software and Publications Distribution, Electric Power Research Institute, 3412 Hillview Ave., P.O. Box 10412, Palo Alto, CA 94303

Chapter 11: The Human Population: Growth and Distribution

Microcomputer Programs for Demographic Analysis (MCPDA)
- Performs a wide range of tests and analyses on demographic data.
- Institute for Resource Development, Westinghouse, P.O. Box 866, Columbia, MD 21044

DYNPLAN
-Calculates the effects that specific health-care interventions and family-planning measures can be expected to have on the demography of a nation.
-Stan Berstein, Department of Population and International Health, School of Public Health, University of Michigan, Ann Arbor, MI 48109

Chapter 12: Air and Air Pollution

Acid Deposition (ADEPT) Model
-Analyzes alternative strategies for dealing with the problem of acid deposition.
-Manager, Software and Publications Distribution, Electric Power Research Institute, 3412 Hillview Ave., P.O. Box 10412, Palo Alto, CA 94303

User's Network for Applied Modeling of Air Pollution (UNAMAP)
-Provides tools to analyze the implications for air quality of a wide variety of possible development projects and programs and for assessing alternative air-pollution control regulations
-Computer Products, National Technical Information Service, 5285 Port Royal Rd., Springfield, VA 22161

Chapter 13: Climate Change and Ozone Loss

Long-Term Global Energy-Carbon Dioxide Model
-Makes long-term global projections concerning energy utilization and carbon dioxide emissions from the energy sector.
-Thomas A. Boden, Oak Ridge National Laboratory, P.O. Box X, Carbon Dioxide Information Analysis Center, Building 2001, Oak Ridge, TN 37831

Atmospheric Greenhouse Model (AGM)
-Analyzes the consequences for the global climate of various scenarios regarding the production of carbon dioxide from fossil fuel combustion.
-Prof. L. D. D. Harvey, Department of Geography, University of Toronto, 100 St. George Street, Toronto, Ontario M5S 1A1, Canada

Chapter 14: Water Resources and Water Pollution

Water Supply Simulation Model (WSSM)
-Evaluates the physical and economic characteristics of a water supply system.
-U.S. Environmental Protection Agency, Office of Research and Development, Water Engineering Research Laboratory, ATTN: Dr. James A. Goodrich, Environmental Scientist, Systems and Cost Evaluation Staff, Drinking Water Research Division, Cincinnati, OH 45268

Chapter 16: Food Resources

Computerized System for Agricultural and Population Planning Assistance and Training (CAPPA)
-Facilitates use of a multisectoral scenario approach to agricultural planning.
-Chief, Development Policy Training and Research Service, Policy Analysis Division, Food and Agriculture Organization of the United Nations, Via delle Terme di Caracalla, 00100, Rome, Italy

Standard National (Agricultural) Model (SNM)
-Analyzes the consequences of domestic or international policy changes for a nation's domestic food situation.
-Director, Food and Agriculture Program, International Institute for Applied Systems Analysis, Schloss Laxenburg, A-2361, Laxenburg, Austria

Chapter 17: Sustaining Biodiversity: The Ecosystem Approach

Range, Livestock, and Wildlife
-Helps decision makers understand and evaluate policy alternatives for rangeland management.
-Paul Faeth, World Resources Institute/International Institute for Environment and Development, 1709 New York Avenue, N.W., 7th Floor, Washington, D.C. 20006

BIOCUT
-Assesses the economic viability of alternative designs and management strategies for wood energy plantations.
-National Technical Information Service, U.S. Dept. of Commerce, 5285 Port Royal Rd., Springfield, VA 22161

Chapter 18: Sustaining Biodiversity: The Species

Biological and Conservation Data (BCD) System
-Provides an inexpensive, effective tool to inventory, rank, protect, and maintain endangered species.
-The Nature Conservancy, Data Systems Divisions, 1815 North Lynn Street, Rosslyn, VA 22209

*Audubon Wildlife Adventures
-Explore wildlife conservation issues of grizzlies and whales using scientific information, state-of-the-art graphics, computerized databases, and on-line guidebooks.
-Advanced Ideas, Inc., 591 Redwood Highway, #2325, Mill Valley, CA 94941 (415-388-2430)

*Wildways: Understanding Wildlife Conservation
-Emphasizes the need for wildlife conservation through integration of biology, geology, and sociology in sections on Earth and life, basic necessities of life, importance of wildlife, population ecology, community ecology, extinction, wildlife management, and citizen action.
-Opportunities in Science, Inc., P.O. Box 1176, Bemidji, MN 56601 (218-751-1110)

Chapter 19: Nonrenewable Energy Resources

ENERPLAN
-Performs basic energy analysis for a nation, province, or community.
-Mr. Nicky Beredjick, Director, National Resources and Energy Division, Department of Technical Cooperation for Development, United Nations, New York, NY 10017

Estimating Fossil Fuel Resources (EFFR)
-Simulates the global exploitation of oil resources and evaluates alternative resource-estimation techniques.
-Prof. John D. Sterman, Sloan School of Management, Massachusetts Institute of Technology, 50 Memorial Dr., Cambridge, MA 02139

OTHER SUGGESTIONS

The computer applications area of environmental experience is growing rapidly. Other areas to explore in this realm include:

—Networking. Networks of people interested in environmental issues are forming. Some include information about environmental topics, current issues of interest, bills being addressed in Congress, who serves on environmentally-related committees, and when important votes are about to take place. Through some, environmental databases of student-generated environmental analyses can be accessed. Some are interactive, with electronic bulletin boards.

One place to start is ECONET, a broad-based international environmental computer network. ECONET, 18 DeBoom St., San Francisco, CA 94107 (Phone: 415-442-0220)

The Global Action and Information Network (GAIN) uses ECONET to disseminate information to help individuals act on environmental legislation and take action in their own lives. GAIN, 575 Soquel Ave., Santa Cruz, CA 95062 (Phone: 408-457-0130)

—National Geographic. The National Geographic GTV: *Planetary Manager* is one approach to using technology for environmental education. This program uses a TV monitor, videodisc player, and optional computer and printer. To order or preview, contact: Optical Data Corporation, 30 Technology Drive, Warren, NJ 07059. Information about other National Geographic computer courseware is available from: National Geographic Society, Educational Services, Washington, D.C. 20036. (800-368-2728)

APPENDIX D

QUESTIONNAIRE ON ENVIRONMENTAL LIFESTYLES, ATTITUDES, AND AWARENESS

It is suggested that you reproduce all or parts of this questionnaire, have students answer these questions at the beginning of the course, and turn their answers in. At the end of the course have them complete the questionnaire again (without looking at their earlier answers). Then have them compare the two sets of answers and mark items in which their answers changed. You could tally the results for the entire class to evaluate the impact of your course. If you do this, we would greatly appreciate receiving a summary of your results along with any suggested improvements in the questionnaire. Send this information to G. Tyler Miller, Jr., c/o Jack Carey, Brooks/Cole Publishing Company, 10 Davis Drive, Belmont, CA 94002.

Answer the questions to the best of your ability. Skip any questions that you feel you really just don't know.

LIFESTYLE

1. Would you rate your waste of water as high, medium, or low?

2. In what ways do you conserve water?

3. Would you estimate that the percentage of calories in your diet coming from meat and meat products (such as milk, cheese, and butter) is high (more than 50%), moderately high (35-45%), medium (25-35%), low (15-20%), or very low (less than 20%)?

4. Is the percentage of the food you eat that is produced organically without the use of pesticides, commercial inorganic fertilizers, growth hormones, or antibiotics high, medium, low, or unknown? Is the percentage of the locally grown food that you eat high, medium, low, or unknown?

5. Do you produce a large, medium, or small amount of solid waste each week?

6. What are the major components of the trash you generate?

7. Do you separate cans, bottles, and paper for recycling for curbside collection, take these materials to recycling centers, or throw them away?

8. What items and products do you reuse instead of recycling them or throwing them away?

9. Do you deliberately try to buy items made from recycled materials? If so, what items?

10. Do you use rechargeable batteries?

11. When shopping do you carry out items in paper bags, plastic bags, or in your own reusable canvas or string containers?

12. In what ways do you try to waste less energy?

13. How many days a week do you walk, ride a bicycle, carpool, or take a bus or subway to your work or school?

14. Do you depend on a car for most, some, or little of your transportation?

15. If you drive a car, what is its average gas mileage?

16. Do you use energy-saving light bulbs (screw-in fluorescent light bulbs)?

17. Do you regularly obey the speed limit (which also saves gas and reduces air pollution)?

18. Are you a member of a national, state, or local environmental organization?

19. Do you regularly read an environmental publication?

20. Have you participated in any groups or activities to improve the quality of your local environment within the last year?

21. Have you written to or talked with a local, state, or federal elected official concerning some environmental issue within the last year?

22. Of the things you buy, would you say that most, some, or few of them are items you really *need* (as opposed to *want*)?

23. Do you buy new clothes, cars, furniture, and other items to keep up with the latest fashions frequently, sometimes, or rarely?

24. Would you rate the harmful environmental impact of your lifestyle as high, moderate, or low?

ATTITUDES

Beliefs about the human population

25. Is the world overpopulated?

26. Is the country in which you live overpopulated?

27. Is your local community overpopulated?

28. Do you favor reducing the population size of the world?

29. Do you favor reducing the population size of the country in which you live?

30. How many children do you plan to have?

31. Do you believe that any person should be able to have as many children as they want?

32. Does your country consume too many resources?

33. Do you consume too many resources?

Beliefs about Policy

34. Do you favor greatly increased foreign aid to poor countries to help them reduce poverty, to improve environmental quality, and to develop sustainable use of their own resources?

35. Do you favor a more equitable distribution of the world's resources and wealth to greatly reduce the current wide gap between the rich and the poor, even if this means less for you?

36. Do you favor debt-for-nature swaps in which poor countries would be forgiven most of their debts to rich countries, in exchange for protecting specified wild areas of their country from harmful and unsustainable forms of development?

37. Would you support a 10% increase in income taxes if you knew this revenue would be used to improve environmental quality?

38. Do you favor requiring all cars to get at least 21 kilometers per liter (50 miles per gallon) and vans and light trucks to get at least 15 kilometers per liter (35 miles per gallon) of gasoline within the next ten years?

39. Would you favor much stricter, twice-a-year inspections of air pollution control equipment on motor vehicles and tough fines for not keeping these systems in good working order?

40. Would you favor a $2 tax on a gallon of gasoline and heating oil to help reduce wasteful consumption, extend oil supplies, reduce air pollution, delay projected global warming, and stimulate improvements in energy efficiency and the use of less harmful energy sources?

41. Would you vote for anyone proposing a program to add a $2 per gallon tax on gasoline and heating oil, assuming all other factors are the same?

42. Would you support laws requiring that all new homes and buildings meet high energy efficiency standards for insulation, air infiltration, and heating and cooling systems?

43. Would you favor such a law for existing homes and buildings?

44. Would you favor a nationwide law requiring a 25¢ refundable deposit on all bottles and cans to encourage their recycling or reuse?

45. Would you support a law requiring everyone to separate their trash into paper, bottles, aluminum cans, steel cans, and glass for recycling and to separate all food and yard wastes for composting?

46. Would you support a law that bans all throwaway bottles, cans, and plastic containers and requires that all beverage and food containers be reusable (refillable)?

47. Would you support a law requiring that at least 60% of all municipal solid waste be recycled, reused, or composted?

48. Would you support a law banning the construction of any incinerators or landfills for disposal of hazardous or solid waste until at least 60% of all municipal solid waste is recycled, reused, or composted and the production of industrial hazardous waste has been reduced by 60%?

49. Should industries and other producers of hazardous waste be allowed to inject such waste into deep underground wells?

50. Would you support a law banning the emission of any hazardous chemicals into the environment, with the understanding that many products you use now would cost more and some would no longer be made?

51. Would you support a law banning the export of any hazardous wastes and pesticides, medicines, or other chemicals banned in your country to any other country? Would you also support a law banning export of such wastes from one part of a country to another so that each community is responsible for the waste it produces?

52. Would you support sharp increases in monthly water bills for all homes, buildings, industries, and farms to discourage water waste?

53. Would you favor requiring that the market cost of any product or service include all estimated present and future environmental costs?

54. Would you support classifying a much larger proportion of the public lands (such as parks, forests, and rangeland) in your country as wilderness and making such land unavailable for timber cutting, livestock grazing, mining, hunting, fishing, motorized vehicles, or any type of human structure?

Beliefs about Other Species, Economics,
Environmental Change, and the Future

55. Do you believe that humans are superior to other species?

56. Do you believe that individuals and countries should have the right to consume as many resources as they can afford?

57. Do you believe that the most important nation is the one that can command and use the largest fraction of the world's resources to promote its own economic growth?

58. Do you believe that the more we produce and consume, the better off we are?

59. Do you believe that humans have a duty to subdue wild nature to provide food, shelter, and other resources for people and to provide jobs and income through increased economic growth?

60. Do you believe that resources are essentially unlimited because of our ability to develop technologies to make them available or to find substitutes?

61. Do you believe that all use of nuclear power plants should be phased out?

62. Do you believe that every living species has a right to exist, or at least struggle to exist, simply because it exists?

63. Do you believe that we have an obligation to leave Earth for future generations of humans and other species in as good a shape as we found it, if not better? Did past generations do this for you?

64. Do you think your environment will be more livable, about the same, or less livable ten years from now?

65. Do you think that humans can bring about a major change within your lifetime that involves helping sustain rather than degrade Earth?

66. Do you believe most environmental issues are overblown by environmentalists and the media?

67. Do you believe that environmental improvement will result in a net loss, a net gain, or no change in the total number of jobs in your country? In your community?

68. Would you be in favor of improving the air or water quality in your community if this meant a net loss of local jobs?

69. Would you be in favor of improving the air or water quality in your community if this meant that you lost your job?

AWARENESS

70. List the following in order of decreasing importance as environmental threats to you: indoor air pollution, outdoor air pollution, depletion of the ozone layer, global warming, toxic chemicals in the air, drinking water contamination, leaking hazardous waste sites, acid rain, air pollution from automobiles, nuclear energy, coal-burning power plants, overpopulation in poor countries, overpopulation in affluent countries, tropical deforestation, soil erosion, pesticides in your food and drinking water.

71. About how many people live in your community? Is it growing or shrinking in size?

72. What have been the major beneficial and harmful effects of the growth or shrinkage of the population in your community?

73. Name five types of trees growing naturally in your area.

74 Name five types of wild edible plants in your area and indicate the season or seasons when they are available.

75 Name five types of wild animals found in or near your area.

76. Name five types of resident and migratory birds in your area.

77. Would you rate the abundance and diversity of wild species in your area as high, medium, or low?

78. Have human activities reduced, increased, or not affected the overall abundance and diversity of wild species in your local area during the last ten years?

79. What species have become extinct or are in danger of extinction in your area?

80. Is the soil around where you live composed mostly of clay, sand, or silt?

81. Is the fertility of soil around where you live high, medium, or low?

82. Is the soil around where you live highly acidic, moderately acidic, or alkaline?

83. Name five kinds of rocks and minerals found in your area.

84. List the major rivers, lakes, wetlands, and oceans within 48 kilometers (30 miles) of where you live.

85. Would you rate the quality of the water in each of these bodies of water as good, fair, or poor?

86. Are any wetlands in your area threatened with development?

87. Is there abundant, some, or little agricultural land near where you live?

88. Are there serious soil erosion problems on cropland, in urban developments, and on grazing land in your area?

89. Does your community have a land-use plan? If so, what are the major goals of these plans (for example, encouragement of population growth and economic development, slow growth and development, preservation of farmlands, forests, wetlands, and other natural areas)?

90. Which, if any of the following hazardous are likely where you live: earthquakes, hurricanes, tornadoes, droughts, floods?

91. Are there any power plants in or near your community? If so, what type are they, how close are they to where you live, and are their safety records over the past ten years good, fair, or poor?

92. What major industrial plants are in your community? How close are they to where you live? What chemicals are being emitted into the air and water by these plants? How many accidental emissions have these plants had during the last 10 years?

93. What are the major hazardous wastes generated in your community? Who generates these wastes? What happens to these materials?

94. Where is the nearest municipal landfill? Is it polluting groundwater?

95. Where is the nearest toxic waste dump? Nuclear waste facility? Garbage incinerator? Hazardous waste incinerator? Are any of these facilities polluting the air or water? If so, what is being done about this pollution?

96. Would you rate the quality of the air you breathe good, fair, or poor?

97. Is acid deposition a serious problem in your area? What are the sources of these acids?

98. Have the buildings in which you live or work been tested for the presence of asbestos and radioactive radon gas?

99. Where does the water you drink and use come from?

100. Would you rate the quality of the water you drink as good, fair, or poor?

101. How is the sewage you create treated? How many times has this treatment process violated federal and state water pollution standards within the last 10 years? Were these violations promptly reported to the public?

102. What percentage of the solid waste you produce is buried? Burned? Recycled? Composted?

103. Is there a recycling program in your community or at your school? If so, is the program voluntary or mandatory? Are there plans for increasing the amount of recycling?

104. Is your house or dorm heated by burning oil in a furnace, burning natural gas in a furnace, electricity produced by nuclear power, electricity produced by burning coal, electricity produced by water flowing through a dam (hydropower), passive collection of solar energy, or active collection of solar energy? Which of these sources is used to heat the water you use for washing?

105. What is the average temperature of your room or house in the winter? In the summer?

106. Would you classify the room or house where you live as well insulated, moderately insulated, or poorly insulated?

107. Would you classify the room or house where you live as very airtight, moderately airtight, or leaky?

108. Would you rate energy conservation on your campus as good, fair, or poor?

109. Would you rate the overall environmental awareness of students on your campus as good, fair, or poor?

110. Would you rate the overall environmental awareness of teachers and administrators on your campus as good, fair, or poor?

111. Would you rate overall environmental awareness in your local community as good, fair, or poor?

APPENDIX E

ANSWERS TO THE REVIEW QUESTIONS OF THE TEXTBOOK

Chapter 1

1. p. 2-16	8. p. 6	15. p. 9	22. p. 15
2. p. 1	9. p. 7	16. p. 9	23. p. 15
3. p. 2	10. p. 7	17. p. 10	24. p. 16
4. p. 2	11. p. 7	18. p. 11	25. p. 16
5. p. 3	12. p. 8	19. p. 12	
6. p. 3	13. p. 8	20. p. 12-14	
7. p. 4-5	14. p. 8	21. p. 14	

Chapter 2

1. p. 20-42	9. p. 26	17. p. 31	25. p. 38
2. p. 19	10. p. 27	18. p. 32	26. p. 37
3. p. 20	11. p. 27	19. p. 32-33	27. p. 39
4. p. 20	12. p. 28	20. p. 33-35	28. p. 40
5. p. 21-23	13. p. 29-30	21. p. 35-36	29. p. 41
6. p. 22-23	14. p. 30	22. p. 36	30. p. 40
7. p. 24 25	15. p. 31	23. p. 36	31. p. 40-41
8. p. 25	16. p. 31	24. p. 36-38	32. p. 42

Chapter 3

1. p. 47-61	9. p. 49-50	17. p. 52	25. p. 56
2. p. 46	10. p. 50	18. p. 53	26. p. 57
3. p. 47	11. p. 50	19. p. 53	27. p. 57
4. p. 48	12. p. 51	20. p. 53	28. p. 58
5. p. 49	13. p. 51	21. p. 53	29. p. 59
6. p. 49	14. p. 51	22. p. 54	30. p. 60-61
7. p. 49	15. p. 51	23. p. 54	
8. p. 49	16. p. 51	24. p. 56	

Chapter 4

1. p. 65-89	9. p. 70	17. p. 76	25. p. 85-86
2. p. 64	10. p. 70	18. p. 79	26. p. 86-87
3. p. 64	11. p. 72-73	19. p. 80	27. p. 87
4. p. 64-68	12. p. 73	20. p. 81	28. p. 89
5. p. 65	13. p. 73	21. p. 81	29. p. 89
6. p. 68	14. p. 73	22. p. 82	
7. p. 69	15. p. 74	23. p. 82-84	
8. p. 69-70	16. p. 76	24. p. 84-85	

Chapter 5

1. p. 93-103	6. p. 95	11. p. 99	16. p. 102
2. p. 92	7. p. 95-96	12. p. 99	17. p. 102-103
3. p. 93	8. p. 96	13. p. 100	
4. p. 93	9. p. 98	14. p. 101	
5. p. 95	10. p. 98-99	15. p. 102	

Chapter 6

1. p. 107-136	9. p. 111-112	17. p. 127	25. p. 133
2. p. 106	10. p. 112	18. p. 127	26. p. 133-134
3. p. 107	11. p. 112-115	19. p. 127	27. p. 134-135
4. p. 107	12. p. 115-116	20. p. 129	28. p. 136
5. p. 107-109	13. p. 116-119	21. p. 131	29. p. 137
6. p. 109	14. p. 119-124	22. p. 132-133	30. p. 137
7. p. 109-110	15. p. 124	23. p. 133	31. p. 137
8. p. 110-111	16. p. 124	24. p. 135	

Chapter 7

1. p. 141-157	7. p. 143-145	13. p. 147	19. p. 154
2. p. 140	8. p. 144	14. p. 147-148	20. p. 154
3. p. 141	9. p. 145	15. p. 148-150	21. p. 155
4. p. 120, 128, 135	10. p. 146	16. p. 150	22. p. 155
5. p. 142	11. p. 146	17. p. 150-151	23. p. 155-157
6. p. 142	12. p. 147	18. p. 152-153	

Chapter 8

1. p. 161-170	6. p. 161-162	11. p. 165	16. p. 168-169
2. p. 160	7. p. 162	12. p. 165	17. p. 170
3. p. 161	8. p. 163	13. p. 166-167	18. p. 170
4. p. 161	9. p. 164	14. p. 167	
5. p. 161	10. p. 164	15. p. 168	

Chapter 9

1. p. 174-199	10. p. 179-180	19. p. 187-188	28. p. 196
2. p. 173	11. p. 180-183	20. p. 188	29. p. 196-197
3. p. 174	12. p. 183	21. p. 188	30. p. 197
4. p. 175	13. p. 184	22. p. 189	31. p. 199
5. p. 175	14. p. 185	23. p. 189	32. p. 199
6. p. 175	15. p. 185	24. p. 193	33. p. 199
7. p. 177	16. p. 185	25. p. 193	
8. p. 177-178	17. p. 185	26. p. 194	
9. p. 178	18. p. 186	27. p. 194	

Chapter 10

1. p. 204-219	8. p. 206	15. p. 210-211	22. p. 215
2. p. 203	9. p. 207	16. p. 211	23. p. 215-216
3. p. 204	10. p. 208	17. p. 212	24. p. 216
4. p. 204	11. p. 208-209	18. p. 212	25. p. 217
5. p. 204	12. p. 210	19. p. 213	26. p. 217-218
6. p. 206-206	13. p. 210	20. p. 213	27. p. 219
7. p. 206	14. p. 210	21. p. 213-214	28. p. 219

Chapter 11

1. p. 223-250	11. p. 229	21. p. 238	31. p. 245
2. p. 222	12. p. 230	22. p. 238	32. p. 245
3. p. 223	13. p. 231	23. p. 239	33. p. 245
4. p. 224	14. p. 232	24. p. 240	34. p. 246
5. p. 225-226	15. p. 233	25. p. 240	35. p. 246
6. p. 226	16. p. 234-236	26. p. 240	36. p. 247-248
7. p. 226	17. p. 236	27. p. 241	37. p. 248-249
8. p. 227	18. p. 236	28. p. 242	38. p. 249-251
9. p. 228	19. p. 236-238	29. p. 242-245	
10. p. 229	20. p. 238	30. p. 244	

Chapter 12

1. p. 256-277	7. p. 260	13. p. 267-268	19. p. 273
2. p. 255	8. p. 262	14. p. 268	20. p. 273
3. p. 256	9. p. 262	15. p. 269-271	21. p. 274
4. p. 256-259	10. p. 262-264	16. p. 271	22. p. 274-277
5. p. 257	11. p. 264-265	17. p. 272	23. p. 277
6. p. 259	12. p. 265-267	18. p. 272-273	

Chapter 13

1. p. 281-301	8. p. 287-289	15. p. 293-295	22. p. 299
2. p. 281	9. p. 290	16. p. 295	23. p. 301
3. p. 282	10. p. 290	17. p. 296	24. p. 301
4. p. 283	11. p. 291	18. p. 296	25. p. 301
5. p. 284	12. p. 292	19. p. 296-298	
6. p. 285	13. p. 293	20. p. 297	
7. p. 286-287	14. p. 293	21. p. 299	

Chapter 14

1. p. 306-342	12. p. 312-313	23. p. 325	34. p. 335
2. p. 305	13. p. 314	24. p. 325	35. p. 336
3. p. 306	14. p. 315	25. p. 326	36. p. 337
4. p. 307	15. p. 316-317	26. p. 326-327	37. p. 337
5. p. 307	16. p. 317	27. p. 327	38. p. 338
6. p. 309	17. p. 317-318	28. p. 328-329	39. p. 338
7. p. 310	18. p. 318	29. p. 329-331	40. p. 339
8. p. 310	19. p. 318-321	30. p. 331	41. p. 340-341
9. p. 311	20. p. 321	31. p. 332	42. p. 341-342
10. p. 311-312	21. p. 323	32. p. 332	43. p. 343
11. p. 312	22. p. 324	33. p. 333-334	44. p. 343

Chapter 15

1. p. 348-373	11. p. 353-354	21. p. 356	31. p. 369-370
2. p. 347	12. p. 354-356	22. p. 362	32. p. 370
3. p. 348	13. p. 354-355	23. p. 362-363	33. p. 370-371
4. p. 348	14. p. 356-357	24. p. 363-364	34. p. 371
5. p. 349	15. p. 357-358	25. p. 364	35. p. 372
6. p. 349-350	16. p. 358	26. p. 364-366	36. p. 372
7. p. 350-351	17. p. 359	27. p. 366-367	37. p. 373
8. p. 351	18. p. 360-361	28. p. 367	
9. p. 352-353	19. p. 361	29. p. 367-368	
10. p. 352-353	20. p. 361-362	30. p. 368-369	

Chapter 16

1. p. 378-406	11. p. 385	21. p. 391	31. p. 399
2. p. 377	12. p. 385	22. p. 391	32. p. 399
3. p. 378	13. p. 386	23. p. 391	33. p. 400
4. p. 378-379	14. p. 386	24. p. 392	34. p. 400-401
5. p. 380	15. p. 386	25. p. 393-394	35. p. 401-402
6. p. 380	16. p. 387-388	26. p. 394	36. p. 402
7. p. 380	17. p. 389	27. p. 395	37. p. 402
8. p. 382	18. p. 390	28. p. 396-398	38. p. 402
9. p. 382-383	19. p. 390	29. p. 398	39. p. 403-406
10. p. 383-385	20. p. 390	30. p. 398	40. p. 406-407

Chapter 17

1. p. 412-444	13. p. 423	25. p. 431-433	37. p. 441
2. p. 411	14. p. 423-424	26. p. 432	38. p. 441
3. p. 412-413	15. p. 425	27. p. 432-433	39. p. 441-442
4. p. 413-414	16. p. 425	28. p. 433-434	40. p. 442
5. p. 414	17. p. 425-426	29. p. 435	41. p. 442
6. p. 414-415	18. p. 427	30. p. 435	42. p. 442-443
7. p. 417	19. p. 427	31. p. 436	43. p. 443
8. p. 417-418	20. p. 428	32. p. 436-437	44. p. 443
9. p. 419	21. p. 428-429	33. p. 437	45. p. 444
10. p. 419	22. p. 429	34. p. 437	
11. p. 420	23. p. 429	35. p. 438-439	
12. p. 421	24. p. 430	36. p. 441	

Chapter 18

1. p. 449-474	8. p. 453	15. p. 462-465	22. p. 471
2. p. 448	9. p. 454	16. p. 464	23. p. 471-472
3. p. 449	10. p. 454-456	17. p. 466	24. p. 473
4. p. 449	11. p. 455	18. p. 466	25. p. 473-474
5. p. 449	12. p. 457-459	19. p. 466	26. p. 474
6. p. 452	13. p. 460	20. p. 468	
7. p. 453	14. p. 460	21. p. 468	

Chapter 19

1. p. 479-502	10. p. 484-485	19. p. 492	28. p. 501
2. p. 478	11. p. 485-487	20. p. 493	29. p. 501
3. p. 479	12. p. 488	21. p. 494-495	30. p. 501
4. p. 480	13. p. 489	22. p. 496	31. p. 502
5. p. 481	14. p. 489	23. p. 496	32. p. 502
6. p. 481-482	15. p. 489	24. p. 497	33. p. 502-503
7. p. 483	16. p. 490	25. p. 498	
8. p. 483	17. p. 490	26. p. 498	
9. p. 487-488	18. p. 491	27. p. 499-500	

Chapter 20

1. p. 507-535	8. p. 512-513	15. p. 520	22. p. 527-528
2. p. 507-508	9. p. 514-515	16. p. 521	23. p. 528-531
3. p. 508	10. p. 515-518	17. p. 522	24. p. 532-533
4. p. 508	11. p. 518	18. p. 523	25. p. 533
5. p. 509	12. p. 518	19. p. 524	26. p. 534
6. p. 510	13. p. 518-519	20. p. 524	27. p. 535
7. p. 511-512	14. p. 519	21. p. 524	28. p. 535

SUGGESTED ANSWERS TO THE CRITICAL THINKING QUESTIONS OF THE TEXTBOOK

Chapter 1

1. No, renewable resources are being used faster than they can be replenished. Yes, many countries in the world live without the enormous resources the United States wastes each year, so it is possible for us to live with less. We can reduce the amount of resources we use and waste each year if we become more aware of our energy and resource consumption and take measures to reduce and change attitudes.

2. Yes, exponential population growth is a major case of environmental problems, so efforts to reduce growth not only can reduce environmental degradation but also improve quality of life for many.
    a. Reduce poverty, especially among women.
    b. Improve health care as well as birth control and family planning programs.
    c. Financial incentives such as no child tax benefits beyond a certain number of children.

3.
    a. While this may be true, the waste of resources and environmental degradation caused by developed countries may outweigh any monetary benefit to developing countries. It is possible to continue economic growth while reducing resource use and environmental degradation.
    b. Economic growth will also slow if resources become so scarce that prices for those resources become prohibitive, which will happen if resources are used up faster than they are replenished. It is more likely that resources will be depleted if the population continues to grow.
    c. Though technology may help find substitutes for renewable resources, which may be environmentally helpful, it may not always find better, cheaper substitutes. Also, loss of these resources means that they would not be available to be used in new ways developed by technology. Reducing waste and consumption would not only allow these resources to remain available but also reduce pollution that may be caused by the use of the resources.
    d. Answer same as above.

4.
    a. Economic growth which favors use of renewable resources, pollution prevention, and efficient, low-waste production.
    b. Economic growth that uses cleanup for pollution control, nonrenewable resources, and inefficient, high-waste production.

5.
    a. Littering
    b. Pouring household substances down the drain that should be disposed of in another way
    c. Collecting rare plants from a state or federal park

6.
    f. I want to do something about this problem.

7. Feelings which might perpetuate the problems: a, b, c, d, e
    Feelings that may help alleviate these problems: f, g, possibly c, e

8. Agree. These five reasons are certainly the most important causes of environmental problems today. Because all of these problems are attributable to rapid population growth, it has to be the most serious root cause of environmental degradation. Another problem is what to do about current pollution problems and how to prevent more pollution in the future.

Chapter 2

1. Disagree. It was obvious from the failure of Biosphere 2 that scientists do not yet understand the intricate interrelationships within and between ecosystems. Earth is made of very complex systems and much work, like that attempted in Biosphere 2, needs to be done in order to understand these systems.

2. Yes, the primary goal of economic systems is based on production and consumption. Alternatives are systems that are based on sustainable growth.

3.
    a. Goods and energy may become more expensive as we transition to a sustainable growth society but eventually costs will stabilize as people learn to live without consuming and wasting as much.
    b. My children would be living in a sustainable society and not have to fear that their actions are polluting the earth and that resources would not be available for their own children.

4. Yes, requiring zero-discharge levels would force industries to recycle or reuse all toxic substances they produce rather than releasing them.

5. Yes, taxing pollution and waste will drastically change the way industries produce products and the way individuals use them.

6. Agree. These proposals are designed to decrease poverty without a negative impact on the environment.

7. I agree with all solutions for shifting to a more environmentally sustainable economy. These principles will ensure that future generations have enough resources and that the environment will be protected.

8. Student diversity will define the variability of answers.

9. I agree with all six principles designed as guidelines in making environmental policy. We should be humble, not do things to the environment that are irreversible, stop activities if there is a least some evidence that it is harmful, prevent problems before they occur, use integrated solutions to solve environmental problems and make sure that environmental risks are equally shared.

10. Most worldviews can be divided into two groups, atomistic and holistic. Atomistic worldviews may be human-centered or life-centered, while holistic worldviews may be biosphere- or ecosystem-centered. Human-centered views have the basic belief that we are in charge and we should manage the planet for our benefit. Life-centered views have an expanded view and believe that all forms of life have inherent value regardless of their usefulness to us. Holistic views, such as the environmental wisdom view, contend that we are not in charge, resources should not be wasted, and our success depends on understanding how the earth sustains itself and integrating these lessons from nature into the ways we think and act. Answers to the last portion of this question will vary.

11. Though we all may have the right to do these things, history has taught us that population growth, consumption and wasting of resources, and lack of consideration of the effects of environmentally degrading land use practices cannot continue if future generations are to have resources, clean air, clean water, etc.

12. Disagree. Understanding how the earth works and improving technology are ways of achieving sustainability, but in order to truly achieve sustainability, the general public must believe that the Earth is an important place to protect and that sustainability practices are worthwhile. Forming an emotional bond with the Earth and its life forms can increase the likelihood that people will work toward sustainability.

Chapter 3

1.
    a. Nothing is ever absolutely proven in science, but the evidence that cigarette smoking can cause death is overwhelming. Therefore, there is a high degree of confidence among scientists and health care professionals that smoking is harmful.
    b. Theory is the strongest idea in science. It is based on a large amount of evidence and is widely accepted.

2. Answers will vary.

3. A scientific law is an explanation of a phenomenon in nature, while a societal law is a man-made law to correct behavior and protect people. A scientific law cannot be broken, while a societal law can be broken.

4. The law of conservation of matter states that matter cannot be created or destroyed but can be transformed into another form. This means that things we consume are merely changed into another form, which often creates problems such as pollution when we consume them.

5. The tree is taking in water, minerals, nutrients, and gases and converting these to carbohydrates, etc., so it is only transforming matter, not creating matter.

6. Everything we know supports the law of conservation of matter, but science must remain open to any new evidence.

7.
    a. No guilt waste
    b. No pollution
    c. Unlimited resources

8. Waste matter is transformed into less noticeable waste but in the process often pollutes, i.e. incineration, burial. Biodegradable waste transforms into recyclable nutrients.

9. $CH_4 + 2O_2 \rightarrow CO_2 + 2 H_2O$
    CO_2 and water vapor, produced from the O_2 requiring burning of methane gas, are both considered greenhouse gases and so may contribute to global warming.

10. Do not invest. This is a misguided or bogus venture because it breaks the 1st law of thermodynamics.

11. The 2nd law of thermodynamics states that energy is transformed into a less useful or lower-quality form as it is changed. Once a barrel of oil has been burned, that energy has been transformed into mostly heat energy and no longer exists as oil.

12. 1st law. Provide excess amounts of energy to areas of the world where it is most needed, transform heat into electrical power, and remove excess heat from troposphere to reduce global warming and convert it to electrical energy. 2nd law. Build recycling engines that convert waste of combustion back into gasoline, perpetual crops that never die, and space travel to set up colonies.

Chapter 4

1.
   a. Plants produce oxygen and carbohydrates that are cycled in living organisms such as us. All of the carbon in living organisms was first incorporated into a plant or other photosynthetic organism. All of the oxygen gas in the air we breathe was produced by a plant or other photosynthetic organism.
   b. Paper, ink, glue. If the bumper sticker were made of recycled items, then it would be a sound application of the slogan.
   c. Decomposers recycle nutrients, which would otherwise be locked in waste material from organisms or dead bodies of organisms.

2.
   a. The aquarium needs soil, plants, water, fish, heat, and light.
   b. It should be able to continue, but as Biosphere 2 taught us, systems can be complex and unpredictable.
   c. The fish will die from suffocation. Plants produce oxygen that the fish requires and also remove nutrients, such as nitrogen, which will also deplete oxygen and create an imbalance of nutrients in the water.

3. The 2nd law of thermodynamics states that when energy is transformed it becomes less usable. When energy flows through a food web most of the energy is lost as heat (low-quality) and so does not end up in the body of organisms in the next level. There is not a true loss of energy at each step since the energy is transformed into heat, so the 1st law of thermodynamics is not broken.

4. The amount of energy and resources used to produce one cow can produce a much larger amount of vegetation. Consequently, people in poor countries grow more crops than raise cattle or other animals.

5. Plants take in carbon from the air in the form of CO_2 but must get nitrogen and phosphorus from the soil.

6. Most organisms that use O_2 and produce CO_2 are more active during the day and, therefore, give off more CO_2 during the day. Automobiles are also more active in the daytime, and they also give off carbon dioxide.

7. Carnivore eating an animal, because much more energy was invested to produce the animal the carnivore ate than the plants the herbivore ate. The carnivore is higher on the food chain, and more energy is required to maintain organisms high on the food chain than those lower on the food chain.

8. Mice eat vegetation and are small; therefore, many more mice can be supported within a given area than lions in the same area, since lions are large carnivores. Lions depend on eating mostly large herbivores, which requires much more vegetation and area than mice.

9.
   a. Nutrients would not be recycled within the ecosystem, and everything would die.
   b. No oxygen would be produced, and no carbon cycling within living systems would occur.

1. Theories are based on large amounts of evidence and are the most accepted ideas in science. Biological evolution is a theory that has stood the test of time and has more evidence and scientific support than ever. It has the same level of acceptance as any other theory in science. While it could be true that over time humans may develop bodies that can better detoxify pollutants, this selection will eliminate an unpredictable number of us as well as other organisms. Rather than facing such an unclear future, it makes more sense to reduce pollution.

2. Many more species have become extinct than are alive today, so if no extinction had ever occurred, there would be many more species today. However, without prior extinction many species would never have evolved in the first place, so there probably would not have been as many species in the past as there have been.

3. Extinction is a natural process, but extinction caused by human activities is not a natural process and may be decreasing the level of biodiversity at such a fast rate that the resulting loss of species may create a mass extinction with unpredictable consequences.

4. The study of environmental science includes the study of biology and biological systems. The study of biology is based on evolution.

5. If no competition existed, then an organism could fill its fundamental niche. Because competition does exist, a species cannot occupy its entire niche but only some portion of it, its realized niche.

6. Humans and cockroaches may live in the same house and eat the same food, but they don't occupy the same niche. Cockroaches, being small, may live in walls or under the floor of a house and can tolerate more drastic temperature differences, lack of food and water, and toxins. Cockroaches also eat a wider variety of food than humans and reproduce at a much greater rate. Humans and cockroaches are somewhat in competition for the same resources, but since cockroaches are small and stealthy, they manage to live in the same area as humans.

7. Humans are generalists because they can eat a wide variety of food and live in a broad range of climates but are specialists because they often create niches for themselves that have narrow tolerances of temperature, food types, etc.

8. There is a need in society for both generalists and specialists. For example, technology and medicine are so complicated that it is necessary to study narrow fields within these disciplines in order to gain expertise. Conversely, it is important for the study of other disciplines, such as education, law, or politics to have broader knowledge about a wider range of topics.

Chapter 6

1.
   a. Little water
   b. Permafrost.
   c. Cold temperatures
   d. Little light
   e. Long, warm summers

2. Both of these ecosystems have much less precipitation than tropical forests. Only smaller, fewer and less diverse vegetation grows in these areas, which cannot support the diversity of life that is supported by the larger, more diverse vegetation of the tropical forests.

3. The floor of the tropical forest has little light or space compared to the tall, dense vegetation. Vertically, there exists a wide variety of niches, with differing amounts of sunlight, which creates specialized plant and animal niches and allows for a large variety of species to coexist.

4.
    a. Eating meat raised on former tropical forestland.
    b. Eating crops raised on former tropical forestland.
    c. Using timber cut from tropical forestland.

5.
    a. Tropical and temperate grasslands
    b. Temperate grasslands

6. This would only be a postponement of the problem. Containers may be damaged by the extreme cold and the salt and may leak, which would allow dispersal of the contents that may be transported by ocean currents and upwelling. Also, little understood, deep dwelling ecosystems may be damaged or completely lost if containers leak.

7.
    a. Vacationing, golfing, boating, or buying real estate along the coast encourages coastal development.
    b. Eating seafood, which results in over-fishing or farming in coastal areas.

8.
    a.
        1. Improve local economy
        2. Provide needed housing
        3. Reduce swampy areas in which insects breed
    b.
        1. Wetlands are the oceans "nursery" and loss of them would reduce numbers of many fish, shellfish, etc.
        2. Wetlands are important breeding grounds for many waterfowl.
        3. Wetlands protect the coast from major storm damage.
        4. Wetlands reduce coastal erosion.
    If the community would greatly benefit from the development of the wetlands and there were not endangered or threatened species in the wetlands, then I may vote for ecologically sensitive development as a compromise. Retention of most of the wetland within the neighborhood, including leaving trees and other vegetation where possible and providing for erosion control, not only would be more environmentally responsible but more aesthetically pleasing as well.

9. Both are regions of high species diversity and should be saved. Coral reefs protect coastlines against major storms, support 25% of all marine species and 65% of all marine fish species, remove carbon dioxide from the atmosphere, provide developing countries with jobs and food, and support fishing and tourism industries. Tropical Forests are home to 50-80% of the world's terrestrial species, provide food for developing countries and medicines worldwide, remove carbon dioxide from the atmosphere, affect the earth's climate, and support the tourism industry. These are only a few examples of the importance of these ecosystems to the world, but if only one can be saved, it should be the rainforest because it is home to more species and has a greater affect on earth's climate.

Chapter 7

1. Tropical rainforests have a higher canopy, more rainfall, and faster cycling of nutrients than temperate forests. This allows for faster growth and more vertical niches, which creates greater species variety.

2. While temperate areas are not as diverse as the tropics, they still have a lot of diversity. Also, they are where many people live and where crops and livestock are grown, so the health and maintenance of these biomes is important for survival of the human species and many of Earth. Though diversity is also not as great in Polar regions, they are home to many uniquely adapted animals and much of the world's fresh water, so it is also important to maintain the health of this and all other biomes.

3. Size and degree of isolation. On a small island the immigration rate is lower and the extinction rate higher than on a larger island, so the number of different species is usually less.

4. Remove debris from the outside of the house, trim shrubs, check foundation for access to the interior of the house. Try to stop the invaders from entering by sealing cracks, chalking around windows and doors, chalking or insulating around plumbing and electrical fixtures, etc. Make sure food is not left out and that the house is clean and dry.

5.
   a. Succession is very slow and a disturbed ecosystem may never fully recover. Also, species may be replaced by introduced species rather than native species.
   b. What is also unpredictable are the effects that destruction or disturbance of ecosystems will have on the organisms, including humans, which live within those ecosystems. An example of this is the emergence of diseases previously unknown or isolated within intact ecosystems.
   c. Research shows that biodiversity is necessary for stability within ecosystems; however, the level of biodiversity required is unclear. Because this is not well understood, it is important to protect biodiversity until we can better understand the effects of reducing it. Old-growth forests are vastly more diverse than tree farms.

Chapter 8

1. Population density or the number of organisms present is not directly affected by abiotic factors, such as light, because abiotic factors are either favorable or unfavorable to organisms but are independent of the number of organism present. Biotic factors such as reproductive rate and food availability have a great affect on the population density.

2. Both exponential and logistic growth are advantageous for species when resources are plentiful because populations can increase in number, but as resources are depleted and growth approaches the carrying capacity of species, logistic growth gains the advantage because, unlike exponential growth, population growth slows as it nears the carrying capacity.

3. One reason pest species are pests are their large numbers. This occurs because of their high rate of reproduction, which is indicative of r-selected species. K-selected species are more likely to become endangered because of low rates or reproduction.

4.
   a. Early loss
   b. Late loss

5. Humans have altered and modified the areas in which they live to avoid environmental resistance factors. Yes, it is likely to continue as technology continues to advance, but hopefully in a more ecologically sustainable way.

6. I agree with all four of the principles and lessons of sustainability because the lessons are simply that we should mimic nature when possible because it has worked for millions of years in a sustainable way. Reliance on fossil fuels that create pollution, lack of reuse and recycling, and wasteful use of resources all violate sustainability principles. Yes, I would like to change my lifestyle, so that it does not violate these principles.

Chapter 9

1. Weathering creates soil but also creates sediment that can pollute water if it erodes. Erosion is a natural cycling process, but too much erosion pollutes waterways and removes topsoil. Plate tectonics, while often violent, have created mountains and other features of Earth's surface.

2. Answers will vary but may include:
   a. The 2nd law of thermodynamics states that energy is degraded to a lower-quality, less useful form as it is used. Extracting most minerals in seawater would require such a tremendous amount of high-quality energy that it would not be energetically feasible to do this.
   b. High-quality energy may be wasted on retrieving low-quality minerals. Minerals will become economically depleted.
   c. This may be energetically feasible, but solar energy may not be useful enough to mine increasingly rare minerals. The loss of nonrenewable minerals should also be considered.
   d. High-quality energy would be increasingly used to retrieve lower and lower-quality minerals. The minerals will become quickly economically depleted.

3. Answers will vary but may include:
   a. Support. Public land should remain so. Leasing may be allowed.
   b. Oppose/Support. Other types of mining operations pay 8–16% of net value, not gross revenue, so hard rock mining should also pay a percent of net value.
   c. Support. As with other types of mining, hard rock mining companies should be responsible for environmental cleanup of the areas mined.

4. Answers will vary but may include:
   Earthquake. Know likelihood of occurrence; whether buildings where you live and work are designed for earthquakes; disaster protocol.
   Volcano. Don't live or work near volcano; know likelihood of predicted occurrence; evacuation routes.

5. Answers will vary but may include: Any activity that increases runoff or loss of vegetation.

6. Inorganic fertilizers are cheaper because they are more readily available, but they don't add organic matter and tend to dry out. Addition of organic fertilizers improves texture and water retention of the soil.

7. Answers will vary but may include:
    a. Reduce use of minerals by finding alternative. Mandatory recycling of minerals.
    b. Levy fines on individuals, businesses, and industries for activities that contribute to erosion. Encourage planting of vegetation.

Chapter 10

1. Answers will vary but may include:
    Agree. Cigarette smoking causes premature death, costs millions of dollars each year, and has no value except to the tobacco industry and tobacco farmers. Many more people would benefit from fewer people smoking than benefit from the industry, and millions of lives would be saved.

2. Answers will vary but may include:
    No. The effects of most chemicals are not known, and it may be too expensive to test each one. Many scientists and health care workers want greater emphasis placed on pollution prevention to reduce risk of exposure to chemicals. This approach, called the precautionary principle, places the burden of proof of safety on the manufacturers who believe it is cost prohibitive.

3.
    a. Chemicals can be safe at certain doses, so avoiding harmful levels is possible and should be pursued.
    b. There are thousands of chemicals, and it is unlikely that we can develop immunity to them all. Millions of people may die in the present from exposure to toxic or harmful levels of chemicals. These chemicals can also affect other organisms in the environment. It is wiser to try to reduce levels of chemicals.
    c. Genetic engineering is not a fix all. It is not known what the impact of genetic engineering will be on the reversal of damage to humans and the environment caused by chemical pollutants.

4. Answers will vary but may include:
    What is the toxicity of the chemical? Where will it be used? Who will be exposed? Does it persist, or bioaccumulate? How will is be disposed?
    a. If an extremely toxic chemical were necessary for industrial purposes and had strict safety precautions designed to protect workers and the environment, then it would be acceptable for that chemical to be used in society.
    b. The level of toxicity of chemicals used by individuals depends on the expertise and need of the individual as long as safety precautions and proper disposal practices are observed.
    c. Only nontoxic levels of chemicals are safe for children.

5. Answers will vary but may include:
    It would be better to err on the side of caution and set the levels to protect the most sensitive people in a population, especially children.

6. Answers will vary but may include:
   The overuse of antibiotics has created bacteria that are immune to the effects of the antibiotics.
   The routine use of antibiotics in livestock should stop. Antibiotics should be used to treat diseased
   cattle only, and the choice of treatment should be other than that routinely used on humans.

7.
   a. Being single, smoking, having unprotected sex and/or multiple sex partners, drinking and
      driving, and not eating a balanced diet are examples of risky behavior.
   b. Urban setting, commuting to work more than 10 miles, crime, air pollution, and water
      pollution are examples of risks from where one might live.
   c. Working in potentially hazardous environments such a medical lab, working in a potentially
      dangerous environment such as manufacturing plant, working night shifts, working long
      hours, and stress are examples of work-related risks.

8.
   a.
      1. Data and models are not always reliable, but experimentation in nature is not always
         possible.
      2. Industry profits and everyone suffers when certain levels of chemicals are allowed in the
         environment. The government, often influenced by lobbyists, determines allowable
         levels.
      3. Both risks are important, and scientific data should be used in making decisions.
      4. Independent scientists should do risk analysis, and a combination of government
         agencies, independent scientists, and public representatives should review results.
      5. A prevention approach should be the primary goal.
      6. Yes, cumulative effects should be considered.
      7. Answers will vary.
      8. No, risk levels should not be higher for workers than for the general public. Workers and their
         families, as the general public, should have a voice in determining acceptable risk levels.
      9. Answers will vary.
   b. Answers can follow the same patterns as in a.

Chapter 11

1. It is rational because it is part of their culture to have large families. Also, women have low status
   in society, and extreme poverty is very common. To reverse this, poverty would need to decrease,
   and women would need more status in society.

2. Providing drinking water for the world. Population growth has caused water to be used faster than
   it can be replenished in many parts of the world, causing shortages and a decrease in quality.

3. If a country has a large number of people in the prereproductive stage, even with replacement level
   fertility, it would take many years to reach ZPG because the birth rate would continue to be higher
   than the death rate until the number of prereproductive people approximately equals the number of
   reproductive people.

4. I don't believe the overall population of the United States is too high except in certain areas,
   especially along the coasts. The loss of habitat and degradation of environmental services in high
   population areas is a direct result of population growth.

5. Those who oppose promotion of reduction in births do so for religious reasons and the freedom to choose how many children they have. Those who promote reduction in births know that one of six people on earth does not have basic necessities and that environmental degradation has been caused by explosive population growth. I support reduction in births until everyone's basic needs are met and environmental degradation is reversed.

6.
   a. If illegal immigration could be reduced, the number of legal immigrants would not be considered a problem. The United States has a tradition of allowing many immigrants and refugees into the country, which should be continued, but the number of illegal immigrants should be reduced.
   b. Agree. Attempts to reduce illegal immigration could include: tighter border control, better attempts to locate and deport illegal immigrants, stiff penalties and fines for those who hire illegal immigrants, and aid to countries from which there are high numbers of illegal immigrants in an effort to improve living and working conditions which drive people to illegally immigrate to the United States.
   c. Disagree. Our population is slowing but not declining, so we should not encourage population growth.
   d. Agree. We are the most wasteful country on Earth. Every additional person in this country adds to that waste. Slowing population growth, slowing waste, and consumption are all necessary to reach sustainability.
   e. Disagree. Humans cannot live sustainability on Earth while consuming and wasting at today's rate. The greatest factor in loss of resources and pollution is population growth, so humans should not be encouraged to have children. In some countries that are facing mass starvation, they may even lose the right to have as many children as they want.

7. An average of 216,438.35 people would need to be shipped off each day. An average of 2,164.38 space shuttles per day would be needed. This is not a logical solution to the Earth's population problem.

8. Developing countries do cause much environmental degradation, but it is mostly local. Developed countries are causing global environmental degradation by their consumption and waste, and they also have better capability and resources to improve their environmental impact.

9. It may be true that there are enough resources for everyone and that distribution is a problem. However, distribution is always likely to be a problem, and though it is important to improve distribution of resources, reducing consumption and waste by developed countries and improving the ability of developing countries to sufficiently support its own population would do more to solve the problems of overpopulation, poverty, etc.

10. High price of operation of the car would encourage use of other forms of transportation. Safe, easy, accessible, and inexpensive alternate transportation would encourage the use of other forms.

11. While it may not be a right, housing certainly is a need, and efforts to provide at least minimal housing should occur.

12. Agree. Subsidies should be used to discourage sprawl. High-density residential development, as long as it is convenient, attractive, and safe, is an effective way to reduce sprawl as well as revitalize downtown areas. It also can create a closer sense of community, reduce use of transportation, and allow for better opportunity for recycling.

13.
   a. Reduce poverty, encourage people to have fewer children, and reinforce trends toward smaller families.
   b. Ecological land-use planning, revitalization of existing towns, and urban growth boundaries.

Chapter 12

1. We also have not proven that cigarette smoking causes cancer, but the evidence is so overwhelming that its use is regulated just as emissions standards for many pollutants should be.

2. Answers will vary.

3. Yes, all tall smokestacks should be banned. While they may improve local air pollution, they create regional air pollution that is devastating areas such as the Appalachian Mountains in the United States.

4. Radiation temperature inversion is a mostly daily occurrence, oscillating as the sun goes up and down, but subsidence temperature inversions depend on weather patterns and can last much longer and are therefore usually more severe.

5. Yes, they have proven effective in reducing pollutants. Because this method relies on self-reporting and monitoring, there is often cheating. Companies should be penalized if they fail to report or monitor properly.

6. I am for establishing stricter emission standards of ultra fine particles. Yes, there is an EPA regulation that was supported by a Supreme Court ruling that will reduce the acceptable size of ultra fine particles, but it has not yet been enforced.

7. *Relying on pollution cleanup rather than prevention.*
    Yes. Pollution prevention not only reduces pollution but also is less costly in the long run.
    Failing to increase fuel efficiency standards for cars and light trucks.
    Yes. Increasing fuel efficiency here would be the quickest, most effective way to reduce air pollution because these are the most commonly driven vehicles.
    Not adequately regulating emissions from inefficient, two-cycle gasoline engines.
    Yes. These include lawn equipment and boating equipment, which are extremely numerous, and are much worse polluters than cars. Also, fuel and oil from them is much more likely to be spilled.
    Doing too little to reduce emissions of carbon dioxide and other greenhouse gases.
    Yes. Though this is expensive, it is necessary. Often the technology that comes from control standards actually stimulates economic growth and can be sold in the marketplace.

8. Agree. Both outdoor and indoor air pollution cause health problems, and outdoor air pollution degrades the environment. For outdoor air pollution reduction, reducing dependency on fossil fuels, improving efficiency, and relying more on renewable energy would help bring about a shift. For outdoor air pollution, increasing the cost of smoking, banning smoking indoors, and reducing poverty are ways to help bring about a shift toward prevention.

9. Answers will vary but may include:
    1. Increase fuel efficiency in cars and trucks.
    2. Increase mass transit use.
    3. Slow population growth.

<u>Chapter 13</u>

1. Every 1°C rise in Earth's average temperature would shift climate belts and change where crops could grow, as well as affecting the makeup of 1/3 of the forests.

2. As the Earth warms, changes in the hydrologic cycle such as glacial melt, droughts, floods, and changes in water availability and quality may affect climate patterns. With a warmer Earth, more plant material will decompose, adding more carbon into the carbon cycle possibly in the form of carbon dioxide.

3. Clearing forests should not affect Earth's albedo because both forests and grasslands are darker surfaces and have low albedo, but converting forests to grasslands will increase temperature because of increases in carbon dioxide and nitrous oxide, which are greenhouse gases.

4. Ocean currents, which transfer heat, may be interrupted by global warming and less heat would be conveyed to Europe and the eastern North America.

5. Answers will vary but may include: Act now as a part of a no-regrets strategy. Everything feasible should be done to slow atmospheric warming to avoid serious potential problems. Slowing global warming by reducing fossil fuel consumption and deforestation, for example, will also have other beneficial effects such as decreased biodiversity loss and pollution. Also, new technologies may arise from developments designed to reduce global warming.

6. I agree with all proposals for slowing atmospheric warming. Harmful effects of not taking these actions would be global warming, which will change climate, sea level, damage crops, increase incidence in skin cancer, and eye cataracts. I also agree with proposals to prepare for long-term solutions to climate change. The consequences of not being prepared are food and water shortages, loss of buildings along the coast, pollution, and loss of habitat.

7. Yes. The United States uses and wastes much more than their share of the world's resources, so they should bear the greatest burden in dealing with high CO_2 emissions. A large part of the world's CO_2 problem has been caused by the U.S.

8. Yes. Developed countries largely created the causes of global warming.

9. Activities such as driving a car, flying, or any other activity that burns fossil fuels and consuming goods that have been grown in deforested areas, especially tropical forest areas, contribute to increases in greenhouse gases. I would be willing to use mass transit transportation and try to purchase products that have been produced in a sustainable fashion, such as timber that is certified as being sustainably produced and coffee that has been certified as being grown under shade trees.

10. If someone has been diagnosed with basal cell skin cancer, then it is likely they have already been excessively exposed to harmful U V-B rays, and since there is a 15–40 year lag between excessive exposure and skin cancer, they are likely to have a recurrence of skin cancer, which would be exacerbated by living in an area which has a lot of sunny days, such as Australia or Florida.

11.
    a.
        1. Increase fuel efficiency in automobiles, improve mass transit systems, and encourage cleaner transportation technologies.
        2. Dramatically slow deforestation around the world.
        3. Reduce industrial greenhouse gas emissions around the world.
    b.
        1. Cut emissions of all ozone-depleting chemicals around the world.
        2. Encourage development of alternate chemicals to replace ozone-depleting chemicals.
        3. Enforce the 1992 Copenhagen Protocol.

<u>Chapter 14</u>

1. Removing ground and surface water for irrigation, energy production, cooling, and manufacturing. Reducing the need for water for irrigation would help the most. Reducing the use of energy and reducing waste in industry and municipalities.

2. Answers will vary.

3. It is the cause of water shortages. More people require more food, which increases the need for irrigation. More people require more drinking water, energy, and products that require water to be produced.

4. Water, like any resource, should not be used faster than it can be replenished. The loss of water, due to overuse, has created an ecological disaster which is creating an economic disaster due to lack of water for agriculture, increased desertification of surrounding areas, salinization of cropland, and increased health problems for people living in the area.

5. Answers will vary but may include:
   Yes, we should raise the price of water. Water is becoming scarcer and is still being wasted. Higher cost will encourage people to conserve and may slow development in water scarce areas.
   a. Initially businesses and jobs may suffer from higher prices of water but with new water saving technologies and conservation, it will rebound.
   b. Crop production will also initially cost more, but with water conservation and growth of plants, which require less water, it should stabilize. It may be necessary to have incentives to encourage conservation rather than higher costs.
   c. Everyone's lifestyle should change toward a more conservation minded, waste-reducing lifestyle.
   d. Poor people would suffer more from increased water costs, and it may be necessary to find a different strategy, such as incentives, to encourage water conservation for this group.
   e. The environment, which supports us all, will be positively affected, which will benefit all organisms on Earth.

6. Various options in answering this questions could include tankless water heaters, use of gray water, etc.

7. Building on floodplains, removing vegetation, and draining wetlands. Slowing or stopping these activities.

8.
   a. Infectious agents – point sources
   b. Oxygen-demanding wastes – point source
   c. Inorganic chemicals – nonpoint source
   d. Organic chemicals – nonpoint source
   e. Plant nutrients – nonpoint source
   f. Sediment – nonpoint source
   g. Radioactive materials – point source
   h. Heat – point source

9. Answers may vary but may include:
   10 ppb. It will be very expensive to reduce the levels to 10 ppb and even more expensive to reduce to even lower levels. The WHO and the National Academy of Science both propose 10 ppb as their minimum standard even though many scientists believe it should be lower.

10. Answers will vary but may include:

Yes, dumping of waste and untreated sewage should be banned. The long-term effects of dumping are unclear, but there is evidence, such as the degradation of the Chesapeake Bay and Gulf of Mexico, that it is harmful and so should be avoided. Sewage wastes can be treated by relatively inexpensive natural methods using natural or artificial wetlands, which would allow even developing countries to treat their sewage waste. Other types of wastes such as radioactive, oil, and hazardous industrial wastes should be disposed of in the most environmentally acceptable way, and tankers that transport hazardous material should be double hulled. Exceptions for sewage waste may occur in areas where there is a small population and using wetlands is not practical. Exceptions for other types of waste should not occur. Heavy fines or incentives for not dumping would help successfully regulate dumping.

11. Irrigating crops more efficiently, using water-saving technologies in industries and homes, and improving and integrating management of water basins and groundwater supplies are three ways to manage the world's water resources.

12. Reducing toxicity or volume of pollutants, reusing wastewater, and recycling pollutants are three ways of reducing water pollution in the world.

Chapter 15

1. Answers will vary but may include:
   a. Agree. Both glass and plastic beverage containers are recyclable, though recycling glass is easier, and recycling would conserve resources.
   b. Agree. Separating materials is the most efficient and inexpensive collection method. In addition, people and businesses will be more aware of how, what, and why to recycle.
   c. Agree. This approach has been shown to encourage recycling.
   d. Agree. Even a nominal fee will encourage conservation and use of reusable shopping bags.

2. The 2nd law of thermodynamics states that energy conversion produces less quality energy. Source-separation requires that items are sorted where they are used, then are transferred to recycling centers already separated. Centralized programs collect mixed waste, which then has to be transferred to recycling centers where large quantities must be separated and which is less energy efficient because it requires more energy to separate.

3. Yes, an eco-industrial revolution will help move toward sustainability, as well as reduce waste and pollution. Yes, it would be possible to phase in this type of revolution in the United States. For example, Ray Anderson has voluntarily implemented many innovative projects to move toward sustainability in his company, and it is saving his company millions of dollars each year. It would be possible for other companies to do the same, though stricter regulations may be required.

4. It costs money to redesign manufacturing processes, so some companies may participate without redesigning their processes to reduce waste because the waste will be used. The problem with this idea is that there could be more waste produced than other companies can use. The point of this plan is to reduce waste as well as reuse and recycle it.

5. Yes, a service flow economy provides profits for companies but reduces resource use and waste. For example, Xerox Corporation leases photocopiers and thereby leases document services rather than selling copiers. The company maintains the copiers and recycles their parts when replaced by a new copier. Yes, it would be possible to convert to a service flow economy. As other companies see the profits made by this method, they may adopt the same strategies; however, other companies may require stricter regulations to accept these changes.

6. No, I would not want these in my community because I would be concerned about pollution and odors. Rather, I would want a reduction in waste and an increase in recycling and reusing resources. If everything was done to reduce the amount of waste then I may accept one or more of these facilities to handle the waste, if they used the most efficient and environmentally safe technology available.

7.
   a. Agree. Charging a tax or fee forces people to develop alternatives.
   b. Disagree. It may be impossible to ban all land disposal and incineration of hazardous waste at this time but charging fees or having incentives to reduce these activities would lead to technologies that may make a ban feasible.
   c. Agree. These incentives would make companies more likely to find alternatives to their current methods of disposal and create new technologies to reduce resource use.
   d. Agree. Countries with large amounts of hazardous waste should reduce or dispose of their own waste rather than ship them to developing countries. Being able to ship waste to other countries does not encourage reduction in waste.

8. Develop products that use less material and energy to be produced; develop production methods that minimize use and waste of raw material, water, and energy; and do no damage to any ecosystem throughout their production and use.

Chapter 16

1.
   a. While cultivating more land may produce more food, most of this land is unsuitable for crops and would require vast amounts of fertilizers and/or irrigation. Also, it would destroy forest resources, reduce biodiversity, and affect water quality and quantity.
   b. About 75% of the 200 commercially valuable marine fish are overfished already; increasing fish catches would only worsen this serious problem.
   c. The high yield in small volumes of water make aquaculture an efficient, cost-effective method of producing fish. However, the concentrated wastes, large land and water usage, and contaminated tanks are drawbacks for this type of agriculture.
   d. Increasing crop yield per acre of land allows for increased production of food without the need to cultivate land, which protects wild lands and biodiversity, and feeds more people. However, the genetically modified plants being developed to increase crop yield are controversial.

2. It would be morally unacceptable not to care about the plight of hungry and malnourished people on Earth. Malnourishment causes mental and physical retardation and disease, and it is perpetuated generation after generation. Reducing poverty, slowing population growth, and giving aid directly to the poor to help them become self-reliant are three ways to reduce hunger both in the U.S. and around the world.

3. Yes, if I were starving, I would eat insects. Many people around the world already eat insects and encouraging more people to eat insects, where malnutrition is a problem, would increase their protein consumption.

4. Energy-intensive agriculture relies heavily on fuel oil, so a dramatic increase in the price of oil would cause prices of crops to dramatically increase also. This would cause my food bill to increase, and I would have to be more selective and less wasteful.

5. Wild grazing animals may require less water and grain and produce less waste than conventional livestock. Though it may not be desirable, I do not think it is unethical as long as the animals are not endangered.

6.
   a. No, subsidies should not all be eliminated for farmers, they cannot control weather, crop prices, pests, etc., and we all depend on them to grow our food.
   b. Yes, the government should subsidize sustainable agricultural practices.

7.
   a. Support. Only a few species of plants and animals are used for 90% of the world's food. Many more of the Earth's perennial plant species could be exploited as food and are often better adapted to regional soil and climate conditions than the traditional crops, and are cheaper to grow. Animal alternatives, such as insects, are readily available and are a good source of protein. Shifting toward poultry, which are cheaper and less environmentally degrading to raise than cattle or sheep, is a more sustainable form of agriculture.
   b. Support. Genetically modified foods need less water and fertilizer, grow faster, require fewer pesticides and are more resistant to disease. The downside is that they may create herbicide-resistant weeds, cause new food allergies, harm beneficial insects, and may have unpredictable genetic and ecological effects.
   c. Support. Perennial food crops can be more adaptive to climate and soil types, do not require tilling or replanting, reduce energy use, save water, and reduce erosion.

8. Answers will vary but may include:
   Yes, I believe that government subsidies should be reduced because they contribute to overfishing. I am sure I would be unhappy if my livelihood depended on fishing, but I hope I would understand that the only way to allow recovery of depleted stocks of fish is to stop overfishing.

9. I would oppose this project. There are large amounts of concentrated wastes as well as destruction of the natural coastal environment, and the tanks often become so contaminated that they cannot be used after five years. To sacrifice coastal ecosystems for limited return seems illogical. If the project does occur, safeguards, such as careful selection of the location and strict pollution regulations, should be in place.

10. No, there are other methods of pest control that do not have the damaging effects that synthetic chemicals have, such as killing organisms other than the target pest, pollution of air and water, and harming wildlife and humans. Genetic engineering of pest resistant crops, crop rotation, and use of natural predators and bacteria are only some of the available methods of controlling pests without chemicals.

11. No, the long-term effects of DDT are too dangerous for it to be used. Making sure there is no standing water, using insect repellents, and encouraging natural mosquito predators are ways of reducing the likelihood of contracting West Nile fever or malaria.

12.
   a. Increase irrigation efficiency, conserve soil and use more perennial crops.
   b. Institute integrated pest management, increase biological pest control and development more pest resistant crops.

Chapter 17

1. Yes, I favor the reintroduction of both wolves and grizzly bears to Yellowstone Park and other public lands because these are their natural habitats and the health of any ecosystem requires its intact natural biodiversity.

2. I agree with the four principles that biologists have suggested. Protection of biodiversity, no subsidies or tax breaks for extracting resources, compensation to the American people for use of public lands, and responsibility for environmental damage by users of public lands are important considerations for public land use in this country. I disagree with the suggestions of developers and resource extractors. Selling public land, cutting old-growth forests, opening parks and refuges to oil drilling, mining, and commercial development, doing away with the National Park Service, and easing protection of wetlands all go against the protection of wild lands and biodiversity that may never be recoverable if lost. It also goes against the purpose of the park system, which is to protect wild places for future generations.

3.
    a. Agree. Banning or limiting grazing in riparian, sensitive habitats and other ecologically unsustainable areas and allowing individuals or groups to purchase grazing permits on public land and not use the land for grazing are ideas that will protect sensitive areas from degradation by overgrazing.
    b. Agree. Longer timber rotations, selective or strip cutting, reduction of road building, certification of sustainably grown timber, etc. will help preserve old-growth and other forest ecosystems.

4. Continue the practice of sustainable timber management and have long-term income. Protection of ecosystems is more important than making money.

5. No, this practice should stop. There are enough private lands to provide needed timber, and subsidies cost taxpayers over one billion dollars a year.

6. I agree with all the proposals for protecting the world's tropical forests. Most of the products from tropical rainforests are used in developed countries, so deforestation is mostly a result of demand from developed countries. To protect these resources, developed countries should fund at least a large percentage of the money needed for preservation of these forests in poorer developing countries.

7. Protect tropical forest areas that are in danger of being lost and are rich in diversity, reduce poverty, slow population growth, phase out government subsidies that encourage unsustainable use, and use debt-for-nature swaps to encourage countries to protect tropical forests. I would try to support all of these activities.

8. I agree with all proposals listed. Protecting the U.S. National Parks preserves them for future generations, and these proposals will sustain and expand the system.

9. Yes, I would support the control burn. Surface fires, which burn undergrowth, can reduce the chance of more destructive crown fires, which burn whole trees and jump from treetop to treetop. Nearby residents should be notified, and the area near the control burn should be closed to the public.

10. Yes, I am in favor of establishing more wilderness areas either by the federal government or private groups. Once these are lost, they will not be replaced, and there is increasing visitor demand for wilderness areas.

11.

    a. Eliminate logging old-growth forests, encourage recreational uses rather than logging, mining, etc. to boost local economies and mandate sustainable logging practices.

    b. Require integrated management, locate parking lots and commercial facilities outside parks and shuttle people in, increase funding to maintain parks, and increase the number of rangers.

    c. Intensely manage popular wilderness areas, permit only skilled wilderness visitors in remote wilderness areas, and eliminate visitors in ecologically sensitive areas.

    d. Establish protected areas, use integrated coastal management practices, and regulate and prevent pollution.

Chapter 18

1. It is true that species become extinct, but if the extinction is caused by humans, it does matter. Loss of biodiversity indicates the degradation of the environment. We should not interfere with the natural world to such an extent that we degrade the environment to the detriment of our own survival and the survival of many other species as well.

2. I believe that all organisms have a place and role to play in their own natural environment. Though it is certainly important that we protect humans, it is also important to preserve ecosystems for the health of the planet. The removal of any species will affect the ecosystem from which it was removed in ways we cannot predict.

3.

    a. Agree, but alternatives to the use of animals in research should always be sought. Millions of human lives have been saved and improved because of animal research. The use of animals should be very closely monitored, and the value of research using animals should be carefully scrutinized.

    b. Agree, but facilities should be thoughtfully and carefully designed to provide habitats as natural as possible. Support for the plight of endangered and threatened animals can be increased by the education and exposure to the public that zoos provide. Also, many zoos use captive breeding programs to increase numbers of endangered or threatened animals.

    c. Agree, but zoos should attempt not to breed animals to the extent of over population. If animals are overcrowded, all will suffer, so it may be necessary to remove excess animals, especially old, weak or sick animals.

4. Use hot water to kill them where it is practical, and use small amounts of pesticides, designed to kill fire ants, directly on mounds to avoid killing any other species.

5.

    e. Wildlife should be protected.

6. I like bats because they are interesting. Bats eat millions of insects every night, including those that carry disease, so they help keep insects in check. I would feel fortunate to have bats feeding in my yard in the evening and would enjoy watching them.

7. Purple cone flower, rat snake, and hummingbirds. I chose the cone flower because I appreciate the beauty of wildflowers, and it is my favorite. I chose the rat snake because I like the chance to see more secretive animals such as snakes, and I know they perform important services in the wild. I chose the hummingbird because they are so bold, fast, and fun to watch.

8. I would encourage the development of tree farms on land that is already cut or degraded. Also, certain types of sustainable logging might be permitted in less sensitive areas so that the squirrel is protected. Timber could be cut, and with sustainable logging practices, more jobs could be saved over a longer period of time.

9. I agree with proposals to improve the ESA and disagree with all proposals to weaken it. Endangered species may be lost forever if protecting them does not work with current laws.

10. *Species 2000* and other similar databases contain baseline information about the Earth's known species. This allows for the study of global biodiversity and will make it easier to determine which areas are more sensitive. Developers and extractors would not want these studies to prevent them from developing and extracting from these areas.

11. Try to plant shrubs, flowers, and vegetables that deer don't eat; put up an electric fence or deer fence to keep them out; or plant so many plants that a least some of them survive.

12. No, if only a few species are hunted, they will soon become endangered also. It is very hard to monitor hunting of whales, so I don't think commercial whale hunting should be allowed.

13. Determine what species and ecosystems we have; locate and protect the most endangered ecosystems and species; and give private landowners incentives to help protect endangered species and ecosystems.

Chapter 19

1. I do not believe it is possible to continue to use oil at this rate indefinitely. To run out of the most commonly used energy source in the United States would dramatically affect the lives of my children and grandchildren. Transportation, climate control, electricity, etc. would all be adversely affected. If waste is decreased and alternate forms of energy are more widely used, we can depend less on oil and not have shortages.

2. Find ways to reduce fuel consumption such as driving less, buying a fuel efficient car, using mass transit, etc.; recycle and compost organic waste; make sure your house is well insulated; turn off appliances, lights, etc. when not in use; and adjust thermostat to use less energy. I already try to do most of these things to conserve energy.

3. The best way to become less dependent on oil imports is to reduce consumption and waste. However, we may need to continue to import oil to meet demand. This can put our economy at the mercy of oil importing countries because a jump in the price of oil can cause a recession or worse. If we don't import, we may be forced to drill in environmentally sensitive areas in the United States. Reducing consumption, reducing waste, and using alternate energy sources would help reduce dependence on oil

4.
   a. Agree, if drilling is not allowed in environmentally sensitive areas.
   b. Agree. People will drive less, and individuals and industries will waste less if gas and oil cost more. Heating oil for homes should be taxed less.
   c. Disagree, until environmentally acceptable methods of dealing with the waste are found, nuclear power plants should not be encouraged. They are also very expensive to operate.
   d. Disagree. All older facilities should be shut down, but newer, safer facilities could continue to operate.

5. No. This pristine area should be protected. It is too risky to explore or drill in this environmentally intact area.

6. It should be buried underground which is the method favored by the U.S. Academy of Sciences.

7. I would not like it, but if I lived in a remote area that was chosen because it was not populated and was not environmentally sensitive, then I might accept it if all precautions for safe transport were taken.

8.
   a. Disagree. Until an environmentally safe solution for waste is developed and cost of the power plants is brought down, nuclear energy is not the best way to solve our energy problems. Reducing waste and consumption as well as developing alternative energy sources are not only more economical but better for the environment.

9. If the nuclear plant has the best safety precautions possible, then I would rather live near it because pollution from coal-fired plants is much more likely to harm me.

10. Yes, nuclear accidents can affect areas hundreds and thousands of miles away and create contamination so severe near the reactors that the surrounding areas cannot be occupied. It is imperative that these reactors be closed to protect people and the environment from a catastrophic accident.

Chapter 20

1. While it may be clean in the house, this type of heat is very inefficient. The 2nd law of thermodynamics indicates that energy conversion degrades the quality of energy. Electric baseboard heat uses electricity from power plants and in the conversion from coal or nuclear energy to electricity that heats the heat strips, so much energy is lost that this is one of the least efficient ways to heat a home.

2. You cannot recycle energy. The 2nd law of thermodynamics states that energy is lost as heat as it is converted and this heat is a much less usable form of energy.

3. CAFÉ standards should increase. SUV's, trucks, and vans may always have lower standards than cars, but they can still be increased. Slowly increasing standards would prompt new technologies to increase fuel efficiency and reduce waste.
   a. If CAFÉ standards increase, this would have positive effects on health because there would be fewer pollutants in the air and less CO_2, a greenhouse gas.
   b. Elimination of CAFÉ standards would have the opposite effects of *a*.

4. Drive a fuel efficient car, drive less, make sure that my house is well insulated, turn down thermostat in winter and up in summer, recycle materials, and compost organic waste. I do all of these except compost organic waste, which I am planning to do.

5. I would build a super-insulated house in the mountains with large, efficient, south-facing windows with large overhangs and small north-facing windows. Instead of traditional lumber, I would use engineered lumber or steel, composite material interior trim, and bamboo wood floors. I would use passive solar heat supplemented with efficient gas heat. My water heater would be heated with natural gas and be wrapped. Other appliances would also be gas except for the refrigerator, dishwasher, and washing machine. Lighting would be with fluorescent bulbs. I could do without the dryer.

6.

    a.   Disagree. Subsidies for cheaper, more efficient forms of energy would encourage their use and development.

    b.   Agree. See *a*.

    c.   Disagree. Private industry development of alternative forms of energy would be encouraged with subsidies. Government support of nuclear and fossil fuel use would encourage the current levels of use and waste and should be discontinued.

7.   I agree with all of these proposals to promote more sustainable energy use. Most of our energy problem is too much consumption and waste. These proposals would discourage consumption and waste and allow future generations to have energy available and protect the environment.

8.   Provide incentives for buying fuel-efficient vehicles, require increased fuel efficiency, reduce energy waste, encourage development of alternate forms of energy, phase out subsidies for production of energy from fossil fuels, and create subsidies for the production of other forms of energy.

APPENDIX F

INTEGRATION OF INTERACTIVE CONCEPTS IN ENVIRONMENTAL SCIENCE CD-ROM

These are suggested discussion topics or questions that incorporate animations and interactions from the Interactive Concepts in Environmental Science CD-ROM. The questions and discussions topics are designed to encourage students to use the CD-ROM.

Chapter 2

1. Two views of economics animation

   a. Use this animation to explore differences between conventional and ecological economics in terms of flow of money, products, and factors of production.
   b. What are some of the ways to reduce the throughput of matter and energy according to the ecological economists?

Chapter 3

1. Feedback control of temperature

   In this animation, what are the stimulus, the receptors, the integrator, the effectors, and the response?

2. Subatomic particles interaction

   a. Which two elements are used in the animation?
   b. How many protons, electrons, and neutrons does each of these elements have?

3. Atomic number, mass number interaction

   Give the atomic number and the mass number of the two elements used in the animation.

4. Isotope animation

   Define isotope and give an example.

5. Martian doing mechanical work animation

   a. What does the Martian do while she is pushing the NASA Rover to the top of the hill?
   b. What happens to the potential energy of the Rover when it returns to the bottom of the hill?

6. Visible light interaction

   What are the levels of energy and wavelength for violet, green, and red light?

7. Half-life interaction

   What are the percentages for parent and daughter isotope when 0, 1, 2, 3, 4, and 5 half-lives have elapsed?

8. Energy flow animation

    a. Where does energy flow start from in this animation?
    b. What happens to most of the energy reaching the producers?
    c. What happens to the rest of the energy reaching the producers?
    d. How does energy flow in this animation?
    e. How do the nutrients flow in this animation?

9. Total energy remains constant animation

    What energy system is used in this animation?

10. Economic types interaction

    a. What type of economy controls waste and pollution best according to this interaction?
    b. What type of economy results in high waste according to this interaction?
    c. What type of economy reuses matter outputs according to this interaction?

Chapter 4

1. Levels of organization interaction

    a. What are the five levels of biological organization presented in this interaction?
    b. What is the relationship between the levels of organization presented?

2. General features of a cell interaction

    Describe the three major regions of the cell.

3. Sun to earth animation

    a. How much of the sun's energy reaches the troposphere according to this animation?
    b. Who is responsible for the natural greenhouse effect?

4. Linked processes animation

    How is oxygen produced and later used in the cycle shown in this animation?

5. Matter recycling and energy flow animation

    a. How are organisms in an ecosystem connected according to this animation?
    b. What happens to most of the energy in an ecosystem?
    c. What happens to most of the materials in an ecosystem?
    d. Who are the players in this animation?
    e. What are the relationships between the players in this animation?

6. The role of organisms in an ecosystem

    a. What are the different types of organisms presented in this animation?
    b. What are the roles of the organisms presented in this animation?

7. Diet of the red fox interaction

    a. What is the diet of the red fox in each of the four seasons as presented in this interaction?
    b. Discuss possible reasons of the differences in diet between seasons.

8. Categories of food webs interaction

    What are the differences between a grazing and a detrital food web based on?
    1. the organisms involved?
    2. the energy flow?

9. Energy flow in Silver Springs animation

    a. If the energy inflow to the system were 3,000,000 kilocalories how much is not harnessed?
    b. Further investigate the numbers at each level of the energy flow.

10. Water cycle interaction

    What is the numerical relationship between the amount of water moved by wind through the atmosphere annually and the amount of water included in the surface run-off and groundwater?

11. Carbon cycle animation

    What are the processes moving carbon from one reservoir to the other?

12. Nitrogen cycle interaction

    Discuss the processes presented in this interaction

13. Phosphorous cycle animation

    Discuss the processes presented in this interaction

14. Sulfur cycle animation

    Discuss the processes presented in this interaction

Chapter 5

1. Stanley Miller's experiment animation

    a. What is the function of the condenser in this animation?
    b. Which organic compounds are produced at the end of this animation?

2. Evolutionary tree of life animation

    a. What were the products of the first major divergence on the tree of life?
    b. How did mitochondria arise according to this animation?
    c. What major divergence is associated with the appearance of the chloroplasts?

3. Adaptive trait interaction

    Answer the questions of the interaction.

4. Change in moth population animation

    What type of selection is demonstrated in this animation?

5. Stabilizing selection animation

    a. Which phenotypes are eliminated in this animation?
    b. Which phenotypes become dominant in this animation?

6. Disruptive selection animation

Which phenotypes disappear in this animation?

7. Speciation on an archipelago animation

Describe the speciation that can occur as the birds colonizes each island.

8. Evolutionary tree diagrams

What does each of the three evolutionary trees in this animation mean in terms of trait changes?

Chapter 6

1. Coastal breezes interaction

What is the principle that drives the phenomena shown in this interaction?

2. Climate and ocean currents map

    a. What factors affect the direction of the currents according to this animation?
    b. Why is the climate in London milder compared to Ontario although they are at the same latitude?

3. Air circulation and climate animation

    a. How is rainfall associated to air circulation patterns?
    a. How are the air circulation patterns associated to the distribution of different biomes?

4. Air circulation interaction

Discuss the results of this interaction.

5. Upwelling along western coasts animation

Which factors are involved in the development of upwelling according to this animation?

6. El Nino Southern Oscillation interaction

    a. What are the changes of trade winds and surface water flow during ENSO?
    b. What are the effects of ENSO on the water temperature?

7. Greenhouse effect interaction

Discuss the effects of low, medium, and high concentrations of greenhouse gasses on the earth's surface temperature according to the interaction.

8. Increasing greenhouse gases interaction

   What are the effects of three chemicals presented in this interaction on the increase of greenhouse gases?

9. Biomes map interaction

   Describe the food web connections between all organisms included in all levels for the web shown in this interaction.

10. Interactions in prairie interaction

    Describe the food web connections between all organisms included in all levels for the web shown in this interaction.

11. Interactions in a rainforest interaction

    Describe the food web connections between all organisms included in all levels for the web shown in this interaction.

12. Ocean provinces interaction

    What are the differences between the provinces shown in this interaction?

13. Lake zonation interaction

    What are the differences between the zones shown in this interaction?

14. Lake turnover interaction

    a. Which layer is constantly mixing in the summer profile of this lake?
    b. What are the differences of the temperature at the bottom of the lake between summer and winter profiles?

15. Trophic nature of lakes interaction

    What are the factors that influence the development of a eutrophic and oligotrophic lake?

Chapter 7

1. Species diversity by latitude

   What are the differences in species richness between the poles and equator for birds and ants according to this animation?

2. Area and distance effects interaction

   Discuss effects of the size of an island and the distance from the mainland on the immigration rate, extinction rate, and number of species.

3. How species interact interaction

   Discuss the five types of interactions shown in this interaction. Compare and contrast between types of interactions.

4. Gause's competition experiment interaction

   What concept is illustrated in this interaction?

5. Succession interaction

   What are the similarities and differences between the two types of succession presented in this interaction?

6. Resources depletion and degradation interaction

   Make lists of vanishing biodiversity, endangered species, and environmental degradation as they are presented in this interaction.

Chapter 8

1. Capture-recapture method interaction

   Each student can estimate the population size five times, and you can then pool the students' estimates to calculate a class average. Discuss the effects of sample size and repetitions in accurately estimating a population.

2. Exponential growth animation

   What are the numbers of mice at 9, 15, and 18 months?

3. Life history patterns interaction

   a. Which type of survivorship curve shows high survivorship, constant death rate, or high mortality?
   b. What type of organism fits each type of survivorship?

Chapter 9

1. Geologic forces animation

   a. What is the phenomenon illustrated in this animation?
   b. What are the differences of what is happening at the trench and the ridge?

2. Plate margins interaction

   What do plate margins and volcanoes have in common according to this interaction?

3. Soil profiles interaction

   Compare the soil profiles among the five biomes presented in this interaction.

4. pH interaction

   Give the pH for each material included in this interaction.

Chapter 10

1. HIV replication animation

   Discuss the biochemical processes presented in this interaction.

2. Life cycle of *Plasmodium* interaction

   a. Which disease is presented in this interaction?
   b. Describe the stages of the life cycle of this parasite.

Chapter 11

1. Current and projected population sizes by region

   a. What are the differences between 2002 and 2025 in terms of population sizes in the size continents presented in this interaction?
   b. Which projection shows an increase or decrease, and why?

2. Examples of age structure interaction

   a. What are the differences between the six age structure examples shown in this interaction?
   b. What are some reasons for these differences?

3. U.S. age structure interaction

   a. What are the differences among the age structures for 1985, 2015, and 2035?
   b. What are the projected age structure changes for the baby boomer generation in this interaction?

4. Demographic transition model interaction

   a. Discuss the death, birth, and population trends for each of the stages included in this interaction.
   b. Which countries are in the postindustrial stage?

5. SF Bay region growth interaction

   What effects do you think this population growth has had on the region?

Chapter 12

1. Formation of photochemical smog

   Discuss the chemical reactions shown in this animation

2. Thermal inversion and smog interaction

   How does the air layer change in this interaction during thermal inversion?

3. Acid deposition animation

   a. Discuss the chemical processes shown in this animation.
   b. What is the role of limestone on the effect of acid rain on soils?

4. Effect of air pollution in forests animation

   What are the surface and underground effects of air pollution on forests?

Chapter 13

1. Greenhouse effect interaction

   Discuss the effects of low, medium, and high concentrations of greenhouse gasses on the earth's surface temperature according to the interaction.

2. Increasing greenhouse gases interaction

   What are the effects of three chemicals presented in this interaction on the increase of greenhouse gases?

3. How CFCs destroy ozone animation

   What is the role of the chlorine atoms in this animation?

Chapter 14

1. Polarity of water animation

   Discuss the three-dimensional lattice shown in this animation. What are the effects of the formation?

2. Threats to aquifers interaction

   Discuss the locations where groundwater overdrafts, groundwater pollution, and saltwater intrusion are present according to this interaction.

3. Effects of deforestation interaction

   Discuss alteration of rates of evaporation, rainfall, runoff, and transpiration due to deforestation as presented in this interaction.

4. Stream pollution animation

   What is the role of bacteria in this animation?

Chapter 16

1. Transferring genes into plants animation

   What is the role of an agrobacterium in the process described in this animation?

2. Land use interaction

   How is land classified and what is the justification for these classes?

3. Pesticide examples interaction

   Discuss the three chemicals presented in this interaction and the way they function.

Chapter 17

1. Humans affect biodiversity interaction

   Discuss the connections between biodiversity loss and food supply and demand, freshwater supply and demand, climate change, and forest product supply and demand.

2. Biodiversity hot-spots interaction

   Give biodiversity characteristics for each of the regions given in this interaction.

Chapter 18

1. Habitat loss and fragmentation interaction

   a. What is the common characteristic among the four animals as it relates to their habitat?
   b. Give reasons for the phenomenon described in this interaction.

Chapter 19

1. Energy use interaction

   Discuss the types of renewable and non-renewable sources of energy and differences between developed and developing countries.

2. Chernobyl fallout interaction

   a. Discuss the timetable of radioactive fallout from the Chernobyl accident.
   b. Which areas of the world were affected?